North American Freemasonry:
Idealism & Realism

North American Freemasonry

IDEALISM & REALISM

Thomas W. Jackson

Plumbstone
WASHINGTON, D.C.

Cover illustrations:
Details of Masonic engravings from Jeremy Ladd Cross,
The True Masonic Chart, or Hieroglyphic Monitor (New York:
J. L. Cross, 1846) and David Vinton, *The Masonick Minstrel*
(H. Mann & Co., 1816).

Interior illustrations:
Masonic engravings from Jeremy Ladd Cross,
The True Masonic Chart, or Hieroglyphic Monitor
(New York: J. L. Cross, 1846).

Copyright © 2019 by Plumbstone.

Publisher's Cataloging-in-Publication data
Jackson, Thomas William, 1934–
    North American freemasonry: idealism and realism
    / Thomas W. Jackson
    686 p. 25 cm.
    ISBN-13 978-1-60302-018-3 (paperback)
    ISBN-13 978-1-60302-017-6 (cloth)
    1. Freemasons. 2. Freemasonry—United States.
    I. Title

Library of Congress Control Number: 2019937175

http://www.plumbstone.com

Dedication

I dedicate these writings
to the memory of two Brothers:

Dr. and Brother Alexander Stewart, PDDGM,
a great friend who influenced me significantly through
his wisdom, dignity and class and who frequently
reminded me that I was here because of him,
since as a doctor, he saved my mother's life
when she was a small girl.

Brother John K. Young, RWPGM, also a great man
of class, wisdom and dignity who represented to me,
everything I would have liked to be.
If there were such a thing as reincarnation
and I had a choice, I would want to
come back as a John K. Young.

[Contents]

PART FIVE • International Masonic Jurisdictions

[Acknowledgments]

In considering how to attribute acknowledgments for this book, my greatest concern was that I might inadvertently miss some individuals to whom I owe much credit. Therefore, I express to all for whom I may have not have acknowledged, my sincerest apology.

First I must give much credit to those brothers who have for over two decades harassed, inveigled, cajoled and threatened me into coalescing my writings into book form. Without their persistence this volume would not have been completed and had I have known in advance how long it would take and how much effort it would require, it would probably still not have been completed.

I therefore, owe a debt of gratitude to brothers Wayne Adams and Claire Tusch, Past Grand Masters of Maine; Richard Curtis, former editor of *The Northern Light*; Wallace MacLeod, the Past Grand Historian of the Grand Lodge of Canada in the Province of Ontario; Ali Razi, Past Grand Master of the Grand Lodge of Iran in Exile; Allen Roberts, noted author and historian on Freemasonry; Richard Fletcher, Past Grand Master of Connecticut and former Executive Secretary of the Masonic Service Association.

I express my gratitude also to brothers Brent Morris, Arturo de Hoyos, and John Bizzack who read the manuscript and offered their advice.

Special thanks go to Dr. Glenys Waldman, librarian at the Grand Lodge of Pennsylvania for her initial editing of the papers. Inasmuch as I am a scientist and far less qualified in the art of writing, this was a Herculean task on her part.

My appreciation goes also to Brother Barry Martz, a Past Master of my Lodge who came to my rescue on several occasions to prevent me from totally destroying my computer.

Finally, my eternal thanks to my wife Linda, who has tolerated my angst and anger when the computer was failing to perform, along with my long absences from home due to my many travels to understand world Freemasonry.

[Preface]

It has been my privilege to be a member of the Masonic Fraternity for over 54 years. During these years I have been given the opportunity to serve in presiding offices of a number of Masonic organizations along with positions in local, state, national, and world bodies.

Finally, following many years of contemplation, I am disciplining myself enough to sit down at my computer and attempting to put my writings into book form, a project that my brothers, colleagues and friends have been requesting, pleading, cajoling and even threatening me, to have me do for nearly twenty years.

Over the last decade I have been receiving considerably more requests from those for whom I have the greatest respect, to compile my papers and lectures into a book before it is too late to do so. Brother Wallace McLeod the well-known Masonic author and lecturer from the jurisdiction of the Grand Lodge of Canada in the Province of Ontario for years has asked me each time he saw me, "Have you written your book?" Brother Ali Razi, Past Grand Master of the Grand Lodge of Iran in Exile along with many other brothers has been constantly encouraging me to do the same.

Around seven years ago, I was sitting in a hunting cabin in northern Maine with several friends including two Past Grand Masters from that jurisdiction, Brothers Wayne Adams and Claire Tusch, a Past Grand Master from Oklahoma, Brother Ron Coppedge, along with Brother Chas Pierro, as fine a cook as I have ever found at a hunting camp.

As might be expected, the evening conversation following dinner along with a bottle of good scotch gravitated to a subject of common interest, Freemasonry. Eventually, the question came up concerning when I was going to write my book. I responded as I generally do, "As soon as I can get the time." Brother Wayne Adams in his diplomatic way then told me, "Damn it Tom, you owe it to the Craft." With this gentle encouragement I began thinking more seriously about the subject but it still took me several more years to reach that stage. Now, seven years later, I found myself working to finish what I started a decade ago.

Being one of the world's great procrastinators and never one to be enamored with the discipline of writing, I found it far more difficult to organize my writings than I might have earlier on. Many of my early talks were given extemporaneously and try as I might; I have been unable to recall them. Eventually as I began to realize that I was forgetting points that I wished to make, I went through a phase where I wrote key points on 3×5-inch cards to remind me of what I wanted to express. Those speeches I have attempted to reconstruct. Finally after receiving numerous requests for copies of what I had presented, I began writing my papers, most of which I have retained in my files.

It was never my intent to write a book. As a result, I did not date papers I had written or record the locations where they were presented and in many cases, did not even title them. This volume includes addresses I have given, along with some articles I have written. The speeches are comprised of those I have been able to reconstruct from the 3×5-inch cards and those that I had written out. If I could recall where and when a speech was first presented, I have given that information. Those that did not have titles, I gave the location where it was presented, if I knew it. I have also included some papers presented as either opening or closing addresses of the World Conference. Unfortunately, some papers I could not locate and some were lost in cyberspace or somewhere else in my computers or my files.

I have tried to the best of my recollection, present them in some chronological order in which they occurred. Because most relate to Masonic subjects and reflect my thoughts and ideas, there is repetition of some subject matter found in different papers. I have attempted to remove repetitions without destroying the intent of the paper. Nonetheless, some remain due to speaking to different audiences. I have also found it prudent to eliminate approximately 25% of the papers that were too similar in content. It is important to understand that each paper was written for a specific audience and I attempted to satisfy the intent of my host without violating my convictions.

They also reveal my change in thinking as I spent more time studying the significance of the Craft. However, as a result of my inability to place the papers in a true chronological order, the evolution of my thoughts is not precisely reflected in that manner.

I have divided the papers into six sections, based on to whom or how early in my career they were given. The first contains most of my early papers reflecting a more positive flavor when my idealism shined through and dealing with the greatness of Freemasonry.

The second part contains later papers, revealing my greater concern on the direction the Craft is traveling, when my pragmatism dominated my thinking. The third part contains papers given to ladies night banquets. Part four features papers presented to non-Masonic audiences. The fifth section is material presented to Masonic organizations outside of the United States and the sixth are miscellaneous papers not necessarily Masonically related.

[Foreword by Arturo de Hoyos]

One of the great secrets of our fraternity is that it is a "center of union" which can "conciliate true friendship among those who may otherwise remain at a perpetual distance." Had it not been for our fraternity, I would have never had the privilege of knowing my dear friend and Masonic Brother, Thomas W. Jackson. In our over twenty years of friendship we've served together as board members in Masonic organizations, attended meetings together in foreign countries, and had countless conversations on Freemasonry and its purposes. The remarkable ability of Freemasonry to cross borders, real and artificial, and to make men into brothers irrespective of nationality, color, or creed, has been proven many times over by Brother Tom, who is one of the best-known and most respected, Masons in the world.

Although Brother Tom's Masonic record is too long to recite here, I will briefly mention a couple of his achievements. Since 1988 he's served as the executive secretary of the world conference of Masonic grand lodges; he served for twenty years as Grand Secretary of the Grand Lodge of Pennsylvania; he's a past president of the Conference of Grand Secretaries of North America; he's an honorary Grand Master and/or honorary member of over thirty grand lodges, and has received more awards than I can count. In his over 50 years of Masonic membership, Brother Tom has also delivered countless speeches, some of which you will find between these covers.

The scope of the articles covered by the book is almost

daunting. Time and again, Brother Tom is a voice in the wilderness, asking us to look in the mirror, and questioning us what we know, what we are doing, and where we are going in the fraternity. He questions how Freemasonry included so many of the world's greatest statesmen and leaders in its fold in times past, and wonders where such leaders are today. He shows us how the principles of the enlightenment were promoted by the fraternity in a time when kings and superstition ruled the world.

With remarkable simplicity and clarity he writes, "The goal of the Craft is to make the man." And so it is. Because the rituals and purposes of Freemasonry are unchanged, we must wonder why we no longer seem to have the quality of people we once have. With frankness he questions whether we have been too liberal in opening the doors to men who seek the fraternity for purposes other than self-improvement and the betterment of society. In our desire to maintain higher membership numbers have we lowered some of our standards? He questions whether the desire for positions, titles and awards is a detriment to the practice of the true Freemasonry.

Brother Tom not only explores the challenges of maintaining Masonic ideas, but he discusses the practical nuts and bolts of preserving Masonic regularity, and why it is important. There's an unfortunate tendency today among some younger, Masonically uneducated, members to presume that the practice of Masonic ritual bestows membership and/or regularity (legitimacy). Brother Tom dispels such mistaken notions by explaining how legitimacy is conveyed and maintained, and why it is important. He correctly celebrates Masonic charities as the byproduct of Masonic principles, rather than the purpose of the fraternity, which is first focused upon the individual self-improvement of each member. He provides a context which explains why

Freemasonry was called "the handmaiden of religion," without being a religion itself.

In brief, this book can said to be an anthology on the relevance of Freemasonry not only to the individual but to society. It is a book which I have enjoyed reading, and which I expect to turn to for inspiration for many years to come. It is uniquely adapted to sharing in lodge, and I am sure its contents will elicit enjoyable, lively, and serious discussions.

Arturo de Hoyos, 33°, Grand Cross, KYCH
Grand Archivist and Grand Historian
The Supreme Council, 33°, SJ

ONE

Idealism

[1]

Why Do We Take This Road?

*Given at the Grand Lodge of Canada
in the Provence of Ontario*

S everal years ago, I experienced these two situations on the same day. First, an attorney from Lebanon with multiple academic degrees was in my office. He wanted to become a Freemason because of how much he thought it meant to the world and how much influence it had. His mother was one of his major sources of information. He was so enthusiastic, that it became the first time I found myself downplaying the power and influence of the Craft. That evening I spoke at a lodge meeting. Following the meeting, a member talked with me and told me that he was considering resigning his membership because of his disappointment with what Freemasonry had become, and I found myself defending it. That day I found myself caught between the idealism and the realism that has become Freemasonry.

The history of the world is replete with the names of men who have led in their country's struggles for freedom and liberty. Some of these names may not be known to all of us but they are household names in their respective countries and areas of the world. In the United States, many of the names of our early patriots who led in its struggles for freedom are well known to most of us.

Canada has had its share of great government leaders

who were also Masons, including six Prime Ministers. The first was Sir John A. MacDonald, and more recently, Right Honorable John G. Diefenbaker. We can add to that list Brothers such as Joseph Brant, John Ross Robertson, and Most Rev. William Lockridge Wright as Masonic greats who helped shape Canada. I also learned from M. W. Brother Bob Davies of the influence of Masonic brothers in the R.C.M.P. who greatly impacted Canada's development.

These men all had at least one thing in common. They were all Freemasons. They were all nurtured in a Masonic Lodge, where they were taught the precepts of freedom, liberty and equality. This is not to imply that it was the Craft alone that made them the great men they became, but nor can it be coincidence that those who led in struggles for freedom in so many countries of the world that has freedom, were Freemasons.

History is also replete with the names of other men who most will recognize. We all know the names of Hitler, Mussolini, Stalin, Franco, Tito and Khomeini. They also had at least one thing in common. They all were enemies of Freemasonry.

Freemasons died by the tens of thousands at the hands of these men's regimes simply because they were Freemasons. Much has changed over the ensuing years, but tyrants remain the enemies of our Craft, and we should have no problem with that. We should wear their enmity as mantles of pride, for to oppose tyranny is to embrace freedom and that is a structural character of the Masonic Fraternity.

Historically, we have always risen above their attacks. It may have taken considerable time in some cases, but we have risen. Where there has been tyranny, Freemasonry has survived only underground, but it has survived the onslaught of tyrants almost from its inception, even flourishing in spite of them.

Of even graver concern, are those who have chosen to become our enemies and who quite possibly have benefited the most because of our existence. What makes this an even greater tragedy, is that their opposition to the Craft is for the very same reasons as that of the tyrant.

It's almost incomprehensible that Freemasonry could have as opponents religious and government leaders of the free world, when they might very well be in those positions because of the efforts of Freemasons. And yet, even as with the tyrants, there have been men in these categories who must rank with the Craft's greatest enemies. They also have had no long lasting effect upon our survival in the past, even though they can be traced back almost to our inception.

However, we, my Brothers, are today accomplishing what none of our enemies from without have been able to accomplish. I know that what I am about to say will be approaching heresy to some, but then, fools rush in where angels fear to tread.

We, my Brothers, are providing the environment for our own extinction. We, the leaders of the Craft for the last twenty years, have aided in the gradual eroding of the quality of the membership, and it is this loss of quality, that is the greatest threat to our survival as a significant institution. This loss of quality is already showing an impact on our quantity and it is counterproductive to that very goal of increasing quantity that is causing it. Why do we take this road?

Many of our decisions in recent years indicate a lack of interest in preserving the quality of the Craft. We seem more intent on redefining and reshaping it, for the simple reason that we, as leaders, do not want to be judged as failures because our numbers have decreased, and yet we acknowledge that this is a sociological phenomenon affecting almost all organizations. It is a phenomenon we cannot change, and it is one, which we must ride out. My Brothers, we cannot afford to continue to evaluate ourselves in terms of quantity instead of quality. To do so offers little hope for a future of an organization that changed this world, and we, as leaders, will shoulder the blame for future generations.

I quote from the book, *Reflections of Masonic Values*, "If we shall not be careful in the admission of candidates and improve the procedure of admission, we are then starting the composition of a funeral hymn for the death of our noble institution. As Freemasons, we should not allow this to happen. If we do, we are doomed for we have just hammered the last nail in the sarcophagus of Freemasonry."

We all realize that the Craft has had its ups and downs, its increases and decreases in numbers during its entire history. Following the Morgan affair in North America, it almost became extinct in some areas, but it survived to flourish again. Nothing the world outside threw against it was able to hold it down for long. Freemasonry in Russia, although little known, is perhaps a classic example of the tenacity of this organization. It might also be used as a study as to what the result could be if our approach in North America continues along the pathway we have been following in recent years.

Margaret Jacob wrote in *Living the Enlightenment*, that Freemasonry passed out of serious scholarship in the late 1940s, and I would suggest that this was the time when we began to lose focus on what we were. It is interesting that it was also the time of our most rapid growth. It was the beginning of our failure to guard the west gate. Even then however, quantity over quality was not promoted by our top leadership as it is today.

In my first dozen years as Grand Secretary, I never saw a resignation for religious reasons. Now we receive them routinely. Opposition by religious leaders is not new to

Freemasonry, but it is becoming more pervasive and effectual. Why do you suppose that is? There was also the time when most of the prominent lay leaders of our churches were also the prominent community leaders, and they were also Freemasons. To attack Freemasonry was to attack the most supportive members of the church and the quality leaders of the community. We are now failing to attract these quality leaders. The church leadership has no longer reason to be concerned about our influence.

We have admitted for years, that only 10% of our membership is active (although I have often wondered where that statistic came from). This, of course, means that 90% is inactive, and yet they continue to pay their dues year after year, knowing full well that they will never be active. There is only one logical reason for doing this. They have a perceived value in being able to say: "I am a Freemason." Take away that perceived value, and we risk losing the 90%, and that is what we are seeing today. The willingness to be suspended for non-payment of dues or the submission of resignations is indicative of a loss of respect for the meaning of Freemasonry by our own members.

We, as leaders, have made more changes in our structure and system in those twenty years than have probably taken place in the last 200 years. This has all been done for one reason: to acquire numbers, and frankly, my Brothers, I don't know if we have even slowed the loss. We may not have stemmed the decline of numbers, but we surely have decreased our influence in society and, with this decrease, our ability to accomplish our purpose.

I find it difficult to comprehend why we are incapable of recognizing that most of these changes made have not only not benefited us, but indeed may have caused considerable harm. I don't understand our attempts to emulate other organizations that are declining at least as rapidly as are we, and with whom we cannot compete to begin with.

Freemasonry has been the best, we were different, and we were unique. Why not build on that uniqueness instead of trying to convert into something we have never been nor ever meant to be? There has never been any organization that could lay claim to being more significant to the world, outside of organized religion, than has Freemasonry. Why not look at Freemasonry in the world where it is succeeding, where it remains influential and try to emulate it? I am not in opposition to change when it is to our benefit, but we must recognize and distinguish what is beneficial and admit when we have failed.

I had some serious problems with the paper presented to the Grand Masters' Conference by the Imperial Potentate at Savannah a few weeks ago, even though he had some valid points. When he said that we should ask how many Shriners are present at our lodge meetings, and then stated that we "will be amazed at the number of Shriners that are now keeping your lodges open and are officers," then I must disagree.

Let it be known now that I am a very proud Shriner, but I became a Shriner because of Freemasonry, and I served as a Lodge officer not because I was a Shriner, but because I was a Freemason. I was not a Shriner keeping my Lodge open. I was a Lodge officer who also joined the Shrine. Without the early requirement of Masonic membership as a prerequisite for Shrine membership, which supplied the quality, the Shrine would quite probably be just another social club today, and a deletion of that quality may make it so.

There is no question that the environment in which we exist has changed. Now we must determine whether we wish to retain our principles and values and lift others to meet our ideals or change to fit into the standards of present day society.

We must also acknowledge that the present-day environment is undergoing a metamorphosis more rapidly than ever in our past. Changes are taking place today in our world, which out of necessity, must cause us to pause and analyze how we will fit in as part of that environment. Freemasonry could and may play a vital role as a stabilizing force in society throughout that metamorphosis. But we surely will not if we can't even stabilize ourselves. We must reexamine our purpose, our precepts, and our philosophy and be willing to make changes in our modes of operation when necessary, but we must be certain that those changes do nothing to damage or destroy the basic principles and precepts with which we were born and with which we flourished.

I cannot believe that a philosophy that sustained us for almost 300 years is not applicable to today's world. Have we become an anachronism in present-day society? Have our principles and values actually had no place for the last quarter century? I think not. Why then do we continue to make a concentrated effort to change into something we are not, and fail to recognize that we are destroying the quality of the Craft that is necessary to support that philosophy? If we truly do believe that our philosophy and principles have a place in the modern world, then we must pull others up to meet our philosophical standards not step down to meet theirs.

John Robinson made an astute observation concerning our Craft well before he became a member. He said that the problem with Freemasonry today is that it does not practice Freemasonry anymore. My Brothers, how can we, when the vast majority of our members do not even know what to practice? We don't need more members. We need more Freemasons.

For the first time in our long and glorious history, historians are finally writing about Freemasonry, but they are not writing about our quantity. They are writing about our quality. What they write in the future is now in our hands. We cannot let it become less than it was, nor less than it can be.

[2]

How Can They Ignore Us?

I recently read the book *Living the Enlightenment* written by a non-Mason, Margaret Jacob. In that book she made statements giving credits to Freemasonry which probably were, at best, only alluded to in the past. For example:

> Perhaps we have finally located the earliest movements in the formation of modern civil society.

> Freemasonry was one of the social practices that put freedom and equality central on the word list.

> Central to Masonic identity was the belief that merit and not birth constitutes the foundation for social and political order.

> Freemasonry assisted in the propagation of mesmerist materialism, and thus laid the foundations democratic thought.

> Modern Civil Society was invented during the Enlightenment in the new enclaves of sociability of which Freemasonry was the most avowedly constitutional and aggressively civic.

For a long time I have been wondering about this Craft, wondering why it developed as it did and wondering why it endured as it has. I have reached the conclusion that Freemasonry is and has for two primary reasons. First it was the probably the first organization to appear upon the scene in a class society where men of all walks of life could sit together as equals. This was of primary importance for this was the age of royalty, of nobility, of merchants, of military, of the working class to sit together as equals even philosophically was unheard of.

Secondly, Freemasonry attracted the greatest minds of the time. Throughout her text, Jacob observed the leadership offered by enlightened minds of those with the potential to lead. If Freemasonry had lacked either one of these characteristics it could not be what it is today.

Now, I have a concern, for I'm looking at a third characteristic, one needed as a sustainer, one common thread which supports the other two: selectiveness. Not selectiveness in regard to occupation, not selectiveness in regard to education, not selectiveness in regard to social class—but selectiveness in terms of quality of the man.

I have been confused as I am sure some of you have been with the absence of reference to Freemasonry in history books.

Before I left for Greece in June, I went to the bank to pick up some Greek currency (Drachmas). Upon returning to my office I said to my secretary, "Look at this currency. It has a picture of a pirate on it!" When I reached the Grand Lodge of Greece I saw pictures of the same individual on the walls of the Grand Lodge and I found out he was regarded as one of Greece's greatest heroes. Talk about judging a book by its cover!

Then I began to think more about some of the other great leaders who lead their countries fight for freedom, men like George Washington in America, Simon Bolivar, referred to as the George Washington of South America, and I just read in the MSA *Messenger* of a stamp being issued honoring Lajos Kossuth, the champion of Hungarian liberty and there are many more.

These men changed the world. How can this organization be ignored? Is it by happenstance that they were Freemasons? No way! Theodore Kokolotronis, that Greek "pirate" whose image is on the currency said, "Blessed be the Masonic lodges which baptized you in the holy water of freedom."

Today, I am reading more and more historical writings giving Freemasonry the credit for what it was and for what it did. There are even those who are looking at the philosophy of Freemasonry as being the origin of modern democratic thought. My brothers, we are being recognized for our past, finally.

But Jacob also observed that sometime between 1945 and now that "Freemasons dropped out of serious scholarship" and this my brothers, could be frighteningly true. When I look at Freemasonry's liberal practices today I ask myself, am I that far out of touch with todays accepted reality? Is this what it is to be accepted by Freemasons today? Is it reflective of our quality today? If it is, is this why we slipped out of serious scholarship if indeed we have — because of our willingness to be less? How will historians write about us tomorrow?

Well, I'm not willing to surrender our character. I'm not willing to resign myself to Freemasonry of lesser quality. Because society lowers its standards does not mean we must do the same. Indeed, we have an obligation to the future to lead the way to what is morally and ethically right, to be more than just average in society: in essence, to be what we have always been. The world must know who we are and what we do as well as who we were and what we have been.

Freemasonry has been an attractive force for some of the greatest men this world has ever known. Freemasonry must continue to serve as that force. There is no alternative. There is, however, a criterion for Freemasonry's greatness and that is to attract great men, for without great men there can be no greatness. We must remember what it was that made our past so great. It was not how many of us there were but how respected we were.

I am concerned with some of the decisions that we are making today which will affect the quality of Freemasonry's future. Some Grand Lodges have gone to open solicitation and I must conclude that if we wish to destroy the Craft that would be a great way to start. Few men in the professions will solicit and eventually there will be no value to them for membership. With that loss, goes our best source of leadership and our image to the outside world. We cannot afford to promote what amounts to short-term survival and long-term doom.

We must prepare to bridge the sociological changes which will continue to occur in our society in the future but we cannot hope to grow or even remain the same by lowering our standards. It was the quality of the Craft that present-day writers are writing about, not the quantity. Freemasonry is more than a group of men, it is an ideal.

I fear that one of our greatest weaknesses is our inclination to point out to others, members who have been known for their greatness and not nearly enough to the greatness of the organization itself.

After writing this paper I received a report from the first World Congress of Grand Masters held in Mexico City in 1995. The Charter of Anahuac was signed by all participating jurisdictions. In it was proposed that Freemasonry be involved in fighting ecological depredation, environmental contamination, social instability and religious commitments in education. I have a serious concern with this charter which I expressed. Freemasonry as an organization cannot become involved in issues involving politics or religion.

I recognize that Freemasonry must have been involved in the creation of great men. Men such as George Washington, Simon Bolivar, Lajos Kossuth, Theodore Kolokotronis, Benito Juarez and so many others who were political leaders, and Masons led their countries as great men not as great Masons.

For the first time, I began to comprehend why Freemasonry is not discussed in history books. Historians write about great men, not organizations. We cannot deny the influence of Washington, Bolivar, Kolokotronis, Juarez, and the other great leaders but it was Washington the man, Bolivar the man, etc., who led their countries—but not as Masons.

And so, it must remain as it has been the goal of the Craft to make the man. The man will make the history.

[3]

What of Tomorrow?

Written around 1980

In the short period of time that I have to address you
tonight I have chosen a subject near and dear to all of
us; Freemasonry. Freemasonry is in trouble my brothers.
Does it shock to hear someone make that statement? It
would for many simply because they do not want to hear
it. They do not want to be dragged out of the comfort of
the shell into which they have withdrawn. They simply do
not want to face reality.

Yes, this great fraternity which we all love so much has
problems and ignoring them is not going to cause them to
go away. In fact the problems are due at least in part to us.
We are facing challenges unprecedented in our history and
our future depends upon are facing up to these challenges
and so far we have not been fulfilling our obligations to
the Craft.

Our Craft has had a phenomenal history. It is properly
known as the world's largest, oldest and most prestigious
of all fraternal organizations. But like every human institution it is subject to forces external to itself and over
which it has no control, forces that in a considerable part
will shape its destiny. Look around you and note the age
of the members. My brothers, we have cause for concern.
What of tomorrow?

We cannot ignore tomorrow. We must be concerned

about the future for we shall spend the rest of our lives there. Shakespeare once wrote, "Tomorrow and tomorrow and tomorrow creeps in this petty pace from day to day, to the last syllable of recorded time."

Well, my brothers, tomorrows no longer creep. Instead they rush past us carrying us forward whether we want it or not into a future radically different from the past that we once knew or the present we now know.

Let us take a look at some of the issues with which we are being confronted. 1. Membership has been dropping precipitously for a number of years. How long can we continue on this pathway without creating a major impact upon our ability to operate? 2. Lack of member interest is becoming a significant problem. I have been amazed in recent years at the number of Past Masters jewels being worn by lodge officers indicating a deficiency of members interested in serving as an officer. 3. Inflation, over which we have no control, is creating and will continue to create challenges in maintaining our buildings and collecting Lodge dues. 4. The church—of whom Freemasonry is perhaps the greatest ally—is continuing to challenge us and our compatibility with them. Out of ignorance, more and more church leaders question our sincerity and purpose. 5. Perhaps the greatest threat of all may be the government's threat against our fraternal integrity. The Department of Health, Education, and Welfare challenge of our Masonic Home's right to operate is one example of the government's willingness to impinge upon our operation by challenging our admission policy.

A number of years ago Dr. and Brother Frederick H. Buck when speaking at a banquet celebrating his seventy years as a Freemason made this observation: "As a farm boy living near a little village in Minnesota where I grew up and where I had no relative who was a Mason,

I became aware of a group of men with great reputations and character. I learned that these men all belonged to an organization called Freemasonry. I saw in this group, good men and true who were leaders of the church and community and I reasoned that Masonry must be good." My brothers, this was Freemasonry of the past. It is Freemasonry of the present but will it be Freemasonry of the future?

Our late brother, Johann Wolfgang von Goethe, the great thinker and philosopher perhaps brought it into perspective when he said, "That which has been bequeathed to us must be earned anew if we would possess it."

We cannot assume because the fraternity is so old that it is eternal. Nor can we assume that leadership and support will always be provided by others. Freemasonry is an old institution; its philosophy has withstood the test of time. It is the product of some of the greatest thinkers of the ages and that philosophy has not changed one iota. Only we have changed. We are the variable.

Knowledge is doubling every 7½ years. In the future we will be eating different foods from different sources, energy will be coming from different sources, space travel will be an accepted norm, cloning will be part of everyday life etc. etc. etc. Terms that just a short time ago belonged only to the scientist will become commonplace. Energy fuels and material shortages may cause chaotic disruptions in our economy. Unpaid dues and material shortages may cause tight economic constraints. Maintenance of our Masonic Temples, Scottish Rite Cathedrals and Shrine Mosques that we value so highly today may become white elephants tomorrow. Preoccupation with personal and business crises may leave little time for fraternal activities.

Examine the impact of the change and urbanization the Western world has already brought. Where the Masonic Lodge was once a highly visible and potent social force in thousands of small towns and villages a century ago it is now relegated to an inconsequential role in the social life of our great metropolitan centers.

To a great majority of our citizens, its visibility is nearing the zero point. Men who a century ago would've ardently sought membership, never give it a thought today and most have not the haziest idea of what it stands for. We today, glory in our history. We place enormous emphasis on the great Masonic personalities of the past, but where are the great Masonic personalities of the present?

Freemasonry does not need architects today. Its structure was made sound by the architects of the past. Today, Freemasonry needs builders. The architects have done their job well; it is up to us now to build. We need operative masons in our speculative Craft. Not operative masons to work in stone but to work in lives.

There is nothing wrong in being proud of our past unless in so doing we ignore the present upon which we must build our future. Today our potentially great personalities say they do not have time to contribute to our fraternity they have too many more important activities they are too busy.

Too busy: Brother George Washington was not too busy. Brother Marquis Lafayette was not too busy. Brother Benjamin Franklin was not too busy. Brother Harry Truman was not too busy.

Are those who are too busy today any more busy than were these great brothers of the past? It may well be time to glory less in our history and begin to create some history. It is long past due for us to recognize what our brothers in the past saw clearly, that membership carries with it responsibility. If we are not willing to contribute to the perpetuation of Freemasonry, then we are not worthy to be called Freemasons. Let us be egotistical enough to recognize that the world needs us.

We must not allow everyday complexities to blur our perspective. Whether modern technology is advancing too swiftly, leaving man behind, is beside the point. Science and technology, barring a universal holocaust, cannot stop. Instead of fearing and confining technology we must learn to cope with it. We must recognize the fact that the environment in which our Masonic organizations are operating has and will continue to change and requires change in our practices to adapt the Lodge to operate within this environment.

Freemasonry lost much of its mutual helpfulness that characterized it for so many years. Perhaps the challenge we are facing now may return us to it. It has served well during so many times of stress due basically to its tremendous inherent strength. We need not fear its philosophy for it has withstood the test of time.

In the allegorical section of the 32° is found one short line of nine words which to me expresses what should be essence of the Craft, "give me to serve and I am doubly blessed." Therein lies the soul of Freemasonry.

We have a tremendous opportunity to serve as an example for a small boy. We have an assumed responsibility to earn anew that which has been bequeathed to us. We have a single obligation to preserve Freemasonry for future generations. We owe that much to our past brothers and we certainly owe it to future generations. If we wish to preserve Freemasonry, then we have no alternative. Let us accept that opportunity, assume that responsibility and dedicate ourselves to that obligation.

Are there any small boys looking at us and from what they see, reasoning that Masonry must be good?

[4]

What Is Freemasonry?

A Reaffirmation of Our Vows

If someone walked up to you today and asked you, what is Freemasonry? How would you respond? What would you say? We all know that answer, don't we? But, can you answer the question?

With all of the time that I have spent in Freemasonry, I continue to find it a difficult question to respond to. It has been defined through numerous sets of ambiguous words and descriptions in trying to grasp a meaningful vision to give to the world.

Historically, we know that the first Grand Lodge was formed in 1717 in London, England. We know that we evolved from operative masons. We know that we are now speculative Masons. But what is a speculative Mason? What really are we? How many of us truly know what speculative Freemasons are? Well, we know that speculative is theoretical rather than demonstrable. It means to consider issues mentally. In theory, a speculative Mason is one whose major effort is directed toward the development of character and improvement of the life and conduct of the individual brother and who has the desire to learn and to improve.

A speculative man is an idealist, not necessarily the man of fact and practice. We as Freemasons do not build material cathedrals; we build cathedrals of the spirit. We are not dogmatic; we build from a universal spirit of brotherhood.

This is what makes us unique and different from religion. It provides for us a greater opportunity to promote the brotherhood of man under the fatherhood of God. From the time of man's creation there has probably existed a need for him to get together with others of like mind. In Freemasonry, this truly has resulted in a brotherhood with the potential to benefit all mankind.

All of us realize that our fraternity is a selective fraternity. We start with the best building material that we can find just as did the operative masons. We build from that material, just as did the operative masons. And, just as the operative masons' cathedrals have survived so to do the cathedrals of the speculative Freemasons.

With knowledge and skill the ancient builders erected the superstructures that were wonders to be studied and admired even to this day. As builders of men, we also have erected admirable superstructures to be studied and admired. Unfortunately, we today find some of the ancient cathedrals beginning to crumble and decay due to lack of use and neglect. They simply are not being maintained.

So to, is our speculative fraternity beginning to display those very same signs and for the very same reasons. We should not forget our past but we cannot afford to dwell upon it. We need today to do more than express lovely platitudes and philosophies. We need to stop referring to the ancient accomplishments. We, in the present, need to accomplish for the future.

Perhaps the time is long overdue for us to re-examine and to reaffirm our vows. We well know that Freemasonry is not for everyone. We also know that none of us were asked to join. We came by own free will and accord and were given the honor of unanimous acceptance. The Lodge has honored its commitment to us — but have we honored our commitment to it?

Our past has been glorious, my brothers. Freemasonry has had a phenomenal history. Probably no organization in the history of man can approach Freemasonry in regard to its success in terms of accomplishment or survivability. But, this is the present and with the present, Freemasonry has lost much of its gloss and glory. We should not forget the past but we cannot dwell upon it. As Longfellow succinctly put it, "Look not mournfully to the past, it comes not back again." But, as we should not forget it neither can we afford to continue to glory in it, ignoring the present. Longfellow also wrote, "Wisely improve the present, it is thine."

What we do now, in the present, will determine our future and we have the rest of our lives to spend there. We of the present day need to bestir ourselves; we need to do something besides expressing lovely platitudes and referring to ancient accomplishments. Freemasonry has been referred to as a sleeping giant and perhaps this is a good definitive description. But, it was not always asleep. If it were it would not be known today and indeed if it is now asleep, it is so because we permit to sleep. We are its only internal variable. Its philosophy is essentially the same as it was at its inception. So why are we less than we were?

There is no question but that our way of life has deprived the fraternity of much of the opportunity of doing those personal and brotherly acts that were the source of its major strength in the past. Today it is not quite as easy to be brotherly as it was in the past. So what do we do? Do we reaffirm our commitment to our vows or do we like Rip van Winkle sleep into a time when we are too infirm to accomplish anything of further value?

What we must do in reaffirming our vows commits us to not an easy task but as Albert Schweitzer once wrote;" anyone who proposes to do good must not expect people to roll stones out of his way." We cannot continue to make excuses to justify our failures and we should not have to worry about defining Freemasonry at all. It was no easier in the past to define it. Freemasonry was its own definition.

So where does this bring us? Are we now able to define Freemasonry to the profane? I doubt it. Freemasonry must be awakened so that its definition may be seen in works, not heard in words. We may not be able to define it but we can live it and our lives then becomes its definition. If Freemasonry could have meant so much to so many great men, can it mean less to us?

By reaffirming our vows and by fulfilling our obligation to the Craft, Freemasonry will define itself. The giant will stir and regain its rightful place in today's world.

[5]

Leadership, Ego, and Freemasonry

Given to a Scottish Rite leadership conference

My purpose as a keynote speaker is to stimulate and inspire and I'm not sure that I can do that. I don't need to inspire you to lead; you are leaders. I don't need to sell you on Freemasonry; you are sold. You would not be here if you were not. I don't need to define your purpose; you know your purpose. So, why am I here? What do I do, what do I say that will make any difference? Well, I hope I can at least define our purpose as Freemasons.

In order to truly comprehend our purpose we must first acknowledge that what we do is for our own satisfaction. We are salving our own egos. I have heard brothers over the years saying that they were active in Freemasonry because of what it does for others but in actuality much of what we do is the result of the self-satisfaction we receive in accomplishment.

There is absolutely nothing wrong with having egos drive us. Indeed, what we achieve in life is a result of it. But, we must contain that ego. We became what we are because of it but the legacy we leave behind will depend upon how well we have learned to control it. Perhaps one of the greatest problems we have in Freemasonry today is a result of leadership failing to control their egos. We have all known those who in life were great leaders but left behind poor legacies.

As a leader you are never going to satisfy everyone but if you can stimulate others to want to work for you, you will accomplish much more than you would if others simply work for some type of reward. To be a leader you must understand the environment in which you lead as well as knowledge of whom you are leading, and be flexible enough to change as the issues change.

When I was working as a sales manager it became my goal to have the customer like me enough that he would feel badly if he purchased the product from another vendor. Before visiting a prospective customer, I researched his occupation so that I could try to deal with him in his terms.

However, when I was in the teaching profession, I was emphatic with my students that my purpose in that class-room was to teach and they, my students (customers) were to learn. I let them know that if I could teach and they could learn when we finished the term and they liked me that was my goal, but if they forced me to make a choice, they would hate my guts at the end of the year. Two totally different environments but in both cases, I was selling myself. My brothers, leadership in Freemasonry is no different. If we are going to lead others we must be able to sell ourselves to them.

But to lead Freemasonry we must first understand it, and few Freemasons can provide a concise understandable definition of what it is.

It has been defined as:

1. The world's largest, most prestigious and most widely known fraternal organization.

2. A natural community of equals bound by shared experience and interest and united in action.

3. An organization to make good men better, perhaps the most definitive;

4. A beautiful system of morality veiled in allegory and

illustrated by symbols, perhaps the most stimulating;

5. A way of life, the most ambiguous;

6. A Brotherhood of man under the Fatherhood of God, perhaps the greatest reflecting our philosophy.

What does any or perhaps all of these definitions, however, tell one outside of the Craft? They would tell me very little to cause me to understand Freemasonry. So what is it, really?

Sometimes it is easier to define what it is not, rather than what it is. We know that it is not a religion yet we have religious characteristics. We know it is not a charity yet we have a charitable tendency. We know it is not an educational organization yet we emphasize the need for the acquisition of knowledge.

Historically, we do know that in 1717 the first Grand Lodge was formed in London, England. We know that it evolved from operative masonry. We know that it is now a speculative fraternity but how many know what it means to be a speculative mason? Probably, even in our fraternity, few know.

Yet, this speculative fraternal organization has created one of the greatest impacts this world has ever known. In its almost 275 years of organized journey, its indelible influence is forever marked upon the human race. The more you study this Craft the more you will realize that. I have learned more about Freemasonry in the past half-dozen years than probably the previous twenty and the more I learn more impressed I am.

Speculative is theoretical rather than demonstrable. It means to consider anything mentally. The speculative man is an idealist not the man of fact and practice. This does not mean that we should not be practical. Indeed today we must be a combination of both. We do not build material cathedrals any longer but we do build cathedrals. We build cathedrals of the spirit rather than of stone and mortar. We are not dogmatic; we build with the mortar of the universal spirit of brotherhood. That is why we are unique. That is what makes us different from religion. Religions out of necessity have a built in bigotry but that does not hamper the universal brotherhood of Freemasonry.

We must realize that Freemasonry is not for everyone. We must continue to strive to remain selective. As leaders we must avoid the self-centeredness which has caused much of our problem today. I recall when setting up a Conference of Grand Secretaries, a Past Grand Master explaining to a hotel manager that there would be 60 Grand Masters in attendance and each one of whom thinks he walks on water. This of course was an exaggeration of the issue but it also reflects a major problem in Freemasonry that we must recognize. Unrestrained ego remains a very ongoing dilemma for our Craft.

Shortly after becoming a Grand Secretary, I sat at my desk and wrote this little prayer. "Dear God, let me never forget where I came from and let me know when to quit." I am not sure whether I will apply it when the time comes but I am convinced that it would be a great goal for each one of us and a great contribution to the Craft.

As builders of men, Freemasonry erected admirable structures to be studied and admired. Regretfully, we find today, some of our speculative cathedrals beginning to crumble and decay due to lack of use and neglect.

My brothers, no one asked us to join. We came of our own free will and accord. We were accorded the honor of unanimous acceptance. We should not forget the past but we cannot afford to dwell upon it. We need stop referring to ancient accomplishments. We, in the present, need to accomplish for the future.

We seem to have a tendency to get caught up in what

should be of little consequence and ignore the larger issues. We cannot see the forest for the trees. We can argue all we want of new changes in practice such as recognition of Prince Hall or recognition of the ladies organizations but the fact remains our philosophy is unchanged.

So why are we, if we are, less than we were? My brothers, we are the members. We are the Leaders. Bringing back into our fraternity the meaning and practice of brotherhood might be a great place to start in becoming what we were. It seems almost a lost ingredient in the present day expression, Brotherhood of Man under the Fatherhood of God.

So where does this bring us? Can we now define Freemasonry to the profane? I doubt it. Why do we have to worry about defining Freemasonry at all? It was no easier to define in the past than it is now. Freemasonry was its own definition. Through fulfilling the unchanging philosophy of the Craft, Freemasonry will again define itself. We don't have to define it, we have to live it. Our ancient brethren did just that, and they did their job well. Now we as leaders hold our future in our hands.

[6]

An Honor You Have Just Received

Given at a Scottish Rite reunion

Congratulations, Sublime Princes of the Royal Secret. You are now 32° Masons. I recall a friend one day bragging to me about his son-in-law. He told me that he was a 32° Mason—*a 32° Mason!* Although not a member of the Craft himself, he was greatly impressed with the idea that his son-in-law had achieved that status. And well you should be also. I cannot convey to you what an honor it is to be recognized by one's peers, and in Freemasonry my brothers, we are all peers.

Words can never express my feelings when I am honored as I am by this valley to have a class named for me. I never cease to be amazed when I receive recognition in any form. When I look back on my life, I see a boy from the country who was helped by so many and to whom I owe so much. I will always be grateful to this valley for this honor which is really due to them. For I am truly a reflection of their influence and my brothers, we are all a reflection of all who influence us.

If Freemasonry were nothing else it would be a journey through knowledge. What you have done today in affiliating with the Scottish Rite is taken a giant step in the acquisition of knowledge. The Craft has so much to offer for those who would receive it.

I have been a member for thirty-six years and am constantly impressed by the greatness inherent in our organization. Since I became a book reviewer for *The Northern Light*, I have become much more aware of the meaning and impact of our fraternity, meaning put there and impact created there by our ancient brethren. We owe so much to them, these brothers of the past and I'm not sure that we are fulfilling our obligation to them.

We are losing that impact, that influence we once had. Why? Freemasonry has always had its detractors. Even before the formation of the Grand Lodge of England in 1717 there were those who opposed us and there are those who oppose us today. Opposition is not new and we must deal with it. Much of the opposition is due to ignorance of what we are. Much is due to jealousy because of what we have accomplished. Today, however, much is due to pure hate by those who cannot build themselves so they tear down others.

I wrote more than twenty-five years ago that we cannot sit back and not defend ourselves, and I am still convinced of this today. Times change my brothers and we must deal with that change. We must adjust to the environment in which we live. We must be seen for what we are; a viable force for good and we must remain a viable force. Even as the environment changes Freemasonry must not lose sight of its purpose.

Make no doubt about it: we are the greatest organization ever conceived by the mind of man. We have impacted the evolution of civil society more than any organization outside of organized religion.

This world is as it is today because Freemasonry lived. We are great because we attracted great men, we supported great ideals and we performed great acts. To remain great we must continue to attract, support and perform

In the first Masonic talk I ever gave thirty years ago, I expressed my concern over the loss of membership quantity. My greatest fear today, however, is our willingness to accept lower quality to gain quantity. For if quantity is lost it may be regained but if quality is lost it is possibly lost forever. Freemasonry has been an attractive force for some of the greatest men this world has ever seen because it not only embraced high ideals and principles but it nurtured those ideals and principles, developed the minds of the members and stimulated aspirations to greatness. We cannot hope to grow or even remain the same by reducing our quality. We must be able to respond. John Robinson's observation was that "The problem with Freemasonry today is that it does not practice Freemasonry anymore.

My brothers, we must strive for excellence in everything, our ritual, our philanthropies, our demeanor but most of our image. We must by our image, cause men to want to be part of us. Each of us individually is part of our future and every one of you is just as important to this Craft as am I.

Am I concerned? YES! Am I pessimistic? No! Freemasonry has been too significant in crafting this world not to be needed but we as present-day Freemasons must make sure the world knows.

I am extremely proud to be part of us, I can only hope that in some small way, I can pass on to others the understanding of just how important we have been to the operation of this world. Others have done it for me. I stand here because of them.

Again, I thank this valley for the recognition of the brothers of the past through this honor to me. Although I receive it, it is theirs, their epitaph etched upon the headstones of eternity. For as long as Freemasonry lives, Freemasons' contributions will never die.

[7]

Why this Lack of Interest?

Given at Affinity Marketing Breakfast

It has been my intent for years whenever I speak to stimulate thought. That is a modus operandi I carry from the field of education. If I can't cause you to think, I waste both our times. I also know that not everyone agrees with what I have to say. I don't expect that. This also is a carryover from my days as an educator.

I recall a biographical sketch in *The Scottish Rite Journal* a few years ago about a member who has not missed a meeting of his Lodge for 46 years. He also had been Treasurer of the Lodge for 35 years. I think this biography illustrates well a thought that I wish to leave with you today.

The man is a Past Master, Past High Priest, Past Thrice Illustrious Master, Past Commander, a Knight of the York Cross of Honor and a 33° Scottish Rite Mason. These accomplishments in themselves, although admirable, are not unique.

He has also, however, sponsored more than 100 petitions in each of these Masonic Bodies, donated more than 100 permanent memberships in the Knights Templar Eye Foundation and more than 100 permanent contributing memberships to the Shrine Hospitals. This is unique.

This Brother is also a Past Potentate of the Shrine, Past Vice Chairman of the Board of Trustees of the Scottish Rite Children's Hospital, Past President of his Masonic

Temple Corporation and Past Master of the District Masonic Association.

He served as President of his Masonic Temple Company for ten years and twice served as President of the Scottish Rite Foundations of Georgia. This list merely touches upon his contributions to Freemasonry.

For many years now we have been making excuses to ourselves for the declining interest in our Craft — stating that men today do not have the time to be Freemasons, that the demands placed upon their time today are simply too great. This excuse is used to justify lowering our requirements to attract them. And yet, with modern labor saving devices, reduced required working hours and increased speed of transportation, modern man has far more free time than did any of our Brothers of the past. No, my friends, all we are doing is making excuses to satisfy ourselves. It is a matter of priorities, not time constraints.

So, back to our Brother. Here was a man who dedicated his life to Freemasonry, a man who found a single niche into which he could direct his energies. Right? Wrong!

This Brother was also Charter President of the Atlanta Law School Alumni Association, President of the Georgia Children's Chiropractic Center, Director of the Joseph B. Whitehead Memorial Boys Club, and Chairman of the Board of Trustees of the Doctors Memorial Hospital for eight years and Vice Chairman for ten years. He is also Past President of the Overland Guarantee and Insurance Agency and an Elder in the Presbytery of his church where at the age of seventeen he became its youngest Deacon. This merely touches upon his contributions to his community and his church.

This man had no more than a 24-hour day, the same as everyone who has ever lived. His priorities provided the initiative for his accomplishments. So, here is a man who surrendered his life to organizational service—a man fully devoted to service to others. Right? Wrong!

In his spare time he served as a Judge in the Criminal Court system and is now Judge Emeritus, Superior Court of Georgia. He also managed to earn L.L.B. and L.L.M. degrees from Atlanta Law School and an L.L.D. from Webster University.

How could one man give so much service to others and, at the same time, accomplish so much for himself? The life he lived, the accomplishments he achieved, the contributions he made are beyond admirable but still not unique only to him. There have been others. So, why do we insist on making excuses to justify a lack of interest in us?

Let us ask this why. Why would a man not be interested in an organization that made this world what it is? And make no doubt about it, my Brothers, without Freemasonry this world would be different, very different.

I relate to you a tale I heard a number of years ago. A little boy one day found a cocoon of a moth and observed movements within it. He realized that the moth was attempting to emerge to its final metamorphic state—that of a vibrant, living adult. The boy decided he would help the moth in escaping the confines of the cocoon, so he cut the cocoon to permit the moth to emerge. To his disappointment, the moth failed to open its wings and develop into the adult he expected and it soon died.

His mother, noting the disappointment on the face of the little boy, explained to him that, in order for the moth to reach its full potential, it was necessary for it to emerge on its own. The struggles of the moth were for a purpose — to enable it to gain strength to rise above the world upon which it used to crawl. The struggle was a necessary part of its life. She told him that because he did not allow it to struggle to mature; it would neither walk nor fly. When the boy reduced the struggle, the moth was never able to achieve its potential.

For generations we have been doing exactly that with the youth. We do our utmost to make life easier for succeeding generations. We don't want our children to experience our struggles, although few of us, if given the chance, would change ours. Much of the pathway that we have paved for them removed responsibility as a requirement for achievement.

I watched this phenomenon occur during the seventeen years I spent in the field of education and in the more than thirty years working with youth organizations. Requirements for advancement and recognition were continually reduced, and I observed a distressing decline in initiative to excel. I firmly believe that this decline is at least in part due to what we as adults required or rather did not require.

The result of our attitude is evident today in the multi-million dollar defaults in student loan programs, the lack of assumption of responsibility to ethical commitments and a declining interest in responsible organizations.

Why should one who was never required to assume responsibility as a youth be interested in an organization based upon an assumption of responsibility? Our attempt to give much while requiring little in return has not only not benefited our youth but also has proven detrimental not only to them but to society in general.

As long as we have the attitude that we can buy the admiration and respect of the young by giving more and requiring less, we have little or no hope of recapturing that admiration or respect. And, we will continue demoting the reason for an interest in us. Those adults whom I remember and respected the most as a youth are those who demanded the most from me. Think about your youth and who won your respect. Why should this be any different today?

We cannot now expect to change a phenomenon of society by making excuses for those who lack the interest in a responsible organization. We must, however, attract those who have that interest.

For years I have been asked what my answer is for the survival of the Craft. And, for years I answered, "I do not know."

Today, I am convinced that our survival will depend totally upon our intent to remain a quality institution. The teaching and requiring responsibility of our youth will go a long way to developing the interest in responsible high-quality organizations in the future.

[8]

Beyond the Ordinary

I received a book written by Henry Clausen, Sovereign Grand Commander of the Southern Jurisdiction titled, *Beyond the Ordinary*, and I thought "What a descriptive purpose of Freemasonry!" We should be beyond the ordinary for we start with the best men we can find and we work to improve that best. One of the greatest contributions Freemasonry has ever made to society was showing men that they are much better than they think they are.

Experience and history teaches us that only a very small percentage of men will ever rise to a level to be termed "beyond the ordinary" but I think that the same experience and history would reveal that percentagewise a greater number of Masons will reach that plateau than will nonmembers. Why? I would like to believe that it is because we as an organization are geared to carry men beyond the ordinary.

It is not for every man to be great as we know it. If it were we would have to redefine the term "greatness," but it is for every man to be greater than he will be. I read recently a book titled, *The 100: A Ranking of the Most Influential Persons in History*. I found with few exceptions one common theme running through that listing; they were concerned with their fellow man. They dedicated themselves to service to others. The few exceptions were as result of the "most influential" in the title not the most positive influential. If we look back at great men who were

Masons, we will see that they were also dedicated to service. They were concerned with others.

We as Freemasons must learn from the examples set by our ancient brethren but we must stop looking back and lamenting that our present is not as great as was our past. Life is for today, not yesterday. We can become today what we want to become but not by dreaming of the past. We know that by becoming a Freemason we took a giant step in our lives, perhaps the first step that could lead us beyond the ordinary.

The poet Edwin Markham expresses well the profound influence that characterizes Freemasonry. "There is a destiny that makes us brothers; none goes his way alone, all that we send into the lives of others, comes back into our own." So too does the value of the lessons taught in Freemasonry lie entirely in the thoughts and inspirations they stimulate in the minds of those receiving them. Maybe this is the answer as to why only some will rise beyond the ordinary.

I had the privilege to teach at an exclusive private girl's college for fourteen years. I listened to a number of my students who came from a relative privileged segment of society complaining about what they lacked. I kept a quotation on a bulletin board in my classroom that stated: "I had no shoes and I cried, then I met a man who had no feet." My brothers, no one rises by crying over what he lacks.

Tomorrow morning I will be delivering a eulogy for one who was one of my best friends for over 37 years. He was a man who had a great influence on my life. He knew more about the philosophy of Freemasonry that almost anyone I have ever met. He was my assistant Scoutmaster when I was a Boy Scout. I became a Mason because he said to me one day "Tom, you should be a Freemason." I had lost interest in joining the Craft eight years prior when I asked someone who was a member of the lodge that I eventually joined, how to join and he never told me.

My friend was a man who never ceased to amaze me. I watched him work two or three jobs most of his life to take care of his family. He was wounded during the Second World War and was in constant pain but he continued to work to care for his family.

The adversities in his life were far greater than we will ever experience. I stood beside him at the funeral of his nine-year-old daughter who had died of a brain tumor. He had another daughter go to prison on a drug conviction and a son who was killed by a police officer in a robbery attempt.

One of the last times I was with him he was unable to stand but he was chopping wood to burn in his stove by dragging a piece over with an ax and then splitting it. He told me that day, "that he had so much to be thankful for. He had a great family, he always had a job to feed his family, and he had great friends."

This man had one other adversity that we have not had to face. He was a member of the Prince Hall Grand Lodge. He was a black man.

We must learn to use what others have to offer us. We are but a composite of all of our life's experiences. We never know what lasting effect may be produced. And remember, there is none in life who can offer us nothing. There is no one from whom we cannot learn something.

How easy it is for us to write off someone who does not come up to our standards. How easy to minimize the worth of one who is less intelligent or from a lower social class or is of a different race, religion or culture. How often we may encounter someone we think as a nobody. But, if we do, we are the poorer for it. What a loss it would have been in my life had I not accepted my friend because he was a black man.

I recall reading somewhere that "There is enough good in the worst of us and enough bad in the best of us that it ill behooves any of us to find fault in the rest of us."

Those who will rise to great heights above the ordinary have probably learned to accept men as they are. They have learned to learn from all regardless of whom or what they were. They're less impressed with themselves than they are with others.

Goethe once wrote, "Treat an individual as he is and he will remain as he is. Treat him as he could or ought to be and he will become as he could or ought to be." The basic structure of Freemasonry is the Brotherhood of man under the Fatherhood of God. Perhaps this is why the percentage of the Craft that will rise beyond the ordinary is above the average.

We can say now, with little reservation, that some here are or will be beyond the ordinary. We also know that probably most will not. We also know that most could. Most of us will make no big mark in the world but we could all leave some mark. Certainly we can all be brothers and perhaps, just perhaps that may today be beyond the ordinary. The American poet Ernest Howard Crosby wrote some years ago:

> No one could tell me where my Soul might be.
> I searched for God, but God eluded me.
> I sought my brother out and found all three.

This fundamental precept of the fraternity probably has contributed to our survival while other organizations have failed. It therefore has led us as a Craft, beyond the ordinary. If we are to continue to survive, we must rekindle that spark of brotherhood. We must indeed, keep Freemasonry beyond the ordinary.

[9]

You

*Given at a Leadership Conference for
the Grand Lodge of District of Columbia*

I never cease to be amazed at what my brethren think I am. I have been introduced a number of times as a noted Masonic speaker, a Masonic author, a Masonic scholar a Masonic Historian and recently in Portugal, I was introduced to the president of the country as an important Masonic philosopher. But, my brothers, I am just a little country boy who became a Freemason and left my farm to become a Grand Secretary. I do not look at myself as a Masonic speaker, author, scholar and certainly not a philosopher. Whatever I have gained in my life; I have gained it because of the contributions of others to me.

I am greatly concerned with the future of Freemasonry. There is a tremendous need today for Masonic leadership and that is what I am going to speak to you about this morning. I hope that what I have to say stimulates you. It is my hope that you will begin to comprehend the need to become better than you are in your leadership role of this Craft. Those of you who are sitting here today are the ones that must expose society and our new members to the meaning of Freemasonry. Leadership begins with where you sit today.

I spent seventeen years in the teaching profession—fourteen at a private girl's college—and there I was obligated to give one-hour lectures. One thing I learned at that time was that my students stopped listening before I stopped speaking. Now I have resolved that issue. I would rather leave you with a few thoughts that you will remember than with many thoughts that you won't. When I wrote this presentation, I started thinking about what I was going to title it and I came up with a very complex title. I titled it "You," and that is what I'm going to speak to you about today; You.

I spoke at a conference down here some years ago and I was told at that time that as a keynote speaker, it was my responsibility to motivate, stimulate and inspire you. I was to cause you to think about what you mean to Freemasonry. Frankly, I don't think that I need to inspire you. The fact that you are here indicates that you must have been inspired somewhere along the line. If you were not leaders already, you would not be here today.

I don't need to sell you on the Craft; had you not been already sold, you would not be here. I don't need to define your purpose; each one of you should know your purpose by now, and that is to lead the Craft. So it is, that there are times that I wonder when I am speaking to a group of leaders like you, why am I here?

First, I am here in part to cause you to think a little more fully about your importance to Freemasonry and bring it into perspective. Because of you Freemasonry continues to do good for others. Freemasonry has been a greater contributing organization to the good of mankind than any other organization that ever existed. You, my brothers, keep the Craft going. But let's be realistic. If we sit here and say that we are active in Freemasonry because of the good that it does for others, we are only kidding ourselves.

We are here today because of the feeling of satisfaction that we get out of the fraternity. We are here because we want that stimulus that we get out of accomplishing something on behalf of ourselves. We are here because of our egos. Fortunately for the world, our activity in Freemasonry cannot be performed without benefiting the world and my brethren there is nothing wrong with egos. Without ego we would accomplish practically nothing. Yet, and this is important, the legacy that we leave behind will depend more upon our ability to control our egos than to use our egos. One of the greatest problems in Freemasonry today is that many of our leaders, and some at the Grand Lodge level, in enhancing of their egos, fail to remember their purpose. If we are not in Freemasonry to serve, we are in Freemasonry for the wrong reasons. What we get out of Freemasonry is a side benefit.

You did not join the Craft for what you were going to get out of it; you joined the Craft for what you could give to it. You accepted this task as an obligation. Before you took the obligation you stated that you were not present for any improper motives. This fact delineates the extent of the Freemasonry I know. My little prayer, "Dear God, let me never forget where I came from and let me know when to quit," was written from having seen many leaders who have forgotten where they came from when they became leaders and having seen many men who were great leaders until they remained too long. I never want to forget where I came from and never want to hang on so long that I am remembered for what I was at the end rather than what I was when I had greater capabilities.

Permit me to tell you about an old man who was a member of my Lodge. He never held an office of any kind that I am aware of but he served on every committee for which he was asked. I never saw this old man turn down a request to serve others. He never drove an automobile, but he rarely missed a meeting. Our York Rite bodies met eleven miles from the town in which he lived and he took a bus three times a month to attend the meetings of those bodies and hoped that he can get a ride back home. Our Scottish Rite bodies were fifty miles from town, and he took a bus each time there was a reunion and again hoped that he would be able to get a ride home. If he didn't, he would go back to the bus station to wait until the bus ran. I never knew a man that was as totally free of ego as was he. He neither asked for nor sought recognition but he offered to help all who were in an active leadership role.

Was this old man a leader? In my opinion, this old man is one of the great Masonic leaders I've known in my life because he served as an example to others. He inspired others to become something better than they would have been. He epitomized to me what is significant as a passive leader. Without men like him, my brethren there could be no men like us. What good would be the greatest leader in the world if there were no followers? When the old man died and I read his obituary, I learned that he was a highly decorated hero from the Second World War. He chose to live his life in the simplicity of service.

The future of Freemasonry, however, is going to depend upon the active and qualified leader. And this is where you come in. You must have the commitment to lead. You must know its purpose and you must understand its importance. You must be more concerned with Freemasonry than you are with your own image. You must have enough ego to be driven but not too much to be overwhelmed. We have had our share in Freemasonry of those with over-inflated opinions of their own importance on all levels of the Craft.

What I am saying very simply to you this morning, my brethren, is if you are here today for you, or if you are here as an officer so you can walk around with a past officers jewel on your breast, you are in the wrong place. Freemasonry deserves better. My brothers, you must understand your place in history. You must appreciate the significance of the position you hold and will hold.

We as Freemasons have inherited an awesome responsibility, but those of us who have chosen to be leaders of this Craft have inherited much more. For we have chosen to help lead the greatest organization ever conceived by the human mind. You have chosen to be not just average. You have accepted a mantle of responsibility that has been borne by predecessors who made this Craft great.

You will never be a leader anywhere else in any other organization, where you will have as much potential power as that which is placed in your hands by Freemasonry. Freemasonry also places upon you a greater obligation than any other organization will ever place upon you and it must be expected that you will assume that obligation.

A simple old adage says, "Leaders are born not made." Well, I don't buy that. Certainly there are some men who are born with a superior leadership potential. It is a fact of life that there are those born with a greater psychological or physiological potential for leadership but I have watched too many men with limited talent go through the chairs of a Masonic body and noted that they came away from those chairs as far better men than they were when they started, to believe that leaders cannot be made.

Yes, leaders can be made. Know it now, my brothers, you can be good, but you must make yourself good. Do not lay back and expect to absorb ability. Do not lay back and expect that you will become a leader by an osmotic phenomenon. This organization has played a major role in developing the potential of many and the result has been great leaders but do not think that it will occur in you without your effort.

Freemasonry offers more than a training ground; it

brings with it a known respect far surpassing that of any other organization. Freemasonry is an elite organization that has helped to produce elite leaders. It has been known by its quality for more years than most other organizations have even existed. Some of our greatest statesmen, patriots, heroes and leaders in all walks of life had their ideals forged and honed in the conclaves of Masonic ideology. These men took advantage of what the Craft had to offer. One of the notable perks of Masonic leadership is the development of the leader.

You are now being afforded a recognition opportunity, but recognition must be earned. The recognition, you realize, will depend primarily on what you do. You can do little, if you choose. You can sit, go through the chairs, and walk out of office with a jewel on your chest, but if you do, you may not be recognized at all. Your wages will reflect your input. You, my brothers, are on the threshold. Yet, we know that not all can become great leaders but all can become better leaders.

Freemasonry is an amazing organization, but frankly my brothers, I don't think we are nearly as great as some of our members' think we are, but we are far greater than the vast majority of the world realizes we are.

Think of what America would be today without the Freemasons of the past. Look at the influence of the early patriots and the great leaders who were Freemasons. Now look at those around the world who are not necessarily as familiar to us but just as important in the struggle for liberty, equality and freedom in the rest of the world. Think what this world might be today if it had not been influenced by men like them.

This world desperately needs Freemasonry. We are an enclave of toleration in an intolerant world. We are a unique organization in a world that desperately needs that uniqueness. We have been a viable force for what is good and right in mankind for centuries. There is no other environment in the world offering the opportunities for all diverse factions to associate together as brothers. Frankly, there is nothing in this world to replace us. Our future is now in your hands.

We need leaders with far-reaching vision but that vision, my brothers, depends upon a sound knowledge of our past. So we must understand who we were and what we are. Learn, my brothers, learn what we have been in the past; learn what we are now and recognize what we can be in the future. Our brothers in the past have blessed us with an unsurpassed legacy. Where it goes from here is in your hands. Each one of you sitting here today is an important part of the puzzle of what the future of Freemasonry holds.

We are too great to fail. If we do the whole world loses. Personally, my brothers, I don't want to be remembered as part of the generation that permitted this Craft to fail. Do you?

It's a great privilege in my life to be able to associate with you. You are the leaders of this day. Freemasonry's future is now up to you. Become better than you are now; if you do, you can become whatever you choose to be.

[10]

Masonic Charities

For many people on this earth, the very struggle to survive supersedes any consideration of what they might do for others. The very concept of charity is nonexistent. This is not true in most educated societies, including our own.

To do just what we can do in life to get by, is not enough. It is not enough to say, I'm earning sufficient to live and support my family. It is not enough to say, I'm a good husband, I'm a good father and I do my work well. There must be something more to life.

Every man should seek to do some good. Every man must seek in his own way to make himself more noble and to realize his own worth. We must give something to our fellow man, even if it's just some little something. Dr. Albert Schweitzer wrote, "For remember, you don't live in a world all your own, your brothers are here too."

Freemasonry provides a great opportunity to us, not only in its teachings but also in its system, for we cannot practice Freemasonry without practicing charity. Even if we are active in Freemasonry for our own self-satisfaction we cannot avoid the charitable character of the Craft. You must remember, however, that Freemasonry is not a charity. We have no charitable classification as a fraternity, yet we are one of the world's greatest charitable institutions.

Masonic scholars believe that this vast philanthropy

began in the middle ages during the construction of the cathedrals. Funds were set aside to care for injured guild members and their families or widows and this characteristic was retained when we became a speculative Craft. It has been known for hundreds of years, that Masons take care of their own. When Freemasonry developed in America it structured its heart in charity.

Over time, Freemasonry evolved into a worldwide benevolent organization with the objective of improving world conditions through improvement of the individual. With that we evolved from a self-centered organization into one with a greater concern for others.

Over the past 150 years the Craft has grown at an astounding pace and yet we make no effort to seek publicity for our endeavors. To relieve the distress of others is a duty incumbent upon all mankind but it has become the special obligation and responsibility of the Masonic fraternity.

Many attempts have been made to determine how much money Freemasons put into charitable objectives. It has been stated to range from 1.3 to 1.6 million per day. My brothers, this equals 50% of the entire United Way Fund. This however is a mythical figure. There's no way we can pinpoint any accurate amount. Individual lodge contributions remain an unknown and charity cannot be measured in terms of money alone, the contribution of time must be considered also.

We do know that our Craft is not a beneficent society unto itself. Sixty percent of all its known charitable funds are available to the general public. One of the greatest of its internal charities is our homes for the elderly. This past year $250 million was used to support these homes and an additional $100 million is used for children's homes. None of those funds were solicited from the public. Pennsylvania homes are possibly the greatest in the world and it cost

Pennsylvania Masons $28 million to operate for that year.

We know about most Pennsylvania Masonic charities. The Pennsylvania Youth Foundation, the Drug and Alcohol Foundation, our children's home, the higher education loan fund, flood and disaster relief loans, the Masonic Service Association, hospital visitation program, and the George Washington National Masonic Memorial.

We all are familiar with the Shrine's Crippled Children's Hospital Program. It is unquestionably the best known and most widely recognized of all Masonic charities. The budget for those hospitals last year was one hundred ten million dollars plus ten thousand a day for the transportation fund. But, my brothers, the Shrine did not make the crippled Children's Hospitals, the Crippled Children's Hospitals made the Shrine.

But, did you know that Freemasonry also supports treatment and research in cancer, arteriosclerosis, heart disease, muscular dystrophy, muscular atrophy, retinal disease, tuberculosis, leprosy, arthritis, lung diseases, cerebral palsy, leukemia, diabetes, aphasia, dyslexia, kidney disease and others.

We have research hospitals, we provide dental care for the handicapped, we provide and deliver food to the poor, we provide tens of millions of dollars annually in scholarships, and we provide hearing dogs for the deaf. This is but a partial list of what is known. Subordinate lodges contribute to many other charitable causes. We gave $6 million for the renovation of the Statue of Liberty. This does not include charitable works that may be done by our members as a result of being stimulated by Freemasonry.

When we add all this up, it is difficult to comprehend America without Freemasonry. The economic burden on the taxpayer would increase dramatically. But the most significant factor would be the loss of that human quality of compassion for our fellow man.

There is no organization that could replace us. There are no organizations being formed today of this magnitude. Freemasons want Freemasonry to survive. Realistically, the free world cannot afford for it to fail.

[11]

Where Is Leadership?

I recently received an article by Dallas historian A. C. Green taken from the *Dallas Morning News* concerning Freemasonry titled, "We Are Brothers for Life." Green writes, "There used to be a time when it meant something to be a Mason. In the past being a Mason was like owning an American Express versus a Master Card. It showed a level of class. But, now that's all over. Masons are just old men clinging to the past. The Masons are a group designed to accommodate men who have accomplished a lot and want to float to the end."

Last year, a Washington newspaper contained a not too flattering article about the George Washington National Masonic Memorial. My brothers, this attitude is reflective of our declining influence and must be a concern to Grand Lodge leadership as well as every member of the Craft.

Today, self-centeredness is a way of life and the demand for our service is on the decline. Anyone can be a leader, at least to some degree, when everything is sailing smoothly. But, now the quality of leadership must improve, for now we must sell Freemasonry where in the past it sold itself.

There was a time when membership in Freemasonry was ardently sought. Anyone wanting to succeed saw an organization of successful men. Those successful men were Freemasons, many of them Masonic leaders. But where are they now? Why can we not find the Washingtons today, the Franklins, the Trumans and so many other great men who took pride in being members of the Craft?

My brothers, we must glory less in our past. We cannot survive on that. Organizations that have done so and are doing so now are withering on the vine. We must improve our present and we must do it now.

I do not agree with the cliché, "Leaders are born not made." There is no doubt we inherit some of our capabilities but the environment plays a vital role in the development of greatness and that includes great leaders. Would we have ever heard of Beethoven had never been exposed to music? Would we have ever known the name, Michelangelo without his exposure to art? Would we know the name, Babe Ruth, if he had not played baseball? Their environment was vital for their greatness in their fields.

At the same time, I could have practiced music all my life, I could have dedicated a lifetime to painting and sculpture, or I could have devoted my life to baseball but my name still would not have been known in any those fields. These men inherited the genetic potential for greatness in their lines of endeavor.

My brothers, have you ever watched a man go through the chairs of the Lodge and fail to come out a better leader? There is another old cliché that says, "He also leads who follows." I think today of two men who I have regarded as inspirational leaders. One was, doctor and Brother Richard Kern. He was a retired Navy Admiral, a retired surgeon, a Past Grand Master of the Grand Lodge of Pennsylvania and Honorary Sovereign Grand Commander of the Ancient Accepted Scottish Rite, Northern Jurisdiction. None could ever deny his significance as a leader.

The second man was a brother of my Lodge who was an old man when I joined the Craft, never drove an automobile but he rarely missed a meeting. He never served in any office that I'm aware of but he never turned down a request to serve on committees or perform any other function that he was asked to serve. He was a man that contributed much to the Craft by simply serving as an example to others.

It takes both of these types of leaders for an organization to be successful. We are losing both. It behooves each one of us to ask ourselves, "Suppose no one did any more than me?

There is a story told of a doctor in a small French village about to retire. For many years he served the citizens of the small village in which he lived and was on-call day and night. It mattered not whether they could afford to pay. It made no difference to this old doctor.

As a day of his retirement approached the people of the village wished to express their gratitude for the man who had devoted so much of his life to them. It was decided that each citizen would bring a pitcher of wine and pour it into a barrel and present the barrel of wine to the doctor.

Following ceremonies on the day of his retirement, the old doctor returned home with the barrel of wine given to him in memory of their love. He poured himself a glass and sat down in a chair to enjoy it but the wine tasted like water and the truth was revealing. Everyone in town reasoned, "My little pitcher of wine will not be missed, I have so little for myself, the others will take care of it." The little water that I substituted won't be noticed.

So, none gave and this, my brothers, is so indicative of Freemasonry today. Certainly, most of our brothers tell you that they value Freemasonry and yet so few are willing to give. We need to, in Freemasonry today, realize that the individual is important. The individual brother is the vessel for carrying the "soul" of the Craft. Today, we make Masons individually, we instruct Masons individually, and we neglect them individually. What we need are leaders to inspire them individually.

Diogenes, the popular philosopher of Athens in the fourth century went through the streets of Athens carrying a lantern while the citizens mocked him. He responded to their inquiries of what he was doing by answering, "I'm looking for an honest man." Freemasonry today is running to and fro looking for a man, for men, for men to lead. My brothers, we must find the man, the real man, the man who will lead.

Why are we no longer attracting the top men of our society? Are we really old man clinging to the past or are we what we think we are and as Daniel Poling described us, "A vital and dynamic force for everything high and worthy?" The philosophy of Freemasonry has not changed one iota. All that has changed is the composition of the membership. Don't ever forget, the only difference between a rut and a grave is the depth of the hole.

We certainly seem to be in a rut today but no organization with quality leadership remains in a rut and certainly none progresses to a grave. We must find the leaders. We must search for those qualities of vision that make leaders great. So, what do we search for, what are those qualities? It is intangible and difficult to find because there are no constants. There is nothing specific to define him as a leader. Leadership is something a person does, not a characteristic that he possesses. Today, the Masonic leader must use his imagination in using modern tools without losing sight of the ideals and principles upon which we were founded.

Frequently a good leader appears due to timing. It is the right man, at the right place, at the right time. Woodrow Wilson led us successfully into World War I because the timing was right and the country was ready, but he failed in his attempt in creating the League of Nations because the timing was not right.

The timing must be right for us today to develop good Masonic leadership but what will that take? During the darkest days of the Civil War a General was captured by opposing forces. A cabinet member went to President Lincoln requesting the promotion of a Colonel to a General. Lincoln replied, "I can promote a Colonel to General by the stroke of a pen but that won't make him a leader." Leaders must create themselves.

Leadership is the ability to inspire others to accomplish what they felt was quite difficult if not impossible. A good leader must be able to use diplomacy, to set an example and to give suggestions rather than commands. With these abilities he can transform potential skills into action but even more he must be willing to do everything he asks of others and more. He must be willing to work longer hours, undertake more difficult tasks than those assigned and withstand stress and adversity while still maintaining his enthusiasm. Above all, he must be willing to give credit to others. Nothing can be more discouraging than to have the leader take all the credit.

We must not think that being a leader is easy. Often, it is a lonely difficult business. As Nietzsche observed, "Life gets harder toward the summit; the cold increases, the responsibility increases, and there is never any guarantee of success."

If Freemasonry is to survive, these traits we must seek. Leadership is there. We must find it.

[12]

We Must Build Bridges

We as Freemasons take great pride in what we are and what we were, and justifiably so. We can, however, spend our time living in this pride and in so doing, decay on it. We should be proud of our past but we must remember that life is for today, not yesterday. What we do today will determine our tomorrows.

It is probably long past-due that we examined ourselves and asked these questions. Suppose no one took any more interest in the Craft than I do. Suppose no one attended any more meetings than I do. Suppose no one supplied any more leadership than I do. Where would the Craft be today? We must not continue to sit back and assume that someone else will always do it.

This magnificent country in which we live today is due to the men and women from our past of magnanimous spirit and unselfish character, willing to work for others and Freemasonry is the magnificent organization that it is today because there have been men with the same character willing to work for others.

There is an adage that says, "He profits most who serves best." Regretfully today, we are living in a society that is becoming extremely self-centered. This attitude is greatly affecting all organizations dedicated to the concept of service. Certainly, Freemasonry is showing the effect of it. Other than religion, there is no organization that does more to establish the brotherhood of man under the fatherhood of God than does our Craft and there are few organizations more devoted to the promotion of love of country. But, Freemasonry today is not doing what it should and could do in the promotion of this brotherhood. We are becoming a passive fraternity. Non-involvement is also becoming a part of our lives.

The English statesman Edmund Burke wrote, "The only thing that has to happen in this world for evil to triumph is for good men to do nothing." The following poem entitled "The Bridge Builder" expresses eloquently what might be an unprofessed goal for the Craft.

> An old man going a lone highway,
> Came, at the evening cold and gray,
> To a chasm vast and deep and wide.
> Through which was flowing a sullen tide
> The old man crossed in the twilight dim,
> The sullen stream had no fear for him;
> But he turned when safe on the other side
> And built a bridge to span the tide.
>
> "Old man," said a fellow pilgrim near,
> "You are wasting your strength with building here;
> Your journey will end with the ending day,
> You never again will pass this way;
> You've crossed the chasm, deep and wide,
> Why build this bridge at evening tide?"
>
> The builder lifted his old gray head;
> "Good friend, in the path I have come," he said,
> "There followed after me to-day
> A youth whose feet must pass this way.
> This chasm that has been as naught to me

To that fair-haired youth may a pitfall be;
He, too, must cross in the twilight dim;
Good friend, I am building this bridge for him!"

I would like to think that Freemasonry is a means by which we may build bridges but we must push against the force of the sullen stream. What a challenge to us as Freemasons, to build a bridge for the youth following after us. To accomplish this goal it will be necessary for us to revert back to a time when serving others was regarded as admirable. To use a Masonic term, we must return to the square. Some time ago Charles H. Brower wrote *The Return of the Square*. In it he pointed out that we in America have always had our share of freeloaders, persons who had rather discuss fringe benefits, more of what they are going to get from life than the extras they are going to give. They prefer to live in the grandstands enjoying the luxury of being spectators while others played the game.

Someone once wrote, "There was a time, when square was a positive word in our vocabulary. An honest man gave a square deal, he got a square meal when he was hungry, and he stood foursquare for the right and squarely against the wrong, when his debts were paid, he was square with the world and he could look you squarely in the eye. Then strange things began to happen to this fine, honest, wholesome word. Some characters bent it all out of shape and gave it back to their children."

We know what a square is today, don't we? He is the poor guy who never learned to get away with it. He is the sucker who volunteers when he doesn't have to. He is the young man so absorbed in his homework that he must be reminded to go to bed. He is the nut who gets choked up with the playing of the *Star-Spangled Banner* and stands at attention when the flag is passing by, one not afraid to say *I believe.*

If all Freemasons are not squares today, they should be. We need dare to be different. The man from Galilee died to go on record that he was not a mere conformist. However, tribes of squares are not thriving well in our climate today. They do not fit into the contemporary group of angle-players, corner-cutters and goof-offs. They are slowed by such old-fashioned ideas as honesty, loyalty and fidelity.

We as Freemasons must dare to do that which is square. We must let ourselves, again become an influence to be felt. Brother and President Theodore Roosevelt wrote, "It is not the critic who counts; not the man who points out how the strong man stumbled, or where the doer of deeds could have done better. The credit belongs to the man who is actually in the arena, whose face is marred by dust and sweat and blood, who errs and comes short again and again, who knows the great enthusiasms, the great devotions, and spends himself in a worthy cause, who at the best knows in the end the triumph of high achievement and who at the worst, if he fails, at least fails while daring greatly. So that his place shall never be with those cold and timid souls who knows neither victory nor defeat."

We must dare to be different, dare to profess our belief, dare to serve our fellow man, dare to be a square. So the challenge is ours. If we as Masons do not accept it then the failure will be ours. I quote the first few lines of the anonymous poem, "The Measure of Man:"

Not—How did he die?
　But—How did he live?
Not—What did he gain?
　But—What did he give?
These are the units
　To measure the worth

Of a man as a man,
    Regardless of birth.

We must be the bridge builders of today. This, my brothers, is Freemasonry.

[13]

What Is Expected from DeMolay

At the time I was asked to speak to this distinguished group of executive officers for the Order of DeMolay on the subject of "What Freemasonry Expects from DeMolay," I learned that M.W. Brother Joe Manning would be addressing the subject of what DeMolay expects from Freemasonry. As a chapter advisor, I was familiar with Joe's subject but never thought much about my subject. I find it an interesting and intriguing question but one without a clear-cut, definable answer.

Freemasonry, indeed, does have a right to expect something from not only the Order of DeMolay as a body, but also from each of the individual components of the body. Simply defined, we have the right to expect a performance from the members of DeMolay that reflects the purpose of the organization.

I never had the opportunity to be a member of the Order of DeMolay since there was no chapter active in the area in which I lived. In fact, I never heard of DeMolay until I became a Freemason. However, I was very active in the Boy Scouts of America for a period of twenty-seven years obtaining my Eagle rank in 1951.

After learning about DeMolay, I have regretted that I did not have the opportunity to participate. The basic principles of both organizations are the same, but I would have loved to have had the opportunity to work with the ritualism of DeMolay, and I have noticed that many of our outstanding DeMolay's have also been outstanding members of the Boy Scouts.

Brother Frank Land, when asked to define the order of DeMolay, stated: "Literally speaking, I would say the Order of DeMolay is a youth organization for young men whose purpose is a building of better citizens."

In trying to define specifically what Freemasonry expects from DeMolay, we should look to the seven cardinal virtues and the vows of a DeMolay. They are after all, indicative of what it takes to become a better citizen. Freemasonry has every right to expect that the purpose will be carried out within the individual member, the chapter, and the order in general.

One of the unique facets of DeMolay which has made it so different has been the first cardinal virtue, filial love. This is a quality never specifically stressed in any other organization with which I am familiar. We have the right as a Masonic fraternity, therefore to expect the members of the Order to demonstrate a respect for their parents and to acknowledge their contribution in their lives.

We have every reason to expect a member of the Order to demonstrate reverence for sacred things. This concept is a fundamental philosophical principle of Freemasonry, and we can accept no less from the Order of DeMolay.

We have every reason to expect courtesy in every way from our young men. Courtesy as a virtue contributes to the uniqueness of the Order, but seems to be a lost ingredient in present-day society.

We have every reason to expect that virtue of comradeship. Indeed, I would suspect that this virtue would be one to become more valuable in the life of a young man with each passing year.

We have every reason to expect a demonstration of

fidelity on the part of each young man who belongs to the Order. Perhaps this is one of the least emphasized virtues in society today, yet one of the most valuable.

We have every right to expect cleanliness of our members in thought, word and deed. This virtue also is one which seems to have been lost in our promiscuous society.

Finally, above all, we should expect no less than an absolute dedication to the concept and display of patriotism. The Masonic fraternity itself emphasizes the need for a commitment of each of us to his country, and we should never expect less than that from members of the Order of DeMolay.

In addition, the vows of the DeMolay require of each member to uphold and aid the public school system, and to honor and protect every woman. Freemasonry has a right to expect to see these vows demonstrated.

To see the more general aspect of what Freemasonry expects, we would have to look at the reaction of our members to specific situations and the reflections thereof, for what they expect to see in the organization they support. It may not be fair and indeed, probably is not, to expect the members of the Order to respond to the image some of our members expect. However, as an active advisor of the chapter, I have heard and I am certain all of you have heard, some of our members complaining about the action of individuals within the Order of DeMolay. These actions can be as minor as simple misconduct in a Lodge Hall to a more major misconduct which can reflect upon the organization as a whole.

Many of our members who have never been exposed to the Order of DeMolay or for that matter to the actions of current young people in general, have a much greater tendency to look with disdain upon the Order of DeMolay because the young men of the Order do not always create the image which they expect to see.

We as Freemasons assumed an obligation that whatever we should do, would reflect positively upon the fraternity. The members of the Order of DeMolay assumed the same obligation. Because the rest of society or the majority of society complies with a certain set of values does not mean that we must comply with exactly the same set of values. What is considered wrong in accordance with Masonic law and Masonic values does not necessarily have to be equal to the values of society, and this applies also to the Order of DeMolay. What is considered un-Masonic conduct does not necessarily constitute conduct acceptable to society.

Therefore, what Freemasonry expects in a general sense of the young man comprising the Order of DeMolay is that they present themselves in appearance and conduct at a level which is higher than what is expected from society in general.

Much of the "sale" of DeMolay to Masons today is based upon their future membership in Freemasonry, and it certainly serves as a selling point and justification for Masonic support for the Order.

However, it is not the purpose of the existence of the Order of DeMolay. Brother Land stated that its purpose was to develop better citizens. If those better citizens then chose to affiliate with the Masonic Fraternity that should be regarded as a side benefit for the support of Freemasonry but it certainly should never be the ultimate end result.

Before closing, I would make several observations regarding M. W. Brother Joe's presentation. I am in full accord with the basic concept of everything he said. I would, however, like to make a few comments regarding it.

The reference to the inability of the chapters to get good members from our Masonic lodges as advisors is well taken. However, we recognize that this is also a problem basic to our lodges as well. We cannot get good leaders to serve as officers within the Lodge.

I am not convinced that by going to leadership outside the fraternity is going to solve the problem. In the twenty years I spent in scouting on troop, district and council levels, the securing of leadership was always a problem, and we had no restriction on scout leaders coming from any source. One advantage to requiring the chapter advisors be Masons is that at least we have some control over who serves in that capacity.

I do not feel that the requirement by a grand lodge that a lodge officer be required to serve as an active member on an advisory board is going to solve our problem. At best, we would probably supply some warm bodies with little value. At worst, it could discourage potential lodge officers by adding requirements to serve.

Brother Joe stated that Masonry should invite representatives of the Order of DeMolay to participate in activities and programs of the fraternity. One of my concerns for some time has been the lack of exposure of our top leadership in DeMolay to State, National and International Masonic organizations.

At the conference of Grand Secretaries in San Diego, I received requests and permitted brothers to present programs to our conference from the National Masonic Foundation for the Prevention of Drug and Alcohol Abuse among Children, the Masonic Renewal Task Force, and the Southern California Research Lodge.

One final comment: I do agree that the Masonic fraternity has a responsibility of providing some degree of fiscal support to the chapters. However I have found that the more that is given, the less the effort is made by the chapters to gain anything on their own. Much more effort should be made by chapters to become more self-sufficient.

The less we require, the less we will receive.

I trust that what I have tried to suggest in this short time has been reflective of what we as a Masonic fraternity should expect from those who compose the order of DeMolay.

[14]

Sleeping or Dying?

Back in 1717, in a world of degeneracy, a world of lost values—where religion was at low ebb and losing its influence, there arose a new giant, a giant based upon the cathedral builders of the past. These new cathedral builders built not cathedrals of stone and mortar but cathedrals of the human soul and spirit, using not stone and mortar but using man's hunger for truth and goodness, his love of God and loyalty to his fellow man. Thus began, our Masonic heritage.

As this giant walked the earth its strength and influence was felt throughout the world and the effect it created was enormous. The influence of Freemasonry in the creation of our nation alone is beyond most influences ever felt anywhere in the world. There were times in its 275 year journey when its influence was less felt than at other times but never in all this time could it be said that it slept. Even at its lowest ebb, its influence could be felt. Now Freemasonry has been referred to as a sleeping giant; a great potential, little felt. But, my brothers, is it sleeping or is it dying?

I cannot help but think of other fraternal organizations which no longer exist or if they do, are of little consequence. Who today hears much of the Grange or the Odd Fellows, two of the few survivors? Maybe they were allowed to sleep too long. If indeed, Freemasonry is sleeping, why is it sleeping and if it is dying, why is it dying? What is different about our fraternity from what it was in the past? Is the fault internal or is it external? I would suggest that both factors are involved but the internal should be readily correctable. Our philosophy has changed not one iota. Only the members have changed.

In my last few years of teaching, I experienced the frustration in trying to justify right as right and wrong as wrong for moral or ethical reasons. I watched young people abandoning accepted standards of behavior in rebelling against most of what we accepted as right and good. Self-centeredness became a way of life. This rebellion against society was also felt by our fraternity as shown by the lack of interest in it.

But, I also found that same group of young people thirsting for guidance, hungering for examples of strength, desperately crying out for someone to guide them and we weren't there. We as a fraternity have failed to attract a generation. Why?

Have we dwelt too much on our past? Have we spent too much time glorying in what we once were and giving no reason to the young man for interest? If this giant Freemasonry is asleep, how do we awaken it? It is about time we stop mourning and begin working. Perhaps, we ourselves have become too self-centered. We are certainly a more passive fraternity compared with what we were.

We have done too much of too little for too long. We cannot survive forever on the accomplishments of our brothers of the past. It is of paramount importance that we begin again to practice the brotherhood we preach. We pronounce our lovely platitudes to others but fail to practice them. Maybe this is why the Giant sleeps.

If we lost a generation because we failed them, we must look to where we failed. We have sought for generations to make life easier for ourselves and for our children. We have sought to give much and require little

I would suggest that we gave too much help and lost a generation. We have removed a requirement for maturation. We have given for too long requiring little effort in return.

In our fraternity, we also have required too little and we have lost much of our potential and permitted the giant to sleep. Recall the story of Rip van Winkle. After his sleep he could no longer accomplish anything of note and had nothing to look forward to but death.

Is this Freemasonry today? Do we have anything to look forward to, but death? I am convinced that we have sold Freemasonry far too cheaply. We gave too much to our youth without a requirement of responsibility and we give too much to our members without a requirement of responsibility. Our ancient brethren saw clearly that membership carried with it responsibility. They also practiced a form of brotherhood that we seem to have forgotten. We must do more for our brothers. We must become a meaning in the lives of others.

So, is the giant asleep or is it dying? If it is asleep, we can awaken it. If it is dying, we can revive it. But we can afford to wait no longer. It can sleep only so long before like Rip van Winkle, it will have no influence when it does awaken. It is up to us, now.

[15]

Freemasonry Is?

I sometimes question my wisdom when I agree to write an article on a subject as challenging as, "Freemasonry is?" It has been defined by some of the great scholars of the Craft along with some who thought they were great scholars of the Craft. It has been defined by some of our greatest adherents as well as by some of our greatest enemies. Because it is an ever evolving entity, a definition today may not fit snugly tomorrow nor did it fit snugly yesterday; yet it is universal and some definitions always fit. To capture its meaning is like chasing the will-o'-the-wisp, and I readily recognize that there are far greater minds than mine still trying to do so.

There have been many definitions of our Craft given by Masonic scholars over the centuries, all of which have a definitive meaning and application as to what we are. They all define the Craft and yet none do so, not totally. With all their meaning, most of them are indefinite, at least to those outside of the membership. One of the most alluring and most frequently used definitions is that "Freemasonry is a beautiful system of morality, veiled in allegory and illustrated by symbols." It is also possibly the most complete definition, but what does it mean to those who are not members and very frankly, also to many of our brothers within the Craft?

And yet, with all the ambiguity of what it is to the

outside world and with the dearth of understanding of its purpose even to our leadership, it is an organization that has changed the course of civilization. What is it that makes an understandable definition so elusive? It is probably because Freemasonry is simply what each individual brother determines it is in his own mind. It will be nothing more or nothing less to each brother beyond what he makes it to be.

I have had the opportunity to travel extensively throughout the world and to experience Freemasonry in a number of jurisdictions. Thus, I have learned that even though the structural philosophy of Freemasonry is universal, the operational philosophy may vary considerably. In trying to classify Freemasonry into what I refer to as "operational styles," I have observed thus far what I perceive to be four distinctive styles: They are philosophical, sociological, political and charitable. These styles are based upon the emphasis placed on them by the jurisdictions where they are located and in turn have evolved into that particular style as a result of societal pressure of the environment. The tenets of Freemasonry were ever present, but the forces driving it made it relevant to the social structure in which it existed. In almost all environments where Freemasonry is found, its character has been shaped by the society. The only exception that I have found to the society shaping the style was in early Russian Freemasonry prior to Catherine the Great, where Freemasonry tended more to shape the society.

European Freemasonry, for example, operates in more of what I refer to as the philosophical style, retaining much of the philosophical and intellectual approach to the Craft from the age of Enlightenment. South and Central America, although retaining much of the philosophical, style are more idealistic as a result of the pressures of their societies, hence I have termed it a sociological style. Mexico has a tendency to be more involved politically, and for lack of a better term I refer to Mexican Freemasonry as a political style. The character of Freemasonry is almost paradoxical in the sense that even as it changes it remains the same. North American Freemasonry has probably deviated more from its roots than any other form of Freemasonry and has developed into an almost pure charitable style to the neglect of much of the philosophical character for which it is known over most of the world. Although we do not normally regard Freemasonry as a spirituality, much of its character tends to edge it into that niche. Any attempt, however, at a universal definition of Freemasonry based upon North America's charitable style could not be successful and yet even as it is different, it remains the same. It continues to be Freemasonry.

In all jurisdictions, there is some fusion of styles. For example, all contain aspects of the philosophical and charitable characteristics and vary only in the placement of emphasis. Indeed, all Freemasonry evolved from a philosophical style. There are probably other styles or variations in the world, but I have been unable to delineate them due to lack of experience and understanding. As a result of the variables in Freemasonry's operational philosophy, any specific attempt at an all-inclusive definition is difficult at best and perhaps impossible to achieve. This is probably one of the reasons for the ambiguity in the definitions that have been written.

No brother can participate in the practice of our Craft without it impacting his life. It has changed the lives of millions, making them more confident and more self-assured in what they wanted to do and what direction they wanted to go. It truly does become a way of life. (Another ambiguous definition.) Freemasonry remains an intangible and almost indefinable manifestation of the potential goodness of man. Its philosophy, if applied, could well serve as a template for understanding and world peace.

So what is Freemasonry? I was asked to write this short article on that subject, and what I have written will give no one a more clear understanding on the subject than what he had before reading it. Indeed, I probably contribute more to the indefiniteness.

When I am asked the question "What is Freemasonry?" I generally respond that it is a fraternity designed to take good men and make them better. But Freemasonry is so much more! More than anything else to me it is an ideal, not any tangible structure with any predetermined purpose. I am not even sure that the Freemasonry is definable, for to define it is to limit it and how can one limit an ideal?

[16]

On Masonic Education

*Given at a Quarterly Communication
of the Grand Lodge of Pennsylvania*

I f you have listened to me or read my writings in the past you know what my feelings are in regard to the need for Masonic education. I am firmly convinced that the future of Freemasonry in North America will depend upon our commitment to educating our members. It will only be through education that we will restore quality to the Craft.

To understand the need, we must first look at Free-masonry outside of North America. The cost to become a Mason and the cost to remain a Mason is exceedingly greater probably everywhere else in the world. The requirements to become a member of our Craft and to remain a member are also much higher. The appreciation and respect both inside and outside of the Craft is also much higher.

In France, the rejection rate is almost 60% and they have had an average 10% increase in membership for ten consecutive years. In Brazil, when I asked concerning the dues to be a Freemason they told me it was equivalent to $50 per month. When in Portugal I learned that the average age of a Freemason was 39 years, they met once a week and two meetings a month were dedicated to education. I learned while at the Grand Lodge of Iceland that they had a six year waiting period to join the Craft. I could continue citing examples but it is significant that the educational requirements far exceed anything we dream of in North America.

The respect shown to our Craft in most countries is much greater than we find in North America. While in Greece I had a prominent medical doctor who insisted on serving as my chauffeur. In Brazil I had a reception given by the Governor of São Paulo. In Ivory Coast, I was welcomed by the ambassador to the United Nations. In Portugal I attended a reception at the Presidential palace and the Prime Minister's palace and again I could go on citing examples. This recognition that I received was not for me but for what I represented. In almost all countries it is far more costly to be a Freemason and learning is a requirement. What I am trying to point out to you, however, is that the respect that is given to the Craft is proportional to the requirements of the Craft.

So to, it was in early America. I can look back over my thirty-eight years and see a continuing decline in what we require to become and remain a Freemason. I made an observation at the Northeast Conference of Grand Masters, Deputy Grand Masters and Grand Secretaries several years ago that upset some of those in attendance. I said at that time that American Freemasons were the most ignorant Freemasons in the world and then qualified my comment when I was challenged by adding that we were not only the most ignorant but also the most cheap. Please note, that I am saying ignorant (lacking in Masonic knowledge) not stupid. What I said at the time I continue to support today.

We have reduced our requirements to become a member and we have reduced our requirements to remain a member. And, what has been the result? We certainly do not carry the image in society that we once did.

Why do you suppose the attacks of the radical religious leaders have become more pervasive and effective? The answer is simple; they need no longer be concerned about our influence. Maureen Dowd observed in her column in *The New York Times*, that "If you require less than you deserve, you will receive even less than you require." There can be no doubt about that when applied to Freemasonry.

We must again practice Freemasonry and we can't practice it, when the vast majority of our members do not even know what to practice. If American Freemasonry is ever again to experience the influence it once had and regain our rightful place in society, it will have to rejuvenate the respect that it once had. That respect must result from masonically educated, quality members.

Historians are finally writing about Freemasonry but they are writing about the quality of our past, not the quantity. I have no doubt that this is exactly what you want but you cannot get it by osmosis and we cannot spoon-feed it to you. It is up to you. You are the future. Freemasonry in North America is in your hands.

[17]

Foreign and Fraternal Relations

Given to the Grand Secretary's Conference

Tis is a subject in which I have a great interest, and with which, I have also been greatly concerned for a considerable number of years. I have become even more concerned, in recent years, due to major changes taking place in Freemasonry. It is a subject with which all grand lodges and certainly all Grand Secretaries should be concerned.

For many years Freemasonry has been a relatively quiescent entity in regard to increasing the number of regular grand lodges in the world. At the same time, irregular and unrecognized Masonic bodies have also been relatively quiet. This period of quiescence has been replaced in recent years with a flurry of activity by both categories of Freemasonry. This activity may be regarded in many cases to have been a beneficial activity to Regular Freemasonry, but certainly not all of it has.

Indeed, our Craft is confronted today with resultant challenges, perhaps of a magnitude never before seen in our history, and we cannot afford to remain ignorant of what is occurring. The way our leadership responds today is going to determine the direction Freemasonry will go in the future, which in turn, if we remain a viable institution, will influence the direction of civil society.

Every grand lodge has an inherent right to make decisions regarding those grand lodges with which they will be in amity. There must also be, however, an assumed responsibility on the part of the leadership to become knowledgeable of, and understand the characteristics of, the grand lodges they are considering. They must also be cognizant of the impact their decisions may have upon World Freemasonry. We, as grand lodges, can no longer function with an isolationist attitude that many of us have chosen in the past.

The approach to Foreign and Fraternal relations has not only been made more complicated by the increase in the number of grand lodges being created, but the picture has been clouded by the creation of competing grand lodges in the same geographical jurisdiction. These competing grand lodges have not always been a result of creation by any regular grand lodge, but of what is regarded as "irregular" Freemasonry.

There has also been a marked increase in schisms within regularly-consecrated grand lodges resulting in two grand lodges in the same jurisdiction, both claiming to be the legitimate, regular grand lodge. The result has been that some mainstream grand lodges recognize one, while other mainstream grand lodges recognize the other. This is an untenable situation, which weakens our Fraternity.

To further compound the problem of recognition, Masonically affiliated appendant bodies have become instrumental in causing some of the schisms to occur. These occurrences should be even more intolerable to us as officers of grand lodges. And yet, we have not only permitted the situations to exist by simply ignoring the issues, but in some cases have even contributed to them.

The result is that today many of the grand lodges in the world have no idea which grand lodges in some jurisdictions are regular and which are not, while most appendant bodies know even less. To give you an example: Several years ago while visiting in the jurisdiction of Greece, I became aware that every grand chapter in the United States recognized a grand chapter in Greece that was not part of the Grand Lodge of Greece in amity with all North American grand lodges. What this amounted to was that our grand chapters recognized the irregular Freemasonry of Greece. I do not cite this is an example to criticize our grand chapter's leadership, but to illustrate the lack of knowledge of what is occurring in other jurisdictions, as well as the need for caution when we make decisions regarding fraternal relations.

Personally, I would like nothing more than to see all regular Freemasonry in the world united as a like-minded brotherhood of men, with a common goal. Such unity would not only contribute to the strengthening of our noble institution, but would increase our potential to be an influence in the ongoing evolution of civil society and search for world peace.

This cannot and will not happen, however, so long as our leadership remains ignorant of, or ignores the protocols of fraternal relations. Nor can it, nor will it happen so long as conformity to these protocols which have sustained us for almost 300 years is not complied with by those seeking recognition. We, as Masonic leaders today, cannot permit ourselves to be seduced into accepting anything less. We cannot offer ourselves for sale to the highest bidders.

So where does that leave us in dealing with this issue of foreign and fraternal relations? First of all, we must recognize and acknowledge as leaders that we cannot, and do not, know everything. This will not be easy for many Masonic leaders, for we just might have the greatest accumulation of egos of any organization in the world. Even the most ardent of us, however, must acknowledge that in this day and age, it is simply not possible for any one individual to keep abreast of the changes that are occurring in our Craft. Most of our leadership today is dealing with demands in their lives, which will preclude any hope of their determining which Grand Lodges are entitled to recognition.

For the sake of Freemasonry, it is therefore imperative that we divest ourselves of our limiting egos, and accept guidance from those whose function it is to make these studies. In our case, that responsibility lies within the Commission on Recognition of The Conference of Grand Masters in North America. They have been charged with this responsibility, and although they are not an authoritative body, having no dogmatic powers, it would behoove our grand lodges lacking the wherewithal to conduct their own independent investigations to look to them for guidance.

We are creating many of our own problems today. By contributing to disunity instead of unity, by supporting the irregular instead of the regular, by reacting instead of acting, and by failing to recognize our ignorance on specific issues, we are not only not helping the perpetuation of our Masonic Craft, we are aiding and abetting its demise. Our leadership should not permit it. Our grand lodges should not accept it, and Freemasonry must not tolerate it.

If our Craft is to have a stable and contributory future, then we must support our requirements of regularity and requirements for recognition. We must also be unwilling to accept deviations from these requirements. Fraternal relations must be limited to Regular Freemasonry. Those grand lodges seeking recognition know what is required. If they cannot accept these parameters, then they fail to gain recognition, and if a regular grand lodge chooses a divergent pathway, then it must risk losing recognition.

Fraternal relations between grand lodges is not a right, it is a privilege. Each grand lodge is free to choose, but if that choice contributes to disunity, then Regular Freemasonry has the responsibility to attempt reunification. Only through unity, can there be unity, and Freemasonry certainly needs that today. The future of the Fraternity depends upon it.

[18]

Our Relevancy in Today's World

*Given at a United Grand Imperial Council of Knights
of the Red Cross of Constantine Annual Assembly*

It is a great privilege for me to be asked by our Grand
Sovereign to speak to you tonight on a subject that has
been to a very great extent, my life for over fifty years; a
subject that has not only impacted my life, but has impacted
the evolution of civil societies for centuries. The subject,
of course, to which I refer, is Freemasonry. Knight Com-
panion Wood granted me free reign to speak on whatever
subject I chose and I titled my paper, "Our Relevancy in
Today's World."

Freemasonry is an old institution as we all know. Indeed,
it is the oldest fraternal organization in existence today but
its origin is essentially an unknown phenomenon. We do
know that the first organized speculative form of Freemasonry can be traced to the year 1717. However, its roots go
back to antiquity, but not the antiquity that some claim.
We did not predate the pyramids. We were not part of the
great thinkers of ancient Greece nor did we celebrate the
rise of the Roman Empire. In fact, we did not even assist
the Druids at Stonehenge. We, however, probably existed
in some form as early as the fourteenth century. While
attending the fourth International Conference on Masonic
History in Edinburgh, Scotland, I was invited to attend
a meeting of the oldest continuously operating Masonic

Lodge in history with minute books confirming that, dating to 1699. That Lodge, although composed of some operative Masons, was chiefly composed of non-operative Masons.

Freemasonry has contributed significantly in the development of civil societies for several hundred years. Many of the members during those several hundred years could be listed as Who's Who on an honor roll of the greatest men who have ever lived. Not only did our philosophical structure aid in creating the concept of a Democratic society, but many of the great leaders who led their countries in their struggles for liberty, freedom and equality were brothers of our ancient Craft.

It would be illogical to consider that so many of the greatest patriotic leaders of the world who led in the fight for the rights of man were Freemasons and were not influenced by its philosophy. Did Freemasonry make them great? Of course not; but neither can it be happenstance that they were all Freemasons. The philosophical precepts of Freemasonry must have influenced their thinking and contributed in some way to stimulate them to place themselves in a position to be leaders for their country's struggles for the rights of their citizens to be free.

Freemasonry may not have made these men great but these men contributed to making Freemasonry great. Without them, and many others whose names are legendary in so many diverse fields of endeavor, Freemasonry could not have risen to its greatness and have had the influence to impact the evolution of civil societies the way that it has for several hundred years. One of its great attributes to its credit is that the Craft attracted some of the greatest men with some of the greatest minds that ever lived. This attractive force was primary in causing our Craft to become a force unlike any other seen in the world to serve as a beacon to developing world societies.

Few countries with freedom that exists today do so without the influence of Freemasons or Masonic philosophy. Freemasonry was one of the significant enclaves that provided the environment wherein great thinking minds could meet with a relative degree of freedom during the Age of Enlightenment. Should we doubt how significant the impact and how relative Freemasonry's influence was, consider that the United States of America is quite possibly a result, along with many other countries, who used the model of democracy created here.

However, the world has changed; and with that change, we must examine our relevancy to it today. Is the philosophy and are the precepts of Freemasonry relevant to the demand of societies of the present day world? Does the visible image of Freemasonry stand out as a significant positive influence as it did in the past? Do we continue to have the influence to impact evolving civil societies? Does our present-day leadership have the long-range vision required to see the potential importance of the ongoing evolutionary development of society? These are very serious questions and our response to them will determine not only our influence on society but our very survival as an institution.

The answer to the first question regarding Freemasonry's relevancy to the demands of society in the present day world is an unequivocal "yes." There can never be a time that the philosophy of Freemasonry and its precepts would not be relevant in any society. The issues challenging Freemasonry in parts of the world today do not lie in the relevancy of its philosophy; it lies in our failure to practice it. I quote John Robinson, the noted author who quite possibly led the charge of the present day plethora of writers on Freemasonry, "The problem with Freemasonry today is that it does not practice Freemasonry anymore."

Robinson, however, was writing as a result of his observance of American Freemasonry. There is a distinct difference between the relevancies of Freemasonry in America when contrasted with most of the rest of the world. Society's evolution in America is slowed by a maturation requiring lesser evolutionary change and plagued by complacency and apathy. Unfortunately, American Freemasonry has been plagued by the same disease.

Several weeks ago I spoke at a symposium in Izmir, Turkey on the subject, "The Challenges Facing Masonry in the Twenty-First Century." When I was asked to speak, the topic was qualified to me with the observation that it is evident that our protocols of regularity, recognition, jurisdictional authority, etc. are not applicable in today's world. When I presented my paper, I served as the devil's advocate debating this observation. These very protocols have sustained Freemasonry for several hundred years and when we begin to lessen their significance, we begin to weaken the fabric that holds us together. I am constantly amazed by many of today's leaders who seem intent on destroying the very qualities of the Craft that not only sustains us but those that contributed to making us significant.

The proposition put forward was that Freemasonry must change to adapt to the technological age. And yet, Freemasonry has thrived for 300 years through evolving societal changes without sacrificing its protocols. Let us ask these questions: Is the societal change required to advance in today's age of technology any more dramatic than the societal change required advancing into the age of the Industrial Revolution? Must Freemasonry become something fundamentally different to remain relevant? Perhaps the changes are not so much needed in Freemasonry as they are in the society in which it exists. With the moral and ethical values promulgated by Freemasonry and with the changes that I have observed in my lifetime of society's evolution, I would suggest it would be more prudent for society to change, than Freemasonry.

There can be little doubt that with the loss of 75% of our membership, Freemasonry in America no longer has the influence that it once had. Our failure to attract great men and professional leaders from our society is indicative of a lack of vision that served as the foundation to the development of Freemasonry in America. It is not the decline in numbers, however, that is the continuing cause for failure of our visible image, but rather it is our response to the issues causing it. Membership numbers have always fluctuated, but never in the past have we been willing to surrender our quality to retain a quantity. We have not only failed to retain the quantity but we have sacrificed an unprecedented quality that will be extremely difficult to regain. It is undeniable that the relevancy of Freemasonry in American society is less than what it is in most of the rest of the world. We have justified lowering the quality of the organization due to the decline in quantity of members. Certainly, our numbers have been declining, but the loss in numbers has not approached the catastrophic loss in numbers during the Morgan affair and we did not find it necessary then to lower our standards to survive.

In today's age, we live in a country that is dominated by a precept of "political correctness" wherein the prevailing attitude has become that every citizen has the right to have the same as everyone else regardless of ability, initiative or work ethic. But, America was also built on sustaining protocols — protocols that provided its citizens with the opportunity and the stimulus to rise above the ordinary and to excel in their lives. The political correctness attitude has resulted in the conversion of many productive citizens of America to parasites living upon society. Unfortunately, much of our Masonic leadership has bought into this political correctness precept with the result of a devastating decline in the quality of the Craft.

I am not suggesting that we become an organization composed of only the "elite" of society. Indeed, a second reason for our greatness was in the organization's intent to accept men from all diverse walks of life and seat them in a Lodge room as equals. Lacking that intent, we could not have risen to the greatness that we have experienced. Nonetheless, we are an elite organization. When we set our goal to accept only good men, we became elitist. There is nothing wrong with elitism. Freemasonry has always been, and must always be, an elite fraternity.

However, a third and lasting reason for our greatness was our commitment to remaining selective as to the quality of the man we would accept. It is our failure to retain that third reason that Freemasonry's significance is declining in America.

I look at the Red Cross of Constantine as being the premier Masonic organization existing in North America today and one of the few bastions of Masonic elitism remaining. Some of you may recall that during my term as Grand Sovereign, I emphasized the need for us to remain selective. That is the primary reason that I encouraged the reduction in numbers of membership limits on subordinate conclaves. We must continue to serve as an example of what a Masonic organization can and should be.

However, my references thus far have been applicable only to the sociological conditions of our country and perhaps a few others, generally, the English-speaking countries.

Let us now take a look at Freemasonry in most of the rest of the world today. We are living in a remarkable age for Freemasonry. The Craft is growing at what may be its greatest rate since its inception. There have been 26 new Grand Lodges consecrated since the turn of the century and the Craft is achieving success and influence in parts of the world where it has not existed in the past or where it has been rejuvenated following the demise of repressive regimes. This perhaps represents the greatest numerical expansion of Grand Lodges in that span of time in our history, and most Grand Lodges in the world are increasing in membership numbers. They are attracting some of the greatest leaders in their communities and Freemasonry's impact upon their societies is considerable. Unquestionably, Freemasonry is relevant to them.

Many of you know that I have been serving as Executive Secretary of the World Conference of Regular Masonic Grand Lodges for the past fifteen years. In that position, I have had the privilege of traveling over much of the world and have been able to observe, Freemasonry as it operates in many different countries. As might be expected, it has been confronted with many challenges for various reasons. In Eastern Europe, the challenge has been in consequence of an ingrained distrust of all organizations as a result of the repressions that they have experienced over many decades. In Africa, it must deal with issues of distrust due to tribal and local fears of it being some type of witchcraft organization. In both areas of the world, it must also deal with resistance from religious leaders that have historically opposed Freemasonry.

I am firmly convinced that the relevancy of Freemasonry in today's world is no less significant than it has been than any time in our past, but I am also convinced that its relevancy in America must be redefined by our members and reinserted into society and its significance reemphasized. Fortunately, this is not the case in most of the world. Freemasonry has always been at its best when it has been challenged the most. This is a primary reason that it is succeeding in most of the world but showing failure in other parts. Permit me to relate to you some of my experiences that will emphasize the relevancy of Freemasonry.

I was in Romania several months ago and had a one-hour meeting with the president of the country, my second meeting with him discussing his interest in the potential contribution of Freemasonry to his evolving society as well as current social issues existing in his country. I also participated on two television interviews while there. Two months preceding that trip I took part in a videotaped interview in Italy.

Over the past decade, I have been received by the presidents of six countries and several prime ministers and have been on numerous television and radio programs in Europe and Africa along with many press interviews. I have addressed a public forum in India and senates and military leaders in Latin America. I participated in a wreath-laying on the tomb of the unknown soldier under the Arc de Triomphe in Paris with a sitting president, also on the grave of a former president of Gabon along with the president of the country, the tomb of O'Higgins in Chile along with the president and at the monument of Benito Juarez in Mexico. I assisted in the dedication of a Masonic monument on the national mall in Valparaiso, Chile, to name but a few of the significant experiences that I have had as a result of the significance of Freemasonry.

Does the visible image of Freemasonry stand out as a significant positive influence as it did in the past? It certainly does in most of the world. Its visible image continues to stimulate leaders of newly emerging societies to inquire as to its potential to participate. It is always astounding to me as to the type of receptions I receive in other countries simply because I represent Freemasonry to them.

I was recently in Montenegro where I attended their Grand Communication. Montenegro, for those who may not be aware, is the southernmost country that resulted from the breakup of Yugoslavia. There are currently seven countries, Serbia, Montenegro, Croatia, Slovenia, Macedonia, and Bosnia-Herzegovina created from this dissolution with a eighth, Kosovo, possible in the near future. I knew then how I would complete this paper.

Yugoslavia had been a country composed of numerous cultures with centuries of distrust and animosities, some of which continue to this day. It has always been amazing to me that one man, Marshal Tito, as a dictatorial power, could hold them together for as long as he did.

What is far more significant, however, is that within the framework of the philosophical precept of the brotherhood of man, Grand Lodges were consecrated in each one of these new countries with assistance from the others. Even now there are thoughts being generated to create a new Grand Lodge in Kosovo. When it is formed, it will also include the Grand Lodge of Albania because of their citizens living there. Each of these Grand Lodges was present in Podgorica and the display of affection for each other permeated the atmosphere of the occasion.

Does Freemasonry continue to have the influence to impact the evolution of civil societies? Just looking at a Masonic Communication in Montenegro should eliminate all doubt. Freemasonry will continue to have a major impact in evolving civil societies. The struggles will continue and the greatest restraints faced will lie within the vision of the leadership and the need to overcome the egotism that will be the greatest restriction.

At that communication, I wore the medallion of the Grand Lodge of Yugoslavia that had been presented to me along with the Grand Star of Montenegro. I wore it as a symbolic reminder of the relevancy of Freemasonry. Even though all wounds have not healed and all animosities dissipated in the societies, the philosophical impression of

Freemasonry on those brothers sitting in the Grand Lodge displayed very prominently the relevancy of Freemasonry in today's world. The feeling of brotherly love generated by Freemasonry does indeed transcend the hate and animosity in the world. Think, if it were possible, to transfer that same feeling to the world, what impact we would have.

[19]

The Universality of Freemasonry

For a number of years I have had the great privilege of being able to travel throughout much of the world and to see Freemasonry at work. I have, perhaps, been able to see it more clearly as an outsider in the regions I found myself, with a vision unclouded by any local emphasis placed upon it by the membership. This has accorded me the opportunity to observe it, analyze it, and compare it to the Freemasonry with which I was most familiar

The first observation I made is that there are considerable differences in Freemasonry in various parts of the world. I found, for example, that the European Grand Lodges retained many of the philosophical qualities that characterized Freemasonry in its early years. It therefore is philosophically oriented. In Central and South America it is more sociologically oriented, while in North America may be said to be more charitably oriented. I would expect to find additional variances in other parts of the world also, but it is important to note that these qualities are found to some degree in all Grand Lodges. The variances seem to be driven by the needs of the society in which Freemasonry exists, or at least as interpreted by the membership. None of these differences, however, impairs its philosophical foundation or the basic precepts upon which it has operated for centuries.

Far more important to society, and to the world are its

similarities rather than its differences, for it is the similarities that most benefits the world. Freemasonry's unanimity of purpose has defined it for generations and is its most important feature to society. Its basic ideals have remained unchanged in its dispersion throughout the world and it is this retention of unanimity of purpose that has made it the world-renowned institution for which it has been known for centuries. This inherent characteristic has caused to a great extent, its uniqueness. It is also this characteristic along with its philosophy and precepts that contributed to making the world what it is today. The Universality of Freemasonry has made it the most important organization in the evolution of civil society outside of organized religion that the world has ever seen.

Freemasonry became the significant organization that it did, and has created the impact that it has, probably for three primary reasons. First it was the first organization to accept all men as equals, and this in a class distinctive society. Visualize if you will and try to conceive how radical a thought such acceptance must have been back in fifteenth century Europe when there was little interrelationship between classes of people. Then there appeared this concept of Freemasonry that accepted all people as equals from Royalty to the Stonemason.

This totally new concept probably fomented much of the thought, which led to the evolution of what became democracy. Indeed there have been a few historians who have credited Freemasonry with the development of modern democratic thought.

Secondly, it attracted some of the greatest minds that ever lived. Much of the freedom of thought that flourished during the Age of Enlightenment was cultured and encouraged in the conclaves of Masonic lodges, and encouraged by Masonic ideology. It served as an attractive force for men whose names are forever remembered for their contributions to the world and to civil society in so many areas of expertise. Men like Voltaire, Franklin, Mozart, and Haydn, are names known worldwide as contributors to today's modern civil society.

Later names of other great men were added to the list of members: Kipling, Burns, Churchill and others. It is, however, in the names of those who led in the struggles for Freedom throughout the world that Freemasonry became most noted.

Thirdly, it remained selective on the quality of the man it would accept. Freemasonry's intent is to start with the best men we can find and through our moral lessons, improve that best. Do we always succeed? Of course not! Freemasonry has, however, been a unique organization in that we have been able to take men from all walks of life socially, economically, culturally etc., and provide an environment where-in the similarities of good are far more important than differences of type. Because of these men, the very course of history was changed. There are very few areas of the world today that truly know freedom that did not obtain that freedom without the efforts of Freemasons or at least the influence of Masonic ideology. I have learned a great deal about the influence of the Craft in my travels and never cease to be impressed by how much this organization meant in each area of the world I visit.

As mentioned earlier, many of the world's great patriots were Freemasons, and led their countries in its struggle for freedom, liberty, and equality. Many countries of the free world have the names of their great leaders etched upon their headstones of freedom who were our brothers, and who led their respective countries in the fight to erect those monuments. You will be familiar with many of those names although they may be from distant places and earlier times.

All of these men are revered in their respective nations as heroes who were at the forefront leading the way for their people to achieve freedom.

There are hundreds of other Freemasons who though lesser known, are none-the-less important and who assisted in these struggles. Freemasons were killed by the thousands for their position and support for the liberty of man.

What is it about Freemasonry that causes it to attract and gather together men of this caliber from all over the world, men who were willing to surrender everything they had including their very lives for freedom for others? What is it about Freemasonry that stimulates the tyrants and despots to try to destroy it? What is it in the philosophy of Freemasonry that has attracted many of the greatest men for hundreds of years to mold the precepts of freedom and provide the leadership to attain it? "What is it in its teachings that might he lacking elsewhere that helped develop this world? What is it that made it Universal?

First and foremost a requirement of anyone seeking to join with us is that he must believe in a Supreme Being. A belief in God creates a unifying bond of all members regardless of where they may be. We do not, however, limit our brotherhood to any one religion. We are neither sectarian nor dogmatic. It is our goal to encourage all men to worship God as their conscience dictates and their religion teaches. With this practice, men of all faiths have the opportunity to sit together as brothers without the divisiveness that tends to exist in so much of the world, and results in so much misery. It is a tragedy of major consequence that most of man's inhumanity to man is done in the name of God.

Freemasonry encourages its members to be patriotic. Dedication of its members to the country in which they live is of primary importance to Freemasons, assuming that freedom to practice its precepts exists there. Where there is no freedom to practice these precepts, Freemasonry cannot exist. Remarkably in spite of the opposition and all persecution, Freemasonry remains, reflecting its noble precepts.

Finally, the teaching of the need for our members to practice toleration of all people and their rights is the major cause of the Universality of Freemasonry. The philosophy of Freemasonry and its teachings of the need of tolerance of others rights and beliefs could very well serve as a model for world peace. The right to be free should be the birthright of all mankind. The respect for this birthright, if practiced, would eliminate almost all conflicts and wars. Peace would then be the accepted norm of the world.

This respect for freedom as a birthright is why there is the Universality of Freemasonry. This is why it has lasted so many years in so many countries. This is why it still lives while most organizations have long ago died. This is why it has attracted great men and helped make men great. Its finest definition is that it is "A Brotherhood of Men under the Fatherhood of God."

Freemasonry played a major role in the development of this world. Its philosophy is simple and eternal. For several centuries, its teaching has led the way in inspiring men to struggle for freedom for several centuries, and hopefully will continue to lead for many centuries to come. This is the Universality of Freemasonry.

[20]

Pride in Our Past, Faith in Our Future

P ride in our past—absolutely. No organization in the history of mankind has more reason in being proud of what it was than does the Masonic Fraternity. Of course, since no organization can be proud, that leaves it to the membership to express that pride. We have overwhelmingly done that. Perhaps today that is our greatest strength as well as our greatest weakness. It is our greatest strength, because it gives us a strong foundation upon which to build as well as a selling point to the outside world. It is our greatest weakness, because we use it today as a crutch to justify our present existence. We have too much of a tendency today to sell our past instead of our present.

Faith in our future — absolutely. With the increasing numbers of Grand Lodges being consecrated, with the increase in the number of members being accepted in grand lodges all over the world and with the spread of Freemasonry into areas of the world where it has never been, we must have faith in our future. Freemasonry has been propelled into the new century as a rapidly spreading institution that will create an impact upon this world. One way or another it will create an impact. The extent and kind of impact it creates is in our hands. It is important, therefore, that we do not dwell upon the pride of our past to the extent that we ignore the present upon which we must build the future. Our predecessors developed our past that built our present, and now we must develop our present to build our future.

Freemasonry has had within its ranks some of the greatest men and minds that have ever lived. Its membership rolls are a list that sounds like a listing of who's who of the world for the past 275 years. The diversity of fields of endeavor for which they are known is almost as diverse as the men themselves. It seems incomprehensible that there could be any force that could be of a strength that would attract and hold them together, and yet Freemasonry was and did. The Fraternity is a large part of the reason this world is as it is.

What was it about our Craft that drew these men together? What was it that kept them together? What was it that caused so many to work toward common goals? What was it that caused these men to create an organization which makes us so immensely proud of our past today? Many organizations — some patterned after Freemasonry — have been created, lived, and died, and left little evidence of their existence. And yet this Craft has been exerting its influence for just less than 300 years. Why?

I propose that first of all it was its' philosophy. The teaching of the acceptance of men from all walks of life was a new philosophical concept in a divided class world. Most organizations were structured around men not only from the same social strata, but also from the same profession, and although, this structure provided attractiveness to many, it lacked the diversity of thinking patterns that could lead to the support of a philosophy that would change the world.

It was the philosophy of Freemasonry that contributed to the thinking, which in turn produced the leadership that led the world. Just consider the names of the men who will forever be memorialized in their respective countries due to the leadership they provided in their struggles for freedom liberty and equality. Was this due to Freemasonry alone?

No, I am not that idealistic nor that foolish to believe that Freemasonry alone caused them to become great leaders. But then I am not so blind as to fail to see and realize that it would be a totally illogical assumption that so many of the great men of the world who were leaders in their country struggles for this freedom came from the Craft. This simply could not have been happenstance, thus the importance of the philosophy.

A second significant feature about the Craft that made us what we are was our commitment to accepting only good men. There is absolutely no way that fine porcelain can be made from poor clay. This is the answer I gave to a religious leader a few years ago when he criticized us for not taking poor men to make them better. There are many organizations devoted to that project, but that is not our purpose. Had it been so, we probably would not exist today, and we certainly would not have had the impact upon this world that we have had. Our future will depend upon our ongoing commitment to this precept.

The Road We Are Traveling

Given at the Grand Lodge of New York

Mere words could never express my feelings tonight, to be able to stand before you and to address you as the recipient of what I have regarded as one of the most prestigious awards given by North American Freemasonry. To have my name included along with those great brothers who have preceded me as past recipients, is an honor beyond what I could ever expect, and my expression of gratitude to the Grand Lodge of New York for selecting me, inadequate for what it means.

Were we to review the biographies of those great men who have received this award, we would find that they were truly outstanding in their fields of endeavor. I suspect that they spoke to you regarding their experiences in those fields and perhaps what Freemasonry meant in their lives. I will speak likewise, but you must understand that Freemasonry has been my field of endeavor for most of my life, so I will speak more specifically to it.

We sit here tonight due to efforts of giants of men, men of courage, men of character, men of wisdom, men of quality, but most of all, men of vision. Consider for a moment the magnitude of what that vision produced: an organization that changed the very course of history. We sit here at their feet, and although they are no longer a visible force, the legacy they crafted for us has been a sustaining force for several hundred years. Without them, we would not, we could not, be here. What a debt of gratitude we owe to them.

Just think, of how much this organization of Freemasonry has influenced your life. I know beyond a shadow of a doubt that without it, I would not be here. I would not be here not because of this being a Masonic function. I would not be here because I would not have had the capability of being here. I am a living classic example of the fundamental purpose of Freemasonry, of making a man better. Freemasonry showed me that I was far more capable than I ever gave myself credit for being. It did much more than that, however. It expanded my vision to see farther, to aim higher, to think greater thoughts, to want more out of life and to want more out of life also for others. It made me more determined; more committed, but it also softened my many rough edges. In short it polished a very rough ashlar. (Not that there are not rough edges left, mind you, but they are fewer). I know there are many of you, my brothers, sitting here who could say the very same thing. Indeed, for those who permitted its influence to be felt in their lives, there can very few who could not express that same sentiment?

I grew up in a relatively poor and undereducated environment. Neither of my parents went past the eighth grade. For them, a struggle was a way of life and I learned at a very young age to work for what I wanted, but I would change nothing of that experience. It gave me the stimulus to think and the opportunity to create my own diversions. But I had much help from others. I recognize that I owe whatever I became and whatever I have achieved pretty much to two organizations: The Boy Scouts of America and Freemasonry, along with a mother who knew well how to handle me, a cadre of friends who cared and a wife who accepts and tolerates my commitments. They molded me into a reflection of their influences on my life. Where I have succeeded, I owe to them. Where I have failed, I owe to my own stubbornness. I suspect this is the reason that I care so much about the road that we are traveling.

My friends, I could stand here tonight and stimulate you to bask in the glory of how great we are; I could stand here and tell you how significantly we impacted the evolution of civil society; I could emphasize how much we altered the character of what this world is today; I could rehearse our attributes that would have, if practiced, make any organization great, and we could all walk away with a warm fuzzy feeling. But, that would be a continuation of parasitizing our past, and we have been doing that far too long. I would also be wasting the great opportunity you have given to me to express what must be our concern for the direction we are taking on the road we are now traveling.

I am well aware that what I say is always open to my critics, but then I have possibly been an outspoken critic in North America for the past twenty years on this road that we are traveling. It is never my intent to be a prophet of doom. Indeed, I have a great faith in the future of world Freemasonry. This Craft is growing in numbers and expanding in geographical area at a far more rapid rate than probably since the early history of our existence. Its impact in the world has a greater potential than it has had for perhaps over a hundred years. This expression of the brotherhood of man under the fatherhood of God is reaching some new unprecedented heights, and its beneficial influence is being felt in the evolution of civil society far more today than it has for many years.

Why then, do we in North America sit in confusion on the road that we are taking? Why in a civil society, perhaps impacted more than any other by the philosophy of Freemasonry, are we losing the influence we had for more than almost three hundred years and losing the potential to recreate that influence? Why are our numbers decreasing when they are increasing in most of the rest of the world? Why Freemasons are still the major players in roles in most countries incorporating civility into a civil society while our roles are decreasing?

We have more reason to be proud of our past than any organization ever created, but we are failing to accept that we have also an assumed commitment to pass on and add to, that reason to be proud. We cannot survive by continuing to sell our past, in spite of the fact that it is more saleable than is our present. We, as leaders, must begin to think greater thoughts than we are thinking today; we must see farther horizons and seek more lofty goals. We must again become a major contributor to the creation of a gentler world. We did, my Brothers, and we were.

We have had within our ranks some of the greatest minds that ever lived. To survey our past membership is like a study of who's who in the in the world of great men. No other organization can even come close to imitating what we were. These brothers were men with a vision, a vision to see far beyond those mundane exercises that we attribute to Freemasonry today.

We, in North America are losing that vision. We have worked to excise from the Craft those intellectual and philosophical standards that have characterized it through most of its existence and for which it continues to be known over much of the globe. We are molding our noble Craft into something it was never meant to be, due to a lack of vision coupled with a lack of knowledge, and because of that loss of vision and that lack of knowledge, we are diluting the potential to be a force for what is just and right in this world. My Brothers, the world cannot afford that loss, not now, not ever. We must stop making excuses to justify our failures and commit ourselves to the application of Masonic philosophy as a guiding light to peace in this world.

I do not buy the excuse that our philosophy is not applicable to present-day society. There can never be a time that our philosophy would not apply to mankind. If that were ever to be true, God help humanity.

I do not accept that modern man does not have the time to be active in Freemasonry. It is not a matter of lack of time: it is a matter of lack of priority.

I do not believe the excuse that the cost of being a Freemason is too high for most workingmen today. Membership cost was a far greater percentage of earnings in our past than it is today, and there probably is not one of us sitting here tonight that is not better off financially than were his parents and grandparents, and that applies to the vast majority of Americans.

I do firmly believe that there will never be a time in any century when there is not a demand for a quality organization like philosophical Freemasonry, and most of the rest of the world is still proving it.

I have enough faith in modern man to believe that if we offer an organization of quality with an environment similar to that of our past, with a stimulus to learn and an opportunity to improve, that good men will want to become a part of it, and my brothers, if the priority is there, the cost is not relevant.

There can be no question concerning the influence that this Craft has had upon the minds of many great men. It simply cannot be happenstance that so many men in so many nations who were at the forefront of leadership, leading in their countries' struggles for freedom and liberty were Freemasons. Freemasonry may not have been the cause of these men's greatness, but it certainly provided the environment to stimulate, encourage and support it.

And I would suspect that many of my brothers who have been honored with this Grand Lodge's Distinguished Achievement award felt the gentle guidance of Masonic philosophy in their lives. Freemasonry may not have made them great, but there can be no doubt that they helped make Freemasonry great.

We now must take the time to examine the road that we are traveling, for we are standing at the crossroads and the direction we take will determine the future of North American Freemasonry. What a tremendous opportunity we are being given, you and I, for we are being given the potential to contribute to the redevelopment of a style of Freemasonry that shaped this world. We are being offered a challenge to alter the future of world society.

I am constantly impressed with the impact of Masonic influence in my travels in the world and I continually emphasize in Eastern Europe and in Africa where Freemasonry in now arising or re-arising, that these brothers hold within their hands the potential to direct their countries in the evolution of a new civil society, one with the moral and ethical fiber to benefit not only their fellow man but the direction of their countries.

We can also influence the future of our civil society as we did in the past. We can help to determine the direction we will travel toward a peaceful future. We can stimulate our brothers to commit themselves to a concern for a future where all mankind can sit as equals without the concern of racial difference or the bigotry of religious distinction, as occurs behind the tiled doors of a lodge room. In essence, our goal must be to impregnate society with this philosophy of Freemasonry.

To do so, however, we must change the direction on the road we are traveling. We must again comprehend that the quality of the member of the Craft is paramount to our potential to restore that influence. We must regain our vision; we must think greater thoughts, set higher goals, see farther into the future, and dedicate ourselves to the perpetuation of a philosophy unmatched in its potential to lead the world to a pathway of peace, and brotherly love.

We should walk tall in the pride of what this Craft has meant in the past for we are entitled to it. We must not forget, however, that this entitlement carries with it, responsibility. Were Freemasonry to fail to achieve its potential, the greatest loser would be the world community. As citizens, we have a responsibility to that community, but as Freemasons we have assumed a far greater responsibility to it.

The time is past due for us take a closer look at that road that we are traveling. In the greatest part of the globe we have altered the course of civil society, but we did not roll over it through the magnitude of numbers. We changed it by the impact of the quality of the brothers whom we influenced, one brother at a time. Let us do likewise.

[22]

The American Enlightenment:
Franklin and Freemasonry

*Given at a Masonic Conference Held at
the University of California, Los Angeles*

I have been introduced many times over the years in a number of different ways and in a number of different categories: Masonic scholar, orator, historian, author etc. While attending the second World Conference held in Lisbon, Portugal, I was introduced to the President of Portugal as a noted Masonic philosopher. At that time I wondered why anyone would think of me as a philosopher. I have thought about it since that time, along with the other categories trying to figure what I really am, and although I still don't know that I fit into any one of those niches, I guess philosopher might be as logical or as illogical as any. The noted author, John Robinson's response when asked what his area of expertise was replied, "I am generally regarded as the world's foremost authority on my own personal opinions—and on nothing else." I suspect that definition probably fits me well, for opinions, I do have.

When I was first approached to speak to you today, I was under the impression that I would be addressing a subject field with which I was familiar and after a little hesitation, I agreed to speak at this symposium.

I talked with the Grand Secretary, John L. Cooper III, about a week later, and I learned from him that my subject would involve the American Enlightenment, Benjamin Franklin, and the Constitution, and these are subject fields with which I definitely have a limited familiarity.

I thought about this for a week or more, called John back, and asked him if he was sure that he had the right person to present this paper. Frankly, I'm not sure I even knew there was an American Enlightenment. I was aware of the period of history involving the Enlightenment, but I had always regarded it as being mostly a European phenomenon, with its manifestation concentrated principally in France and England. Oh, I related specific Colonial Americans such as Benjamin Franklin and Thomas Jefferson to the Enlightenment, but I never thought much about the expression of this movement being exemplified in North America.

I told John that if I had any area of expertise in Freemasonry, it was in the field of contemporary Freemasonry. I also expressed a probably totally illogical opinion based upon some definitions that the Enlightenment never fully ceased to exist in all areas of the world. In my travels, I continue to encounter those individuals, especially in Third World countries, who stand out so significantly that they would fit very comfortably into the niche of the Enlightenment. I suspect, therefore, that if the Enlightenment is limited in time, it must have been not only specifically a movement, but also must have existed in that restricted frame of time and is therefore where the American Enlightenment fits.

Well, Brother John, for whom I have the greatest respect, in all his wisdom, convinced me that I was qualified to speak, and that I might continue the subject into contemporary Freemasonry. I do wish to qualify to you, however, that I am no expert on the American Enlightenment, or on Benjamin Franklin or on the Constitution. Nor am I a research scholar. I vowed when I completed my last academic dissertation, that my life of research was finished. Time has never been my greatest resource, and as you all well know, research takes time. Now, after working to complete this paper, I am firmly convinced that I still am not a research scholar and that my time of research is now finished. I also understand more fully why I have such a great appreciation for good Masonic scholars.

Following agonizing weeks, for me, of studying the American Enlightenment, I received a copy of the program, and my topic was listed, "Franklin and Pennsylvania Freemasonry." I again talked with John and learned that it broadened my field from which to draw, since I am a Pennsylvanian. Having already completed a third of the draft, and recognizing that Franklin, the Enlightenment, and Pennsylvania Freemasonry are permanently intertwined, I shall not attempt to untangle them and with my apologies, you will be subject to all three. I will also interject some pertinent observations and how they may be applied to, or impact Freemasonry.

I have spent very little time in my life studying the age of Enlightenment per se. I've simply known that it existed and regarded it as that period in history when man finally escaped the bondage of ignorance that was forced upon him by civil and religious hierarchies of the day. I looked upon it as a spirit set free, to seek knowledge for the sake of acquiring knowledge, to learn for the sake of learning, and to use the freedom of thought so long denied him. Kant regarded the Enlightenment as "a search for truth and the freeing of human knowledge from the chains of suppression and superstition with which it had long been bound." For me, that was just about defines my impression of it.

Now, I find that the Enlightenment, and especially in the American colonies cannot be categorized this simply. Ned Landsman, in his book, *From Colonials to Provincials*, discusses recent historians' approach, regarding not only "The High Enlightenment" of the philosophers, to which I relate it, but also a form, termed "The Low Enlightenment" of the middling to lower classes. In addition, they've created terminologically, a moderate Enlightenment, radical and skeptical Enlightenments, genteel and evangelical Enlightenments, along with Enlightenments of the province, of the aristocracy, of the tradesman, and of women.[1] Henry May refers to the Moderate, Skeptical, Revolutionary and Didactic Enlightenments.[2] With these systems of categorization; it becomes much easier to consider the significance of the Enlightenment in early America.

I, of course, owe a great debt of gratitude to those research scholars who blazed a trail so that I might use their knowledge, as well as to a number of my friends and brothers who freely offered their advice. I will not try to name them, lest I neglect anyone, but one in particular did set my mind to thinking on the subject when I first started: and I do thank Brother Robert Davis from Oklahoma for his interest and motivation, and I must thank Dr. Wayne Huss, author of *The Master Builders* (the three-volume history of the Grand Lodge of Pennsylvania, published 1986–1989) whom I came to know while he was researching in our Grand Lodge, for much of the available data I used.

In preparing this paper, I discovered how illogical it is to consider the creation of the United States of America and fail to comprehend the influence that enlightened minds must have had upon its establishment. The attributes of the Enlightenment became manifest in principle in almost every direction early American leaders took. This manifestation, probably modeled on the European Enlightenment became the foundation of American society. Indeed, it might not be far-fetched to say that the United States of America is a living manifestation of the Enlightenment.

The argument can be effectively advanced, however, that the Enlightenment was not an American phenomenon, but was rather a result of the enlightened minds of men imported from Europe because, excluding Native Americans, all were only a few generations, at best, removed, from being imports. The enlightened minds of early America included both those born inside and those born outside the colonies.

In a very great sense, early America had an opportunity not to be found in those countries with established governments where the age of the Enlightenment was in full bloom. No powerful monarch or pontiff with his armies sat on the doorstep in America to suppress freedom of thought regarding civil or religious liberties. Not to minimize the power that Britain had over the colonies, nor for that matter, the commitment that the colonists had to Britain, but it had to be easier to think more freely, to voice opinions more openly and to act more aggressively, in the colonies than it would have been in Britain or any other European nation. The American colonists also had the opportunity to start from scratch, so to speak, and there can be little doubt that what is known today, as modern American civil society was a product of that opportunity.

New concepts of freedom, justice and human rights were smoldering in a new age of thought. These concepts were providing stimuli for early Americans to defend against what was regarded as an encroachment of tyranny upon human freedom. New world idealism developed by enlightened minds finally resulted in a rebellion against the authority of the monarchy, and the absolutist state, as well as the powers for religious restraint. The result of this idealism was the creation of a whole new nation, with a whole new concept of what a nation should be.

This movement resulted in what we know today as modern civil society and can in truth be said to be an invention of the Enlightenment. It presented new concepts of freedom, justice, human rights and human tolerance. If the American Revolution was not at least the high point of the American Enlightenment, it was the end result, and the development of the Declaration of Independence and the Constitution, surely then was. The American Revolution became a synonymous expression for the American Enlightenment.

Although I have not been a student of the Enlightenment, I have not been ignorant of its relationship to our Craft. By its very philosophy, Freemasonry found a comfortable fit into this age. Indeed, it is not possible to separate Freemasonry from Enlightenment. Margaret Jacob expressed it well in *Living the Enlightenment*: "Modern civil society was invented during the Enlightenment in the new enclaves of sociability of which freemasonry was the most avowedly constitutional and aggressively civic."[3]

Freemasonry was a major participant in the Enlightenment, and the Enlightenment was a dominant factor in the success of Freemasonry. Very frankly, I have been convinced for some time, that without it, Freemasonry could never have achieved the eminence in the world for which it is known.

I am also just as convinced that a major cause for the decline of North American Freemasonry today, is the result of our loss of any semblance of enlightened thought guiding us. In making this observation, I am not denigrating our present leadership; I am observing a marked difference in intellectual style. Dr. Jacob also observed that, "Freemasonry dropped out of serious scholarship between 1945 and now, with some exceptions."[4] Observing North American Freemasonry today, it would be difficult to disagree. However, from my travels, I am more acutely aware of these exceptions continuing to exist in some areas of the world today.

The Masonic lodge in early America found itself in a unique position to develop enlightened thought more than was true of the lodges of Europe. It had the opportunity of gathering together men from different countries, with different ideologies, opinions and religious backgrounds to be fused in enlightened thought. These men, in turn, brought with them new ideals concerning the rights and freedoms of man.

The lodge provided an environment wherein the enlightened minds could gather, along with a stimulus to fertilize and encourage those minds to range beyond their prior limits. It was an environment where these new ideals could be openly discussed. It was an environment that could be political without being partisan, where governmental reform could be presented as an improvement without threat of personal condemnation. Through the ritual and teachings of the Lodge, these early American Freemasons learned via its orations, the values of the Enlightenment, with the freedom of thought and expression not necessarily found outside the doors of the Lodge. Freemasonry was an organization of equals wherein one could experience an environment of order, harmony and charity without fear of suppression. The enlightened minds it attracted, in turn, enabled Freemasonry to gain a pre-eminence, it could never have achieved without them. The Masonic lodge in America epitomized the American Enlightenment and the Enlightenment became synonymous with the American Revolution. European Freemasonry was a valuable contributor to the enlightened age, but in early America, it may have been a driving force.

In essence, the Lodge may well have served as a study in microcosm of what could be, wherein representative government and self-disciplined leadership was understood and practiced, creating a template for what was to become the nucleus of modern civil society of the United States of America. Freemasonry, of course, did not stand alone as an enlightened organization, but it probably accepted a greater diversity of adherents than did others such as the Royal Society. Freemasonry purported to do for the world of social interaction, what the Royal Society did for the world of science. This would have been of greater significance to the colonists if for no other reason than they had a far greater diversity from which to draw.

It was heartening for me to note from my reading, that I was far from alone in my application of the Enlightenment as a European phenomenon, in which America observed from a distance or took part in, only as individuals. With the understanding that such a movement was not relegated to those with a rare affinity to great thinking, it becomes a simpler matter to place early Americans squarely into the mainstream of enlightened thought. It also becomes easier to understand the significance of the influence of Freemasonry in the development of that thought.

To consider Freemasonry operating in early America and ignore the potential to interject enlightened thinking would be the ultimate disregard of organizational influence in the evolution of our civil society. Yet, until recent years, historians have chosen to write about the man who creates history and to ignore the organization that creates the man. Freemasonry, in America perhaps more than any other single organization, played an integral role in the development of the man and therefore the history.

The Masonic Lodge, for many, became a focal point where men could gather together and discuss various issues free from the constraints of politics and religion, and where men could acquire knowledge simply as knowledge, and not as a support to religious or political ideology. It provided a deistic atmosphere wherein there existed no religious limitations other than the belief in a higher power, and wherein the brotherhood of all men was based upon moral worth rather than theological dogma.

Having established that Freemasonry cannot be separated from the Enlightenment, we now must acknowledge that Benjamin Franklin cannot be separated from Freemasonry. He was perhaps, second only to Washington, the most recognized of the early American Freemasons, and in all probability, had far more influence. Indeed, his influence remains like a thread woven throughout the development of early American thought and the tapestry of early American Freemasonry. His contributions to America's development with all its diversity, possibility created an impact unmatched by any other, of any period in our history.

Pennsylvania Freemasonry was first established officially along with New York and New Jersey as one of the three British North American colonies on June 15, 1730 with the deputation of Daniel Coxe as Provincial Grand Master. The first written evidence of it functioning in the colonies was to be found in the *Pennsylvania Gazette*, of which Benjamin Franklin was the editor, on Dec. 8, 1730, although St. John's Lodge is known to have been in operation in Pennsylvania at least as early as 1727. St. John's Lodge along with the other lodges operating in the colonies at this time must have been "time immemorial" lodges, and must have been recognized by the Grand Lodge of England, or the deputation of Coxe would not have been forthcoming. It is worth noting that the first exposé of the ritual of Freemasonry published in America was published in the same issue of the *Gazette*. Modern Freemasons, thinking they have created a new phraseology, have hastened to emphasize to the general public in recent years, that the great secret of Freemasonry is that there is no secret at all. Franklin made the same observation in 1730 in that same issue.

Dr. Wayne A. Huss in his research for the three volume set, *The Master Builders: A History of the Grand Lodge of Free and Accepted Masons of Pennsylvania*, gives evidence that the Grand Lodge of Pennsylvania was meeting in Philadelphia as early as June 24th, 1731, with William Allen as Grand Master.[5] Although this date is accepted by the Grand Lodge of Pennsylvania as the beginning of Independent Grand Lodge functioning in that jurisdiction, it remains unclear as to its actual creation. "If Coxe authorized it, it should more properly be referred to as a Provincial Grand Lodge but if organized without the specific approval of the representative of the Grand Lodge of England, which is also possible, it should be termed an 'Independent' Grand Lodge. Whether Allen was appointed by Coxe or elected by the brothers one year earlier is of little significance. Either way, the authority of the Grand Lodge of Pennsylvania to act, rested on a secure foundation."[6] Nonetheless, the issue remains clouded, and continues as a point of good-natured controversy between the Grand Lodges of Massachusetts and Pennsylvania to this day.

Henry S. Borneman in *Early Freemasonry in Pennsylvania*, states that the "Grand Lodge of England empowered The Provincial Grand Lodge of Pennsylvania to elect a Provincial Grand Master every other year on the feast of St. John the Baptist day."[7] On June 24, 1732, William Allen was either reelected or perhaps elected to replace Coxe as Provincial Grand Master. Either way, the Grand Lodge of Pennsylvania is the oldest Grand Lodge operating in North America and the third oldest in the world following England (1717) and Ireland (1725). (Keep in mind; this is a Pennsylvania Freemason speaking.) According to Pennsylvania records applied to the Grand Lodge, it operated as a Grand Lodge of the Moderns until the year 1761, a period of thirty years. During that span of time eight different Grand Masters presided over the Grand Lodge with William Allen serving 17 of those years, 1731–32 and 1747–61 and more than 700 brothers claimed membership.

Benjamin Franklin was entered into the Craft in St. John's Lodge, Moderns N⁰ 1, a time immemorial Lodge in Philadelphia in 1731, and the year the Grand Lodge of Pennsylvania claims as its origin. Although he published an exposé on Freemasonry in 1730, his commitment to the Craft after joining was beyond question, and that exposé was the last unfavorable comment concerning Freemasonry published in the *Gazette*, although many Masonic articles were published. It is thought that the exposé may have been written to attract the attention of the Freemasons. If so, it worked, for he became a Freemason several months later.

Brother Franklin was elected Junior Grand Warden in 1732 and served as Grand Master of Pennsylvania (Moderns), in 1734 and again in 1749, being appointed Provincial Grand Master by Thomas Oxnard of Boston. He shared the year 1749 with William Allen after being deposed due to a dispute, which he lost, but was immediately appointed Deputy Grand Master by Allen. He also served as Deputy Grand Master in 1750, 1755, and 1757.

While traveling in Europe, he visited lodges in England and Scotland and affiliated with several lodges in France. He served as the second Venerable (Worshipful) Master of the notable Lodge of the Nine Sisters in Paris from 1779 to 1784. It was in this lodge, known for its prominent intellectuals, that Franklin was identified as a significant member of the American Enlightenment along with being a major influence in the American political and cultural movement of the colonies. Franklin was not the only early American colonial to be affiliated with this lodge — John Paul Jones being among the more notable American members. It was also in this lodge that Franklin served as guide in making

Voltaire a Mason. This was not an insignificant act on the part of Franklin, as both men were highly regarded as icons of enlightened thought. Esmond Wright in, *Franklin of Philadelphia*, states that "His meeting and embrace with Voltaire at the Academy were seen as a high point in the Enlightenment. How enchanting it was said 'to see Solon and Sophocles embracing'."[8]

Although Freemasonry was integrally involved in most aspects of the Enlightenment, there was probably no other Lodge so purposefully dedicated to enlightened ideals or to securing for membership men related to it. Franklin's ongoing interest in Freemasonry is further strengthened by his numerous communications, concerning the Craft and Masonic references in the *Pennsylvania Gazette*.

Pennsylvania Freemasonry was not immune to the internal dissension that was creating fragmentation within the Grand Lodge of England, and although Pennsylvania appears to have experienced less of it, the ultimate result was the eventual dissolution of the Grand Lodge of the "Moderns." Pennsylvania leadership was evidently unaware or unconcerned when they began to accept new British Freemasons into the lodges, that they had been made Masons in the Grand Lodge of the Ancients in England. With the appearance of these "Ancients," who were more aggressive in the support of retaining ancient ritual and tradition, many members of the Moderns switched their allegiance to that Grand Lodge. These included some of the more prominent members of the older Grand Lodge, but did not include Franklin or any of the other Past Grand Masters.

Even though remnants of the "Modern" Grand Lodge persisted into the 1780s, the Grand Lodge of Pennsylvania became classed as an "Ancient" Grand Lodge on its records in 1761 after having received an "Ancient" warrant in 1759 electing William Ball as Grand Master in 1760. (He was also appointed Provincial Grand Master the same year). Ball served as Grand Master from 1761 until 1782 and again in 1795, for a total of 22 years. British Freemasonry resolved the Moderns and Ancients issue by merging the two Grand Lodges in 1813 to become the United Grand Lodge of England. Pennsylvania had the issue resolved for them through the dominance of the "Ancient" Masons and the gradual disappearance of the "Moderns." It is interesting that William Ball initially joined a Modern Lodge in 1751, and then an Ancient Lodge in 1760. He belonged to both until 1763, even while serving as Grand Master of the Ancients. The Grand Lodge took a final step of declaring full independence from The Grand Lodge of England in 1786 under Grand Master William Adcock.

With the declining numbers, North American Freemasonry is experiencing today, and our obsession with keeping low dues and fees, it is worth noting that "the admission fee in these early lodges was equivalent to thirty days' wages and over half the estimated annual food budget of an unskilled laborer. In addition it was expected that they were to pay their share of food and drink and charitable contributions."[9] Worth noting also, with the changes we are making in the Craft today, the mature age of a candidate was regarded to be the age of 25 years.

Even as Franklin cannot be separated from Freemasonry he cannot be separated from the Enlightenment. He was unquestionably the most visible example of the Enlightenment in colonial America, as well as the most visible example of the American Enlightenment in Europe. It was his relationship with the Enlightenment, however, that fostered his exposure to the world outside of Freemasonry. His interest in science, and his natural curiosity alone might have given him this exposure, but his interest in public affairs and commitment to the plight of others placed him squarely in the mainstream of enlightened thought. This concern for others is revealed in the effort he put into scientific experimentation. Most was to the benefit of the people.

Franklin was a man with vision ranging far beyond the average. He had the ability to see the larger picture and the capability through his congenial personality to influence others to a cause. "His lack of pretentiousness pointed him out as a symbol of republican simplicity. To Europeans he was the American." The role he played in Paris fit him well, and the role he played at home impacted, not only early American society, but continues as an influence to this day. Turgot said of him, "He seized the lightning from the sky and the scepter from tyrants."

Brother Franklin was a founder of the American Philosophical Society; participated in the founding of the Library Company of Philadelphia, the first free library in America; the College and Academy of Philadelphia, now the University of Pennsylvania; and the Pennsylvania Hospital. He was involved in organizing the first fire company in North America, the first fire insurance company, and was even involved with the paving and cleaning the streets of Philadelphia. His interest in science led him to the invention of the bi-focal, to experiments in electricity and to the invention of a more efficient stove.

He became committed to public affairs that led to multiple positions in the colonies, including clerk of the Assembly, Judge on several courts, member of the Provincial Assembly, Postmaster General of the British North American colonies, agent for Pennsylvania in London, president of the Pennsylvania Committee of Safety, member of the Second Continental Congress, president of the Pennsylvania Constitutional Convention, Minister to France, signer of the Treaty of Paris, delegate to the Constitutional Convention, signer of the Declaration of Independence and of the United States Constitution. No other American of his age can match his contribution to American thought.

Franklin was a prolific writer not only for scientific publications, but also "on politics and diplomacy, moral philosophy, religion, population growth, trade and commerce, and the abolition of slavery." In recognition of his many intellectual contributions, "he was made a member of the Royal Society of London, received a Master of Arts degree from both Harvard and Yale, as well as from William and Mary, a Doctorate of Arts degree from St. Andrews, and a Doctorate of Civil Law from Oxford."[10] Not bad for an uneducated colonial printer.

The Grand Lodge of Pennsylvania takes great pride, and justifiably so, in claiming the association of Benjamin Franklin in their Masonic heritage. Amongst the tragedies of the schisms in Freemasonry, however, was the failure of the Pennsylvania brotherhood, to recognize Franklin's membership in the Craft at his death in 1790. The Grand Lodge was by then an Ancient Grand Lodge, and Franklin never severed his ties with the Moderns. The Grand Lodge of the Moderns had ceased to exist and the Grand Lodge of the Ancients did not carry him on their roles, for he had never changed his allegiance. As a result Freemasonry was not represented at his funeral. As a redress of a wrong, the Grand Lodge of Pennsylvania did take a major part in the celebration of the 200th anniversary of Franklin's birth in 1906, 116 years later, and in 1981 the Grand Lodge held a special commemoration for the two-hundredth anniversary of his initiation into the Craft.

Still, we struggle into the present times with similar bad decisions and illogical thinking. We have continued until recent years, to thrive upon the contributions of those enlightened Brothers who established the reputation for which we were known. Now, we no longer thrive, due to a lack of contributions of style that made us great. We are struggling against a sociological apathy for which we have found no cure. We no longer generate an influence that drives or directs an ongoing evolution of civil society, and the fault lies with us, for we have lost our vision.

Be it commitment to a cause, ego of the leadership, or simply failure to understand the significance of the Craft, North American Freemasonry is failing to attract the great thinkers of the present generations; and we cannot rise, my brothers, by continuing to parasitize our past. At best, this can only be a blueprint for extinction. Although the impact of the Enlightenment lives on in the Craft today, it shines much more brightly in other parts of the world. North American Freemasonry needs an injection of the enlightened thought that characterized much of its past. We need some Franklins to infuse visibility into what is becoming an almost dormant institution for influence in North American society. The future of Freemasonry depends upon it and the future of society will be impacted by it.

LITERATURE CITED

1. Ned C. Landsman, *From Colonials to Provincials: American Thought and Culture* (Ithaca: Cornell University Press, 1997).

2. Henry F. May, *The Enlightenment in America* (New York: Oxford University Press, 1976).

3. Margaret C. Jacob, *Living the Enlightenment: Freemasonry and Politics in Eighteenth-Century Europe* (New York : Oxford University Press, 1991), 15.

5. Wayne A. Huss, *The Master Builders: A History of the Grand Lodge of Free and Accepted Masons of Pennsylvania* (Philadelphia: The Grand Lodge, 1986), 1:2.

6. Ibid., 1:32-35.

7. Henry S. Borneman, *Early Freemasonry in Pennsylvania* (Philadelphia: The Grand Lodge, 1931).

8. Esmond Wright, *Franklin of Philadelphia* (New York: Hill and Wang, 1970), 269.

9. Wayne A. Huss, *The Master Builders*, 1:53.

10. Esmond Wright, *Franklin of Philadelphia*, 269.

The Significance of Regularity

Given as a St. Albans Lecture in Texas

Freemasonry as a regular institution has been operating under a set of protocols that has sustained it as a speculative Craft for almost 300 years. By accepting and maintaining these protocols our institution has become, perhaps, the most significant factor in the evolution of civil society outside of organized religion. Today historians are acknowledging the impact that Freemasonry's philosophy has had on individuals, and in turn, those individuals have had on the development of the standards by which society is judged. Our Craft has been a major player for several hundred years in creating the stimulus for men to learn and to develop and has served as a catalyst to bring together great men and to contribute to making men great. We have taken good men and have made them better men while instilling in them a dedication to the rights, freedom and equality of all men. World Freemasonry today, however, is in a greater state of instability than it has been for probably the greater part of its existence, and for a number of reasons.

First Freemasonry is expanding more rapidly than it has for probably well over 100 years, and maybe 200 years. With the re-emergence of Freemasonry in the Eastern bloc countries in Europe and the development of new Grand Lodges on the continent of Africa, Freemasonry is experiencing a surge of growth unseen for many decades.

It is significant that irregular forms of Freemasonry are also expanding probably more rapidly than they have in their entire history, not only into these areas, but also into areas where regular Freemasonry already exists. This is a major concern for the stability of Regular Freemasonry. It has become almost competitive to see which style of the Craft can be established first.

Second, ignorance of the Craft and its purpose has become a way of life to many Freemasons. This is certainly true in North America and North American Freemasons represents a majority of Freemasons in the world. This presents a tragic commentary for an organization that changed the world.

Third, the Internet has become a valuable tool to spread misinformation and the ignorance of others to our brothers and anyone else who reads it. The vast majority of those who read it lack the knowledge to reject it.

My brothers, the subject of regularity in Freemasonry is not a recent phenomenon, although there are some of our members today who think they have discovered something new in the Masonic world. It was probably one of the first major considerations to confront early speculative Freemasonry. As a result, specific criteria have been established to which any Masonic Grand lodge must conform to be regarded as regular. Today, we acknowledge that a Grand Lodge's regularity is contingent upon it having been created by another regular Grand Lodge, or by the action of three or more regular subordinate lodges. Regularity is also dependent upon adherence by a Grand Lodge to established practice and compliance to specific requirements. These include the belief in a Supreme Being, the presence of the Volume of the Sacred Law upon the altar, the limitation to males only in membership, the avoidance of discussion of religion and politics within a lodge, a restriction of fraternal intercourse with irregular Freemasonry, and the respect of jurisdictional territory of other Grand Lodges, amongst others.

The Craft established the system of granting warrants to Grand Lodges and lodges and created a method early in Speculative Freemasonry that was adhered to as a worldwide standard. Regularity of Freemasonry is the structural base upon which we have erected our edifice to project a constancy of purpose to the world outside of our Craft. Those Grand Lodges not operating within these standards, have not adopted or have eliminated some of the basic landmarks upon which we exist, i.e. the required belief in a Supreme Being, the Volume of the Sacred Law upon the altar, the avoidance of involvement in politics and religion as an organization and the restriction to male only membership.

Regularity in Freemasonry has been accompanied by irregularity since close to its inception. There have been, and are Regular Grand Lodges in origin that became irregular in practice. There have been, and are Grand Lodges that comply with some of the requirements for regularity, but not all, and there exists Grand Lodges that have never been regular in either origin and or in practice. Masonic leaders have dealt with these issues effectively for almost 300 years. Now, there are some of our members who have developed an attitude that regularity is not significant to the Craft.

I met a young Ph.D., a journalism professor in Romania several weeks ago who wanted to give me a copy of a book he had written on Freemasonry. He had studied the Craft for many years before he became a member and understood much of its philosophical foundation. He related this story to me. The first lodge created in that country following the fall of communism was operating under the Grand Orient of France, an irregular Grand Lodge that did not require a belief in God. He was approached to join and was told that belief in God was not a requirement because they felt that men should be free to not believe in a Supreme Being if they chose, and still become a Freemason. Knowing what this requirement had meant to Freemasonry for centuries, he declined to join, even though he had waited for years until he had the freedom to become a member. Here was a man willing to give up his dream to become a Mason rather than become part of a group not requiring this fundamental of the Craft for regularity.

Now however, there is a pervasive attitude beginning to permeate our Craft regarding regularity and fraternalism that none of us can choose to ignore. There are those within the Fraternity today, predominantly in North America, who have developed the attitude that anyone calling himself a Freemason should be regarded as a Freemason. There are those, even including a small segment of our leadership who feel that almost 300 years of history, practice and tradition is no longer applicable in today's world. These brothers probably have no idea how many Grand Lodges exist in the world. The last I heard there were 91 grand lodges in Italy alone. There are 17 known grand lodges in New York City. Twice while I was Grand Secretary, members of another grand lodge came to me seeking support in breaking away from their grand lodge and forming another.

Unquestionably, this results from the ignorance of the majority of Freemasons concerning Masonic history, its contributions to the world and even its purpose for existence. Couple this ignorance with ego and we have a blueprint for disaster. Our leaders should be informed enough to know better, and it is difficult to comprehend the motives, that inspire these men to conclude that our Brothers of the past were so wrong when they accomplished so much.

Lack of knowledge is certainly a major factor, but ego

and arrogance are others, and present-day liberalism is probably a third. Whatever the motives, we cannot afford to ignore their actions. If permitted to continue, it will destroy Freemasonry as it has been known for almost three centuries. We simply cannot permit these attitudes against our protocols to exist in our membership. Our members, who choose to violate their obligation as Freemasons, should be removed before their destructive thinking is spread farther.

For many years our Craft has been a relatively quiescent Fraternity in regard to increasing numbers of regular grand lodges in the world. During this period of time, irregular and/or unrecognized Freemasonry has also been relatively quiet. This period of quiescence has been replaced in recent years with a flurry of activity by both categories. The result is that present-day leadership is being confronted with the need to make decisions that will impact our fraternity far into the future, and many are ill equipped to deal with these decisions due to a lack of knowledge, not only in procedures, required for recognition, but also concerning the grand lodges in question. Grand lodges outside of North America have been dealing with these issues for centuries, but leadership in North America has rarely faced it, and now it is in their hands.

Freemasonry is the most successful fraternal organization that has ever existed and if there was a way of determining it may very well be the most successful organization of any kind that ever existed. It has impacted the world well beyond any other institution created by the mind of man. It has existed longer and has grown larger than any other. It has caused change in the direction of the development of civilization. It has promoted civility, in civil society. And now, there are those in our Fraternity today with the impression that they have a wisdom superior to our past brethren who have created and sustained it for 300 years.

Several years ago, I saw on a website an evaluation by one of our members, of the Commission on Information for Recognition of the Conference of Grand Masters of Masons in North America. The member making the evaluation determined that after his thorough study he had determined that the Commission had outlived its purpose in today's world. Upon checking with this member's grand lodge, I found that he had been a member of the Craft for all of three years. Consider that, a three-year member with the brilliance and knowledge outshining brothers of the caliber of the men who made us. What arrogance. What ignorance. The problem is that there are those who read it and believed it.

There has also been a marked increase in schisms in regularly consecrated grand lodges resulting in two grand lodges in the same jurisdiction, both claiming to be the legitimate regular grand lodge. The result has been that some grand lodges recognizes one, while other mainstream grand lodges recognizes the other. This is an untenable situation, which weakens our fraternity and presents to the world an unstable organization worth little note.

To further compound this problem, Masonically-affiliated appendant bodies have become instrumental in causing some of the schisms to occur. There are also appendant bodies promoting recognition of irregular forms of Freemasonry including those not requiring a belief in a Supreme Being, not requiring the Volume of the Sacred Law upon the altar and or who admit female members into the Craft. Those bodies must be stopped before the harm they cause becomes irreversible.

Craft Masonry created the appendant organizations and they are subject to grand lodge control. Any organization that requires Masonic membership as a prerequisite for membership is subject to grand lodge rule in the jurisdiction in which they operate. My Brothers, Craft Masonry is what impacted this world, and these actions should be intolerable to us as members. Historians are writing about Freemasonry today and its impact on civil society, but not about appendant bodies.

Grand Lodge officers must not continue to permit interference in Regular Freemasonry by organizations subordinate to grand lodges. Violations of our accepted operating protocols must be recognized and confronted. If we fail to face and resolve these issues, we have absolutely no hope that Freemasonry will ever achieve the full potential for its existence nor come close to emulating its past.

I have heard recently, that an attempt will be made to create a form of irregular Freemasonry that will preside over all of North America. We cannot ignore, nor accept, our members supporting this or any form of irregular Freemasonry or any appendant body that supports it.

Interestingly, the use of the Internet is now creating problems that just may be for us, of a magnitude perhaps unseen in our past. It is not only a tool for our enemies to attack us, but it also has become the major mechanism by which erroneous information is disseminated throughout the membership by our own members. Those members who have read it and assumed it was factual have spread it much farther.

Not all of it is spread in error, however. It is being used today by those within the Craft who feel they have a vision for the future of Freemasonry that lies beyond the parameters of what made and sustained our greatness. It is within this small cadre of our own membership that perhaps the greatest threat to our survival as a viable institution lies, and again we cannot choose to ignore it.

Personally, I would like nothing more than to see all regular Freemasonry in the world united as a like-minded brotherhood of men dedicated to a common goal. Such an entity could only contribute to the strengthening of our noble institution. It would increase our potential to be an influence for the ongoing evolution of civil society and world peace. This cannot happen, however, so long as we remain ignorant of, or ignore the protocols of fraternal relations. Nor can it, nor will it happen, so long as those seeking recognition do not comply with conformity to the protocols, which have sustained for almost 300 years. We cannot be seduced into accepting anything less.

For the sake of Freemasonry it is therefore imperative that we become capable of divesting ourselves of our own limiting egos and goals of creating self-perpetuating images and become more aware of the foundations upon which we have thrived for hundreds of years. We must become more concerned about the future of Freemasonry, and less about our own images.

The subject upon which I speak may be the greatest single threat to our survival as a viable institution capable of impacting society in this millennium. Yet, the problem confronting us is one that we ourselves are causing, by creating or permitting disunity within the Craft, by supporting irregular instead of regular Freemasonry, by reacting instead of acting, and by failing to recognize our own ignorance on specific issues. We are not only failing to help the perpetuation of our Masonic Craft—we are aiding and abetting in its demise. Our grand lodges should not accept it, and Freemasonry should not tolerate it.

If our Craft is to have a stable and contributory future, we must support our requirements of regularity, and requirements for fraternal recognition. We must also be unwilling to accept deviation from these requirements. We must be prepared to remove from our brotherhood, those who choose not to conform to its protocols. Fraternal relations must be limited to regular Freemasonry. Those grand lodges seeking recognition know what is required. If they cannot, or will not accept these parameters, then they fail to gain recognition, and if a regular grand lodge chooses a divergent pathway, then it must risk losing recognition.

We must remember that fraternal relations between grand lodges is not a right, it is a privilege. Every member has a right to accept what he chooses, but he must also accept that this choice will determine his right to membership. Each grand lodge is also free to choose, but if that choice contributes to disunity, then regular Freemasonry has the responsibility to attempt reunification.

Freemasonry has been facing a loss of image in present day-society for decades and, my Brothers, we are the cause. The philosophy has not changed. We are the variable. We have not only permitted but stimulated a decline in the quality of the membership. We have required too little to attain membership and far too little to retain membership. We have caused ignorance to become the norm in an organization that has always encouraged an acquisition of knowledge. We have cheapened our organization by being cheap ourselves, and now we are permitting egos rather than brains to drive us.

We must now decide whether we wish to survive as an institution that will impact future society, or if we choose to continue to slide into history as a once great society of men who changed this world, but which no longer exists. What do you want my Brothers? It will be you who will decide.

[24]

Association of Masonic Boards of Relief of the United States and Canada

Presented at the Grand Secretaries' Conference — 2004

Perhaps one of the best-known characteristics for which those outside of it have noted for Freemasonry over the course of our history, is that Freemasons takes care of their own. For good or for bad, this mantle has cloaked us for several hundred years, and it began long before we became a speculative Craft.

I can recall that at a military supply facility near where I lived, it was generally inferred that advancement was dependent upon Masonic membership. I thought that this type of inference was disappearing, but then, just a few weeks ago, a young man came to me and told me that he was interested in joining Freemasonry. He said that it was his intention to become a State Police Officer and that he was told that it would be to his advantage if he were a member of the Craft.

I am comfortable in assuming that many of you have heard the same innuendoes. Such inferences, right or wrong, have been helpful to Freemasonry, in the sense that they have created a public perception that has given a status to the Craft—because of a commitment of our brothers.

This is not the full meaning of, "taking care of our own," however. We have been known far better by the expression of the care and brotherly love extended to one another.

It is probable that no other organization has professed this sentiment nor encouraged its practice, more than has Freemasonry. It has been a stimulus for those outside of us to want to become part of us. Historically, this kindness and care exemplified by Brother to Brother preserved a reputation upon which we now live. It is this characteristic of the Craft that has been responsible for helping tens of thousands of our brothers and their families over the years.

Unfortunately, it is a characteristic that is waning in present-day North American Freemasonry. In our modern-day world, we as individual Masons tend to forget the needs of our brothers, not necessarily only in the extension of financial aid, but also in the extension of fraternal assistance.

There is, however, a Masonic organization dating back to 1885, whose sole purpose is precisely that. There have been brothers for almost 120 years who, through their unselfish devotion and commitment, have carried the torch of this characteristic of the Craft to those who needed it, and by doing so, have aided in keeping alive a fundamental component of Freemasonry. This organization is the Association of Masonic Boards of Relief of the United States and Canada.

At a board meeting, held in Seattle this past year, one of the subjects for discussion was whether they can continue to operate, given the decreasing support from Grand Lodges. We certainly recognize that financial constraints have made it increasingly difficult for Grand Lodges, and it is easier to delete a line item from the budget in supporting a less visible organization.

Yet, this Association perhaps generates a longer lasting visibility and emotional impact than do many of our other appendant bodies, but they do it so quietly that it is seldom seen. As a result, the Association is not well known to much of our leadership. I am speaking on their behalf today, seeking your support in educating those Masonic leaders with whom you come in contact, of the significant role played by this Association in perpetuating a Masonic fundamental.

It is structured with a slate of officers comprising the Board of Directors serving two-year terms. There's also an Executive Committee composed of 13 members. It is the responsibility of the Board and Executive Committee to conduct the purposes of the Association. The Executive Secretary, one of the officers, functions as the day-to-day liaison and it is his responsibility to keep the records of the Association. He is the "Grand Secretary" of the Association, with all that goes with it, and as Grand Secretaries, you all know what that is. There are more than 125 separate "sub" associations and service bureaus scattered throughout North America operating under the guidance of the Association. All income to the Association is through contributions of Grand Lodges, subordinate lodges, these associations, and individual members of the Craft.

Over the years this Association throughout the United States and Canada has provided assistance to our members and their families in need of financial help as well as personal assistance. There have been innumerable instances where our sojourning or transient brothers were provided aid, when there was nowhere else to turn.

This, however, is only an infinitely small segment of what the Association has provided. More than a hundred years ago, they began tracking imposters who were preying upon the beneficent character of the Craft. They have conducted thousands of Masonic funeral services for traveling as well as local Masons when there was no one else to do so. They have run Masonic employment agencies, administered blood banks and provided burial plots for destitute members. They operate lending agencies for hospital and home care equipment, as well as visit Masons in all hospitals. They assist Masonic widows to find housing and provide food until they can take care of themselves. They have filled prescriptions when the family no longer had the money to do so. They have provided the manpower to repair housing for destitute brothers and widows. They have helped locate missing persons and provided assistance in seeking legal advice. Many traveling foreign Masons have found the expression of brotherly love and affection exemplified in North America through the Association of Masonic Boards of Relief. In short they do what Masons are supposed to do.

This is the essence of the Craft. Even as the greatness of Freemasonry may have been crafted in the minds of great men, its soul was crafted in the hearts of those like us. And, even if we do not see specifics of what is done, we as a Craft are the benefactors of it. The request for Grand Lodge support is small compared to the largeness of what they accomplish. I only wish there was a way for everyone to learn the sagas of the Craft, many performed through this Masonic Association.

Now, however, the Association must take a close look at its possible future. Perhaps, after almost 120 years, the expression of brotherly love and taking care of our own has become an anachronism, no longer serving a useful purpose to the Craft. Perhaps, the Association has outlived its usefulness in modern-day Freemasonry. Perhaps, the time has come to close the doors of another Masonic institution.

But, if the Association of the Masonic Boards of Relief represents a vestige of the glory that was ours, exemplified in the expression that Masons take care of their own, then it is certainly to our benefit to do all that we can to support those Brothers who commit thousands of hours of their time helping others. The cost to us is small compared to the immeasurable return upon the investment.

If you feel as I do, that we can ill afford to continue to lose those characteristics that contributed to our greatness and our renown, then all we ask, is for your help in preserving those characteristics by supporting the Association and informing others.

[25]

The Grand Lodge of Iran in Exile

Given in 2003

It is a distinct privilege and pleasure for me to be invited to address this Grand Lodge. I have developed a great respect for the representatives of your Grand Lodge whom I have had the privilege to meet, and you honor me by inviting me to be here. You and your Grand Lodge represent a present-day example of the tenacity for which Freemasonry has been historically known, and although few may recognize it today, I am confident that historians will acknowledge it as such, in the future.

When we peer into the annals of Freemasonry, we find an organization not only unique in its structure, but also unique in its capacity for survivability. It has confronted onslaughts by its enemies even before it existed in present-day form. We have survived when hundreds of organizations, many patterned after Freemasonry long ago ceased to exist. There is probably no organization in the history of mankind outside of organized religion that has existed as long as have we and this in spite of ongoing attacks by despots who would destroy the peace of the world and dissect the liberty and freedom which has been a fundamental characteristic of our Craft.

Freemasonry has encouraged toleration, when toleration was almost an unknown. It has encouraged freedom of thought, in environments where such freedom was an anathema to those in power. It has promoted an equality of man, where such equality was not an accepted norm. In essence, it has espoused its philosophical purpose for existence, to take good men and make them better in a Brotherhood of Man under the Fatherhood of God where all men are free and all men are equal. My Brothers, there are those of you sitting here today for that very reason.

You now represent to the world what many of your brothers represented in the past, survivors of a tyrannical power. You represent a willingness to sacrifice for what is just and right in our world. You are living examples of the effects of tyranny and evil in man, and living proof of the need of the philosophical purpose of our Craft, of toleration in an intolerant world. My Brothers, you are now part of an ongoing standard, by which history may judge our organization as being, in the future.

For a little over a decade now, historians have finally been taking note of the influence that Freemasonry may have had on the development of not only some of the world's greatest leaders, but some of the world's greatest achievements. This is a relatively new phenomenon and although it took a long while, I think I now understand why. Historians dealt with men, not with organizations that contributed to the development of the men. Now, however, they are starting to realize that the two are inseparable. Even as evil can create evil men to perpetuate that evil, good can create good men to perpetuate that good, and the philosophy of Freemasonry certainly is geared to receive and to create good men.

We find scattered throughout history the Kahns, the Hitlers, the Mussolinis, the Stalins, the Francos, the Titos, and yes the Khomeinis, whose control over their countries and influence on the world has been one creating despair, hopelessness, and suffering. Where men of this genre have been in power, Freemasonry has suffered and Freemasons have paid a price.

Fortunately, for the world, for almost 300 years, there have been those willing to pay the price. For many, that price was life itself. Our brothers have been killed by the tens of thousands, simply because they were Freemasons. For many, that price was freedom. Many thousands more were imprisoned for the same reason. For others, like some of you here today, that price was being forced to leave your homeland and settle elsewhere. The liberty, freedom, and equality of man are a fundamental cornerstone of Freemasonry, but even as we can list the tyrants of the world, we can also list the heroes, and many have been members of our noble Craft. Men like Franklin, Washington, Voltaire, Mozart, Kipling, Churchill, Truman, Bolivar, Garibaldi, and a multitude of others have been major players in the ongoing development of civil societies.

Freemasonry has functioned for centuries as a magnet drawing into our brotherhood good men who were attracted to a philosophy that espoused not only the belief in a power higher than ourselves, but also in diffusing the light of that power and knowledge throughout the world, for the welfare of all mankind.

As a result, Freemasonry became in itself, an environment where good men of all professions, all beliefs, all social levels and all walks of life could sit together as equals promoting precepts which, if universally accepted, could serve as a template for world peace. Its membership rolls reads like a listing of who's who of the world for almost 300 years in fields of endeavor as diverse as the men themselves. It seems almost incomprehensible that there could exist any force of attraction that could bring and hold together this number of diverse and good men. But, my Brothers, it did exist, and from this environment there arose men, our brothers, whose names are etched upon the headstones of freedom throughout the world, where freedom exists.

Their names became part of the clarion call of mankind to make this world a better place, a fit abiding place for man to live. It is probable that if freedom exists anywhere on earth, it exists as a result of efforts of Freemasons or the influence of Masonic philosophy.

There's probably no organization in the history of mankind that has a greater reason to be proud of its accomplishments than has Freemasonry. We should be proud of what we have meant to the world, and there is also probably no organization whose membership expresses that pride more. It is our greatest strength because that pride gives us a strong foundation upon which to build as well as a selling point to the outside world. It is also, however, our greatest weakness because we use it today as a crutch to justify our present existence. We have far too much of a tendency to sell our past instead of our present, far too much of a tendency to ignore the present upon which depends our future.

We now must recognize, especially in North America, that our influence in society is waning, and it is doing so as a result of lack of knowledge of the Craft on the part of our leadership on all levels. I have found in my travels throughout the world that we here know less about our Craft than probably anywhere else in the world. Our ignorance of Freemasonry is appalling and detrimental to our very existence.

In the name of political correctness, we have changed elitism into an unacceptable term, but my Brothers, Freemasonry is elite. When we state that our goal is to take good men, and make them better, that is elitism, and it is not bad.

We now need the clarion call to waken us to our needs

if we are ever again to participate in making this world a better world. We cannot afford to continue to dwell upon the greatness of our past members and parasitize their contributions as justification to our present existence. If we continue to fail to build positively upon the foundation they established, then we are not worthy of the respect of the world or of our past.

Many citizens of this world lost their right to be Freemasons because of tyrannical oppression and are just now reclaiming that right. These Freemasons truly appreciate the meaning of being members of our Craft.

Some of you sitting here today probably understand more than most the meaning of the loss of freedom, and the desire of man to live without the oppression of those who took that freedom. You, also probably understand more the meaning and philosophy of Freemasonry, as well as the need to share it with those who do not.

While attending the 275th anniversary of the United Grand Lodge England, I listened to an old man who was the Grand Master of a recently reconstituted Grand Lodge of an Eastern European country. This brother had been the Grand Master of his Grand Lodge before Hitler closed them down in the 1940s. With intense emotion, he spoke of the significance and importance of Freemasonry to him and to the other brothers in his country. There were very few sitting in the audience that day that listened with dry eyes. I only wish that every North American Freemason could have had that experience. Then, maybe, just maybe, they might understand.

The freedom we know has given me the privilege of accepting your very kind invitation to be with you today. Not everyone in the world has that privilege. That freedom, also gave you the opportunity of inviting me.

[26]

Debate: "Resolved, That the Internet Will Make Grand Lodges Redundant"

Held in Washington, D.C.

More than three years ago, I made an observation to some of my colleagues regarding Freemasonry and the Internet. My observation was that because of the Internet, Freemasonry would never be the same. I think the short time span since bears out the accuracy of my observation.

I am constantly inundated with hard copies of Masonic material sent to me by members who pick it up from the Internet. Many are from those seeking information that I have neither the time nor the manpower in my office to answer. Most are valid questions which should be answered; the writers probably think are being ignored. Many are written by well-intentioned Brothers who don't know what they are talking about and who supply erroneous information on a worldwide level. Many are from the anti-Masons who use the World Wide Web as a platform to continue their campaign of hate. None of the above can benefit the Craft.

The concern, however, in this discussion is where Grand Lodges will fit into the world of the Internet or where the Internet will fit into the world of the Grand Lodges. The Internet is here. For better or for worse, it is here.

There is no doubt that Grand Lodges are being bypassed today by ignorant Freemasons. And ignorant Freemasons constitute the majority of our membership. Please note that I say ignorant — not stupid. Grand Lodges, however, have always been confronted with the challenge of working with Members who have no knowledge of protocols and little knowledge of Freemasonry. In the past, however, the mechanism to handle the challenge was also there, but it is lacking with the Internet. Realistically, very few of our Members are qualified to answer any but a small number of the questions presented.

If our membership chooses to remain ignorant, and there is little evidence to indicate otherwise, there must be some hierarchy to at least attempt to disseminate information in an organized fashion and hold together the vast amount of accurate knowledge that exists.

Perhaps it can be justifiably argued that this was not the purpose of the creation of grand lodges in the first place, but it certainly has evolved into a purpose, out of necessity. We must not fail to remember that grand lodges did not create lodges, lodges created grand lodges. The grand lodges then developed through the increasing demands of the lodges.

It has been my contention for years that subordinate lodges have become too dependent upon grand lodges. I have watched this phenomenon continuing during my years as Grand Secretary. For a long time, functions that lodges used to perform for themselves are now being performed by grand lodges because of either the inability or the lack of initiative of lodges to do for themselves. They will continue to become more dependent until the leadership and the commitment of those at the lodge level improves.

Without the grand lodge structure, there would never have been a worldwide uniformity of Freemasonry. The world knows Freemasonry and Freemasons because of this uniformity. Lacking it, each lodge would be known only unto itself. There would be no universal Freemasonry.

Unarguably, Freemasonry was the influential power it became because of a strong central authority directing it in the past. It was the grand lodges that coordinated the interest of the members on the lodge level with those of other lodges. The problem with the World Wide Web is that there is no central authority of any type, therefore no mechanism for coordination or control; thus, no uniformity. The result is evident because of the poor quality of much of the information fed into it. Without grand lodges, there would still be a lack of coordination.

Perhaps with this same logic we can also justify the elimination of the hierarchical structure of religions. Maybe there was and is no need of any organizational structure above the local level and how about our justice system? Are we wasting our resources of time and money by maintaining a structural level above that of a "local judiciary"?

To consider the concept of redundancy of the grand lodges, let's consider the operation of the United States of America with no federal or state governments and the potential for redundancy. Should we eliminate the federal government or the state governments?

This concept would parallel what this resolution proposes: operating Freemasonry without grand lodges. The result would be chaotic, like a many-headed organism running in uncoordinated directions with little ability to accomplish anything of significance. Is there anyone who honestly feels that this country or for that matter any country, could function effectively with no strong central government?

Look what happened to Yugoslavia when the central control fell. Right or wrong, the amazing aspect is not that the historic enemies reverted to fighting over ancient causes, but that they could have been held together to function as a country at all.

This analogy certainly displays what power can lie in central direction. It is indicative of what can be accomplished by capable leadership with authority to lead. Whether good accompanies the power depends upon the direction of the leadership. Without some type of central authority, however, there can be no coordinated response of any magnitude. Every organization with no central direction will continue to diverge until it becomes unrecognizable with respect to the original.

Now look at Freemasonry and the differences of opinion that have characterized it historically, as well as the challenges that confront it daily all over the world: i.e. the P2 lodge in Italy, the Southern Baptist leadership challenge in the United States, the questions of the membership of police officers in England, etc. There is absolutely no way subordinate lodges could respond to challenges of this magnitude—any more than can isolated group opinions guide religious belief or dictate jurisprudence.

Brother Wallace McLeod, in his evaluation of grand lodges, covers several valid points. "Grand Lodge ensures that our ritual, our so-called secrets, our procedures, our requirements, our beliefs, our tenets or fundamental principles, are uniform throughout the jurisdiction, and are of such a nature that Freemasons all over the world can identify with us."

Grand lodges may not always function in a manner that pleases all of the membership, but then what organizational leadership does? Without them, however, there would be no organization. Appendant Bodies would become independent bodies unrelated to Craft Masonry. With no means of a correlated effort, this would probably eventually also apply to many Subordinate Lodges.

Consider Freemasonry today with all of its ritual variations among grand lodges (no two are exactly alike) and think what the result would be if there were no central direction from grand lodges. The breakdown in standard ritual within a present jurisdiction would vary by the number of lodges within the jurisdiction. All ritual today contains the similarity to convey the same lessons that characterize Freemasonry. It is these lessons, through ritual, that made the Craft unique.

There would be a total lack of quality control not only of the ritual work, but even of the quality of the member. With no clearinghouse for membership, a man rejected in one lodge could simply petition another and another until accepted. How long could the Craft survive as the organization we have known?

There must be some mechanism to enforce the accepted standard of Craft Masonry. Our tenets and fundamental principles have made us and thus far sustained us. I'm not even sure that it is a debatable issue that they would not fail if not enforced, and there is no way they will be enforced on a subordinate lodge level.

I could cite numerous specific examples of tragic breakdowns even within grand lodge enforcement. Requirements must be maintained, our tenets transmitted in some form or risk falling into the category of legend.

How much of an impact could Freemasonry have created on this world without a mechanism to disseminate and coordinate information and efforts through grand lodges? How much impact could we hope to create in the future without them?

How well known would Freemasonry have become if each independent lodge had developed its own purposes and promoted its own programs? What kind of charitable purpose could we support with a fragmented leadership? Where would our Masonic Homes, our Shrine Hospitals or any other charitable endeavor be? Do we honestly think they could have existed or continue to exist supported by an unorganized group of subordinate bodies?

Where would the Craft receive direction and guidance concerning the thousands of questions today directed to grand lodges, from the Internet? And, don't ever doubt that the thousands of questions exist. Even today, I am hard pressed to keep up with them.

Even if we accept that there are no secrets in Freemasonry unwritten today; there remains the right to privacy. This maintenance of a member's right to privacy has been an ongoing challenge to grand lodges for years. There is no privacy on the Internet.

Can we honestly believe that the great men who were members of the past would have been attracted to an organization which lacked even the ability to define intelligently and consistently its purpose and direct its energies? Freemasonry attracted great men, and these great men contributed to the greatness of Freemasonry.

Freemasons must always serve as an example of what is better than that which is promoted by the social climate of the time. This example must then be disseminated to the world, and it cannot be accomplished without collective organization.

The Internet will make us change if for no other reason than to maintain damage control. It will force us to get off our collective duffs and do something. It will stimulate some of us who have rarely thought, to think. But, it will not result in redundancy of the Grand Lodge. Indeed, it will probably increase Freemasonry's need to maintain stability into the future. Instead of redundancy, I see the Internet establishing a greater need for Grand Lodges in the future.

[27]

California Freemason Magazine

When I was requested to write this article relative to the customs, practices and differences with Entered Apprentices in different parts of the world, I responded to the associate editor that I felt unqualified to write on this subject. I have probably never experienced an E.A. degree conferral in any foreign jurisdiction, but I told him that I was somewhat familiar with some of the requirements to receive this degree and to pass to the degree of Fellow Craft. This, he requested me to address. I must emphasize, however, that even on this subject, I have limited knowledge. I, therefore, point out that what I discuss in this article is an extremely superficial observation of the subject.

There is an old cliché with which you are probably all familiar: "You only get one chance to make a good first impression." This cliché is probably more significant in its importance to Freemasonry than to any application in any other organization. Consider how you felt when you were first received into a Masonic Lodge and experienced that E.A. degree. Have you ever felt a greater impact with anything else you have experienced? I would suspect that many of our former brothers, who are no longer with us, were lost on that first day due to a less than great impact. It is significant for us to realize that the Entered Apprentice degree is quite probably the most important degree that the member will ever receive or that we can ever confer.

I have had the opportunity to witness the conferral of a number of Master Mason degrees and many opening and closing rituals in other Grand and Subordinate Lodges. Most of these were conferred in a language that I did not understand. Nonetheless I was able to follow fairly well the process that was taking place. What I learned is that there are probably no two jurisdictions that are exactly alike in their ritual conferral, and yet for those who are familiar with the ritual of Freemasonry, there exists a universal understanding of what is taking place.

The greatest similarities among Grand Lodge rituals probably occurs in the North American Grand Lodges, most of whom practice the Webb ritual; but even they have made at least subtle changes from the original. All Freemasons should make the effort to visit other Grand Jurisdictions, even in North America, to experience the diversity in practice and ritual.

It is important to understand, however, that the end result of all degree ritual is essentially the same. This is true of any of the Blue Lodge degrees. It is of paramount importance when applied to the Entered Apprentice degree, for it is here that we create that first impact. The diversity in jurisdictional ritual is like taking multiple pathways to reach the same destination. This is a part of the beauty of Freemasonry, for we can take men from all stations of life and through our ritual even with jurisdictional variables, lead them to our ultimate goal of making them a better man. With this philosophical approach we have changed the world.

Perhaps the greatest jurisdictional differences that exist in the Entered Apprentice Mason degree are not in the conferral of ritual, but rather in the requirements even to qualify to receive that first degree or to pass from it to the degree of Fellow Craft. The stringent requirements in most jurisdictions of the world are far greater than those of any North American Grand Lodge. They have remained committed to the precept of accepting only the best men they can find and requiring a commitment from them to attend, to study and to learn. In addition, the cost to be a Freemason is considerably higher.

In some South American Grand Lodges as well as in other foreign jurisdictions, the candidate must wait for a minimum of a year so that his reasons for an interest in joining and qualifications to become a Freemason can be determined. After he has received his Entered Apprentice degree, he must present several learned papers on Freemasonry to be qualified to take the exam for passing. This is also required before advancing to become a Master Mason. There are very few foreign jurisdictions in which a man can become a Master Mason in less than a year after he is initiated, and some take several years.

The result of the stringent requirements, of course, means that the brother in most jurisdictions is not only qualified by a proper interest in the Craft, but is also far more knowledgeable of the philosophies, precepts, history and purposes for which we exist.

Freemasonry has endured in an organized speculative form for almost 300 years. It has attracted some of the greatest men this world has ever known. The initiatory experience must have had a considerable impact in the minds of millions of our brothers. Its influence and theirs have changed the course of civil society. Historians are just now catching up on how much this influence has meant to the evolution of civilization. This all began with that first step in becoming an Entered Apprentice Mason — even with all the jurisdictional diversity.

[28]

Affinity Marketing Breakfast—2013

My distinguished colleagues, it is a great pleasure for me to speak once again at the Affinity Marketing breakfast. I spoke at this breakfast fifteen years ago and it is a privilege to be asked to speak again.

In those fifteen intervening years I have traveled to many countries for the purpose of Freemasonry, have had the privilege of speaking in more than thirty countries and had the honor to meet some of the greatest men I will ever know. These travels have given me the opportunity to understand more fully the significance of Freemasonry in the historic evolution of the societies of the world. Writing the book reviews for *The Northern Light* magazine for twenty-three years has aided me in comprehending much of the thinking of current Freemasons.

I am going to be somewhat candid with my comments this morning, not meaning to be offensive, but with the realization that I am getting older and my clock is running down. In the limited time I have left, I will try to stimulate you to think more emphatically upon the direction we are going with Freemasonry; to think about what we are and to what we should and can be, and cause you to understand a little more of world Freemasonry. It is always my goal when I speak to cause you to think.

I realize that I could stand here and reiterate to you how great we were or even how great we are. I could rehearse the enormous accomplishments that our brothers in the past have made to this world. I could review a list of those Freemasons whose influence changed the direction of civil societies and what the probable influence the philosophy of Freemasonry had on their lives. I could do all of this and you could walk away happy, satisfied and content with what I said. But what value would that be to you? You have heard it all before.

My brothers, we are living in a remarkable age for Freemasonry. Our Craft in much of the world is achieving continuing success, by growing in quantity and quality of the membership and expanding into geographical areas where it has either not existed in the past or where it is reappearing following the fall of oppressive regimes. Indeed, we are perhaps growing more rapidly now than at any time in our history. There have been 26 new Grand Lodges consecrated since the turn of the century and they are attracting some of the more prominent personages in their societies. It is impressive to observe the quality of these new brothers, along with the attention of government leaders concerning the potential impact of the Craft on the development of their societies.

And yet, while we are thriving and expanding in some areas of the world, we are declining in others, becoming less visible and less influential in society.

I have been looking at divisive issues in Freemasonry with great concern for this decline. There are numerous factors that are contributing to our increasing failure, but the greatest problems facing Freemasonry today are quite different from those which we faced even fifty years ago. The lack of vision in too much of present-day leadership is causing us to concentrate more of our effort on mundane exercises of little consequence to the philosophical purpose of Freemasonry. In so doing we lose the opportunity to make contributions of those magnitudes for which we have been known for centuries.

We have lived for decades parasitizing the glory of our past and of what value has that been to us? We have lost three quarters of our membership in North America. We have surrendered our societal influence. Whereas we once were prominent, we have become almost invisible.

The time is long past for us to recognize that our attempts to regain our prominence in society over the past 30 to 35 years have failed. We cannot continue to emphasize and concentrate on what we were in our past. We must accept the responsibility that we assumed when we were given the privilege of becoming Freemasons.

We must confront the challenges of the present. In the past our greatest challenges were external. Our supreme enemies have historically been repressive government leaders and oppressive religious leaders. Please note, I said leaders of governments and not governments and leaders of religion and not religions. It is leaders who create the opposition—not the governments and not the religions.

It is also significant that the opposition of the leadership of both these entities opposed us for the very same reason: a need to control the minds and bodies of those under their influence. They would take from their adherents everything that Freemasonry stands for.

Now, however, they are not the greatest obstacles that we are facing. The greatest threat to our future lies not from without but from within. There are far more divisive issues for Freemasonry today existing within the egos of the leadership of the Craft than from challenges from forces outside. No repressive governmental system or any oppressive religious regime has been able to defeat the philosophy of Freemasonry. They certainly have tried and they have temporarily impacted us, but none has destroyed us. We now are accomplishing what they could never do. Over the past several years, we have watched the ego of one Grand Master almost totally destroy a very prominent and significant Grand Lodge and that was simply the most visible incident.

In much of North America over the past 30 to 35 years, we have excised most of the intellectual and philosophical qualities of the Craft, eliminating the stimulus to learn and removing the requirements to do so. Tragically, the result has been an erosion of our image along with a decreasing interest in the Craft. In doing so, we have surrendered the qualities that made Freemasonry such a unique entity. Our uniqueness is what made the Craft what it is; the most outstanding and significant organization ever created by the mind of man and in turn, Freemasonry made this world what it is today. Freemasonry was one of the primary enclaves that provided the environment during the age of Enlightenment that attracted great minds and laid the framework for a democratic society. The United States of America is one of the results.

The greatest threats to Freemasonry's integrity worldwide today have been the impact of appendant bodies interfering with Grand Lodge operation, the spread of irregular forms of Freemasonry and our willingness to accept it, along with encouraging an increased exposure of Freemasonry to the public.

We must never accept that any organization appendant to Freemasonry has any influence over the operations of a Grand Lodge. The Grand Lodge is the supreme authority in all jurisdictions and any interference by an appendant body is unacceptable. The greatest challenges to the success of Freemasonry in Eastern Europe and Africa have been a result of interference by organizations that require Masonic membership for affiliation. Higher degree numbers does not mean higher status in Freemasonry. There is no higher degree than a Master Mason's degree.

Irregular Freemasonry has been relatively quiescent and has offered little challenge to our success. Now, however, it is expanding into jurisdictions that have had regular Freemasonry for centuries. Our concern must be with the Masonic leadership today being willing to accept and grant recognition to these irregular bodies.

Finally, our willingness to tell the world all they want to know about us has had a major impact on those who were attracted by the mystique and the unknown of the Craft. When we take away the mystique we take away a stimulus for many who might have petitioned. Many of our leaders today feel the need to expose to the public that which we kept concealed or attempted to keep concealed for several hundred years. This created an aura that surrounded us and tended to lift us to a higher plane than that of other fraternal organizations.

Approximately twenty years ago, I took part in a debate on the proposition that the internet would make Grand Lodges redundant. I was on the side that took the opposing view and made the observation that it would not make Grand Lodges redundant but would certainly change Freemasonry's visible image to the world, and indeed, it has done that.

We live in a society dominated by a concept of political correctness today, the attitude that everyone should have the same as everyone else regardless of ability, initiative or work ethic. Masonic leaders have bought into that concept with a devastating effect upon the quality of the Craft; and as quality declines, so too does our image and our ability to impact the ongoing evolution of civil society.

In the internet, our enemies have found a fertile field in which to plant the seeds of doubt as to what is our true purpose and our intent. However, our misinformed membership probably does more harm to us than do our enemies. I never cease being amazed at the misinformation that is offered by our brothers on the web who think they know and by those who have been members for a short period of time having all the answers, yet never having heard the questions. I recall a quotation I heard many years ago, "Let he who does not know, shut up and learn."

For the last fifteen years, I have been attempting to place the Freemasonry of the world into what I refer to as styles based upon their operational philosophy. The structural philosophy of Freemasonry is universal and unalterable, but the operational philosophy depends upon the response to the sociological pressures of the environment in which it exists. Thus far, I have differentiated five styles and all have experienced levels of success. However, there are those that are beginning to fail in both numbers and influence due to the lack of vision and comprehension of Freemasonry's significance. With the possible exception of the Freemasonry in Australia, North American Freemasonry is today leading the way in this failing.

Every style that exists today came from an origin emphasizing an intellectual foundation based upon emphasis on learning and with the philosophical intent to improve the individual man. It is when we began to lose sight of the real meaning of Freemasonry that we began to observe the failure of its influence.

The more I study this Craft the more impressed I become with how much its presence meant to the development of civilization. Freemasonry made this world what it is today. It made it by taking the best man it could find and improving that man. I look at the results of our early leadership with their magnanimous long-range vision to produce what we have inherited. Then today, I observe not only the lack of that vision but even of the understanding of our significance to the world. It is sad to see our willingness to lower the quality of the membership simply to maintain the quantity. It is sad to watch our efforts to support programs of a consequence that will never approach those of our past and it is sad to watch those leaders whose abilities will never match the size of their egos seriously damage our potential to set an image to this world.

Freemasonry is a unique organization. Its uniqueness is what made the Craft into what it is; the most outstanding and significant organization that the mind of man has ever structured. There has never been an organization that could approach the positive influence that Freemasonry has had on the evolution of civil societies. This influence was not generated by the quantity of the membership; it was generated by the quality of its members. It was generated by the wisdom and the long-range vision of its leadership; it was generated by the dedication of those brothers who saw in the philosophy of the Craft the opportunity to change this world into something better than it was. It laid the foundation for democratic thought and provided the environment to stimulate it.

It is time now for us to lay our egos aside and contribute to restoring regular Freemasonry to the prominence it once had. I well know that no matter how important I may ever think I am to this world, a year after I am dead, the world will ask, "Tom who?"—and my Brothers, the same applies to all of us. We each have achieved what we have because we have an ego driving us. Our legacy will survive us, but whether that legacy is a benefit or detriment to the Craft will depend far more upon our willingness to limit our ego than to use our ego.

We, the present day leaders of our heritage, have assumed responsibility of perpetuating it. This heritage is the result of taking one good man at a time and making him into a better man. It was then, that better man who generated all that we have, all that we are. But it was not Freemasonry that made this world a better world. It was that better man that made this world a better world through the philosophical precepts of Freemasonry. If Freemasonry is not succeeding it is not the fault of Freemasonry's failing, it is a result of Freemasons failing. Freemasonry does not fail Freemasons fail.

I trust my comments this morning will cause you to pause and to think about our responsibility not only to Freemasonry but to our past brothers who gave us this heritage and to a world that needs it.

[29]

The Significance and Potential for the Craft

Presented to the Valley of Allentown

I congratulate each member of the class for the decision to continue his Masonic journey by becoming a Scottish Rite Mason. The Scottish Rite represents a path in Freemasonry leading out from the Blue Lodge providing an opportunity for each brother to expand his horizons through the moral and ethical lessons dramatized by dedicated brothers.

Each of the twenty-nine degrees under the auspices of the Supreme Council of the Ancient and Accepted Scottish Rite of Freemasonry conferred upon Master Masons conveys a moral and ethical lesson that prepares us to truly be Freemasons.

Freemasonry is not simply an organization that we have had the honor to belong to; it constitutes a commitment for each of us to the philosophy and principles of an organization that directed the pathway of civil society. The names of many of our brothers could very well be listed on an honor roll of the greatest men who have ever lived. But, my brothers, we cannot spend our lives basking in the glory of their greatness. We must assume the responsibility of accepting the lessons that we are receiving and applying them to the betterment of all mankind.

One of the principal admonitions of Freemasonry since its beginning has been to stimulate the membership to acquire knowledge. Indeed, there is an increasing amount of evidence that the oldest and most distinguished scientific society in the world designed to stimulate thinking and to share knowledge was founded and structured by Freemasons; The Royal Society. This is impressive, my brothers. The Royal Society is responsible more than any other organization in ushering in the world of scientific thinking.

This stimulus and even requirement for Freemasons to study and to learn is an emphasis that is applied stringently in Freemasonry in most of the world today. Unfortunately, for us in North America very little emphasis is placed on this basic characteristic of our Craft and as a result, we have lost much of our image in society.

Over the past twenty years, I have had the great opportunity and been given the privilege of participating in a number of educational programs throughout the world. I was privileged to give the opening keynote address last year at a symposium in Romania on the subject "Freemasonry, Fraternalism, and the Rise of the Idea of Liberty in Central and Eastern Europe." There is a considerable interest in the potential for Freemasonry to contribute to stability in emerging societies. I have met with several presidents and prime ministers to discuss that potential. Their knowledge of the possibilities of the Craft is impressive considering the short term of the Masonic existence in their countries.

Such potential for the Craft's contribution can exist only in a membership that has the knowledge of what we were, what we are and what we can be. This understanding will be paramount for us in North America if we have any hope of regaining our rightful place in our society.

About a month ago I was visiting the Grand Lodge of Chile and I asked the question, "What is required for a man to become a Freemason in your jurisdiction?" This is the answer I received. When a man petitions a Lodge for membership, a one-year investigation will take place and if he is found worthy, he will be entered. Over the next two years he is required to attend all meetings of his Lodge and the lodges meet once a week. He is also required to be present an hour earlier than the other members for Masonic education purposes. If then found qualified, he will be crafted, when the same requirement will take place for the next two years. There can be little doubt that these brothers will be far more knowledgeable on the subject of Freemasonry than what we know in North America.

Realistically, however, such a stringent requirement would be extremely difficult to apply to North American Freemasonry. This realization, however, does not minimize the significance of the need for our brothers to learn of the importance of Freemasonry in the ongoing evolution of the civil society of the twenty-first century. It takes very little understanding of the issues confronting the world today for us to comprehend the importance of a philosophy like Freemasonry's to serve as a modifying force for perhaps, even to the survival of mankind.

None can be unaware of the declining interest in Freemasonry in North America over the last fifty years. Our membership has dropped from over 4 million to approximately 1½ million, and where we were once a visible and highly respected organization, we are now almost invisible and ignored.

There is no one factor upon which to place the blame for the ongoing decline of interest but there can be no question concerning the lack of a fundamental educational system as being a contributing factor. Freemasonry continues to be held in high esteem in most countries of the world where there is freedom to practice it, even though they have had to struggle far beyond what we have ever known to even exist as a fraternity. One glaring feature about Freemasonry as it is practiced in most of the rest of the world is that their members are required to study and to learn. The acquisition of knowledge as has been universally professed in our Craft has not become a lost art as we have made it in North America. How can we possibly expect there to be an interest in an organization in which so few of the members themselves even knows what we are or our purpose?

I find nothing in our Freemasonry to compare with the stimulus for scholarly discussion that tends to permeate Freemasonry in most of the world. Sadly, this lack of challenge to our members tends to diminish the intellectual quality for which Freemasonry has been historically known. As a result, we have lost much of our allure to a segment of society that structured and gave Freemasonry its societal image.

Today only a relatively small percentage of our members truly understand the significance of the purpose or of the worldwide impact of the Craft. They may understand the words but words are simply words. Understanding must transcend the words and today this is a great failure on the part of North American Freemasonry. Unless we understand the meaning of the words how can we possibly understand the purpose for which we exist?

Regrettably, in the name of political correctness, we have developed an attitude that everyone deserves the same as everyone else. We live in an environment that rewards mediocrity so well that there is little incentive to rise above it. We live in a society that desperately needs a stimulus to excel beyond the norm. We live in a society that lacks a leadership to see beyond their own image and we live in a society that is in desperate need of an infusion of civility and logic into civil society.

Unfortunately, Masonic leaders have bought into this

political correctness concept and as a result we have seriously damaged our image in society and reduced our effectiveness to make future contributions. We need direction with vision to see beyond self-satisfaction and a dedication to rising above the mediocrity of today's social structure. We need a comprehension that Masonic education is a vital component for our survivability. We need a Freemasonry with many of the characteristics of our past.

This Craft played a vital role during the age of Enlightenment as one of the principal organizations in America that provided an enclave wherein great thinking minds from different social strata met and created the concept of a democratic society based upon the structure they found in Masonic lodges. I recommend a book for you to read called, Revolutionary Brotherhood: Freemasonry and the Transformation of the American Social Order 1730-1840. The author, Stephen Bullock, a non-Mason presents very effectively Freemasonry's influence on the development of American society.

For three centuries Freemasonry impacted this world by improving good men, by making them better men and we made them better by infusing into each, the realization that he was far more capable than he himself considered possible. We stimulated him to want to be better and incited his intellect to want to become more knowledgeable, to want to become more capable and to want to participate in improving the society in which he lived.

It was then the better man, the more knowledgeable man, the more competent man that impacted the evolution of civil society. Freemasonry became the educational tool that provided an environment wherein men, great thinking men crafted the ideas that created the ideals of a democratic society.

This world is as it is today because Freemasonry lived

and Freemasonry lived because it undertook the responsibility of taking the good man and making him a better man by teaching him the precepts and philosophies of Freemasonry. These better men then became the leaders that created modern-day civil society. The evidence of its success is revealed in the simple fact that it has thrived when hundreds of other fraternal organizations have long ago ceased to exist.

We can no longer choose to live in the glory of our past. We can no longer have our survival depend upon the claims of how great we were and point with pride to the greatness of our past brothers. We must now decide what we want to be. If we wish to be an organization that will be remembered in history as one that contributed to the greatness of America, if we wish to continue the heritage that was bequeathed to us by our past brothers, then we must make the decision that our current membership deserves it and develop programs whereby we educate them concerning that heritage.

This organization of Freemasonry has to rank as one of the most unique and significant structures that was ever crafted by human intelligence. Its unwavering unanimity of purpose has defined it for generations. Its basic ideals have remain unchanged in its dispersion throughout the world and it is this retention of unanimity of purpose that has made it the world renowned institution for which it has been known for centuries. Its influence on the development of civilization and on its leadership in the evolution of civil societies is unrivaled in the annals of any other organization.

Even as the age of the Renaissance lifted the veil of ignorance from the European world, Freemasonry needs an age of Renaissance in America today. Historians like Stephen Bullock are writing today about the greatness of Freemasonry of the past and its influence on not only the development of America but of world civil society.

We have now been given an opportunity that we may never see again through the writings of Dan Brown. This interest has created a potential to re-create an image of Freemasonry that has been lost to America. It will, however, require that we use it as a stimulus to re-create our lost image and to educate these new men on the potential of Freemasonry's contribution to the ongoing evolution of civil society.

The young men that are showing an interest in the Craft today are seeking much more than we have been providing. They are searching for a quality organization with a character far above the mediocrity of present-day society and they are searching for knowledge in a system that will provide it for them. They know more about Freemasonry before they petition a Lodge than any of us have had who preceded them. What they know however is what they have learned about the Freemasonry of the past. It is now up to us to provide for them that for which they search. The future of our Craft in America may well depend upon our acceptance of this challenge and the future of American society could well depend upon the Craft even as it did 250 years ago.

[30]

Sovereignty and Territorial Jurisdiction: How the World Meetings Will Benefit Freemasonry

1999 Conference of Grand Masters

Today I'm going to present a paper that should address two major concerns which I have heard expressed regarding the World Conference. The first concern was the need for such a conference, and the second was how would it impact grand lodge sovereignty? At the third conference held in New York City this past year a basic operational Constitution was adopted. At that time I accepted, with reservation, the position of Executive Secretary of the conference.

I regard it as a great privilege to be able to address the Conference of Grand Masters of North America. You represent an assembly of significant world Masonic leaders. I do wish to make it clear that what I am going to say today is the result of observation and analysis of what may be perceived as a definitive threat against the integrity of our noble Craft. It is not directed in any way toward any individual or grand lodge action, although I think we must admit that Freemasonry has been damaged in recent years by decisions and actions which, in retrospect, would have been better left unmade or undone.

Several weeks ago, a probable peace accord was reached in the country of Ireland. This accord was worked out through a process of discussion, a process which involved the use of verbal skills and a willingness to sit down and talk with one another. Regretfully, as we all know, this willingness to talk was preceded by years of bloodshed, bloodshed which might have been avoided had dialogue been tried earlier. I do not think there would be one logical thinking individual who would say that the bloodshed was worth it. Certainly those whose families experienced the loss of life would not. That the loss of life was the result of man's unwillingness to talk to one another and is a tragedy of monumental proportions.

One of the major obstacles preventing full cooperation and unity in Freemasonry today lies in our unwillingness or inability to talk with one another resulting in a strain in relations between grand lodges and an embarrassment to world Freemasonry. This limits our ability to use our influence for the good of mankind.

It is important for all of us to understand that there is a distinctive difference in Freemasonry's operational practices as well as its influential philosophy in different areas of the world. A failure to recognize these differences makes it difficult for us to effectively work toward common goals.

Our Craft is today confronted with monumental problems concerning our integrity. Many of these problems have their origins outside of the Craft, but many originate from within. All those that have originated from within should be more readily resolvable, but it is simply not happening.

We are entering into a new millennium, and we are entering it with possibly more divisiveness on a worldwide level than ever in our past. When we need to work together in harmony, we are arriving at decisions causing disharmony. When we should be concentrating all of our efforts to impress the world of our unanimity of purpose, we seem to be intent on fomenting discord amongst our grand lodges. When we most need communications between grand lodges, we seem to be building barriers to communication.

We must also recognize that we are living in an environment today that is undergoing a metamorphosis at a rate more rapid than we have ever experienced in our past. Changes are taking place today in our world that out of necessity must cause us to pause and analyze how we will fit in as part of that environment. It must cause us to re-examine the way our institution operates in that environment, and we must be willing to make the necessary adjustments in our modes of operation. It is imperative, however, when we enter into these changes, that we do nothing to damage or destroy the basic principles and precepts upon which we were born and matured and which made Freemasonry what it became. This, out of necessity, will require that we meet, talk and respond to reason. We are no longer an entity isolated within the confines of our own grand lodge. With modern technology, what was once a grand lodge consideration is now worldwide knowledge.

This is where the World Conference can play a vital role. It can provide the forum wherein discussions can take place and problems resolved while avoiding the conflicts, which has to result in a loss of our world esteem. After all, how can we expect the world to seriously accept us as the institution we claim to be, a Brotherhood of Men, when we don't even act as brothers to each other.

In dealing with the issue of sovereignty of grand lodges, we must recognize and accept that each grand lodge is an independent sovereign unit unto itself, and in that mode has the right to make decisions and take actions which it deems appropriate within its operation. This is an undeniable and inalienable right of a grand lodge. However, the leadership within grand lodges in using that right must assume the responsibility that the decisions made will be a benefit to

Freemasonry as a whole or at least not a detriment. The World Conference can never speak as the voice of grand lodges, and therefore, can never be dogmatic or policy-setting for Freemasonry. We as grand lodge leaders have an assumed responsibility to contribute to maintaining its viability as a world influence.

In past years there have been decisions made which at first glance may have seemed innocuous enough but which in retrospect created serious problems for the Craft. Perhaps talking may not have resolved these issues but then again, perhaps it would have. We will never know because we never tried.

Freemasonry as we all realize is an extremely complex organization. The very issue of legitimacy is perhaps one of its greatest complexities. Grand Lodges have not even been able to resolve the question of what constitutes territorial jurisdiction and therefore, the claims of their sovereignty over which they have a legitimate authority. Were I to enforce my own obligation to not sit in any tiled lodge meeting with an unrecognized Mason present, there are very few grand lodges in the world that I could ever visit outside of North America and in many cases not even in those. Realistically this is an impractical precept for operation and is damaging to Freemasonry. At the same time, we cannot rush in independently without forethought and destroy an operational procedure upon which we have survived for hundreds of years. Again, this is where the World Conference could play a vital role in dealing with these dilemmas before they become major worldwide issues.

We in the North American Conference have operated in the Masonic environment of what is referred to as the "North American Doctrine" wherein only one recognized grand lodge could exist in a geographical area, and that grand lodge claims jurisdiction over every resident living therein. It was revealing to me, when I found that most grand lodges outside of North America claim jurisdiction only over the members of their grand lodge and not any territory. As we are aware today, the North American Doctrine has been challenged in many jurisdictions and has been negated by the recognition of Prince Hall Grand Lodges. At the present time there seems to be no serious ramifications from this change in our long-held policy. I do not mean to justify or condemn the actions; I merely make an observation.

A major issue which is seriously threatening Freemasonry on a worldwide level today, however, is the operation of competing grand lodges in a jurisdiction in which a recognized grand lodge is already in operation and no mutual recognition exists. The public exposure which has accompanied these situations is totally unacceptable to legitimate Freemasonry. If we cannot sit and resolve the issues, we have absolutely no hope that Freemasonry within the boundaries of those jurisdictions can ever achieve the full potential for its existence. There has to be a concern of every one of us because its effect is felt far beyond the jurisdictional boundary of the grand lodge involved. With the attacks from without today, we can ill afford attacks from within.

It is my perception, which is supported by many world leaders, that a major cause of Masonic disputes today is a lack of a leadership commitment to Masonic ideals caused by a superimposed ego of the individual. We must be willing to surrender our personal ambitions for the sake of our future. If we are to solve our internal problems and indeed if we are to solve our external problems, we will accomplish it only through a unity of effort. No matter how important we may think we are, there is not one of us so important that we can afford to accept actions detrimental to the

Craft. A worldwide dialogue can never cause us harm, but the lack thereof certainly might.

This world desperately needs the organization of Freemasonry. There is no other environment which offers the opportunity for men of all diverse factions to associate together as Brothers. There is no organization to replace us. If we are observed as being incapable of working with each other, we cannot expect the world to respect us for what we purport to be.

We must have dialogue; we must work together. We must become what we claim to be: A Brotherhood of Man under the Fatherhood of God, dedicated to making good men better. If we make good men better, we succeed in our purpose and these better men continue to lead the world in its ongoing search for freedom, liberty and equality. If we fail the whole world is a loser.

[31]

Legacy of Liberty:
Masons, the Path to Freedom,
and Contemporary Masonry's Role

Presented at the XVIth World Conference

This is the 14th World Conference of Regular Masonic Grand Lodges, as it is now known. I have attended 13 of them. I presented a paper at the second held in Lisbon, Portugal and the third held in New York City. Other than the opening and closing addresses, this is the first paper that I have presented since being elected at the third as Executive Secretary.

When Chip and I were asked to present a paper at this conference on legacy and liberty, we agreed. Chip was to focus on early Masonry's role and I on contemporary Masonry's role. In developing this paper, I reached the conclusion that Chip received the easier assignment. There are thousands of volumes upon which to draw information of early Masonry's role in the legacy of liberty. However, I found that the only resource material I could draw upon in writing this paper, was my own thinking and a limited number of contemporary articles. This represents a dearth of resource references.

Please note that when I refer to Freemasonry's responsibility and commitment, I am referring to Freemasons. It is not the responsibility of the Craft to improve the world. It is the responsibility of Freemasonry to change the man through the making of good men better. It is then, the Freemason's responsibility to improve the world.

It is not possible to discuss contemporary Masonry's role without looking back at its role in the past, for even as our past impacted our present, the present will impact our future. This paper, therefore, will allude to the past as a preface to the present and the prospect for the future.

This is an incredible age for Freemasonry that we live in today. Probably, not since the creation of the first speculative grand lodge in 1717 has Freemasonry been given the opportunity to impact such a large area of the world and influence such a large number of its citizens. There have been twenty-eight new grand lodges consecrated since the turn-of-the-century, most of them in countries that are struggling to present or re-present themselves in world society. This offers to Freemasonry, a great potential and perhaps an unprecedented opportunity to contribute to a future legacy of liberty on the path to freedom in a large portion of the world.

As many of you know, I have been actively involved for many years in participation with the leadership in multiple grand lodges in numerous countries to find Freemasonry's role in their societies. I have been greatly impressed with the interest of the leadership of governments in the potential of Freemasonry to contribute to the positive evolution of civil society in their respective countries. I have met with presidents, prime ministers and other leaders to discuss Freemasonry's possible role in their countries, as well as promoting a progressive form of evolution into a more stable society. In addition, I have been interviewed on a number of television and radio broadcasts along with press interviews, all relating to Freemasonry's relationship in their countries

I must assume, this interest was generated by the knowledge of Freemasonry's influence in the past in creating a viable image of a stable democratic society wherein individual citizens could improve their status while at the same time contributing to an improved environment for all citizens.

Freemasonry has historically set a standard and worked to achieve an equality based upon the quality of the individual man for several hundred years. Indeed, it is not inconceivable that the present-day concept of democracy was promulgated by the philosophical intent of Freemasonry. Our Craft played a major role during the Enlightenment by providing an environment wherein those with great thinking minds with humanitarian concern, might gather together in "relative" peace with a "limited" fear of repressive government restraint or religious oppression, resulting in the promotion of the inherent rights of man. (I use the words 'relative' and 'limited' as in context of the time.) Indeed, Freemasonry was one of the greatest promoters of democratic thinking that left behind a legacy of liberty with a defined pathway to freedom.

There are those brothers sitting here today, representing their grand lodges, who thirty years ago could not have dreamed of that privilege. There are brothers sitting here today, who have experienced first-hand, life under a form of oppression that prohibited the freedom even to be a Freemason. There are those brothers sitting here today who can look back at a clouded past, but forward to a brighter future. Freemasonry could and should play a major role in that future!

I recall an experience that I had approximately 16 or 17 years ago, when I was sitting in a piano bar in Sofia, Bulgaria along with the Grand Master of Romania and the Grand Master of Bulgaria. I noticed that the Grand Master of Romania had tears in his eyes. I asked him what was wrong. His response was, "I cannot believe that

I am sitting here in a piano bar in Bulgaria with you." My brothers that was an inconceivable possibility even a few years before that date and a moving and revealing moment for one who did not experience his past. The appreciation of being a Freemason is not lost on those who were denied that privilege for so many decades.

As a new vista for Freemasonry opens, also opening with it is an opportunity to leave behind a lasting legacy for which our Craft has been known in the past and will be known for in the future. My brothers, each of us has an opportunity to play a role in that legacy. What a privilege to be placed in a position to impact the future of the countries in which we live. What a privilege to be a Freemason in the contemporary world!

For those brothers, living in environments where Freemasonry is just emerging or reemerging, the potential is enormous. I have had the privilege of traveling in many of your countries where the mantle of responsibility assumed by each of you as Masonic leaders is perhaps as great as has been faced by any Freemasonry in the past. You hold in your hands the responsibility of commitment, not only to your countries but to Freemasonry's legacy. Each of you is the visible example of the Craft to your country.

It places a tremendous responsibility upon the shoulders of those who were denied that privilege, to join now with millions of other brothers to contribute on the continuing path and to leave behind a legacy of liberty in their countries. That legacy of liberty to which we now refer has established a standard by which we the contemporary Freemasons must constantly strive to uphold and renew.

There exists, today, a broader spectrum of opportunity for the Craft than has existed for many decades. However, the window of opportunity is open for a limited time. A greater impact may be felt early in any transition. But, even as the potential to influence society arises in the world, the prospect for leaving a legacy proves challenging.

In a short span of three decades for Eastern European countries, we have learned that the pathway to creating one is not easy. It was not easy in the past and we have no reason to assume it would be easy in the present. Contemporary Masonry's role has not changed from what it was in the past but the environment in which it works has changed. It took very little time for me to recognize that the mindset with which one must deal in Eastern Europe is distinctively different from that of the rest of the world. This, realistically, is the result of living under decades of restricted freedom. There appears to be an almost inherent distrust by the current citizenship of all organizations at any level. This simply offers another hurdle to get over in creating your legacy.

Interestingly, I was talking with a young brother in Russia this past July and I learned something from him concerning the challenge in Russia for Freemasonry. It is somewhat different than the challenge for Freemasonry and the rest of Eastern Europe. In Russia the distrust is of influence of the Western world rather than an organization.

I have had the privilege of traveling in a number of African countries where there has been considerable expansion of Freemasonry within the indigenous populations and have watched with great pleasure the influence that it has created in a nucleus of leadership. From my experience, however, I am well aware of the challenges the Craft there faces, due to the uniqueness and diversity of the populations of that continent. Again, the opportunity of challenge, if successfully met, will provide a great legacy for the citizens of Africa.

I remain convinced that the greatest future for Freemasonry presently, lies in Eastern Europe and on the continent of Africa. Freemasonry in these locations provides some of the greatest challenges and gives the Craft its maximum opportunities to create a lasting impact.

My greatest concern in the countries which experienced great repression or in countries where Freemasonry is a recent phenomenon is that it will be seen not as a great contributor to the positive evolution of society but as a means to gain social or political status for the individual. There must be concern that the appreciation for Freemasonry may cause some to attempt to utilize it to promote themselves rather than promote the precepts and the rights of the citizens. Was this to occur, Masonry may be looked upon as a negative contributor to a legacy of liberty.

Regrettably, the potential to greatly impact society in most of the Western world today is limited, simply because the need of Masonic philosophy is not as great in those societies. They have achieved a degree of political, economic and social stability such that societal evolution is less needed. That does not mean that Freemasons in Western societies have no role in maintaining a legacy for freedom. Indeed, the confrontations that we see every day in the contemporary world, place an enormous responsibility upon our Craft to promote the ethical and moral values that must exist in all civil society for it to thrive and for which we have been historically known for several centuries.

There are many countries today that although Freemasonry has existed there for many decades, continue to struggle against the pangs of poverty and hunger, threats of rebellion, oppressive religious leaderships and government restraints. These struggles will continue to repress philanthropic values and restrict commitment to others. However, these challenges must be looked upon as opportunities for Freemasonry to make its greatest influence felt through the dedication of each individual brother.

In reflecting upon our past we cannot help but acknowledge that some of the greatest men who ever lived, chose to be Freemasons, not for what it did for them but for the opportunity that it provided to make a contribution to the development of world civilization. All we need do is to look at the names of the great men emblazoned upon the headstones of freedom who contributed in the struggles for a legacy of liberty. Look, and recognize how many were Freemasons.

Hundreds of thousands of Freemasons paid with their lives for simply believing and professing the philosophical premise of the inherent rights of mankind. Many, perhaps all sitting here today, can do so as a result of commitment of Freemasons.

To that list of brothers whose names are listed upon those headstones can be added thousands of others in such diverse fields of endeavor that it would be difficult to list them, but whose contributions to society are innumerable. They also played a major role in the past that has supported the pathway to freedom.

Consider how many countries existing today experience freedom and liberty won principally by the contributions and leadership of Freemasons or built on Masonic philosophy.

Permit me to quote from an address of the first president of the Philippines. "The successful revolution of 1886, was Masonically inspired, Masonically led, and Masonically executed. And I venture to say, that the first Philippine Republic of which I was the humble president, was an achievement we owe largely to Masonry and the Masons." Speaking of the revolutionist, he added, "With God to illumine them and, Masonry to inspire them, they fought the battles of emancipation and won."

We can look back at the commitment of our past brothers and their contribution to the legacy of liberty they bequeathed to us. We can acknowledge and experience the liberty in which we now live as a result of their commitment. They also however, left for us a legacy of respect. It is now the responsibility of Freemasons of the contemporary age to assure the world that we are worthy of that respect.

We cannot achieve this by parasitizing our past. Freemasons today, have too much of a tendency to point out to the profane world the great men and the great contributions they made as justification for their respect. To paraphrase Goethe, "That which has been bequeathed to us must be earned anew, if we would possess it." It is now our responsibility to earn anew, the legacy of our past if we would possess it.

We are very aware of the influence and contributions, over several hundred years, that our members have made to the development of civil societies. We should be very realistically aware of the impact that our members have made in the world's struggles for the freedoms and rights of man. It cannot be a simple coincidence that they were Freemasons. The examples are far too numerous to dismiss the probable influence of Masonic philosophy and precept upon their commitments

So, where do we, as contemporary Masons, fit on that pathway to liberty? What role will we play, or are we playing to fulfill our commitment on our path to leave a legacy? What are the greatest challenges that we face if we are to repay the debt we owe to our brothers of the past and to preserve what they have created?

The challenges we are facing today are no more daunting than they were in our past. Not all areas of the world face the same obstacles nor will all grand lodges be confronted by the same challenges. Some challenges, however, are universal.

Whereas the greatest challenges that confronted Freemasonry in the past were external, generally caused by leaderships of governments and religions, the greatest challenges facing us today are internal, caused by our own membership and our leadership.

This is a different world we live in today, my Brothers but the world is always different from that of the past, and it has always changed. The changes that have occurred throughout our history have been dramatic and yet the stability of Freemasonry in support of its fundamental philosophy has not wavered. We have not surrendered to the demands of the profane world to fit into what they perceive we should be.

Freemasonry has evolved since its inception 300 years ago. Its operational procedures have changed and yet its philosophical commitment remains unaltered. Its commitment to the moral and ethical values of a civil society have not been affected as the world changed. The only variable in Freemasonry is the membership. Freemasonry is the greatest organization ever structured by the human mind. Its only major weakness is that of being composed of human beings. It is that variable that causes its practice to sometime fail. Remember, my Brothers, Freemasonry does not fail. Freemasons fail.

One of the greatest challenges Freemasonry is facing in this contemporary age versus earlier ages, is the attempt of leadership to change the basic structure of the Craft which they feel is necessary for us to be part of modern civil society. That, my Brothers, may also be one of our greatest threats to survival. Today's political correctness has impacted our fraternity probably far more than we would like to admit. Too many of our leaders have bought into the attitude that everyone should have the right to be a Freemason. This has caused us to weaken the quality of our membership and surrender much of our respect to the outside world. Mark it well, however, my brothers; not every man deserves to be a Freemason.

There perhaps have been more changes made in parts of the world over the last thirty years than all years prior to it. Are we to assume therefore that for over two and a half centuries we have lived in a static world? And what has been the result of these changes? Our membership numbers in parts of the world are on the decline and our influence has been much lessened. Where membership was once ardently sought by those wishing to affiliate with a highly successful, visible and influential organization, today we are largely ignored.

Freemasonry has always changed. It has never been a static organization. The changes however were as a result of our intent, not driven by the demands of the profane world who fail to understand us or our intent.

A second challenge that confronts us is the lack of the intellectual giants who crafted our organization at its inception. Consider that many were members of the Royal Society, a society that remains the single most significant scientific organization in the world. They were leaders of their time, whose names are imprinted upon the history of man and they were Freemasons. There were, however, those visionary leaders who followed them, who continued to provide the leadership and whose names are also inscribed on that same history.

Perhaps, within our Craft this caliber of man continues to exist and perhaps at some future date their names will also be acknowledged by historians for their contributions. If they exist today as members of our Craft, however, they have chosen to remain invisible and silent.

A third and perhaps the most significant challenge with which we are confronted today in creating a legacy of liberty lies within the leadership whose egos exceed their abilities. We all have watched brothers assume leadership roles with good intent but have permitted their egos to destroy their legacies.

All of these challenges will have a dramatic effect upon our potential to leave a lasting legacy for future generations. Fortunately, they do not impact the Craft in the entire world. There remain in this world, Masonic leaders who have dedicated themselves to perpetuating the philosophical intent of our early brothers; of promoting moral and ethical values, of teaching and of learning, and in supporting the needs of our brothers and of world society. For much of the world, this is the perception that has been created and the one that we are obligated to support.

We are fortunate, for the Freemasonry from our past has left us with a great heritage to draw upon to build a legacy for the future. It remains our role as contemporary Freemasons to continue that legacy. Freemasonry historically has risen above all challenges that it faced. Contemporary Freemasonry must do the same if we are to leave a legacy of liberty; and in spite of us, we will.

TWO

~

Realism

[1]

What Are We Trying To Save?

I recall a quotation I heard many years ago, "When you place your hand in a flowing stream, you touch the last that has gone before and the first that is yet to come." A man's relevant position in history and our position in Freemasonry is as that hand. We stand today as the hand in the flowing stream of Freemasonry, touching the last that has gone before and the first that is yet to come. There is a distinct difference, however, between the hand in the water and us. The hand has no power to change the ultimate destiny of the flow of the water. But we, my brothers, have the capacity and the power to change the ultimate destiny of Freemasonry.

I want to make it totally clear that I speak to you today expressing my views and my opinions, and mine only. I speak for no Masonic body. I do speak, however, as one who has spent 36 very active years in Freemasonry, 18 of them as a professional. I speak as one who has made some effort to study this Craft and have a great concern about its future.

Freemasonry has existed in some form probably at least since the fourteenth century—we think. In its organized speculative form it has existed since 1717—we know. Although we cannot be sure of what it was originally—we think we know what it is now. But do we?

Freemasonry has been defined in many glowing terms, by Freemasons for a long period of time, and in less than glowing terms by its detractors for an equally long period of time. The Definitions are there, and yet there are precious few who truly know what we are and that includes us.

We look with regret at not being as significant in today's world as we were in yesterdays because our numbers are not as great. We evaluate ourselves in terms of quantity instead of quality. That is an unfortunate appraisal of the Craft, for it has caused us also to lose sight of what we were. Our attempt to return to former influence may therefore be unachievable, for if we don't know what we are, how can we hope to become what we were? One thing is certain however, if we continue to change from what it was that made us great, we reduce the chance to regain that greatness.

Think for a moment of how much time and money you have invested in this Craft. Now multiply that investment by tens of millions. The resultant figures are astronomical. Why have we done this? There has to be some stimulating factor that has caused the Craft to be carried for almost 300 years. I would suggest that it was the constancy of its purpose.

We have for the last two decades been concentrating our best leadership ability on an issue which we acknowledge to be the greatest threat against what we perceive we are—the loss of our quantity.

It is significant that we are not a static organization. Freemasonry is an ever evolving entity, and change cannot be opposed because it is change, but nor should it be accepted for its own sake. We each have an obligation to be certain that any change we make will be a benefit to the Craft or more importantly, at least not a detriment. In analyzing this evolution we find one constant denominator that did not vary through all its years—the emphasis on the quality of the membership, which in turn probably has been the primary reason for most member affiliations.

We projected to the world an image of which good men wanted to be a part.

We have probably changed Freemasonry more in the last twenty years than was done in the prior 250, and what have we accomplished? We certainly have not stopped the decline in numbers for which reason we made most of the changes. We have, however, managed to reduce our attractiveness to the professional class which comprised much of our membership.

Perhaps the time has arrived for us to examine more closely what has been done and what has been the result. Let's take the time to analyze what we have accomplished and honestly answer and acknowledge where we have failed. We have not stopped the bleeding of numbers, but we surely have reduced our influence from what it once was.

I propose that Freemasonry became as great as it did, and remained as great as it has, for three primary reasons. Reason number one: it was probably the first organization to accept, at least philosophically, men from all stations of life as equals. Reason number two: it attracted some of the greatest minds that ever lived. Reason number three: it remained selective concerning the quality of the man it would accept.

The deletion of any one of these reasons would have prevented the Craft from becoming what it did or remaining as it has, and I am convinced that the loss of any one will also destroy it, at least in the historic form for which it is known. It, therefore, behooves us to ask, what are we trying to save?

Freemasonry has impacted the evolution of civil society beyond that of any organization outside of organized religion. There can be little doubt that without Freemasonry the civilized world, in its present form, probably would not exist.

Recognizing these facts, my Brothers, we have inherited

an awesome responsibility, one of more than just keeping the name Freemasonry alive. We must keep it viable, a force that can display to the world, what is good and right in mankind, an enclave of toleration in an intolerant world, a unique organization in a world that needs that uniqueness, an organization known by the quality of its membership.

We are making many decisions today that seem to indicate a lack of intent in preserving the integrity of the Craft. We seem more intent on redefining and reshaping it in almost any manner to fit into what we perceive to be what society wants us to be. But, we must be more than that. Freemasonry leads, not follows.

We have attempted to become more family oriented, and yet the Grange, a purely family-oriented fraternity, is rapidly fading from view. We have attempted to become more social in our operation, but the social clubs, such as the Elks and Moose, are struggling to operate. We have attempted to become more civically involved, while the community oriented "fraternities" such as Kiwanis and the Lions are declining more rapidly than are we.

Perhaps we must consider these characteristics but why are we attempting to emulate organizations that are declining as least as rapidly as we are? If we are not succeeding by emulating, should we not be considering building upon our uniqueness? We have always been distinctively different from any other organization. Why should we attempt to change into something someone else wants us to be? It defies logic to put so much effort into programs that are geared to emulate the principal purposes of other organizations. Not only can we not hope to be more significant than they in their field of endeavor to begin with, but none have ever reached the pinnacle of greatness that we have.

First, however, we must understand the cause of the decline. We look at the loss of membership and interest and have the tendency to blame ourselves for what we deem to be a failure in our structure and our leadership. My Brethren, I honestly do not believe that any difference in our structure or our past leadership would have shown results much different than they do today.

The loss in membership can neither be blamed solely on inadequacy of leadership nor failure of our system. Our purpose and precepts have carried us through changing societies for centuries. Why should it now be judged a failure because our numbers fluctuate even as they have fluctuated in the past? We are no different in terms of membership decline than almost all other organizations today, including most religions. The clime of society today simply is different and not geared to organizational interest that place restrictions on its activities.

Because society lowers its standards does not mean we must do the same. Indeed, we have an obligation to the future to lead the way to what is morally and ethically right, to be more than just average in society. In essence, to be what we have always been.

I feel strongly that we are looking at a sociological phenomenon, one probably created by our attempt to make life easier for each succeeding generation and which must run its course before we find a redevelopment of interest in our way of life. We must realize that there is no immediate or spontaneous solution to our decline in numbers. We must acknowledge that this is a problem not localized to either area or organization. It is time for us to recognize that our decrease in numbers is due to a sociological condition of the time and not to our inability to cope with change.

The pendulum will swing, my Brothers; there will be a renewed interest in a quality organization based upon our philosophical principles. But, will Freemasonry as a quality organization be there to accept those interested?

Historians are finally writing about Freemasonry, but they are writing about the quality of the organization not the quantity. Freemasonry for generations has been known by those outside of it for its constancy of purpose and as A.C. Green said, "A level of class." We the leaders of the present have made us as we are perceived by the public today. We are the internal variable. Freemasonry, my Brothers, is more than a name. It is an ideal. So what are we trying to save: the name or the ideal?

We have evolved into the world's greatest charitable organization, but Freemasonry is not a charity. Its avowed purpose is to take good men and make them better. By making good men better, we improved the quality of the world. Of what value will be our charitable nature if we fail to survive to support the charity? We cannot continue to concentrate most of our efforts on raising money to give away. We cannot buy admiration and respect. We must focus greater effort on Freemasonry's survival as the world's premier organization. To be charitable is an admirable quality, but our charitable characteristic must be secondary to our primary purpose.

Freemasonry's goal has always been to start with the best we can find and improve that best. This goal, out of necessity, implied selectiveness. The selectiveness was based upon the quality of the man. Our Craft has been unique in that it has been able to take men from all walks of life socially, economically, culturally, etc., and provide an environment wherein the similarities of good are far more important than differences of type. I suspect the quality of the man is perhaps the major intangible force which, though unseen by the world outside the Craft, is what brings and holds us together. Freemasonry carries the concept of good men associating with good men much farther than any other organization.

It is a natural, instinctive desire to associate with those of similar kind. This is why in nature we find flocks, herds, schools, etc., of animals, and it is no less true of man. This is why we have found in Freemasonry, lodges of good men. Without quality men, there can be no quality organization. Quality will attract quality, and quality will ensure survival. We cannot hope to grow, or even remain the same, by lowering our standards.

We acknowledge that only 10% of our members are active. That, of course, means that 90% are inactive. Yet they retain their membership. They pay their dues each year knowing full well that they will never participate in lodge activities. There is only one logical reason they do that. There is a perceived value in being able to say, "I am a Freemason." Take away the perceived value of association with a quality organization and we risk losing the 90%.

Freemasonry has had in its ranks, men whose names are etched on the headstones of eternity—names not to be forgotten. What was the force which drew them in? I suggest it was an organization which embraced high ideals and principles, nurtured those ideals and principles, and stimulated aspirations to greatness. Thus we became great with them. One feeds upon the other. Great men make great organizations, and great organizations can make men great. Likewise, the loss of one must result in the loss of the other. Freemasonry must never resign itself to be less than it can be. We must always seek the great man and seek to make men great.

Our vision must be expanded. We must stop looking at long-term planning in spans of 5, 10, or 25 years. We must look in spans of 50, 100, or 200 years. We are simply too important to the world to limit our vision. We, as leaders, must not only truly understand our past, but see our potential for the future.

There is no question that the environment in which we exist has changed. Now we must determine whether we wish to retain our principles and values to lift others to meet our ideals or change to fit into today's environment and thus step down to meet present-day standards.

Do we truly believe in the philosophy upon which we existed for close to 300 years? Have we become an anachronism in present-day society? Have our principles and values actually had no place for the last quarter-century? I think not. If we truly do believe we are right, if we truly do believe that our philosophy and principles have a place in the modern world, then we must continue to pull others up to meet with us, not climb down to meet with them.

I am convinced that we are creating one of our greatest problems by making membership in the Craft too easily obtainable and retainable. Of what value can anyone be to us if he lacks either the interest or the ability to be a Freemason except in name, and if his projection to society is not positive?

During all the low points in Masonic history, and there have been some, there is no evidence that decisions were made which affected our basic precepts or reduced the quality of the Craft. Nor was it necessary to make major procedural changes in our methods of operation to recover from membership loss. We seem intent today in reducing all barriers for membership numbers regardless of cost, and the result is evident. We have required less, and less we have received.

When we evolved from a fraternity of the practitioner to the fraternity of the idealist, we forged a character that was idealistic. What is happening to that idealism, that noble philosophical precept of the Craft today, when we no longer believe that if we are great we do not have to ask others to join with us? Are we no longer capable of projecting the image that carried us for centuries, the one that stimulated others to want to become part of us?

Gotthold Lessing, in the 1770s, argued that "if we know a Freemason by his deeds, then he must leave his mark on the world." Is our mark not enough to encourage others, or do we not wish to leave a mark?

Where Freemasonry goes from here is up to us. Our hand is in the flowing water of the Craft. If we are trying to save a name, we may succeed. If we are trying to save an ideal, we are not succeeding. This Craft will not be measured in the future by its quantity any more than historians are measuring it today by that standard. It will be judged by its quality. If we cannot have both, then we must choose.

We are confronted today with monumental problems concerning our integrity as an institution. Many of the problems are originating outside the Craft but, regretfully, most originate from within. We, as leaders, must be willing to sacrifice our egos for the Craft. We must be willing to surrender personal ambition for the sake of the future of Freemasonry.

The quality of the Craft must not be permitted to continue to decline. We must recognize that the organization is much larger than the sum of all of its component parts. We say we are a brotherhood of men under the fatherhood of God, a fraternity designed to make good men better. If this is what we are trying to save, we should re-examine our approach. If we make good men better, we succeed in the purpose of the Craft, and these better men will then continue to lead the world. If we fail, the whole world loses, and I personally don't want to be remembered as part of the generation of leaders who destroyed the Craft.

Give it some thought, my brothers. What are we trying to save?

[2]

Do We Even Care?

Presented to the Grand Secretary's Conference

When the chairman of your agenda committee asked me if I would address the Conference concerning World Freemasonry, I readily said yes. Fortunately for me, our distinguished brother and a good friend from Ireland—Grand Secretary Michael Walker made my job much easier when he agreed to speak on the same subject. I had the privilege of reading his paper in advance and he will say in better words, what I would have liked to say. In fact, I will address much of his topic in Madrid at the World Conference in May.

I was sitting at home at the computer, a few weeks ago trying to think of what to say without becoming repetitious. I have spoken on this subject and to this Conference many times, and most of you know how I feel. I regard the lack of Masonic knowledge by our membership to be the greatest threat to our survival, because that, along with our obsession with numbers, is leading to the destruction of the quality of this, the most significant organization ever created by human thinking.

At that time, a thought struck me that I had never openly contemplated before. Even though I have certainly been aware of, and even in a minor way participated in, the rapid expansion of Craft Freemasonry over the world, I had never coalesced my thoughts into any logical analysis. I will use my small amount of time now to cause you perhaps to think a little more on the subject of what is happening with Freemasonry in the world today, for even as numbers of Grand Lodges are increasing, the number of members and the influence of the Craft in North America, is decreasing.

I wonder how many of us, as Masonic leaders, have spent any time contemplating how much change has taken place in Freemasonry over the last decade and a half. I wonder if we have even tried to comprehend the expansion of the Craft in the world with the consecration and re-consecration of Grand Lodges. I wonder if we are considering what this means to our organization, or more importantly, to its image and its influence in the world. And frankly, with the inflated egos by which we are driven today, I wonder how many of us really care. I know this sounds harsh, but Freemasonry is suffering because of it and we cannot continue to ignore this lack of caring! Freemasonry desperately needs a style of leadership today that is more committed to the philosophy and purpose of its existence than to perpetuation of a self-image.

There has probably been no period of time in our history, except shortly following our origin as a speculative Craft, that there has been more widespread expansion and interest in Freemasonry than there has been in the last decade. With the reemergence of the Craft in the former Soviet Bloc and other dictatorially controlled countries, along with the consecration of Grand Lodges in Africa, Freemasonry has been projected into the new millennium as a rapidly spreading institution which will, one way or another, create an impact upon the future of this world, and frankly, my Brothers, we are not prepared to deal with it.

Grand Lodges are arising with a leadership understandably limited in both knowledge and experience concerning philosophical Craft Masonry. Their problems are being compounded in many jurisdictions by the creation of appendant bodies while a concentrated effort should be given to the development of Craft Masonry. Serious harm is occurring to these Grand Lodges, as we should expect, if for no other reason than the dilution of the leadership pool. What should be even more alarming to us as Grand Lodge leaders is their interference in Craft Masonry that has even resulted in the creation of competing Grand lodges. My Brothers, I have said it before and I will repeat it now, if it affects Freemasonry anywhere today it affects Freemasonry everywhere. And yet we seem to be either oblivious to or uninterested in what is happening in the rest of the world.

Some Grand Lodges are far more knowledgeable than others concerning what is occurring. General ignorance of the meaning and purpose of Freemasonry, however, coupled with the concentration on quantity rather than quality is limiting our vision of the significance of World Freemasonry, as well as of what Freemasonry means to the World.

Emphasis on increasing numbers rather than educating those that we have has become a way of life to North American Freemasonry. The result is totally evident in the erosion of the general quality of North American Freemasonry and the creation of an organization ignorant of its own purpose. This increasing ignorance is followed by an increasing rate of decline in membership numbers, a phenomenon that was totally predictable. Those who retained membership due to the advantage of belonging to a highly respected organization and this represents the vast majority, are observing this deterioration along with their very reason for belonging.

New Grand Lodge numbers are increasing and probably covering a wider geographical area, at a rate which has been unprecedented for well over one hundred years. We know this phenomenon is occurring but not only are we not prepared to deal with it, we don't even understand the significance of it. We do not understand reasons to recognize or not recognize these new Grand Lodges. We do not understand the regularity or irregularity of them, and we certainly do not understand the political motives driving them or their creation. This is important to Freemasonry, because these Grand Lodges are going to project an image into the future of what we are that will represent Freemasonry to the world.

With modern technology, it is far more important today for us to set the guidelines and the standards than it was in the past. Information that took days to be disseminated even ten years ago, now takes seconds. We do not have the luxury of time that we once had to decide if an issue affects us and how we may want to respond to it. If we are to have a future, we must extend our vision and prepare our leaders of the future. And regardless of how we may wish to rationalize it, educating our membership about our past and our purpose is paramount in preparing our leaders of the future. How can they lead if they don't even know what they are leading? We, as leaders, cannot continue to be constantly worried about issues, which, although not trivial, are of less importance to this organization than worries as to how many members we can count or how much money we can raise and give away.

Freemasonry did not contribute to the development of this world through these issues, and, my Brothers, do not doubt that we did play a major role in its development. We must be concerned as to what is happening beyond our back yard. We must expand our horizons. We must have a much more far-reaching vision than we have now. We must divest ourselves of our organizational limiting egos for the sake of the Craft, but more importantly for the sake of the world. Remember, our legacy will depend upon our commitment to the Craft, not our obsession with our image.

I am going to draw no conclusions nor make any suggestions, but please think a little about it before you forget it.

[3]

The Difference Between
American and European Freemasonry

I have been requested to present today, two papers on subjects that are difficult to separate in content. The first subject is, *The Difference between European Free-masonry and American Freemasonry*. The second subject is *What Is Wrong with American Freemasonry?* These papers will be relatively short since they are closely related, overlapping subjects and there is a limited number of observations that can be made regarding them. Keep in mind that what I express are my opinions, I speak for no grand lodge nor are they necessarily the opinions of grand lodge officers.

I do speak, however, with the experience of over fifty-two years as a member of the Craft; twenty years as a grand secretary of a grand lodge, two additional years as grand secretary for foreign relations and 16years as Executive Secretary of the World Conference of Regular Masonic Grand Lodges. I served as presiding officer of eighteen Masonic bodies and have traveled over a great portion of the world just for Freemasonry, spoken in over thirty countries on Freemasonry, and have been involved with numerous television, radio and press interviews.

We must first separate North American Freemasonry from the American Freemasonry south of our border. Both America and Mexico as well as Canada are part of North America, but they are quite separate entities in the way the Craft is practiced.

Secondly, we must acknowledge that the difference between European Freemasonry and American Freemasonry, to some extent defines what is wrong with North American Freemasonry. Keep in mind, however, that what we may regard as wrong is based upon a measurement of present-day success and what we even determine as success. For clarification, when I refer to American Freemasonry in this paper, I will be referring to North American Freemasonry.

Many leaders of American Freemasonry today tend to qualify success on the basis of how many men we can attract (qualified or unqualified) for membership, and how much money we can raise for charity instead of on the intellectual foundation and the quality they bring into the Craft—characteristics of the Freemasonry of our past — as well as on our improvement of the good man. In this regard, what we define as success possibly constitutes the greatest difference between North American Freemasonry and European Freemasonry.

If we choose to judge success solely upon numbers of members, there is no question that North American Freemasonry has been far more successful than has European Freemasonry. Keep in mind, however, that Europe is composed of many countries whereas American Freemasonry is one country composed of many states.

If we choose to judge success on the massive amounts of money that we have given to charity then again there can be no doubt that, American Freemasonry is a magnificent success.

If we choose to judge by the past impact that the Craft has had on the development of its civil societies, then perhaps again, American Freemasonry has been more successful. Certainly the impact of early North American

Freemasonry has been monumentally involved in the establishment of the concept of democracy and in the creation of America. This criterion is more difficult, however, to assess because again, we must consider many countries and their development in Europe compared to one country of many states.

We must also recognize, however, that European countries have been in existence much longer and were required to compete with existing civil and religious oppression long before Freemasonry appeared upon the scene. North America had the opportunity to make a start with a "clean slate," so to speak, without competing with pre-existing regimes. Thus, the Masonic enclaves in America were able to meet with a far greater degree of freedom from persecution than did those in Europe. No powerful monarch or pontiff with his army sat on our doorstep in America to suppress freedom of thought regarding civil liberties. Even much farther into history, during both world wars, American Freemasonry never suffered the traumatic attacks that resulted in the death of over 100,000 Freemasons in Europe.

The struggle of Freemasonry outside of North America, indeed most of the world, has universally been far more severe than anything we could ever have conceived. Being tempered in the flames of adversity has driven European Freemasons to a greater appreciation of what this Craft means to them. Their measurement for success is based on far different criteria than on what we Americans base ours. As a result, the dedication of European Freemasons to the foundation precepts of intellectualism, brotherhood and appreciation of the seven liberal arts is much more deeply ingrained than in America.

The Craft in Europe has retained far more of the basic characteristics that formed its philosophical foundation and from which we evolved than has North American Freemasonry. Certainly, practice of this philosophical foundation was true in early North American Freemasonry. Consider the contribution that early Freemasons made to the evolution of our civil society. We were the epitome of a civic intellectualism that contributed to crafting the Constitution of the United States of America and forging those ideals that led to the very precepts of a democratic society.

Perhaps the greatest difference therefore, between European Freemasonry and American Freemasonry is that European Freemasonry has retained much of those ideals while we have surrendered most of ours.

North American Freemasonry is showing evidence of passing through a state of complacency into one almost of apathy. This state is probably the result of the lack of challenge to its existence. We have never had to struggle, never been tempered in the flames of adversity and never were required to place our lives on the line to simply say, "I am a Freemason."

Whereas the Freemasonry in Europe has been able to retain its image as a highly respected and visible entity in their societies we have become a little respected almost invisible entity in our society. Where we once were the visible image of power and influence we now appear too much of the general public as simply a collection agency for public charities.

It would be well for us, as Freemasons in America, if we wish to recapture the image that we once had, to reassess the criteria of what constitutes success. If we wish to continue to recognize success in terms of dollars and numbers, then all we need to do is to continue the way we are going. If we wish to once again become that highly respected organization whose members are admired for what they are, then we must take a serious look at what we are doing.

If we continue to state that we cannot require of our

membership what the rest of the world requires, then as Maureen Dowd said in *The New York Times* a number of years ago, "less is what we will receive."

[4]

Freemasonry's Relationship with Religion

On February 17, 1981, the Vatican's Congregation for the Doctrine of the Faith of the Roman Catholic Church reaffirmed its centuries-old ban against its membership affiliating with Freemasonry, and imposed the threat of excommunication.

As would be expected the fraternity reacted with some alarm and consternation. Undoubtedly, this reaffirmation would have created some effect upon the Craft had it been enforced, especially upon our present Catholic members. It was doubtful, however, that it would have produced any pronounced long-lasting effect. In January 1982, the Roman Catholic Church broadly revised its Code of Canon Law. The revision replaced the 1917 Code and went into effect on November 27, 1983. In the sixth book of the Code, the prohibition against joining our fraternity has been deleted.

There is no way of determining what effect the initial Papal Bull has had on Freemasonry for the past 245 years but history relates that the Craft has flourished in spite of it. I would suggest that the current Protestant trends pose a far greater threat to Freemasonry, yet we have shown a little alarm.

If you were asked to design an organization that would emphasize and reinforce support of religion, could you design anything superior to Freemasonry? If you were to try to develop a philosophy that would promote the concept of the brotherhood of all men, could you conceivably improve upon the philosophy of the Craft?

Robert Frost in his poem, "Mending Wall," has the old farmer saying:

> Before I built a wall I'd ask to know
> What I was walling in or walling out,
> And to whom I was like to give offence.
> Something there is that doesn't love a wall,
> That wants it down.

Perhaps we should seek to find within our churches what they are walling in or walling out. There appears to be an attempt to wall out freedom of thought and choice, and wall in the membership so as to avoid influences outside of itself.

Albert Pike wrote:

> It is the crowning glory of Freemasonry that, requiring only that a candidate shall believe and put his trust in a living and personal God, the beneficent and protecting Providence, to whom it is not folly to pray; and shall believe the continued existence of the soul of man after the death of the body, it receives into its lodges the Christian of every sect, the Hebrew, the Moslem, the Pharisee and unites them into the holy bonds of brotherhood.

> Masonry is not a religion.... But Masonry teaches, and has preserved in their purity, the cardinal tenants of the old primitive faith, which underlie and are the foundations of all religions.

It would be difficult for any religion to find anything objectionable in these precepts, but many Christian leaders feel that if we are not a supporter solely of Christianity, we are anti-Christian. I quote from the booklet The Antichrist in the Lutheran Church, "Masonry is acknowledged to have a creed, but it is not Christian, therefore it is Antichrist."

We are not now and never could be defenders of only the Christian religion, but of all religions professing these precepts. For this very reason, we have been able to develop a brotherhood that no single religious faith could ever hope to. Masonry is said to be the realization of God by the practice of brotherhood, but it also promotes the brotherhood of man by developing the manhood of the brother. There can be no denying the religious relationship of Masonry but we are not a religion. Religions are many; religion is one. In this respect, Masonry supports religion.

The time is long past due for us to question the motive of church leadership who oppose Freemasonry. It is not a new attitude. It is, however, far more pervasive and vicious, at least in America than it has been in the past. We know that Freemasonry has not changed; therefore the change must lie within church leadership.

Freemasonry has no quarrel with any church but there will always be within the clergy those who desire a monopoly on financial contributions and time of their parishioners and will express resentment against any organization which they determine are competing with them for the fulfillment of this desire.

Even before becoming a member of our fraternity, I was well aware of the anti-Masonic attitude taken by the Roman Catholic Church, and it became evident shortly thereafter that some Protestant denominations also profess similar settlements. A brother with whom I was entered, passed and raised, a minister of a Protestant denomination was discharged from his church for his association with Freemasonry.

This trend is not altogether a recent phenomenon but it appears to have gained momentum recently. In the "Introduction of Freemasonry, and Interpretation," we find, "we have long since felt that the secret societies system, with Masonry at its head is responsible in a large measure for the rationalistic negative criticism of the Bible that is threatening ruin to the church of Christ."

This is no longer the situation. It was well documented in the early nineteen sixties, the position the United Lutheran Church took in its reorganization concerning affiliation by its ministers. This restriction is based upon article VII, section 4 of the Constitution of the Lutheran Church of America which states:

> No person who belongs to any organization which claims to possess in its teachings and ceremonies that which the Lord has given solely to his church shall be ordained or otherwise received into the ministry of this church, nor shall any person so ordained or received by this church be retained in its ministry which subsequently joined such an organization. Violation of this rule shall make such minister subject to discipline.

Other Protestant churches have advanced similar anti-Masonic overtures.

Some Masonic scholars find no threat present, because it affects only those in the ministry and they see no possibility of its encompassing lay members. Other Masonic scholars who are also ministers of the church feel otherwise. For those who feel that such a force could not be created by the leaders of the church, it would be well not to lose sight of the fact that in 1738, when Pope Clement XII issued the first Papal Bull against the fraternity, a large percentage of its members were Roman Catholics.

Why is this attitude becoming influential enough today to cause major changes in church policy? If the change does not lie within the fraternity, it must lie within the church. I am suggesting that we make a more critical analysis of our church leaders and use our influence more substantially as a guiding force, before we find that we have lost our capability to do so. We have a tendency to cover our church leaders with an aura of infallibility because of their very relationship with the church, and thus accept decisions affecting our lives which we would never accept from other bodies. Try to visualize, for example, our reaction to a governmental decree telling us that we could not associate with the fraternity. Yet our defense to just such a decree by the church is at the very best weak, indeed.

It might be well if our church leaders were to recognize that there is a possibility that their decisions may be a factor affecting loss of support and not outside influences. I am not alone in my resentment of such actions as antigovernment demonstrations in violation of our government laws by the clergy nor to their championing causes to which we are opposed. The church's contributions to the "World Council of Churches" are being used to promote anti-American propaganda in third world countries. Terrorism is an antithesis to both religious and Masonic philosophies. Many have become greatly disillusioned with the leadership of our churches and find it difficult, in good faith, to continue to support them.

Inasmuch as I am far from alone in my sentiments, I would suspect that this reaction carries a much greater impact of the loss of church support than they would care to admit. The basic precepts of Freemasonry are in direct opposition to any actions in violation of our country's laws and anti-patriotic involvement, and whereas we tend to attract those who follow these precepts, it is only natural that we as individuals should oppose actions or decisions of this nature.

The objection expressed by the Roman Catholic Church and also to a degree by some Protestant denominations is that we are a secret society, and the church objects to secret societies. Certainly, we are not a secret society. All Masons should know that the only secrets we harbor are some portions of our ritual and our means of recognition, but even if we were to fall into this category, why should this factor generate church opposition. Is it justification enough for the church to oppose any organization it does not understand?

The objection most frequently promulgated today is that Freemasonry is in competition with the church. For those of us who know Freemasonry, the very thought of such competition is an absurdity. Masonry has no quarrel with any church, Protestant or Catholic.

Perhaps the following excerpt from the booklet, "The Antichrist in the Lutheran Church," published by the National Christian Association relates most accurately the feelings leading up to our current conflict:

> Those who have joined its [Freemasonry's] ranks paying yearly dues, do so to the detriment of the Christian church, for to remain in good standing in this anti-Christian organization, the member must pay the stipulated dues and also the high initiation fees if he desires to advance, while he permits the church to worry along as best it can.

The Moody Monthly, a publication of the Moody Bible Institute of Chicago, has Freemasonry listed in its "A

Catalog of Cults." The list is prefaced with these words: "Jesus Christ's deity is what truly separates Christianity from a cult."

There is probably no organization in the world which encourages more church support and devotion than our gentle fraternity, but recent actions by the clergy makes this increasingly difficult to do so.

Objections expressed by church leaders must either be due to ignorance or envy and resentment of the support that the fraternity has been able to generate from its members. It is possible that there are lessons the church could learn from our fraternity. There is no organization even approaching in magnitude the philanthropic work of Freemasonry. Recently it was revealed that in one year, as nearly as could be determined, Freemasonry contributed a sum in dollars for its philanthropic work, equivalent approximately to 50% of the entire United Fund's goal in the nation.

Freemasonry has withstood many assaults in the past and has emerged with no greatly reduced strength, the most notable being the anti-Masonic political movement during the early 19th century. During this period in our history, however, there were those who continued to fight and resist this movement.

To give an insight in how venomous the attacks by some church leaders against the fraternity are, I give you one more quote. This is from the last paragraph of an article titled "The Anti-Christ in the Lutheran Church" by William Meyer. He says: "I hate this secret Lodge, especially Masonry, the whore-mother of all lodges, but my heart goes out to the erring brother, who has never heard his pastor say to him, 'this is the way, walk ye in it.'"

If nothing else results from this affront to our Craft, it should cause us to re-examine ourselves and our place in history. Make no doubt about it, it is great. Freemasonry has been an attractive force for some of the greatest men this world has ever produced and now we deal with a concern that action by the Southern Baptist Convention could impact 15 million of their members, for whom Freemasonry has been one of their greatest supporters.

A century ago, the Grand Lodge of New York proposed the following summary of the teachings of Freemasonry, later known as the Creed of a Mason:

> Masonry teaches man to practice charity and benevolence, to protect chastity, to respect the ties of blood and friendship, to adopt the principles and revere the ordinances of religion, to assist the people, guide the blind, raise up the downtrodden, shelter the orphan, guard the Altar, support the government, inculcate morality, promote learning, love man, fear God, implore His mercy and hope for happiness.

Is this not worth fighting for? The world needs our influence as perhaps never before. Let us seek to find why our churches are building walls and what they fear and why.

There are many within the ranks of our leadership who feel that we should not disagree with church leadership. But, let us recognize clearly that there is no religion that is an enemy of ours, there are religious leaders who are enemies of ours and there is no infallibility in religious leaders. It must be remembered that in the church, the Bible is not the supreme authority in matters of religious faith and practice. The church and not the book has the final say and the Ministry is the spokesperson of the church.

We will not involve ourselves in quarrels, but we must not refuse to use our influence as a guiding factor in establishing church policy. We cannot sit back and allow our potential membership to be diluted without any attempt to generate an understanding with church leaders of the compatibility of Freemasonry and the church. We must not remain passive while the richest source of future membership is removed from us. We owe this much to our brethren of the past and to the future of our great fraternity.

[5]

Panel Presentation for the Supreme Council, Southern Jurisdiction

With the loss of 65% in membership numbers and the ongoing declining interest in Freemasonry in the United States, it might be difficult to comprehend the remarkable age that Freemasonry is experiencing in the rest of the world. There have been 26 new grand lodges consecrated in this century and they are attracting some of the more prominent members of their societies, whose influences are contributing to the development of their countries. At the same time, many of the older grand lodges are also achieving successes in both numbers and influence.

Freemasonry is expanding and establishing roots in relatively untouched environments. There has been a rebirth of interest in the potential of our Craft to contribute to a new societal evolution in much of the world.

This does not mean that there are not challenges that must be faced in the 21st century. In fact, the challenges we are facing now may be the most crucial in our several centuries of existence. For the past several hundred years, the greatest challenges to our existence have been external and have come from oppressive government leaders and domineering religious leaders. In spite of all the attacks that we have experienced from them, they have been unable to do us serious lasting harm. The greatest challenges we are facing in the 21st century, however, will be internal and they will be much more difficult to resolve than those from the outside world.

With very few exceptions, the challenges to North American Freemasonry are possibly the most critical. Freemasonry in the United States has been failing more rapidly than any other area of the world than perhaps Australia, and our challenges are much different in many ways from those that we faced in the past, and very different from those of most of the rest of the world.

I possibly belong to as many appendant Masonic bodies as anyone in this room and have great appreciation for their contribution to our Craft. However, I am also possibility much more aware than anyone here of the issues that have been created by appendant bodies as a result of working with them for the past fifteen years. The greatest obstacle to success of Freemasonry where it has been newly consecrated is a competition with leaders of appendant bodies. Newly-consecrated Grand Lodges must be permitted the time to establish themselves as the supreme authority over Freemasonry in their jurisdictions before having to deal with the egos of leaders of organizations appendant to Freemasonry. This regretfully has not happened in many jurisdictions. The ongoing challenge to Freemasonry in these grand lodges will be to establish their position with those who feel that higher degree numbers mean higher rank and status.

Grand Lodge supremacy of Freemasonry in North America has rarely been challenged and yet, in spite of all of the success that Freemasonry is experiencing in the world, Freemasonry in North America continues to decrease in numbers and lose influence in our society.

I recently completed an analysis of Freemasonry in the United States regarding its decrease in membership numbers from 1959, when it reached its highest membership number of over 4 million, through 2009 when it numbered just over one and a half million. During that period of fifty years, Freemasonry in the United States lost 64.78% of its membership. However, from 1959 to 1979 the loss totaled 18.10%. Over the next twenty years to 1999 it lost 42.16% of those remaining and over the next 10 years it lost an additional 26.55%.

Although there are multiple factors contributing to this loss in membership there can be little doubt that we have lost our attractive force to the segment of society that provided the leadership of our past and created the visible image for which we were known and respected and stimulated others to want to become part of us. This rapid loss in membership numbers beginning 30 to 35 years ago is a result of our loss of vision of the need to maintain the quality of the organization. It was then that our leadership put their greatest effort on securing numbers. It was also that time in our history that we began to try to buy back the respect we lost through large contributions to charity.

We are indeed experiencing an identity crisis and it is one of our own making. Where the public once saw an organization composed of the prominent leaders of society, they now see an organization almost devoid of these men. We have gone from an organization that attracted some of the greatest men and noted leaders in society who ardently sought membership to one almost soliciting anyone willing to sign a petition. We also changed from an organization known for its support of its brothers to an image of a collection agency for public charities.

This decline in the general quality of the Craft has resulted in a loss of interest by society. Our concentration on numbers and charity has been counterproductive to what we were trying to accomplish and destructive to the image of American Freemasonry.

Over that period of thirty years we have conducted many studies, developed numerous programs, instituted many changes and spent millions of dollars to salvage what we had lost — with no success. And yet, in spite of all of the evidence showing failure for thirty years to confront the challenges successfully, we continue to beat that same dead horse.

Although the challenges we are facing on a world level are different, the cause is the same: egos exceeding abilities. Over the last three years we watched the ego of one man, the Grand Master of the National Grand Lodge of France almost totally destroy that Grand Lodge. It may take decades to recover. It has caused a reconfiguration of European thinking and a new pattern of thought presenting two sides. This has the potential of dividing the Craft on the continent.

If we in the United States are to reestablish our identity as a highly respected and influential organization dedicated to improving good men, it is going to require a new pattern of thought of our leaders of the Craft. We must admit that what we have been doing for the last thirty years is a failure. To continue to surrender the protocols that made us great and ignore our commitment to taking only good men and making them better, we will continue our descent into obscurity. Our concern today cannot rest upon the challenges of the changing environment that we blame for our problems but rather our reaction to these changes.

Freemasonry has survived and flourished for three centuries in a constantly changing environment, by maintaining our philosophical precepts and our protocols. Now, we seem to have adopted the prevailing protocols of the profane world. The political correctness attitude of American society today has infiltrated the thinking of Masonic leadership but all men are not equal and every man does not deserve the same as everyone else unless he earns it; thus, every man does not deserve to be a Freemason.

Freemasonry is an elite organization in spite of those who feel that "elitism" is a dirty word. When we set our protocol to accept only good men, we became elite and we must remain elite.

Too many of our leaders today have developed the attitude that the Freemasonry of the past is not suitable for today's American society and that we must change our operational precepts to adapt to the new society. Well, looking at us and looking at modern-day American society, I would suggest it would be more advisable for society to change to fit our precepts than for Freemasonry to change to fit society's precepts.

I well understand that all bodies appendant to Freemasonry must acquire their members from Craft Masonry, so there is a tendency to support programs that will increase the membership numbers in the blue lodges. But, lack of selection has impacted membership numbers of appendant organizations even more than Craft lodges. The greatest hurdle we must get over is the lack of vision and failure to understand the purpose and significance of Freemasonry in too much of the American leadership.

Now we must decide which identity we wish to project to the world. Is it the image of our past as a powerful and influential contributor to the liberty, freedom and equality of mankind, that supported the moral and ethical standards upon which a successful society could be built, or is it an organization that has outlived its usefulness? The future is in our hands and the greatest hurdle to get over will be us.

[6]

Charity as a Core of Our Craft

The Relevance of Charity in the Masonic World

As you might expect, one of the most striking characteristics of Freemasonry is the similarity of its principals and precepts. It is quite evident that its basic philosophical reasons for existence are universal. This feature is the glue that holds it together, and has done so for centuries. The universality of Freemasonry on a world scale is totally dependent upon maintaining these principals and precepts. That is not to say that there have not been differences between, or variances within individual Grand Lodges, but Regular Freemasonry has not deviated from its basic philosophy.

One unexpected observation that I did find, however, was that the operational philosophies of Freemasonry did vary; dependent upon the part of the world in which it existed. The tenants of Freemasonry were ever-present, but the forces driving it, made it relevant to the environment in which it existed. Jasper Ridley, in his recent book, *The Freemasons*, made the same observations, historically. His observations, however, tended more to define individual Grand Lodges, or limited geographical regions. The observations I made covered continents.

I found in Europe, for example, that Freemasonry has retained much more of its philosophical quality that characterized it in its early life. This is not very difficult to understand since its origin was in Europe, and there was a greater degree of stability due to the age of the countries, and therefore a lesser stimulus to diverge. Hence, European Freemasonry displays a more philosophical form of Freemasonry than is found in the rest of the world.

In contrast to this philosophical style, Central and South America have a form of Freemasonry more driven by the sociological demands of its environment. It retains the basic tenants of Freemasonry, while its operational practices tend to take on a more idealistic and progressive approach in establishing the goals of the Craft, to meet the needs of the society in which it exists. Its idealism causes it to seek more lofty goals than are generally found elsewhere in the Masonic world. Hence we find a more sociological style of Freemasonry.

While Mexico mirrors much of the sociological style, it does not seem to fit comfortably into it. Freemasonry there has a tendency to become more involved in the political factions of the country, and therefore is more political in style.

In North America excluding Mexico, we have lost much of the philosophical qualities by which the Craft is known, probably due to an acquired complacency coupled with a lack of a force driving it. Certainly this has been true in recent years. Perhaps this complacency is a result of an absence of the same social needs as those in the countries to our south. What we have evolved into however, is an organization that places much emphasis and effort on raising money and funding charities. The resultant recognizable image of Freemasonry in North America is one of being a charitable organization. Although charity is a core value of the Craft, it is not the core value. We have other core values that have crafted an organization the likes of which the world had never seen before, nor has it been matched since.

We, as a North American Craft, seem to have developed a driving need to raise money for charity, and as a result, I find myself out of step with much of North American leadership in this regard. I feel strongly that this mantle of charity with which we cloak North American Freemasonry, does a great disservice to the philosophical intent of the Craft, and has led to a general dilution of our influence in society.

There are many organizations designed for the specific purpose of promoting charitable objectives, but I know no other, whose professed purpose is to take good men and make them better. My Brothers, think of how unique we were, how unique we are. Think of how much and for how long, we have altered the direction taken in that ongoing quest for civility in a civil society. Even most of the organizations modeled after us have long ago ceased to exist. There can be little doubt, my brothers that our success and survival rests upon the uniqueness that characterizes Freemasonry.

Before I go farther, let me emphasize that I have absolutely no objection to Freemasonry's commitment to helping others. Indeed, it would be difficult to comprehend how we could involve good men, and avoid helping others. This is not, however, the reason for our existence, and we depend too much upon this single feature to generate our image to society. We, therefore limit ourselves to niches that many other organizations have inhabited longer, and were designed to do better. And yet, long before we adopted this approach, we created more of an impact on the evolution of civil society and this world than any organization ever conceived by the mind of man. This has truly been the glowing accomplishment of Freemasonry, and is what historians are finally acknowledging about us today.

We have, in North America, evolved into one of the

world's greatest charitable organization, but my brothers, Freemasonry is not a charity. It did not originate as a charity, it did not function and survive as a charity, it is not recognized by government agencies as a charity, and it certainly did not change the world as a charity. Its avowed purpose is making good men better. By making good men better, we improve the quality of the man and therefore the quality of the world.

We readily admit that we are declining, not only in numbers, but also as a visual image in modern-day society. Even as our numbers are decreasing, even as our buildings are crumbling, even as the quality of our membership is waning, we continue to dedicate much of our effort to raising money for charity. We cannot continue to concentrate our energies on raising money to give away. We cannot buy admiration and respect, and my Brothers; this is exactly what we are attempting to do. To be charitable is an admirable quality, but our charitable character must never cloud our singular most important purpose, to make good men better.

There is another consideration upon which it would behoove us to pause and deliberate: As Dr. Ryan stated in his very succinct observation, "If we become a charity, which we are certainly tending toward, and the government assumes that role which it is tending toward, then our purpose for existence will no longer exist."

History is littered with the remains of organizations, many patterned after Freemasonry, that were forced out of existence for the very reason that the government assumed the role for which these organizations existed. Take time to look back at North America and its fraternalism. I was astounded when I began to comprehend how many hundreds of fraternal organizations were created, existed, and died, many as a result of policy changes instituted by our government.

Freemasonry has not been exempt from these changes. This is one of the reasons why we may be less attractive to current generations than we were to those of the past. The need for brotherly love and dependence upon one another is not nearly as great today as it was in our not too distant past, simply because today the public is taxed to do what we did for free for generations. The Grand Lodge of Pennsylvania for many years operated the Patton School for orphan boys. We prided ourselves in the quality of the young men we were graduating, some becoming significant leaders in society. Notwithstanding, we were forced to close the school when the government took over the responsibility by providing foster homes at taxpayers' expense. The fact that we did it better, and at no cost to the taxpayer, was not relevant.

David T. Beito notes in his book, *From Mutual Aid to the Welfare State*, that "Fraternities have declined in influence since the depression, especially as providers of mutual aid and philanthropy" and that "We have yet to find a successful modern analog to the lodge." He also observed that "We were moving from the character of Fraternalism to that of Paternalism," and "In order to attract members the leadership was willing to de-emphasize their commitments and abandoned the qualities that had made them distinctive." Please note that last comment, my Brothers, for he may be quite probably hitting upon a major cause of the decline of the Craft, both quantitatively as well as qualitatively. He definitely reinforced, with that observation, the contention that the leadership lost sight of the qualities that made Freemasonry, Freemasonry.

Those charitable organizations that have survived, have survived with intent toward a specific charitable objective. Freemasonry and its affiliated organizations, however, have taken on the support of so many different charities, that most of our members are not even aware of them. Few realize, for example, that in addition to our Masonic homes for children and elderly, we support in some form, research or assistance programs involving the diseases of cancer, arteriosclerosis, heart disease, muscular dystrophy, muscular atrophy, retinal disease, tuberculosis, arthritis, lung disease, cerebral palsy, leukemia, diabetes, aphasia, dyslexia, schizophrenia, kidney disease, and that does not cover them all. We also have research hospitals, we provide dental care for the handicapped, we deliver food to the poor, we provide hearing dogs for the deaf and we support major scholarship programs. I am confident that if it were known, there are probably many other charitable projects undertaken by our subordinate lodges and affiliated bodies.

Now, if we don't know what we support, I wonder how many outside of the Craft know. They do know, however, about The Cancer Society, The March of Dimes, The Heart Disease Foundation, The Muscular Dystrophy Foundation, and all the other charities that were designed for the specific purpose of collecting funds just for that disease. What we are doing, is contributing our efforts and funds to support charities that will get the credit for spending those funds.

How did Freemasonry in North America develop into a world's greatest charity? There are several factors that probably influenced this evolution, but we must remember, that according to many scholars, our philanthropic character was taken on in the middle ages prior to our becoming a Speculative Craft. During the construction of the great cathedrals, the stonemasons set aside funds to care for their injured members and their families and widows. Even today, it is still known that, right or wrong, "Masons take care of their own." Note, however, this was not a public charity; it was taking care of our own.

For many people on the earth, the daily struggle to survive supersedes any consideration of what they might do for others. The very concept of charity is nonexistent, but when Freemasonry came to America it eventually found a new soul in charity. Unfortunately, over time, it lost sight of the realization of our purpose, that of improving the world through the improvement of the man. Our long-range vision had become drastically shortened and significantly clouded. We are now not seeing the forest for the trees. We have shrouded ourselves in short-term and less significant functions and lost our understanding of those great potential achievements that the Craft is capable of, and that the World deserves. We are not only failing to recognize the impact of our past, but also the potential impact of our future.

I would suspect by now that most of you sitting here have developed the opinion that I'm opposed to Freemasonry's involvement with charity. Nothing could be further from the truth. The charitable nature of Freemasonry has been an integral part of it, as I have noted, since prior to its conversion into its speculative form. Without its concern for its members as well as for society in general, it could not have become what it has. A Brotherhood of Men under the Fatherhood of God would be a lifeless shell indeed, if it lacked the essence of a charitable concern for our fellowman.

The concern I express is not what we do for charity, but what we do not do to fulfill our purpose because of the concentration of effort we put into charity. We might argue that by supporting charities we are making men better, and this is not untrue, but if this is all we make of Freemasonry today, we are failing our heritage. My Brothers, Freemasonry made this world, and did so by providing much more than charitable gifts. It made men better men than it took in — one man at a time.

It is imperative that we place, and keep in proper perspective, the relationship of charity to Freemasonry. If our charitable objectives, in any way distract us from the primary purpose of the Craft, it must not be tolerated.

Freemasonry in North America is at a critical crossroads in its life. We, the leaders of today, are being forced to determine what it is that we really want the Fraternity to be and where we really want it to go. For over thirty years, we have declined in numbers and reduced our image in society. We have neither lessened the loss nor improved our image by increasing the amount of money we give to charity, although we have surely tried.

The time has come for us to look at ourselves, to become more introspective, to realize that if we fail to look out for ourselves, we may very well lose our ability to look out for others. Rest assured, there will be no one looking out for us when we need help. It did not happen in the past, it will not happen in the future. Regretfully, for all that we have meant to the world, for all that we have given, there have probably been considerably more of the citizenry of the world looking for us to fail than to succeed.

We must become more cognizant of just how important we have been in the development of civil society. There is perhaps no organization more ignorant of its past, than North American Freemasonry. We cannot afford to allow ignorance to consume us while we concentrate our efforts on programs that do not fall within the purview of our reason for existence. We cannot continue to allow our buildings to become eyesores by which the public may judge us while we use our resources for other purposes. We cannot continue to emphasize the need of more members, instead of more quality members. We must also generate an image so that those outside will see us as more than a source of funding for other organizations.

One of Freemasonry's greatest charitable accomplishments has been through the efforts of our members rather than through the contribution of our dollars, and those efforts were stimulated through the teaching of Masonic ideals and the encouragement for Freemasons to participate. Thus, we fulfill our charitable commitments while fulfilling our professed philosophical purpose. We take good men and make them better. If we can fill that purpose and continue to be the world's greatest charity, then so be it. If a choice must be made, however, let us never fail to make good men better. That is more than our duty, that is our privilege, and it is our purpose.

[7]

Limitation of Vision of Masonic Leaders

I am not quite sure how I came to present a paper at this time, especially on a subject lacking in research-able substance. Someday I guess I will learn to keep my thoughts to myself, and yet this is a subject that has concerned me for a number of years. I do hope, however, that it will stimulate some thought.

We, as leaders, have for a considerable number of years been on the cliché bandwagon of the "need for long-term planning" for the future of Freemasonry. This, of course, is an absolute must even though our very operational struc-ture makes the concept, at best, difficult. With short-term leadership and the lack of continuity, working a long-term plan to its completion is not always likely. Every Grand Master has an agenda; as well he should, so concentration of effort on long-term plans will always vary. One absolute prerequisite for our continuing success, however, is a total commitment of all Masonic leaders to the welfare of the Craft.

This, however, is not the concern I wish to express at this time. My concern is the limitation that we as leaders put into our conception of what is "Masonically long term."

Speculative Freemasonry has been around in its present organized form for 281 years and in some speculative form for an undetermined number of years before that. It has endured and, indeed, has flourished for a longer period of time than any Fraternity or any organization that I know of outside of organized religion. Freemasonry is far beyond that cliché of long-term planning that permeates the world of business where it originated. There the concern is relegated to profit and loss statements, not to a philosophical concept that impacts the world. We, as leaders, cannot afford to limit our vision to those terms of time that are taken from the world of business and industry.

I don't have to tell you about the impact Freemasonry has had on the world and the evolution of civil society. This Craft has been a major player for a long, long time. The world is as it is because Freemasonry lived.

Let's look at it now in terms of time. Do you know of many businesses which have existed for an equal period of time? Freemasonry's longevity has been the result of an enduring philosophy and enlightened leadership. Our influence could not have been what it was if our term of existence had been as short as that of other organizations. Even the best of intentions and motives take time to mature, evolve and influence. Granted, we have lasted long enough that we have matured, but maturation is ever ongoing. We have evolved so that our influence is felt. We also have been losing that influence, and, unless we can work a plan that will be long term, and I emphasize long, we will continue to do so. We cannot keep "changing horses in the middle of the stream."

And yet we leaders have the tendency to look at long-term planning for the Craft in terms of probably five to no more than twenty-five years. I don't know that I ever heard of goals established beyond that span of time, and few even for that long. For Freemasonry that span of time, although significant, is too finite for projection into our future. We, as leaders can actually be counterproductive to the purpose of the Craft by our failure to look at Freemasonry in longer terms and as a whole entity including the great diversity of influences it generates. We cannot afford to continue to dwell upon segments of the contributions for which we are recognized. These contributions, each and every one, are significant and important, but our significance to the world must encompass the whole of Freemasonry.

Margaret Jacob wrote in *Living the Enlightenment* that Freemasonry passed out of serious scholarship in the late 1940s, and I would suggest that this was the time when we began to lose focus on what we were. It is interesting that it was also the time of our most rapid growth. Perhaps it was the beginning of our failure to "guard the west gate."

Why do we choose to limit our range of vision?

It is my opinion; the restriction of vision is principally the result of two factors. Factor number one is that few leaders truly understand the full scope of Freemasonry. If Freemasonry and its significance are not fully understood, it is very easy to neglect portions of it resulting in a diluting of its global influence. Reason number two is that most leaders are so concerned with the number of Members that their concentration is placed upon that one facet, and they, therefore, limits their vision of the full meaning of the Craft. Look at the major programs of most Grand Lodges and where the greatest concentration of effort is.

Over the last fifteen years I have made a more concentrated effort to study Freemasonry and, as a result, have developed a far greater appreciation of what this Craft has truly meant to the world. I also am cognizant of the time I put into this study and realize that very few Members are willing or able to devote this amount of time and energy. This is not a criticism; it is simply realism, and certainly it is a devotion not expected. It has caused me to develop a great appreciation of the true scholar of Freemasonry. I only wish I had a greater knowledge of the Craft than

I have, and I wish there was a way of infusing it into all of our leaders. To fully appreciate, one must understand; to understand, one must know, and to know, one must be willing. We unfortunately today lack the willingness.

Without a fuller knowledge of the evolution and impact of the Craft, there is no way we can expect ourselves to fully understand the significance of the need to remain a viable force and how to do so. Our vision may be long term in that range which we have been trained to accept, but it is short-sighted in the range for Freemasonry. What truly is the value of the survival of Freemasonry if we lose our potential to remain a viable influence in the world?

We, as leaders of the Craft, must be capable of looking at the full spectrum of Freemasonry. It should be like looking into a transparent globe with the Craft as a nucleus in the center. We can then see the radiating influence that we have provided to the entire sphere. Unfortunately, today we tend to look only at a limited number of ways Freemasonry has created an impact and as a result, never understand the full extent of its meaning.

We have been known to the world by our acceptance of toleration, our embracement of patriotism, our support of religion, our development of leaders, our encouragement of the acquisition of knowledge, to name a few, and each was actively pursued and encouraged.

By failing to understand the full picture, we fail to support Freemasonry's full influence and thereby damage the ability of the Craft to continue fulfilling its potential. This is a disservice to the Craft, to our past and to the world.

We as leaders must make a greater effort to understand the Craft and its needs to carry into the future. It must, however, be a long-term future. We must expand our vision. If we fail to do so, we limit our hope to be the force that characterized our past. We, the present, are a result of our past.

The future will be the result of us. Let's at least look beyond twenty-five years.

[8]

Masonic Education—Looking to the Future

Given by request to five grand lodges, two regional
Masonic conferences and the opening of the Grand
Secretary's Conference

This title for my paper is an interesting subject for me on which to speak and to write. You might expect that one as outspoken as I have been concerning the lack of Masonic education in American Freemasonry would be well prepared to speak on it, but even though I have been critical of our lack of education and strongly supportive of the need for it, and even though I have written many papers for Freemasonry, I cannot recall writing a paper or speaking specifically on the subject of Masonic education in the past.

Around twenty years ago, I made the observation at the Northeast Conference of Grand Masters, Deputy Grand Masters and Grand Secretaries that American Freemasons were the most ignorant Freemasons in the world. Some of the Grand Masters present took offense to my remark, so I clarified, that ignorance does not mean stupidity; it means lacking in Masonic knowledge.

Much water has flowed under the bridge since that time, and many changes have been wrought in North American Freemasonry, but I stand here today and make that same observation with no reservation. Indeed, with all my traveling in recent years, I've become even more emphatic with it. With all of the changes that we have made to North America to alter the image of the Craft and to change the direction that we have been traveling, we have done precious little to educate our membership. Thus we remain the most ignorant Freemasons in the world and we have done little to alter that fact.

There is no one factor upon which to place the blame for the ongoing decline of the interest in Freemasonry in North America, but there can be no question concerning the lack of an educational commitment as being a major contributing factor. How can we possibly expect there to be an interest in an organization in which so few of the membership itself even know what we are or our purpose? For the last 25 years, very few major programs conducted by the leadership in North American Freemasonry have been for other than to increase numbers or to raise monies to give away to charity.

About ten years ago, I was speaking at a symposium in Argentina that was attended by approximately 500 Argentinean brothers. The symposium was being held over a period of five days, and I asked my host what these men did for a living that they could take five days of their time to attend this symposium. Argentina is a large country and it meant traveling for many hundreds and in some cases thousands of miles for some to attend. I can only recall a few of the occupations of the brothers that he pointed out around the room, but I do recall that he told me two men were neurosurgeons, one that was a nuclear physicist and one that was the conductor of the Philharmonic Orchestra in Salzburg, Austria. My Friends, he pointed to many brothers the like of which we can only dream of having in our Craft in North America today; but such men were members of the Craft in our past.

This past September, I spoke in Romania where I serve

as honorary president of the cultural organization and on the academic committee, on the subject of "Freemasonry, Fraternalism, and the Rise of the Idea of Liberty in Central and Eastern Europe." I spoke for the same Grand Lodge last year at a symposium that presented a series of intellectual discussions relative to Freemasonry and its involvement in current civil societies. These programs attracted some of the greatest thinking leaders in Eastern Europe. I also was given the privilege of addressing a public forum on the subject of Freemasonry in New Delhi, India. These programs were not only for the purpose of educating the membership, but also the general public.

I do not mean to imply that there is no place in Freemasonry for we ordinary individuals; indeed one of the primary reasons that Freemasonry became as great as it did, is because men from all walks of life are accepted as equals, but I am certainly cognizant of the fact that another of the primary reasons was because it attracted some of the greatest minds that ever lived. Even to this day we continue to point with pride to these great men but where are they in North American Freemasonry today?

Last November, the World Conference of Regular Masonic Grand Lodges was held in Gabon, Africa. Presidents of four countries were present for that conference. At least seven presidents of African countries are members of Freemasonry, two of them serving as Grand Masters. I attended the consecration of the new Grand Lodge in Mozambique, also last year, where the Prime Minister was installed as the Grand Master.

Freemasonry continues to be held in high esteem in most countries of the world, even though they have had to struggle far beyond what we have ever known even to exist as a fraternity. One glaring feature about the Freemasonry as it is practiced in most of the rest of the world is that their members are required to learn. The acquisition of knowledge that has been universally professed in our Craft has not become a lost art as it has in North America.

I find nothing in our Freemasonry to compare with the stimulus for intellectual discussion that tends to permeate Freemasonry in most of the world. Sadly, this lack of challenge to our members tends to diminish the intellectual quality for which Freemasonry has been historically known. As a result, we have lost much of our allure to the segment of society that structured and gave Freemasonry its societal image.

Regretfully, today only a relatively small percentage of our members truly understand the significance of the purpose of the Craft. They may understand the words but words are simply words. Understanding must transcend the words. Today this may be the greatest failure on the part of North American Freemasonry. Unless we understand the meaning of the words, how can we possibly understand the purpose for which we exist?

My friends, in the name of political correctness today we live in a society where our leaders feel that everyone should have the same as everyone else regardless of initiative or ability. We live in an environment that rewards mediocrity so well that there is little incentive to rise above it. We live in a society that desperately needs a stimulus to excel beyond the norm. We live in a society that needs an infusion of civility and logic into our civil society. Unfortunately, Masonic leadership has bought into this political correctness concept, and as a result we have seriously damaged our image in society and reduced our effectiveness to make future contributions. Of what value is an organization that made this world what it is, if it has lost its capacity to do so? We need more than ever a leadership with a vision to see beyond self-satisfaction and with a dedication to rising above the mediocrity of today's social structure. The future of Freemasonry in North America may very well be dependent upon the leadership's realization that Masonic education is a vital component for our survival. After all, how can we possibly convince society of how significant we are if we ourselves do not even know what we are? We live in a society that needs the Freemasonry with the characteristics of our past.

Historians are finally acknowledging the influence that our Craft has had on some of the greatest leaders that the world has ever known at a time when we are failing to educate our own membership of this influence.

Freemasonry played a vital role during the age of Enlightenment as one of the principal organizations in America that provided an enclave wherein great thinking minds from different social strata met and created the concept of a democratic society based upon the structure they found in Masonic lodges.

I also learned in Argentina, however, that when a man petitions a Lodge in that jurisdiction he will be investigated for a period of a year and if he passes the investigation he may be entered. Upon being entered, during the next year he will have presented a minimum of three learned papers on Freemasonry to the Lodge and then stand examination to qualify to be crafted. Upon being crafted, he will go through the same procedure prior to raising. My brothers, the members in Argentina know more about Freemasonry when they are raised than the vast majority of our members will know in their lifetime about our Craft.

This is far more characteristic of the Freemasonry of the rest of the world than of the Freemasonry that we have known in America over the past 25 to 50 years. In that period of time, we have excised from the Craft most of the intellectual and philosophical qualities for which it has been known to history and for which it continues to be known in most of world today.

Is it not an incomprehensible phenomenon that an organization of the likes of Freemasonry with the avowed purpose of improving the man and in stimulating a desire for him to seek to acquire knowledge should lack any major system for substantial education like we do here in America? Instead of trying to raise our standards and to improve our image in society, we continue to reduce our standards and to lower the requirements to become a Mason, and to remain a Mason. And what have we accomplished? We have not even slowed the rate of loss in our numbers.

I cannot convince myself that the Freemasons of today are any less capable than were our brothers in the past, but we are definitely more ignorant; more ignorant of our past, more ignorant of our present and definitely more ignorant of our purpose. If it be true, that our brothers of the present day are just as intelligent and just as capable as were the brothers of the past, then lack of Masonic education must be a root cause of a declining interest. The responsibility for this failure lies at the feet of the leadership of the Craft.

I emphasized in Russia several years ago when addressing the Grand Lodge that we must never forget that Freemasonry did not impact this world by rolling over it with the vast quantity of the membership. It impacted the world through the influence of the quality of its membership. It also did not impact this world by massive contributions to charitable organizations. We can never buy admiration and respect. Nor did it impact this world by expounding upon its greatness in public venues. We do not need to expound upon how great we are. If we live the philosophy of the Craft, the world will know that.

Freemasonry impacted this world by improving good men, by taking one good man at a time and making him a better man. We made him better by infusing into him the realization that he was far more capable than he himself considered possible. We stimulated him to want to be better and incited his intellect to want to become more knowledgeable, to want to become more capable and to want to participate in improving the society in which he lived.

It was then the better man, the more knowledgeable man, the more competent man, who impacted the evolution of civil society. Freemasonry became the educational tool that provided an environment wherein men like Washington, Franklin, Wren, Newton, and Voltaire (even though he was a member for just a short while) and many others like them crafted the ideas that created the ideals of a democratic society. God knows this world needs men like them today, and Freemasonry should play a vital role in crafting these men. Fortunately, it continues to do so in many countries.

This world is as it is today because Freemasonry lived, and Freemasonry lived because it undertook the responsibility of taking the good man and making him a better man by teaching him the precepts and philosophies of Freemasonry through a process of Masonic education. These better men then became the leaders that created modern-day civil society. It has lived when hundreds of other fraternal organizations have long ago ceased to exist.

We can no longer choose to live in the glory of our past. We can no longer have our survival depend upon the claims of how great we were and point with pride to the greatness of our past brothers. We must now decide what we want to be. If we wish to be an organization that will be remembered in history as one that contributed to the greatness of America but one that slipped away worthy of little note, then we continue the path we are walking today. If we wish to continue the heritage that was granted to us by our past brothers, then we must make the decision that our current membership deserves that heritage and develop programs whereby we educate them concerning that heritage.

Even as the age of the Renaissance lifted the veil of ignorance from the European world, Freemasonry needs an age of Renaissance in America today to lift the veil of ignorance of our membership.

These young men that are showing an interest today are seeking much more than we are providing. They are on a quest searching for something that society is not providing to them. They are searching for a quality organization above the mediocrity of present-day society. They are searching for knowledge and a system that will provide it for them. They know more about Freemasonry before they petition a Lodge than have any of their predecessors.

Freemasonry is being given an opportunity that it may never see again. The writings of Dan Brown along with a couple of movies and television programs have stimulated an interest in Freemasonry that has not been seen for decades, even perhaps for a hundred years or more. This interest has created a potential to re-create an image of Freemasonry that has been lost to America. It will, however, require that the leadership uses it as a potential to improve the quality of the Craft and not simply as a recruitment tool to improve the quantity of the Craft. History has proven that when quantity is lost it may be regained but if quality is lost it is extremely difficult ever to regain. This re-generated interest in Freemasonry is giving us that opportunity.

I have probably expressed quite clearly my opinion on the subject of Masonic Education: Looking to the Future. This world truly needs an organization based upon a foundation of the philosophical purposes of Freemasonry. If we are deserving of our heritage, then we must undertake a program of educating ourselves and our membership. The legacy of our past brethren deserves that respect and respect given to the Craft will be proportional to the educational requirements of the Craft.

[9]

The Acacia is Wilting in North America

Society of Blue Friars Lecture

I give you a quotation that I kept in my classroom for many years when I was teaching, "When you place your hand in a flowing stream, you touch the last that has gone before and the first that is yet to come." A man's relevant position in history and our position in Freemasonry are as that hand. We stand today as the hand, in the flowing stream of Freemasonry, touching the last that has gone before and the first that is yet to come. There is a distinct difference, however, between the hand in the water and us. The hand has no power to change the ultimate destiny of the flow of the water. But we, my brethren, have the capacity and the power to change the ultimate destiny of Freemasonry.

Approximately thirty years ago, I presented a paper to a subordinate lodge that began with the statement "Freemasonry is in trouble." At that time I was referring to the decline beginning to show in the quantity of our membership. It was a time when few of our brothers were willing to believe it and even fewer wanted to hear it.

Well, time has not improved our situation and we are still in trouble with the quantity of our members, but I have a far greater concern today with the quality of the member we have been willing to accept in a vain attempt to sustain the quantity. A major distinction between then and now, however, is that none can deny it whether wanting to hear it or not.

The decline in our numbers began and unquestionably continues as a sociological phenomenon affecting most organizations in North America. It was simply the result of a change in the interests of American society. This was not a new phenomenon to Freemasonry. Societal interests have never been static, and have always impacted the Craft. Our leadership did not cause the loss of interest, but are probably responsible for accelerating it. What is even more alarming is that the rate of decline is probably going to continue to accelerate.

This situation is a tragedy of monumental proportion because our response to it is resulting in the deterioration of the image and the influence of Freemasonry in North America. The image and influence of the Craft have not waned as a result of the decrease in numbers, they have plummeted as a result of our response to it, and our subsequent failure to attract the quality men who projected our image in the past and were chiefly responsible for exerting its influence.

Our willingness to accept those who, not too many years ago, could never have hoped to become members, will continue to serve to keep the quality men away in the future. We, the leaders, must bear the weight of the responsibility for not only permitting the deterioration, but to some degree actually stimulating it.

The rapidity of the decline in numbers of members is not as great as it was during the Morgan affair, but the dilution of the quality of our institution and its ability to influence society did not follow the pattern after the Morgan affair, that it has with this decline. As a result, recovery will be less likely. The major variable causing this difference has been an internal not an external as with the Morgan affair, and to a great extent, is the result of our reaction to the number loss.

We have the opportunity to control our destiny, and our survival as a viable institution, but it depends upon our commitment to sustain an organization that has the capability to continue to influence society, not simply as an institution with the name Freemasonry.

Freemasons have used the acacia, symbolically, as an emblem of immortality for many years. It has exemplified our commitment to a belief in a power higher than ourselves. Freemasonry, however, is not immortal, not any more immortal than any of the hundreds of other extinct organizations that died before it. It remains subject to the influence that we place upon it. We are the hand in the flowing stream of Freemasonry, and because of us, the acacia is wilting in North America.

We have admitted for years, that only ten percent of our membership is active. This conversely, means that 90 percent is inactive, and yet they pay their dues each year knowing full well that they will probably never be active. There is only one logical reason for a man to do this. There is a perceived value in being able to say, "I am a Freemason." Take away that perceived value and we take away the reason for him to belong. Those who retain membership due to the advantage of belonging to a highly respected organization, and this represents the majority of our membership, are observing the deterioration of a quality organization, along with their very reason for belonging.

We can readily see the effect of these observations today. We are not only failing to attract, we are failing to retain. The rate of suspensions for nonpayment of dues, as well as resignations is rising in almost all jurisdictions, and is not a result of the sociological condition of the time. It is the consequence of a vision failure on the part of the leadership and our response to this issue. Suspensions and resignations are resulting from a loss of respect by our own membership, and it was predictable. Now, if we are losing the respect of our own membership, how can we expect respect from those outside of us?

Even though the leadership must assume responsibility for part of our failure today, I do not mean this observation as a condemnation of those who try. We are the product of a style of Freemasonry that de-emphasized much of the structural integrity upon which the Craft was formed and in which it excelled. We, in North America have excised from the Craft those intellectual and philosophical standards for which it was known throughout its existence, and for which it continues to be known over much of the globe. We have made elitism a dirty word when applied to the Craft, and yet it is elitist by its very definition of, "taking Good men." We have diluted the requirements for admission and advancement, along with the stimuli for learning, to the extent that North American Freemasons today know less about the Craft than any other Freemasons in the world.

We have evolved into a form of Freemasonry ignorant of its own heritage, its purpose and its potential. As this self-perpetuating ignorance increases, it is followed by an ongoing erosion of the general quality of the membership, followed by an increasing rate of decline of not only our image, but of an interest in membership, a phenomenon that was also highly predictable. We have created many of our own problems by making the Craft too easily obtainable and retainable. Emphasis on increasing numbers rather than educating those whom we have has become a way of life to North American Freemasonry.

Today our leaders rarely extend thought beyond the acquisition of members and the raising of money to give away to some other organization. North American leadership seems to have acquired a type of syndrome that results in an attitude that large numbers represent success and that we can buy admiration and respect. Thus, even while our membership is decreasing, our lodge buildings crumbling and our image deteriorating, we continue to concentrate a major portion of our efforts in soliciting numbers and raising money to give to charities that will receive the credit for spending those monies. We have inherited from our brothers of the past, a respect probably unmatched by any organization that ever existed and now we are losing it. We cannot buy it back; it must be earned.

It would behoove each of us to ask ourselves: "Would I have joined this Craft when I did, if it was then what it is today?" If you have any doubt my brothers, as I definitely do, you are probably looking at the major cause for our failure to attract the quality man, who himself would then attract quality men. What has happened to the community leader, the professional man, the man visible in society who represented a large segment of our Craft in the past and served as a living image to stimulate others' interest in joining us?

Now ask yourself this question: "What do we offer today, that would attract this type of men to us?" We do not offer much, and this also is not the result of the sociological condition of the time, it is the result of our failure to understand our heritage and our purpose as well as to provide an environment wherein a man might wish to participate and learn.

We must stop looking for excuses to justify our failure, accept the responsibility for what we have created, and develop ways to change it without reducing the quality of the organization or deviating from its philosophical principles. Of what value will we be, if we no longer are capable of influencing civil society?

I was watching a program on the history channel discussing secret societies. One of the societies presented was Freemasonry. As is generally the case, a considerable amount of the information provided was inaccurate, blatantly accusatory of our motives and outright lies.

In the past, I would have sat there highly incensed that this type of inaccurate propaganda could be broadcast on public television, but instead, this day I found myself almost appreciating what these men were saying, because they were giving recognition to a power we never had. They actually had me feeling proud that I was part of an organization that they were implying as having the kind of influence I wished we had.

Isn't it sad even to think of taking pride in an untruth that was tending to support the image of the greatest organization ever created by the mind of man, and taking that pride because we are losing the image? Freemasonry has never needed anything more than its own philosophy, its own reputation and its own membership to support it or its image. What should be even more important to us is that this still holds true in most of the rest of the world.

The simplest and most definitive explanation of the purpose of Freemasonry is that it is designed to take good men and make them better. If we succeed in that purpose, we fulfill our obligation to the Craft, to our heritage and to the world. There is nowhere within that definition, a requirement for large numbers. We have assumed an obligation to make a man a better man, and as in our past, we can do that one man at a time.

One of our glaring weaknesses as leaders today is our inability to see the big picture of the Craft. We have become so enmeshed in issues of lesser magnitudes that we ignore the great ones for which the Craft is known and we became so engrossed with issues that are not paramount to the purpose of Freemasonry, that we have ignored those that are. Our hang-up in North America with the need for large membership numbers is causing us to ignore what is paramount to the Craft's survival. We did not impact this world because we had great numbers; we impacted this world because we had the quality member who could impact it.

Decisions are being reached today that are restructuring and remolding our noble institution into something that it was never meant to be. The results are evident in the dilution of our influence which enables us to use our philosophies and precepts in the development of what is good and right in the evolution of civil society. We, as leaders of Freemasonry, have an assumed obligation to do all within our power to curtail this dilution, to contribute to the perpetuation of our ideals and to cause them to be diffused throughout the thoughts of future generations. If we fail in this purpose, we fail in our commitment to our Brothers of the past, whose contributions are etched upon the headstones of eternity. More importantly, however, we fail in our commitment to society in general and to world peace and understanding.

It is difficult to comprehend the motives which cause the conclusion to be reached that our brothers of the past were so wrong when they have accomplished so much. How can 300 years of practice and tradition be no longer applicable in today's world? Are we that different? Has society been static for that long, or are we being dissected by ignorance, egos, and present day liberalism? We must not lower the standards of the Craft to fit into present-day society.

Freemasonry is experiencing an unprecedented surge of growth and interest, more than has been seen for well over 100 years. With the emergence of Freemasonry in the Eastern European countries and the development of the

Craft in Africa, Freemasonry is appearing or reappearing with a newfound vigor. And yet, instead of being able to bask in the glory of this growth, we in North America find ourselves struggling to stay alive.

We must return to the roots that made us great. We must refrain from requiring less and begin to require more. Even as the future we are entering will require more from its great men, we must require more from our members if we are to participate in that future.

How we respond now, will determine how we are perceived in the future. Let each of us as leaders seriously ask ourselves how we want to be remembered. My brothers, the acacia is wilting. I do not want to be remembered by historians as part of the generation that destroyed North American Freemasonry. Do you?

[10]

Masonic Restoration Foundation
Symposium

New Hampshire—2013

It is a great privilege as well as a definite personal pleasure for me to speak at this the Fourth Annual Masonic Restoration Foundation Conference. I have been a member of the foundation board since its inception but have in recent years been unable to participate in many meetings and I have sincerely regretted that I have not been able to make a greater contribution to the foundation. I am firmly convinced from my experiences and studies of Freemasonry, and have expressed this opinion many times, that unless a better approach be developed, our greatest hope of survival as an institution resembling Freemasonry in North America will be through the structure of "Traditional Observance" lodges. Realistically, this requires the creation of new lodges with a different style of Freemasonry than we have been practicing in North America for many years. There may be some existing lodges willing to transition into what we call Traditional Observance lodges, but I do not think our future lies in that potential.

It is important for North American leadership to understand that we are not attempting to evolve into something new and different; we are trying to revert back into something that we were. What we are now certainly is not what we were. What we were was a highly visible and extremely well respected fraternal organization that led in the creation of modern civil societies. What we are now is an almost invisible organization with little influence on any level of society.

This will require innovations for some grand lodges that have not incorporated some traditional practices. But it will also require, as I think we now realize, flexibility on our part to work within the parameters of grand lodge laws.

Many of you know that I have been one of the more vocal critics of what we have done and what we are doing to North American Freemasonry. My goal any time that I speak is to cause you to think. It is not so important that you agree with what I have to say. I ask only that you think about it.

There was a time when we in North America were looked upon as perhaps the greatest example in the Masonic world of the success of Freemasonry. We were large numerically, we were wealthy financially, we built some of the most magnificent structures in the Masonic world, and our influence in society was as significant as any grand lodge in the world, and now, perhaps excluding the grand lodges in Australia, we are failing at a far greater rate in numbers, in wealth and certainly in societal influence than any other style of Freemasonry in the world. In spite of all of our excuses that we have promoted to justify our failures, the fault is ours.

Although our numbers have been in decline for over five decades they have been in freefall for the past 30 to 35 years. Approximately 20 to 25 years ago I made this observation in a paper I wrote: "We have admitted for years that approximately only 10% of our membership is ever active and yet they continue to pay their dues year after year knowing that they will never be active. There is only one logical reason for a man to do this. There is a perceived value in being able to say, 'I am a Freemason.' Take away that perceived value and we risk losing the 90%." What we are now seeing is the loss of the 90%.

Freemasonry in the United States reached its highest membership numbers in 1959. From 1959 to 1969 our membership decreased from 4,103,161 to 3,868,854 a loss of 5.71%. From 1969 to 1979 it decreased to 3,304,334 a loss of 13.14%. From 1979 to 1989 it decreased to 2,682,537 a loss of 20.17%. From 1989 to 1999 it decreased to 1,967,208 a loss of 26.66% and from 1999 to 2009 it decreased to 1,444,823 a loss of 26.55%.

This total loss of 2,658,338 represents a decrease in membership of 64.78% from 1959 to 2009. However, 1959 to 1979 (20 years) our loss represented 18.10%. From 1979 to 1999 (the next 20 years) our loss was 42.16% of those remaining and from 1979 to 2009 (30 years) the loss was 41.45%.

Certainly, this dramatic loss of members within our Craft can be attributed to multiple factors, such as increased number of deaths, sociological changes of the environment, and self-centeredness of the populace. The 18.10% loss from 1959 to 1979 was probably primarily due to these factors. However, these factors fail to explain the dramatic decrease in numbers beginning approximately thirty years ago. It was, however, the period in our history when our concern with the loss of numbers caused a loss of vision, resulting in a gross failure of our comprehension of the purpose and significance of Freemasonry and what is required to retain it.

It was the beginning for the first time that we began to ignore the quality of the members we were taking in and began to concentrate on the quantity of the membership. It was also a beginning of our attempt to buy back respect and increase our numbers by making large contributions to public charities and it continues to this day. It was the beginning of the freefall.

All viable studies will show that we not only failed to curtail the freefall, we caused its acceleration. What must be an even greater concern was the impact created by the loss of an attractive force for that segment of society that provided the vision and leadership of our past.

When we lost the attractive force for the leaders of our communities, we lost the positive visible image of Freemasonry. We gave up the meaning for the pride in being able to say, "I am a Freemason" and for thirty years we have continued to beat the same dead horse. What has happened to that magnanimous vision of our forefathers?

There was a time that suspension from Freemasonry for nonpayment of dues would have been a 'black mark on a man's soul' and now we can count thousands of them annually. The perceived value is gone.

When I became a Grand Secretary in December 1979 it was rare to see a brother brought up on un-masonic conduct charges. Today, they are an ongoing occurrence and many others are permitted to resign to avoid trials. This can only be a result of our failure to guard the west gate.

My brothers, Freemasons have bought into the political correctness attitude of today's America and the result has been devastating to our Craft. Freemasonry in the United States has been transformed from an organization that attracted some of the greatest men and noted leaders in society who ardently sought membership to one soliciting almost anyone willing to sign a petition. In our attempt to buy back the respect that we surrendered, we changed from an organization known for the support of its brothers to an image of a collection agency for public charities.

One of the attributes of Freemasonry that created its greatness was that it accepted men from all social strata and placed them in an environment where they were regarded as equals. However, it also attracted some of the greatest thinkers and leaders of the world and seated them in that same Lodge room. It was these men that created the visible image of Freemasonry to society. This attraction was primary in causing our Craft to become a force unlike any other seen in the world; one that has served as a beacon to developing world societies. Without these men, it is doubtful that we would have survived to the present time. The Craft may not have created their greatness, but they have created the Crafts greatness. The philosophical precepts of Freemasonry influenced the thinking of great men and provided a stimulus to contribute to the development of world civilization.

Now, Freemasonry in the United States, for the first time, is no longer attracting this caliber of man and that failure has developed over the past three decades. It is our generations that must assume the responsibility for where we are today. The philosophy of Freemasonry has influenced the evolution of civil societies for several hundred years because of the quality it maintained and the respect it generated. Now, we have been willing to sacrifice the quality and surrender the respect simply to increase our quantity.

Freemasonry in the United States is not alone in its need to confront challenges in this millennium, but the challenges facing Freemasonry in our country is uniquely different from what is faced in most other parts of the world although the cause of most of the challenges has been essentially the same, inflated egos.

My brothers, Freemasonry has thrived for 300 years through constantly evolving societal changes without the need to sacrifice its protocols. I continue to be confounded by those leaders today who seem intent on destroying the very qualities of the Craft that not only have sustained it but contributed to making us significant.

Many Masonic leaders today are proposing that Freemasonry must become something fundamentally different to remain relevant in today's world and to adapt to the technological age. Are the environmental changes of the modern world so much different from those of the past that the philosophical precepts of Freemasonry are no longer applicable? Why must we now change to suit society to remain relevant? The Crafts relevancy has not declined over the past three centuries, nor was it required to change to remain significant and it did not prostitute itself to maintain its significance. Indeed, it thrived because it maintained those moral and ethical values upon which it was structured and which it disseminated to the world, and refused to submit to a society of decreasing values.

This does not mean that Freemasonry has not evolved throughout its history. It has evolved and flourished in a constantly changing environment for close to three centuries and has been a dominant player in the evolution of civil society during that period of time. But the evolution was not due to pressures from the profane world. It was because we wanted changes that benefited the Craft and consequently the society. It has changed over these three centuries but never in the form or magnitude that we are seeing in the present age.

Perhaps changes are not so much needed in the precepts and protocols of Freemasonry as they are needed in the society in which it exists. Acknowledging the moral and ethical values supported by Freemasonry and after having observed society's evolution in my lifetime, it would be more prudent for society to change than for Freemasonry to change. Freemasonry has never been a stagnant institution. Change has been inherent since its inception but we must curtail our willingness to change to satisfy the "political correctness" attitude of present-day society.

As illogical as it may sound to us in the United States, Freemasonry is in a remarkable age. For the first time in many decades, there has been a regeneration of interest by leaders of governments in the potential of our Craft to participate in the societal evolution in their countries.

The Craft is expanding and establishing roots in relatively untouched environments. Its expansion into Eastern Europe now encompasses almost every country following the collapse of oppressive Communist rule. Many of these new grand lodges have been re-consecrations but it also includes countries that have never had Freemasonry in the past and the expansion of the Craft into African countries involving its indigenous populations has been significant in the last three decades.

The success of Freemasonry, however, has not been limited to newly consecrated grand lodges. Grand lodges with centuries of existence have also been growing and attracting some of the most significant individuals in their societies.

In spite of the successes that we can observe in the growth and expansion of our Craft, its attraction for significant individuals and its influence on evolving societies in much of the world, we in North America have continued to experience a decline in numbers and a loss of influence unmatched since the Morgan affair. Our concern today should not be so much in the challenges of the changing environment in which we operate but rather our reaction to it.

There seems to have developed in much of our leadership in America, the prevailing attitude that the Freemasonry of the past is not a good fit for modern American society and that we must change our operational precepts to adapt to that society. However, all of the studies that we have made, all of the changes that we have instituted, all of the monies we have invested and all of the programs that we have developed to reshape Freemasonry to fit into this "modern" world have achieved precious little success. Indeed, if we look at the broad picture, we have not only failed but we have accelerated and assured the failure. We have become far too willing to surrender the integrity and character of the Craft that made us prominent and visible to begin with, simply to retain numbers and to satisfy demands from the profane world.

As we proceed into the 21st century, we now face challenges that will be unlike many that we faced in our past. Historically, the greatest challenges that confronted Freemasonry over the past 300 years have been external and have come principally from oppressive government leaders and dominating religious leaders.

Our greatest challenges in this century are chiefly internal. There are far more divisive issues existing within the inflated egos of Masonic leadership and the liberal attitudes of the membership than those from challenges outside of it. We are now accomplishing what the oppressive government leaders and the dominating religious leaders have never been able to accomplish, the defeat of the success of Freemasonry.

For years I have been emphasizing what I perceive to be several of the greatest threats to our integrity as an institution. These are the interference of appendant bodies with Grand Lodge operations, the expansion of irregular forms of Freemasonry and our willingness to accept it and our enthusiasm to encourage exposure of Freemasonry to the public.

To this list should be added those leaders of the Craft whose egos have exceeded their abilities and the members of the Craft, whose ignorance of its philosophical purpose have reduced our potential to contribute to the evolution of world society.

Interference in grand lodge operations by any appendant organization requiring Masonic membership as a prerequisite is unacceptable, but it is becoming a greater threat to the stability of Freemasonry in today's world. There have been far too many grand lodges in recent years, struggling to compete with these organizations whose members feel that higher degree numbers means higher status. There is no Masonic degree higher than that of Master Mason. All other degrees are superfluous to the third. One of the greatest threats to the success of Freemasonry in Eastern Europe and Africa has been a result of the creation of appendant Masonic bodies and they are now causing schisms in grand lodges in Latin America where Freemasonry has existed for centuries.

Irregular forms of Freemasonry have existed almost as long as has regular Freemasonry, but they have now become a greater competitive threat and are spreading into environments where regular Freemasonry has existed for centuries. Of a greater concern must be the willingness of some present-day leadership to accept and grant recognition to those bodies that are not governed by the same protocols as are we.

Regularity of origin is a constitutional assurance that those seeking recognition are indeed, Masonic. Regularity in practice forms a basis for granting recognition and assures us that grand lodges remain in compliance with the principle landmarks of the Craft. Regularity is a right based upon origin and practice. Recognition is a privilege granted by each individual Grand Lodge and must be based on regularity.

In America in recent years, there has been a willingness to submit to the demands from the profane world to lift the veil of mystique and secrecy that has made us such a unique organization. That uniqueness is what helped to differentiate us from other organizations and made us the most outstanding and significant organization that the human mind has ever structured.

Now many of our present day leaders feel the need to expose to the public that which we have concealed or attempted to conceal for several hundred years, diluting our uniqueness and eliminating the aura that surrounded us and tended to lift us to a higher plane than other fraternal organizations. This newfound motivation has had a major impact upon those who were attracted by the mystique and the unknown of the Craft. The result has been that many who might have petitioned for that reason have no longer the stimulus to affiliate.

Ignorance of the membership of the true significance and purpose of Freemasonry aided by their access to the Internet has facilitated the decline of the mystique. It is appalling to read some of the information that is put on the Internet by well-meaning brothers, who have all the answers but have never heard the questions.

Inflated egos of far too many Masonic leaders today, along with their exposure to the public, have negatively impacted the historic image of Freemasonry by society. We have watched in recent years, a Grand Master almost totally destroy a highly respected and honored grand lodge. This became the most visible image of the damage that can be inflicted by one man but there are numerous less visible images scattered throughout the Masonic world.

We have faced internal challenges in the past but none that has created the impact and the potential for destruction as we now face. The internal dissensions that are tending to divide grand lodges, the increased egotisms that are tending to weaken grand lodges and the advancement of modern technologies that are providing for the diffusion of misinformation along with our willingness to surrender our protocols should be our greatest concerns.

It is long past due for us to deposit our egos at the door and dedicate ourselves to the unity of regular Freemasonry. It is time for us to repay our brothers of the past for the unsurpassed legacy left to each of us and to the world. We, the present day leaders of this heritage, must assume the responsibility of perpetuating it, and carrying it into the future.

The twenty-first century could very well be the most critical period in our existence. We have, in this century, the potential to accomplish great successes but we also have the potential to accomplish what no other entity has been able to do, facilitate our own extinction. We have spent far too much time parasitizing the greatness of our past. Our concern must now be with the potential greatness of our future and our greatest hurdle to get over, will be us.

The work that the Masonic Restoration Foundation is doing may very well be that of laying the foundation and erecting the structure upon which the future of Freemasonry in North American will be built. I have found the greatest supporters of our way of thinking today to be the older brothers who have experienced the Freemasonry of the past and the good young men coming in who are seeking the Freemasonry of the past.

If Freemasonry is not succeeding anywhere in the world, it is not the failure of Freemasonry, it is a failure of Freemasons.

[11]

Masonic Restoration Foundation

Philadelphia, Pennsylvania—2015

It is a great privilege for me to once again address the Masonic Restoration Foundation. I spoke at our meeting two years ago in New Hampshire and I am speaking to you today only because we are meeting in my home Grand Lodge. This time I have the pleasure to welcome you to Pennsylvania and I have been given the opportunity to say a few words.

In contemplating what I had to say, I continue to realize that it becomes more and more difficult for me to keep writing something new and different. I find myself presenting the same thoughts wrapped in a different package. It did, however, cause me to think about how many addresses I have given and in how many countries. In tallying the count, I found that I had spoken in over 40 countries. I have also addressed audiences in the majority of the grand lodges in the U.S. and Canadian Provinces.

The messages that I attempt to convey are structured for the countries and or grand lodges, lodges or other organizations to which I am speaking. In many locations there are specific subjects that I am asked to cover and I try always to speak in support of their programs.

However, in North America, I have been fairly consistent over the past thirty years on what I had to say. In compiling my writings into a book, I have become aware, that they have evolved from expressions of "how great we are" to expressions of concern of how we are "losing that greatness."

I have had great apprehension for many years in the direction that North American Freemasonry is traveling and much of my writing and speaking has been reflective of that apprehension.

I am a great supporter of the Masonic Restoration Foundation and have been involved from the beginning with its creation and support for its operation. At the present time I see no programs on the horizon to offer any greater hope for survival of a viable Masonic institution in North America, than the creation of a "Traditional Observance" style of Freemasonry.

We must be aware and recognize however, that we are not a panacea for all of our ills. Nor can we permit ourselves to think that we are. One of the greatest obstacles that I have observed to our success today is that we may present ourselves as superior to other Masonic operations and in some cases there is justification in this thinking.

There are those who imply that we look at ourselves as an elitist organization. My brothers there are nothing wrong with being elite. Freemasonry itself is an elite organization but we must not allow ourselves to become arrogant or complacent with any success that we have achieved, for we have a long, long way to go. Many of us will never live to see the end result of what we are attempting to do but hopefully we can rest assured in the comfort of knowing we are doing something for our future.

I have been a member of Freemasonry for fifty-two years and have been a student of the Craft for the largest portion of those years. I have presided over eighteen Masonic bodies and have written book reviews on Freemasonry for twenty-five of those years. I served twenty years as Grand Secretary of the Grand Lodge, two years as a Grand Secretary for foreign relations, sixteen years as Executive Secretary of the World Conference of Regular Masonic Grand Lodges and am now Honorary President Ad Vitam for that organization.

What I have learned in that period of fifty-two years, is just how little I know about this Craft. The experience however, has given me a unique opportunity to see Freemasonry with all its greatness as well as its foibles; its successes as well as its failures, its potentials for a great future as well as its potential for a less than great future. I have had the privilege of meeting some truly great men but I have also watched men assume leadership positions who could have been great leaders, permit their egos to destroy their legacy and diminish the very body they were leading.

What we are today is not what we were and we were better in many ways than we are today. Our image was better; our influence was better, our vision was better, and based upon our average quality of composition, our quality was better. This observation is not meant to belittle the membership of today's Freemasonry but we certainly are not attracting the great thinking minds or the visionary leadership that we once did.

It has not been many years ago that membership in Freemasonry was indicative of a success story. To be a member was a sign of acceptance by a segment of society of successful and respected men. Today far too few professional men belong, resulting in an unfortunate dearth of visionary leadership.

There are leaders today promoting almost any change they deem necessary to increase numbers of members and imply that American Freemasonry is stagnating due to a lack of willingness to change to fit into the modern-day world. My brothers, what we are now is a result of change.

American Freemasonry has probably changed more in the last 30 years than it has in the previous 250. Those changes have resulted in a catastrophic impact on the quality of the Craft as well as on the quantity of the Craft. The loss of quantity has created an impact, simply because we have less funding to support our operations. The loss of quality, however, has impacted our own recognition of our purpose to exist.

It is long past due for us to recognize that all of the efforts that we have been placing on increasing numbers and raising monies for public charities has not benefited the Craft. The time has come that we must become more introverted and concentrate our efforts to restoring the dignity, the image and the respect that was bequeathed to us.

How long will we fail to admit that we have been following the same pathways of so many other fraternal organizations that led to their extinction? How long will we sit and watch our buildings crumble, our image decay and our influence wane before we acknowledge that we must change our approach for survival?

Over the last 30 to 35 years we have divested the Craft of almost any intellectual pursuit. The commandment that we should be a lover of the arts and sciences, has been swept away in lodge meetings dedicated to mundane exercises totally irrelevant to the philosophical intent of Freemasonry.

We have failed to accept the fact that there is a cost to be a Freemason. In our ill-fated attempt to increase our numbers, we have kept our dues and fees absurdly low and now we wonder why we cannot even maintain our buildings. Over the last thirty years, loss of members through suspension and demit can be measured in the tens of thousands. And yet to be suspended from Freemasonry in the past for nonpayment of dues, was almost regarded as a "black mark on a man's soul." Masonic membership to them is no longer a priority. We have taken away the pride in saying, "I am a Freemason."

Our buy-in to the political correctness attitude that permeates our country, of the right of every man to have what every other man has, even to be a Freemason, regardless of his quality has changed the Craft in North America, from being a predominantly "white-collar" fraternity to a predominantly "blue-collar" fraternity. This observation does not mean that the Craft in the past was composed of only the professional class; that would be denying our origins. One of the most renowned qualities of Freemasonry was its commitment to take men from all social classes and set them in a lodge room as equals. But, nor can we deny that our prestige as a fraternity was structured by great thinking men from the professional class. Society will always judge us by our composition.

Freemasonry faced challenges to its existence almost since the time of its inception. Many of those challenges were serious, resulting in the Craft being outlawed in some countries and over those several centuries Freemasons have been put to death by the thousands simply for being Freemasons.

These challenges to our integrity as an institution generally originated within rulers, governments and religious leaders. In each case we were looked upon as being a challenge to their right of domination. American Freemasonry was almost unique in that the only serious challenge that we ever faced was during the Morgan affair. We did not have to deal with dictators, pontiffs or kings and we thrived. Even following the Morgan affair, we thrived.

Now, however, we are not thriving. With the exception of the somewhat insignificant challenge by radical fundamentalists in recent years, we have not faced any serious threat to our existence, and yet we have lost three quarters of our membership? Why have we become an almost invisible entity within American society?

If we are to restore credibility to this fraternity; if we are to regenerate respect of society, then we will have to again attract the class of individual who will serve as an attractive force for others of vision and if we are seeking a criteria to measure the lessening of the average quality of our composition, all we need do is look at the marked increase in trials for un-Masonic conduct taking place in our lodges and grand lodges. When we restore the quality, we will restore the quantity.

It has been a pleasure to be with you again and I thank you for listening to me. Welcome to Philadelphia.

[12]

Grand Lodge of Montana

Before I begin my talk, I want to read to you an email that I received just yesterday from a brother in Massachusetts because it is relevant to the subject that I will speak on this morning. He writes to me, regarding one of my papers published in the last issue of the *Knight Templar* magazine.

Dear Sir Knight Jackson, Thank you so much for your article "Crafting the Mason" in the issue of the *Knight Templar* magazine. Although my grandfather, great grandfather and great-great grandfather were Masons, as soon as I became a Mason some twenty years ago, I have often wondered why I joined an organization that was only good for making friends and donating money to charities. I thought that surely once there was more to Masonry than that and occasionally I noticed another Mason who felt a similar lack in Masonry. Feeling as I do, is it any wonder why I never encourage another man to become a Mason? It is no wonder that Masonic organizations in my State find it difficult to increase their membership. Although it is still in some of our ritual, Masons in my state are not even encouraged to assist brother before non-brothers. Apparently to non-Masons, we are just another charitable organization.

The Grand Master asked me if I would be willing to attend this Grand Lodge Communication and speak to you concerning my views and observations on Freemasonry and it is a great privilege to do so. I do want to clarify before I begin, however, of my perceived position and purpose in our Craft.

I have been introduced over the years in a number of categories including; as a Masonic scholar, author, orator and historian. I was even introduced to the President of Portugal as a noted Masonic philosopher. I thought about this introduction for a long time wondering why anyone would refer to me as a philosopher. Then I began to comprehend that a philosopher was one who had developed opinions and I certainly have been known over the years for my opinions. So perhaps, I am as close to being a Masonic philosopher as any of the other categories.

A few of you here know that I live on a small farm in south-central Pennsylvania with a stream bordering the farm. A friend of mine, across the stream raises prime Holstein cows. He kept several bulls on his farm to service the cows, a big bull, a medium-size bull, and a little bull. Those who understand the pecking order of animals recognize that the big bull got most of the cows, the medium-sized bull had a few and the little bull had just one.

My friend decided that to improve the milk production of the herd, he would bring in a Grand Champion bull. For those who may not understand, the bull has a major influence on the milk producing capacity of the resulting cows through breeding. When word got around the barnyard that my friend was bringing in a Grand Champion bull, the three bulls got together to discuss it. The big bull said, there probably go some of my cows, the medium-size bull said, well there goes most of mine and the little bull said I sure hope he lets me keep my one.

When the day came for the Grand Champion bull to be delivered, the three bulls were standing on a hill overlooking the barnyard when the cattle truck backed in, the ramp came down and this massive big bull came walking down off that truck. The big bull said, my God, there goes all my cows. The medium-size bull said there sure goes all of mine and with that little bull started to snort and slobber and paw the ground. The other two bulls looked at him and asked, have you gone out of your mind what do you think you're doing challenging that great big bull? The little bull said, challenge him, challenge him hell, I'm just making sure he knows I'm not a cow.

I use that little story as an analogy to cause you to realize that I am not the cow either. It is significant to know what one is not and I have never looked at myself as fitting into any one of the categories by which I have been introduced.

One of the primary reasons that Freemasonry became as great as it did, is because it attracted some of the greatest minds that ever lived. Consider for a moment how many great men comprised early Freemasonry and as a result stimulated other great men to want to become part of it. Consider men like Washington, Franklin, Revere, Voltaire, Mozart, Wren, Bolivar, Garibaldi, Priestley and we could go on listing literally hundreds of others who have contributed to making this world as it is today. They also, however, contributed to making Freemasonry what it is today in most of the world.

Realistically, however, I realize that I am, have always been and will always be just a country boy who developed a great appreciation for this Craft. I realize that no matter how important I may ever think I am, I will never serve as an example to stimulate great men to want to become a Freemason. I perceive my purpose in the Craft as being; to do all that I can do to preserve it until great minds come along again to inspire it.

Chief Rahnami Abah wrote in his book, *Light After Darkness*, "Even if my thoughts and ideas may be controversial or, in certain respects, open to question, I shall have succeeded in my attempt if these ideas have generated further thoughts on the main substance of Freemasonry in the search for universal truth" and so mote it be with me.

It is always my goal when I speak to challenge you to think. So today, it is my goal to cause you to think, to hopefully stimulate you to learn a little bit more about this noble institution and to cause you to, as the Grand Master expects, introspectively examine what each of you can do to benefit Freemasonry.

I have been extremely fortunate over the last twenty years or so to be able to travel the world as a Freemason and to experience Freemasonry as it operates outside of North America. In these travels I have been able to observe Freemasonry in many foreign countries and compare it to the Freemasonry of North America. I have been able to see where it works well, where it continues to increase its membership, where it continues to attract some of the greatest men in their jurisdictions, indeed where it remains an organization whose members are the movers and shakers of their societies.

I have experienced new Grand Lodges being consecrated and extinct or suppressed ones being re-consecrated following the fall of dictatorial regimes. I have watched Freemasonry rising on the continent of Africa and its members occupying some of their countries dominant positions. In fact, two of the presidents of African countries are also the Grand Masters of their Grand Lodges.

At the same time I have watched the struggles of these new Grand Lodge officers trying to cope with the challenges of operating an organization that promotes the freedom and equality of men in environments where freedom and equality were unknown for decades and where individual struggle to achieve success was, at best, a muted phenomenon.

I have become familiar with the requirements of foreign Grand Jurisdictions for a man to gain membership and to remain a member of our Craft, both of which are far more stringent than anything we know in North America. I have become more consciously aware of the universality in Masonic philosophy and precept that dominates Freemasonry globally while at the same time observing definitive differences in the operating philosophies in different sociological environments.

I will emphasize some of the observations that I have made in various areas of the world regarding the evolution of Freemasonry and the resulting differences that characterizes the Craft in those areas along with my opinions as to why Freemasonry is declining in North America while it is thriving in many other parts of the world. I will also relate to you some of my personal experiences demonstrating the significance of the fraternity in other parts of the world.

None of us can be unaware of the decreasing interest in our Craft and decline in influence that North American Freemasonry has experienced over the last fifty years and especially over the last twenty-five. One of the first Lodge addresses that I gave over thirty-five years ago dealt with my observations of the decrease in the quantity of our membership. North American membership has gone from over 4 million to approximately 1 1/2 million. It does not take much thought to recognize that Freemasonry's future in North America is bleak if we continue with this loss of membership, at least Freemasonry as it is historically known.

I have however, in more recent years, been far more concerned with the decreasing quality of the membership than in the quantity of the membership. The decrease in the quality is a major contributing factor in the decrease in quantity today. Every person likes to be affiliated with a quality organization. Freemasonry in North America has been losing its attractive force for quality professional men over the last 25 to 30 years. This is not the case in almost every foreign Masonic jurisdiction. One of the most impressive observations that I have made in my travels is in the quality of the brothers that I meet throughout the world.

In my studies of the Craft, I have found that the philosophical purpose of Freemasonry is universal and unalterable but the operational philosophies are dependent upon the environment in which it exists. Freemasonry has been driven to evolve into a form that fits most comfortably into the environment in which it must operate.

For the last fifteen years, I have been attempting to classify the variations in these characteristics and place Freemasonry into what I refer to as styles. As a result, I have to the present time found five specific styles.

European Freemasonry has retained much of the basic philosophy and intellectualism that characterized early Freemasonry. There is a continued emphasis on the acquisition of knowledge and programs to stimulate thought. European Freemasonry has not been forced to diverge from its roots by societal pressures that have been found in some other areas of the world. I put European Freemasonry into what I refer to as a "philosophical style."

I have for a long time placed English, Scottish and Irish Freemasonry in the same philosophical style although recently I am tending to place that Freemasonry into what I refer to as a "social style." Although similar to the philosophical and intellectual characteristics of European Freemasonry it also includes the retention of more of the social relationships that tended to characterize the early

Freemasonry of the British Isles.

South and Central America although also retaining much of the philosophical style of Europe has evolved into a more unique style stimulated by the sociological pressures of the environment. I find it to be more idealistic and perhaps even more intellectually challenging than the philosophical style. It also tends to establish goals that are more difficult to attain. I refer to this style of Freemasonry as a "sociological style" because of its character being impacted more stringently by the sociology of the environment.

Mexican Freemasonry although existing in an environment not totally dissimilar than that of South and Central America, has a tendency to become more directly involved with the political climate in which it exists. For this reason I have placed it into a style all its own which I refer to, for lack of a better term, as a "political style" of Freemasonry.

There is no doubt that Freemasonry will continue to evolve and although I have traveled for Freemasonry in the Far East and Africa, I have yet to differentiate any specific style. It would be interesting however to look back fifty years from now and observe their style of the Craft and its impact on the development of their societies.

North American Freemasonry, excluding Mexico and perhaps Canada, has developed a style unlike that of any other. It is a style that evolved into being to the greatest extent over the last 25 years. In that span of time we have surrendered most of its intellectual and philosophical qualities, eliminating the stimulus to learn and excised the requirements to do so. We have directed most of our energies toward becoming an organization dedicated to raising monies for outside charities. Hence I refer to North American Freemasonry as a "charitable style" of the Craft.

Tragically, the result has been an erosion of our image in society and ironically we evolved into this approach in an attempt to buy back the respect and admiration along with that image we were losing. As a result we have surrendered the qualities of Freemasonry that made it such a unique entity. There are hundreds of organizations dedicated to specific charitable objectives but there are precious few that were dedicated to improving the man and this constituted much of the uniqueness of Freemasonry. Our uniqueness is what made the Craft into what it is; probably the most outstanding and significant organization ever created by the mind of man and in turn, Freemasonry made this world what it is today. It made it by taking the best men it could find and improving the man. By so doing, it changed the direction of civil society. Freemasonry was one of the primary enclaves that provided the environment during the age of Enlightenment that attracted great minds and laid the framework for a democratic society.

The more I study this Craft the more impressed I become with how much its presence meant in the development of civilization. And now I look with great sadness to the loss of both quantity and quality in North American Freemasonry. I look at the results of our early leadership with their magnanimous long-range vision that produced what we have inherited and then observe not only the lack of that vision today but even of the understanding of our significance in the world. The vast majority of our Grand Lodges have not produced a major program over the last 25 years other than programs designed to increase numbers or raise monies to give away to charities, both of which have been detrimental to us and my friends that is not the purpose of Freemasonry. I emphasized to the Grand Lodge of Russia several years ago that we did not make this world by rolling over it with vast numbers. We made this world by making good men better, one man at a time.

Unfortunately for Freemasonry we live in a country that

is the great equalizer. In the name of political correctness today, we have developed an attitude that everyone deserves the same as everyone else regardless of ability, desire, initiative or work ethic. As a result, the stimulus for one to rise above the level of mediocrity has been diminished in our society and Masonic leadership has bought into it. We refuse to raise initiation fees and dues because we feel that the average American could not afford it, the same average American who would spend at least an equal amount on something to smoke or drink or on entertainment and not give it a second thought. It is not a matter of cost; it is a matter of priority.

We in North America have absolutely no concept of what it means to be a Freemason in the rest of the world. The financial cost to affiliate with this organization in most of the world is in the thousands of dollars and the time requirement to become a Master Mason is measured in years, not in months let alone in days. While we in North America are lessening our requirements to be Freemasons, much of the world is increasing theirs or at least not decreasing them.

I was in Brazil about ten years ago and I asked what the dues were in their jurisdiction and they told me $50.00. When I expressed surprise that their annual dues were that cheap, they told me it was $50 a month not $50 a year and there are some jurisdictions where the dues will run as high as several thousand dollars a year.

I was speaking at a symposium in Argentina about eight years ago and following a Lodge meeting, we retired downstairs for the customary toasts then went to a restaurant for dinner. Following dinner the Grand Master spoke and the floor was open for discussion. Around three o'clock in the morning they finally took me back to my hotel and after they dropped me off were walking across the street and I asked them where they were going now and they said they were stopping for a drink and to continue their discussion. The next day I asked the Grand Treasurer how late their meetings normally ran and he told me that sometimes they don't get home until it's time to go to work the next morning. Can you imagine that in our country?

In addition, attendance at meetings in many jurisdictions is not an option, it is a requirement. A dozen years ago when I was attending the second World Conference in Portugal, a Portuguese brother told me that their Lodge met every week. Three of those meetings a month were for the purpose of Masonic education and one for the purpose of conferring ritual and conducting business. The average age of a Portuguese Freemason at that time was approximately 39 years. The Grand Lodge session was delayed for almost an hour so that they could expand the size of the room at the hotel to seat all the brothers attending.

The National Grand Lodge of France rejects approximately 60% of the petitions received and their membership has increased an average of 10% a year for the past 12 years. The rate of rejection in almost every jurisdiction in the world far exceeds anything we know in North America and most of these Grand Lodges are increasing in membership while facing far greater challenges to their existence than we have ever known.

Unfortunately in North America and again in light of political correctness we have determined that elitism is a dirty word and yet when Freemasonry stated that their goal was to take good men and make them better we became elitist and my friends there is nothing wrong with elitism. Elitism played a major role in bringing together the great minds of the age of Enlightenment. It was these men with great minds and capable of great thoughts that made it an influential segment of society.

There is no question but that quality will attract quality and if we wish to be a quality organization then we must have quality members to attract more quality members. I do not mean by this observation that there is no place in Freemasonry for the average man. Indeed, a second reason Freemasonry became as great as it has was that it was able to take men from all classes, occupations and social structures and place them in a Lodge room as equals.

The third major reason that caused Freemasonry to excel beyond all other organizations, however, was that it remained selective on the quality of the man that it would accept. My brothers, this is perhaps the major difference that I have found in other jurisdictions. We, in North America have become willing to accept almost any one in a failing attempt to increase our numbers. As a result the public now sees a different image of Freemasonry and society will always judge on the worst, never on the best.

Yet, we must be realistic. It is doubtful that any of us would ever serve as a major attracting force for those like the great men that I cited earlier but we can serve as an example to stimulate quality men to want to become part of us. How many of you sitting here today were inspired to petition the Craft because of men whom you knew who set an example to you and who were Freemasons? I was! We also must realistically recognize that our greatest hope for leadership will come from the professional environment. They are the men with the training to be leaders before becoming Freemasons.

We may argue all we want that these other foreign jurisdictions that I referred to have too stringent requirements in costs and demands for America but I guess it all boils down to what we want to be. Do we want to be an organization with the capability of impacting the ongoing evolution of our society and being highly respected and admired or do we want to be a dying organization of little note.

Let me take a few minutes and give you some examples of what I have experienced in my travels over the past twenty years. The first time I went to Greece I had a brother who drove me to wherever I wanted to go. He would not even let me open the car door, insisting that he open it for me. Just before I left Greece someone told me that he was regarded as the greatest surgeon in Greece and yet he was insisting to wait on me.

At the final banquet in Abidjan, Ivory Coast an older brother came up to me and told me that if I ever came back to that area of Africa, I never again stay in a hotel. He told me that he had a large home, his children were gone and he would be honored to have me stay with him and that his home was my home. When he walked away, a brother asked me if I knew who he was and I said no. He told me that he was the ambassador to the United Nations.

At the fourth World Conference in São Paulo, Brazil, a young man was assigned to look after me for seven days taking care of all my needs. He sat behind me at every meeting in case I needed anything. He drove me wherever I wanted to go and insisted on providing for my every want. I found out the day before I left Brazil that he was a pulmonary surgeon and professor of pulmonary medicine at the University of São Paulo.

I have been on a speaking agenda with the president of Chile and had lunch seated to his right at the presidential palace. I have been received at both the President's and the Prime Minister's palace in Portugal. I was invited to hunt with the Prime Minister of Romania. I participated in laying a wreath at the tomb of the Unknown Soldier under the Arc de Triomphe in Paris along with the presidents of Gabon and Congo. I have met with members of the royal families of Europe and had several dinners with the princess of Yugoslavia. I was made a chief of the village of Nigua-saff in the Ivory Coast. I had dinner at the home of the Commanding General of the Gabon military and attended a beach party at the retreat of the Minister of Defense. I participated in the dedication of a Masonic monument at Valparaiso, Chili where the monuments of the great Chilean heroes are erected. Can you imagine that happening in this country today?

These are just a few of the experiences that I have been privileged to participate in as a result of my affiliation with Freemasonry. It is extremely important, however, that you understand that none of this was for me; it was because of what I represented to Freemasonry and what Freemasonry represented in their country. And the President of Chile and the President and Prime Minister of Portugal are not Freemasons.

It would be extremely prudent for the leaders of the Craft in America to take a serious look at those Grand Jurisdictions that are experiencing the greatest success and begin to consider the logic in trying to emulate their blueprint for succeeding. We must stop playing the "numbers game" and trying to buy back respect through charitable contributions and begin to realize that by improving the quality of the Craft we will improve the quantity of the Craft and regain the respect. We as individual members must set a positive example as to what this Craft means to society. We are the living examples of what Freemasonry is.

As a result of the recent publicity that we have received through Dan Brown's books and a couple of movies and television programs, Freemasonry is being given an opportunity of resurrection of significance in today's society. Young men are knocking at the door of Freemasonry seeking to pass through the portals of an organization dedicated to priorities of improving the man and challenging the mind.

They are seeking something that society is not offering and now we must be willing and able to satisfy their quest. We may never again be given this opportunity. The question is; are we willing and are we able? The world deserves a positive answer as do our predecessors.

[13]

The World's Freemasonry

Given to the Masonic Society

It is a great privilege and pleasure for me to be able to address the Masonic Society. I look at the membership of this organization as being part of the more intellectually elite or at least more intellectually interested in the future of the Craft than the average Freemason. Although I am a Founding Fellow of the Society, I am not a dedicated researcher. Nor do I consider myself as being an historian. I have been introduced as both along with being a Masonic scholar and a Masonic philosopher but in reality, I am just a country boy who has been given the privilege of knowing and associating with those who are.

I have, however, been a member of the Masonic fraternity for fifty years, twenty of those years as Grand Secretary two additional years as Grand Secretary for foreign affairs and am now serving my fourteenth year as Executive Secretary of the World Conference of Masonic Grand Lodges. There has been only a period of three months in my fifty years that I did not sit in an office of at least one Masonic body.

The 21 years that I have been writing book reviews for the Scottish Rite has resulted in an ongoing examination of our Craft. I have been afforded the great opportunity and privilege of being able to travel over much of the world and to observe Freemasonry as it exists today. I therefore look at myself as a student of contemporary Freemasonry.

I tell you this not to inflate my significance, for I well know that no matter how important that I may think I am to this world, a year after I am dead, the world will ask; Tom who? I tell you this to qualify why I speak to you today on the subject of World Freemasonry.

Freemasonry is growing at a more rapid rate than perhaps any time in our history. There have been 24 new grand lodges consecrated since the beginning of this century and there are others that will be consecrated in the not too distant future. The Craft is emerging in Eastern Europe in countries that have either never had it or in countries in which it is been repressed for decades. In Africa with the general exception of the existence of Provincial or District Grand Lodges, Freemasonry is establishing roots in relatively untouched environments. What this can mean to the world is immeasurable.

In many stable societies, however, the potential influence of Freemasonry has become less than what it once was. This is simply a matter of fact, due to those societies having evolved to a level of stability where future evolutionary change will be limited or at least slowed in its development. This does not mean that the need for the philosophical purpose of the Craft has in any way become lessened but its ongoing influence will be more subtle than in the past.

There can never be a time, no matter how long this world may exist, that Freemasonry's philosophy would not be applicable to any society. It simply means that the need for dramatic societal change is no longer paramount in these environments. In addition, a change in leadership style has reduced our philosophical influence in some areas of the world and made us less visible in society. But where Freemasonry is now arising there exists the fertile fields to be cultivated by those dedicated to a society in need of the gentle guidance of our Craft.

Freemasonry has impacted the evolution of civil society for several hundred years. It has changed significantly, the course of civilization. It has influenced the development of some of the greatest men who have ever lived and there-in lays our purpose beyond any other, to continue to contribute to the development of great men. These great men will then influence the ongoing evolution of civil society.

I firmly believe that Freemasonry on the continent of Africa has probably the greatest potential to impact its peoples, to contribute to the evolution of its societies and probably to alter the future of this world beyond any other. It has the opportunity to show to the world what a philosophy like ours can contribute to mankind.

It also, however, is perhaps going to meet some of the greatest challenges that it has ever experienced. For it must deal with not only what might be one of the greatest diversities of societies, cultures and religious beliefs located on one continent, but must also deal with the pressures which will be impressed by outside influences.

But, the philosophy of Freemasonry has always and must always transcend the variances with which it will be confronted in the environment in which it exists. Because of the universality of its purpose coupled with the constancy of its zeal, it has risen above those restrictive barriers that have hindered societal evolution for several hundred years. The very fact that it continues to thrive throughout the free world is un-debatable evidence that its purpose is universal and undying.

For most of our existence, even though there was that "Mystic Tie" binding us together in a universal brotherhood, there was a great tendency toward a provincial attitude of our Grand Lodges. We operated in a form of hierarchal isolationism. Today, however, modern technology has driven us to become a more visible organization, forcing us away from our isolationism and causing us to be more exposed and subject to more external examination.

What were once regarded as Masonic "secrets" can today be found by any computer or in any public library. This, however, in no way decreases our capacity of exerting our influence on society. What it does mean, however, is that we must face reality, confront the complexities it brings with it and adapt to using the technologies to further our goals which in turn must contribute to the betterment of mankind. We first, however, must understand ourselves and our goals.

I have traveled extensively throughout the world for the past two decades for the purpose of Freemasonry and have been afforded the opportunity that few have, to study our present-day Craft and its methods of operation. I have been granted the privilege of meeting with some great men and in developing some of the greatest friendships that one could ever wish for. In doing so, I have observed the universality of the philosophical purpose of our Craft regardless of where it operates in the world. This I refer to as its structural philosophy.

I also, however, have become very cognizant of the differences that exist in the operational philosophies of Freemasonry. These operational variances are worthy of note, especially in areas where Freemasonry is in a developmental stage. From my studies and observations I have concluded that the personality of Freemasonry in different parts of the world is driven and shaped by the environment in which it exists. This is true historically in most jurisdictions.

Based upon these operational variations I have been attempting to categorize the Freemasonry in different parts of the world in what I refer to as styles of the Craft. Thus far, I have distinguished five distinctive styles but

I am sure that others, perhaps less distinctive, may exist or evolve into being. Please keep in mind that these styles are my creation and there could be those who disagree with me. North American Freemasonry has diverged farther from its roots than any Freemasonry in the world. Much of the intellectual elitism that contributed heavily to the creation of what might arguably be referred to as the most influential organization ever conceived by the mind of man has been sacrificed in a pursuit of a static equality with a support of charitable objectives. If any external force is influencing Freemasonry today in America it's our buy-in of political correctness.

Before I go farther let me clarify what I mean by elitism as it impacts Freemasonry and intellectual elitism as it has impacted Freemasonry. My brothers, there is a tendency today for many to frown upon elitism. I have found myself at odds with some North American leadership by the use of this term. And yet, the day that we said that our goal was to take good men and make them better, we became elitist and there is nothing wrong with that form of elitism. In addition, one of the greatest reasons we became the major influential organization that we have, is because we attracted some of the greatest minds that ever lived and that, my brothers, is intellectual elitism. Subtract that factor from the equation and we are not what we are nor could we have been what we were.

Present day Eastern European Freemasonry has not been in existence long enough to show whether it will retain the philosophical style of its Western European creators. A different mindset seems to exist in these countries as a result of fascist and communist suppression that might stimulate it to evolve into something distinctive as a result of the different societal pressure where it exists.

Although I have spent some time in the Far East,

India and the Philippines as well as in Africa, I have not discerned a specific style which differentiates and defines it. In these locations, as a result of operating as Provincial or district Grand Lodges or lodges for a prolonged period of time, there has been a tendency to take on the characteristic of the mother Grand Lodge but we should expect a modification

If it is the intent of Freemasonry to remain a driving intellectual force in the evolution of civil society, if we wish for future historians to acknowledge our contributions in the developing world for the betterment of mankind, if we want to continue toward our goal of taking good men and making them better, then whatever style we choose must lead us on a pathway to that end.

Upon examining the different styles, we can measure degrees of success in World Freemasonry.

The Philosophical/Social Style has been in existence for the longest period of time and has paved the way in every other environment. Therefore differences in style have all evolved from it. It has certainly stood the test of time and has impacted the world in general, probably more than any other. It was this style that became an integral part of the cornerstone of the Enlightenment and it was the Enlightenment that served as a pathway out of the ignorance of the dark ages.

The Sociological Style found in Central and South America has not deviated extensively from it. The infusion of the idealism has not in any way harmed the Craft's potential in the society in which it lives. I am not convinced, however, that it could thrive as well in other parts of the world. The strength of this Freemasonry is a result of the continuing struggle to operate within its environment. I have great respect for both the Philosophical/Social and the Sociological styles of the Craft.

As I have indicated earlier, I do not really understand Mexican Freemasonry but I do have a fear that it places itself in jeopardy by coming close to violating a basic Masonic protocol. Keep this in mind my brothers. We do not fear Freemasons becoming involved in political activity but we must never permit Freemasonry to become involved.

I look at Canadian Freemasonry although part of North America as a modified version of both the Philosophical and Charitable styles. They retain more of the Philosophical style from their origin but have been greatly influenced by the Charitable.

Freemasonry in the United States, however, is purely a Charitable Style today. Interestingly, the change into this style took place over the last 30 to 50 years. It began its life as a philosophical style as brought over by the early settlers from the British Isles and the European continent. There can be no doubt that its impact on the creation of the United States of America was extraordinary. The intellectual stimulus of the Enlightenment played a vital role in the idealistic structuring of this country and more than a few of the enlightened thinkers who played a role in this structuring were Freemasons.

It has changed, however. As a result of never having to face the great challenges to be a Freemason that most of the world has faced, it has not only failed to become stronger, but as a result of complacency, it has become weaker and has now evolved into apathy. Much of the present-day leadership lacks the vision of our forefathers who structured our great society. Today our goal is not to change society but simply to become visible to society. We were an organization, respected beyond any other in America and one whose members were responsible for structuring a society that has been emulated by many others.

Freemasonry for the past thirty years in the United

States has concentrated the vast amount of its energies on recruiting membership and raising money to give away to charities. We have become one of the greatest charitable organizations in the world at the sacrifice of our intellectual integrity and influence in society. We are trying to buy back, through charitable programs, that which we lost through loss of vision. The result is the membership has declined over 70% and we have lost most of our influence and prestige in society.

This does not mean that charity has no place in Freemasonry. Indeed, charity has been a core value of the Craft from its beginning but this charity started as support of its brothers, wives, children and widows. Now, however, it has become the core value in North America with a face almost of a public charity.

Numbers of members and financial wealth is not a visible sign of success in Freemasonry. The United States had both and now is rapidly losing both. So in studying the styles of Freemasonry we must not become blinded by the number of members or by the magnificence of structures. Freemasonry changed this world not by rolling over it with large numbers or by buying its influence. Freemasonry changed the world by improving good men one at a time.

In reviewing the history of World Freemasonry it doesn't take long to realize that it had its detractors and enemies almost from the beginning of its existence. Among those who became its greatest enemies were political leaders and leaders of religious institutions. Upon discovering the motivation for what caused this enmity in such different entities, you will find that they are the same. Both have a desire to control the bodies and minds of those under their dominion.

Almost universally, dictatorial and despotic governments and religious leaders have opposed the Craft but it is significant that no religion opposes Freemasonry, religious leaders oppose it. The major objection that they indicate is that we accept membership from all monotheistic believers while requiring only a belief in a Supreme Being.

Even though this opposition from both groups continues to exist today, Freemasonry has never been destroyed by the forces of either. It has been suppressed at times, driven underground and even forced to cease operation in some areas but it has risen like a phoenix from the ashes when the tyranny was eliminated.

Looking at the condition of Freemasonry on a world level today in general, and disregarding the English speaking jurisdictions, we find a thriving organization continuing to exert influence in the evolving society. There does seem to be greater problems in some English speaking jurisdictions, especially in number loss. Perhaps it has been willingness in these Grand Lodges to lower standards and to adopt a more charitable style of the Craft that has resulted in the decline and loss of influence in society. This is unquestionably true in North America.

I have been greatly impressed almost everywhere I travel, not only with the quality of the men I have found comprising the Craft but also in the positions of influence that they hold in their societies.

Now, however, Freemasonry is being confronted with challenges unlike any that we have faced in the past and will require a continuing re-examination of our methods of operation. The greatest enemies threatening us today lies not in the leadership of governments or religious institutions although some remain enemies of the Craft. Our greatest enemy today is ourselves.

The three greatest challenges that I see confronting Freemasonry today are expansion of Irregular Freemasonry development of modern technology and ignorance of our membership.

Of course, Irregular Freemasonry is nothing new in the Masonic world. It has been around almost as long as has Regular Freemasonry and it has never been a major obstacle to us. The concern regarding it today is the rapidity of its growth and expansion and the tendency to become more organized than it has in the past. What was once a quiescent separate form of Freemasonry, it is now developing into a competitive threat to mainstream and Regular Freemasonry. It also is appearing in jurisdictions that have been occupied by Regular Freemasonry for years. It has become a major obstacle in stabilizing Freemasonry in Eastern Europe and is making its appearance felt in Africa. This is an issue that we cannot choose to ignore because it presents a different face of the Craft to society, one not bound by the protocols that define the Freemasonry we know.

What is of an even greater concern and is something totally new to our noble Craft is the impact that is being felt via the use of the World Wide Web. The Internet has created a new atmosphere that is causing considerable problems for us and is one that is not going to go away or one that we can eliminate.

Grand Lodges today are being bypassed by ignorant Freemasons, and ignorant Freemasons constitute the majority of our membership. Please note that I said ignorant, not stupid although today from what I read on the net, I am not sure anymore.

I never cease to be amazed at how much misinformation is placed on the web by some of our members who become impressed with what they think they know. I now spend a considerable amount of time responding to brothers who have become "instant experts" on the Craft. The lack of Masonic knowledge by our own membership has become a great threat to our survival. For an institution that impresses upon its membership the need for the acquisition of knowledge, the Internet reveals a considerable dearth of success on our part.

In addition to the damage that is being caused by our own membership on the web, whose voice because they are Freemasons, is accepted as fact by the non-Mason as well as our own members, is caused by those who would destroy us. Our enemies have found fertile ground on the web to dissipate their vitriolic hate of our fraternity. This we cannot contain any more than we could contain it in the past but we must understand that it is there and educate our membership concerning it.

We have been fortunate to have carried our isolationist attitude into almost the present day. But, my brothers, like it or not it is over. This modern technology along with present-day leadership's attitude is removing that choice from us.

One of our glaring weaknesses as leaders today has been our inability to see the big picture of the Craft. We have a tendency to lose sight of the great accomplishments for which Freemasonry has been known, and concentrate our efforts on issues not paramount to our existence and of little consequence to society. This is not a viable option. We simply cannot afford to fail to understand the diverse impacts that we have created and continue to create on human society.

For 300 years our past brothers worked to develop an un-paralleled organization whose philosophical purpose could easily be used as a template for world peace and there has probably been no time in our existence that the influence of that philosophy was anymore needed in the world than it is today.

As we acknowledge and recognize our place in the world as Freemasons we must also acknowledge and recognize our responsibility to the world as Freemasons. Our brothers of the past have done their job exceedingly well. They have placed it in the forefront as an elite organization, one respected highly for its contribution in developing world society. It is now up to us to continue to build upon what they established. The very least we must do as Freemasons to contribute to a better world is to live as Freemasons.

[14]

Masonry—Yesterday,
Today, and Tomorrow

Presented to the Valley of Rochester, New York

W hen I started to think about the topic, I figured that even with all my deficiencies, with this broad a subject, I should be able to speak for several weeks. Consider the numbers of volumes written about the Freemasonry of today and many being written on the projection of the Freemasonry into tomorrow. Logically therefore, anything that I say and indeed anything that all of us on the agenda put together today can say will be a superficial rendering of what could be said. Recognizing also, that the Fair is open to both members and non-members, we must speak to what is pertinent to all.

I offer my congratulations to the Valley of Rochester for hosting this "Masonic Education Fair." It has been my contention for years that North American Freemasons are the most ignorant Freemasons in the world. After traveling extensively throughout much of the world over the past two decades, visiting lodges and grand lodges, I find that we in North America teach less and consequently our members know less than Masons anywhere else that I traveled.

For that reason, I am convinced that Masonic education must play a significant role on the pathway to reclaiming our rightful position in society. We cannot afford to continue to ignore what had been a cornerstone of North American

Freemasonry and remains a cornerstone of Freemasonry throughout the rest of the world.

Regretfully, we in North America have lost our appreciation for the Craft simply because we do not even know the Craft. Ignorance of its structure and its purpose has become a way of life to many Freemasons. So little is required from the member that lack of knowledge has become the accepted norm. It is a consequence of no small magnitude that the admonition that we received — of a commitment to the acquisition of knowledge has been lost in our almost pathological quest for numbers.

It is only common logic that when one examines Freemasonry that he is dealing with far more yesterdays than todays and perhaps with even more than the potential for our tomorrows. The Freemasonry of most of our past reflects a glowing heritage from which a template could very well be forged for all of our tomorrows. For that heritage to be of value to us, however, we must deal with the issues of today. It matters not for how many centuries we may continue to survive into the future; the philosophy of Freemasonry can never outlive the needs of human existence. It is inconceivable that our philosophy would not always be applicable to the ongoing evolution of civil society.

I have been able to travel, far more than most, throughout a large portion of the world and to observe the Freemasonry of today, most of which is the result of an evolution from the Freemasonry of the past. From those travels, I have made the observation that even though the basic philosophical premise of the Craft is universal, the operating premise varies depending upon the environment in which it exists. For us to fully appreciate the diversities of its influence, we must understand the variations of its operating premise. We must also understand the evolutionary changes that have taken place during its history.

The Freemasonry of today is indeed different from the Freemasonry of yesterday, and yet the purpose for its existence has not changed. What has changed, however, is the intent of the leadership, and that, in North America, has played a major role in the decrease in the numbers of our members and the decline of our image in society. We must also, however, acknowledge that the sociological condition of the time has played a major role as well. That we could not change, but it has been our response to the sociological condition that has had the greatest impact on our potential in the future.

Is not my intent today to speak to our yesterdays. There are far too many with far more knowledge and far more capabilities to speak to our past than have I. It is also not my intent to dwell extensively upon the Freemasonry of the rest of the world, although I suspect that I am as well-versed in the subject as most of my contemporaries. I will speak principally to Freemasonry today and its potential for tomorrow.

I am probably most well known in the Masonic world for speaking my mind on the condition of the North American Freemasonry of today and the need for change in preparation for an influential Freemasonry of tomorrow. I will, therefore, speak principally to those issues.

It is an undeniable fact that today's Freemasonry lacks the influence that it once had in shaping North American society. Much of that loss can be attributed to the change in society itself, but much also has to be attributed to the lack of vision of our leadership in recent years. One of our glaring weaknesses as leaders today is our inability to see the big picture of the Craft. We have lost sight of the great accomplishments for which Freemasonry has been known, and concentrate our efforts on issues not paramount to our existence and of little consequence to society.

I do not make this evaluation as a condemnation of present-day leadership. We are simply representative and what amounts to the culmination of an evolutionary process that changed North American Freemasonry from an elite, philosophical, learned, highly respected society into a less than elite, almost ignored organization devoted to charitable objectives. We have managed to excise from the Craft those intellectual and philosophical standards that characterized it for most of its existence and for which it continues to be known over much of the globe. And yet, our potential to impact the future evolution of civil society remains within our grasp. It will require, however, a dramatic change in vision on the part of the leadership in North America.

For those who may be present and are not affiliated with the Masonic fraternity or are not well versed in its history, it is important that you understand that there is probably no organization outside of organized religion that has impacted the evolution of civil society more than has Freemasonry. In doing so, Freemasons have been killed by the tens of thousands for their support and leadership in the world's struggles for the freedom, liberty and equality of man. Some of the greatest minds who ever lived were attracted to its precepts and were our brothers. What I express is therefore due to a concern for our potential to continue to impact into the future.

I have been a member the Craft for almost half a century? and have been in at least one leadership capacity in all but three months of those years. Twenty years were spent as a Grand Secretary and even today, following retirement; I probably average better than a fifty-hour week in the study of Freemasonry. For that reason, I feel that I possess some qualifications to look at where we are, where we are going and what we need to change for our future.

In my travels and observations, I have concluded that there are two major threats to the stability of the Masonic institution, as we know it. One is impacting the Craft on a worldwide scale; the other is more specific to North America.

World Freemasonry today is in a greater state of instability than it has been for probably the larger part of its existence. I have been watching with great concern the spread of irregular Freemasonry with an aggressiveness not seen in the past. It is not only expanding into regions where Freemasonry is just being established, but also into areas where regular Freemasonry has existed for decades or even hundreds of years. In addition, various irregular forms of Freemasonry are establishing relationships that did not exist in the past.

This trend offers a definitive threat to the character of our ancient Craft because they possess the opportunity to grow more rapidly, since they are not hindered by some of the protocols of regular Freemasonry. These protocols have characterized our institution with little variation since our creation and remain standards by which we are known. A required belief in a Supreme Being, the Volume of the Sacred Law being upon the altar, the noninvolvement of the discussion of politics or religion in the Lodge and the restrictions on the admission of females into the Craft, among others, have been universal standards that have supported our organization for several hundred years.

Regularity of Freemasonry is the structural base upon which we have erected our edifice to project a constancy of purpose to the world outside. Those Grand Lodges not operating within these standards, have not adopted or have eliminated some of the basic landmarks upon which we exist are regarded as irregular.

In addition, we are facing challenges to the stability of

regular Freemasonry by a leadership either ignorant of, or willing to violate, operating protocols that has sustained our organization throughout our existence. The result, regretfully, is a tendency toward fragmentation, an erosion of our unity and a lessening of our influence in society to work toward what is good and just in mankind.

I recently received a second e-mail from England requesting my assistance in creating a new constitution by breaking away from the United Grand Lodge of England. The senders had read one of my papers published in Freemasonry Today, an English publication, in which I expressed my concerns regarding the emphasis we place on charitable objectives today. Although I appreciate their concern, as it is the same as mine, I responded that all efforts must be made to work with the existing Grand Lodge and that fragmentation can do nothing but weaken our ability to achieve the goals of the Craft.

A major cause for these issues facing us at this time has been the development of modern technology. The worldwide web has become a fertile medium used by those who oppose the Masonic fraternity and for whom stating the truth has never become a limiting factor in their use of it. The Internet has simply become a valuable tool to spread the lies or the ignorance of others to our brothers or to anyone else who reads them and lacks the knowledge to reject them, and this is the vast majority who read it.

Of just as great a concern to us, however, should be the misinformation that is placed on the web by well-meaning brothers who simply do not know. I never cease to be amazed by those who have been members of our Craft for a period of a few years or even a few months who think they have all the answers but have probably never heard the questions.

These issues will impact Freemasonry for many decades

into the future. The way our leadership of today responds will determine the extent of our influence in that same future.

The second major threat to our integrity as an institution is relegated more to North American Freemasonry than to most other areas of the world.

North American Freemasonry has evolved into a form that concentrates its efforts in supporting charitable objectives. Although charity has been a core value of Freemasonry probably even before its evolution into a speculative fraternity, it is not the core value of the Craft. It was a common practice among operative masons to provide relief and assistance to injured or ill companions and to their widows and children, but that was not their purpose for existence.

Although charitable objectives project an admirable quality, it is not a quality that provides the capability to change the course of civil society. We have other core values that have crafted an organization the likes of which the world had never seen before, nor has it been matched since. Unfortunately, over time we are losing sight of the realization of our purpose, that of improving the world through the improvement of the man.

Dr. E. Scott Ryan in his book, *The Theology of Crime and the Paradox of Freedom*, observed, "the wonderful work of Masonic charities is by no means synonymous with the wonderment of Masonic spirituality and that's a shame, when one considers how many fine charities there are and how few fine spiritualities there are." He made another very succinct observation when he stated, "if we become a charity, which we are certainly tending toward, and the government assumes that role which it is tending toward, then our purpose for existence will no longer exist."

History is littered with the remains of organizations, many patterned after Freemasonry, that were forced out of existence for the very reason that the government assumed the role for which those organizations existed.

Just think how unique we are and have been in the world of fraternal organizations. Think of how much and for how long, we have altered the course taken in that ongoing quest for civility in a civil society. There can be no doubt that our success and survival continues to rest upon the uniqueness that characterizes Freemasonry. Leadership in North America is being confronted with the need to change its focus of concentration on what is significant to the future of our Craft.

We in North America have compounded our problems beyond what issues are confronting most other jurisdictions of the world. We not only face the issues created by the Internet, the spread of irregular Freemasonry and the failure to maintain protocols, but we must also face the need to change an operating premise that has come to characterize us as a Craft, for we have created a different and autonomous image of Freemasonry by which we are now known and that is distinctive to North America.

Because of that creation, Freemasonry in North America is at a critical crossroads in its life. Leaders of today are being forced to determine what it is that we really want to be and where we really want to go. The way that we respond to this challenge today, will determine all of our tomorrows.

Freemasonry is far too important to the world for the leaders of North America to continue to follow the same road that we have chosen to follow over the past half-century. Very little effort has been applied to any major programs within the Craft other than programs designed either to increase membership or to raise monies to give away to charity. Regretfully, this counterproductive road has led to a declining membership and a devastating loss in our image.

So, what about our future? I spoke in Washington,

D.C., several weeks ago on the subject of *Crafting a Mason*. This program also included Brothers Robert Davis from Oklahoma and W. Kirk MacNulty from Virginia, both distinguished Masonic scholars. The purpose of this program was to analyze the same issues that we are looking at here today: the past, the present and the future. More specifically, we were looking at the significance of the initiatic experience in the crafting of North American Freemasons. There can be no doubt that our minimizing the initiatic experience has decreased the impression that we create upon our new members — and that has impacted their commitment to the Craft.

We need, however, to examine the whole experience of North American Freemasonry to determine what changes must be made on the road that we are traveling, for Freemasonry once again to play a vital role in North American society. We need to change our attitude from transforming the Craft into something society wants, to restructuring the Craft to working for what society needs. I suspect, this character of the Craft might well be paramount for our past success.

Several years ago, when addressing the Conference of Eastern European Grand Lodges in Moscow, I emphasized to the Grand Lodge officers present, that Freemasonry did not impact the evolution of civil society through large numbers of men. Freemasonry impacted society by the quality of the man that comprised it. This Craft has been composed of some of the greatest minds, in a diversity of fields that the world has ever known. It was through these men and men like them in the Craft, that the philosophy of Freemasonry influenced the ongoing evolution of civil society.

It is imperative for our future that we once again develop long-range vision of where we want to go and once again comprehend the need for the quality of member, not the quantity of the members to fulfill that vision. Our goal must be restored to the fundamental purpose of taking a good man and making him better.

There has been a foundation established in North America, for the purpose of creating a Traditional Observance style of Freemasonry, with the intent of restoring a more philosophical form of the Craft. I am thoroughly convinced that the creation of this different style could lead to a change in the operating premise and the reconstruction of a prestigious and influential fraternity as exists in most of the rest of the world. We currently have Traditional Observance Lodges working in six states, and interest in this program is building. I am impressed with the number of members who are concerned with the restoration of North American Freemasonry back to a more traditional style, especially in the new, younger members.

So again, what about our future? My brothers, Freemasonry is expanding in the world at a more rapid rate than it has for perhaps 200 years. Grand Lodges are being consecrated in Africa and consecrated or re-consecrated in Eastern Europe, bringing Freemasonry into environments in which it never existed or where it was suppressed for decades by tyrannical rule. Its influence is once again being felt in Eastern Europe and being felt for the first time in much of Africa. Freemasonry is impacting the evolution of societies in these environments.

In North America, we hopefully, are beginning to comprehend that the programs that we have instituted over the past quarter-century to rejuvenate Freemasonry have at best, failed, and in many cases were counterproductive to the very goals of the programs.

Freemasonry is the oldest fraternal organization in the world. It remains the largest and the most prestigious organization that ever existed. Its impact on the evolution of civil society is unquestionable and unmatched. Its past is filled with heralded glory, its present with couched anticipation, and with our commitment, its future should be secure.

[15]

Regularity and Fraternal Relations

The subject of regularity and fraternal relations, certainly is not a new topic for discussion to anyone of you sitting here, nor is it a recent point of contention within the Masonic fraternity. Indeed, it is perhaps, one of the first major considerations to confront early speculative Freemasonry, and specific criteria for what constitutes regularity has been established and adhered to by grand lodges during most of Freemasonry's existence.

Today, we acknowledge that grand lodge regularity is contingent upon it having been created by another Regular Grand Lodge, or by the action of three or more regular subordinate lodges to create a grand lodge. Regularity is also dependent upon adherence by a grand lodge to established practice and requirements. These include the belief in a Supreme Being, the presence of the Volume of the Sacred Law upon the altar, the limitation of males only in membership, the avoidance of discussion of religion and politics within the lodge, a restriction of fraternal intercourse with irregular Freemasonry, and the respect of jurisdictional territory of other grand lodges, amongst others. This last requirement has been altered recently to granting recognition to more than one grand lodge in a territory where the grand lodges in the territory recognize each other.

The issuance of warrants is a long held prerogative of grand lodges. Brother Michael Walker, Grand Secretary of the Grand Lodge of Ireland pointed out in a paper he presented to the Pennsylvania Academy of Knowledge recently, "The issue of Warrants commenced about 1731," and "the application for, and the granting of, a warrant rendered the Lodge regular and was the origin of the term used so casually today."

Thus, a basic process was created early in our existence and was adhered to with a constancy that produced a world-wide standard for the regular Freemasonry we know today. Regular Freemasonry is the only structural base upon which we can erect our edifice to project a constancy to the world outside of our Craft. Any deviation from these established criteria can only serve to weaken the Craft's image to the world. I again quote Right Worshipful Brother Walker relative to this subject, "One can either stand fast with colours nailed to the mast and demand full compliance with established practice or one can compromise one's position by accepting less with ever-increasing demands for lower and the lower standards. This is a sure receipt for disaster." I can only endorse fully, Brother Walker's observation.

Regularity in Freemasonry has been accompanied by irregularity since close to its inception. There have been, and are regular grand lodges in origin that became irregular by practice. There have been, and are grand lodges that comply with some of the requirements for regularity, but not all. And, there exists grand lodges that had never been regular in either origin or practice. Masonic leaders have dealt with these issues effectively for almost 300 years.

Now, however, present-day leadership is being confronted with a need to make decisions that will impact our Fraternity far into the future, and many are ill-equipped to deal with these decisions due to lack of knowledge, not only in the procedure of recognition, but also concerning the grand lodges in question.

There is a pervasive attitude beginning to permeate our Craft regarding regularity and fraternalism that none of us can choose to ignore. There is a small segment of our leadership who feel that almost 300 years of history, practice and tradition is no longer applicable in today's world. Lack of knowledge on their part is certainly one factor, ego and arrogance is another, present-day liberalism is probably a third. Whatever the motives, we cannot afford to ignore their actions. If permitted to continue, they will destroy Freemasonry, as it has been known for almost three centuries.

Our Craft is now confronted with resultant challenges perhaps of a magnitude never before seen in our history and we cannot afford to remain ignorant of what is occurring. Nor can we choose to ignore what is happening. The way our leadership responds today will determine the direction Freemasonry will go in the future, which in turn, if we remain a viable institution, could influence the direction of the ongoing evolution of civil society.

Let us establish that every Grand Lodge has an inherent right to make decisions regarding those grand lodges with which they will be in amity. There must be, however, an assumed responsibility on the part of the leadership to become knowledgeable of, and understand the characteristics of, the grand lodges they are considering. They must also be cognizant of the impact their decisions may have upon world Freemasonry. We, as grand lodges can no longer function with the isolationist attitude of our past. The decision of any grand lodge today, regarding regularity and recognition, will reverberate throughout the others. Consider the impact created by the decision made by a North American Grand Lodge this past year. It is, therefore imperative, that unanimity of intent and action by regular grand lodges be applied, before a wedge is driven that will divide and weaken us, thus seriously damaging our ability to serve world society.

In preparing a paper recently, I became awakened to the fact that Freemasonry is expanding more rapidly today than it has in many decades as a result of the reorganization in Eastern Europe and expansion into Africa. Even as we note the spread of regular Freemasonry, however, we cannot ignore the expansion of irregular Freemasonry. The result is that Masonic regularity finds itself competing with irregular Freemasonry. The problem becomes compounded when leaders within regular Freemasonry grants recognition to irregular grand lodges.

There has also been a marked increase in schisms in regularly consecrated grand lodges resulting in two grand lodges in the same jurisdiction, both claiming to be the legitimate, regular grand lodge. The result has been that some mainstream grand lodges recognizes one, while other mainstream grand lodges recognize the other. This is an untenable situation, which weakens our fraternity, and presents to the world an unstable organization worth little note.

To further compound the problem of recognition, Masonicly affiliated appendant bodies have become instrumental in causing some of the schisms to occur. These actions should be intolerable to us as officers of grand lodges. And yet, we have not only permitted these situations to exist by ignoring the issues, but in some cases have even contributed to it.

The result is that today many grand lodges in the world have no idea, which grand lodges in other jurisdictions are regular and which is not, while most appendant bodies know even less. Craft Masonry is what impacted this world. Craft Masonry created the appendant bodies. How can we as officers of grand lodges continue to permit interference in world Freemasonry by organizations subjective to grand lodges? Violations of our accepted operating protocols must be recognized and confronted. If we fail to face and resolve these issues, we have absolutely no hope that Freemasonry will ever achieve the full potential for its existence.

The internet has also created problems that have never been seen in our past. I have been appalled recently when I saw what misinformation is on the world-wide web. What makes it even more frightening is that those who do not know are being accepted as experts in the Masonic world on the web. Of an even graver concern must be the presently small cadre of members who feel that all "Freemasons" should be regarded as brothers regardless of how they were created, and what they practice. These men probably have no idea of how many irregular grand lodges exist in the world today. We simply cannot permit these attitudes against our protocols to exist in our membership. Our members who choose to violate their obligation, as a Freemason should be removed from our Craft before they spread their venom farther.

We as Masonic leaders today cannot permit ourselves to be seduced into accepting anything less. We cannot offer ourselves for sale to the highest bidder. We must insist on regularity of recognized grand lodges. We should also, however, be doing all within our power to work with those grand lodges who were regularly constituted, but are irregular in practice, to bring them back to conformity and recognition.

So where does that leave us in dealing with this issue of regularity and fraternal relations? First, we must recognize and acknowledge that as leaders we cannot and do not know everything. This will not be easy for many Masonic leaders. Even the most ardent of us, however, must acknowledge that in this day and age, it is simply not possible for any one individual to keep abreast of the changes that are occurring within our Craft. Most of our leaders today are dealing with demands in their lives, which will preclude any hope of their determining which grand lodges are entitled to recognition.

For the future of Freemasonry it is therefore imperative that we become capable of divesting ourselves of our limiting egos and goals of creating self-perpetuating images and become more aware of the foundation upon which we have thrived for hundreds of years. We must become concerned more about the future of Freemasonry, and less about our own images.

This subject upon which I speak may be one of the greatest threats to our survival as a viable institution capable of impacting society in this millennium. Yet, the problem confronting us is one that we are causing, by creating disunity within the Craft, by supporting irregular instead of regular Freemasonry, by reacting instead of acting, and by failing to recognize our ignorance on specific issues. We are not only not helping the perpetuation of our Masonic Craft; we are aiding and abetting its demise.

If our Craft is to have a stable and contributory future, then we must support our requirements of regularity, and requirements for fraternal recognition. We must also be unwilling to accept deviations from these requirements. Fraternal relations must be limited to regular Freemasonry. Those Grand Lodges seeking recognition know what is required. If they cannot or will not accept these parameters, then they fail to gain recognition, and if a regular grand lodge chooses a divergent pathway, then they must risk losing recognition.

Fraternal relations between grand lodges is not a right, it is a privilege. Each grand lodge is free to choose, but if that choice contributes to disunity, then Regular Freemasonry has the responsibility to attempt reunification. The future of the Craft is now in our hands. Where it goes in this century is up to us. For the sake of the world, let us not fail.

[16]

Freemasonry's Dilemma

Templum Fidelis Lodge—Canada

It is a great privilege and pleasure for me to be able to address this "Traditional Observance Lodge." I have been serving on the board of the Masonic Restoration Foundation since its inception and the more I travel this world and study Freemasonry, the more impressed I become with what we were and the impact that we had on the evolution of civil society

I am firmly convinced that the future of Freemasonry in North America will depend upon our ability to recapture the significance of our past and once again practice Freemasonry. I am also convinced that to do so we must become fully aware of what created that significance and why we lost it.

It will be difficult to regain what we have lost when the vast majority of our members today have no idea what it is that we have lost. Education of our membership must become a priority and I look to the creation of Traditional Observance Lodges as perhaps our greatest hope of reversing this descent into ignorance and for the salvation of North American Freemasonry.

I have spoken in over thirty countries on the subject of Freemasonry, have appeared on numerous televisions and radio programs and participated in a number of press interviews. I have been introduced over the years as a Masonic historian, author, orator, and even as a philosopher. In reality, I am a little country boy who has been fortunate to have had the privilege of knowing and associating with those who do fit these categories.

The twenty-one years I have been writing book reviews for the Scottish Rite have resulted in an ongoing examination of our Craft. I have been afforded the great opportunity of being able to travel over much of the world as a Freemason and to observe Freemasonry as it exists today. I therefore look at myself simply as a student of contemporary Freemasonry. I tell you this not to inflate my significance, for I well acknowledge my insignificance in this world. I tell you this to qualify why I speak to you today on the subject of the dilemma of World Freemasonry.

A change in leadership style has reduced our philosophical influence in some areas of the world and made us less visible in society. But where Freemasonry is now arising there exist the fertile fields to be cultivated by those dedicated to a society in need of the gentle guidance of our Craft.

Freemasonry has impacted the evolution of civil society for several hundred years. It has changed significantly, the course of civilization. It has influenced the development of some of the greatest men who have ever lived and therein lays our purpose beyond any other, to continue to be a factor in the development of great men. These great men will then influence the ongoing evolution of civil society.

Freemasonry on the continent of Africa has probably the greatest potential to impact its peoples, to contribute to the evolution of its societies and probably to alter the future of this world beyond any other. It has the opportunity to show to the world what a philosophy like ours can contribute to mankind.

It also, however, is perhaps going to meet some of

the greatest challenges that it has ever experienced. For it must deal with not only what might be one of the greatest diversities of societies, cultures and religious beliefs located on one continent, but must also deal with the pressures which will be exerted by outside influences.

The philosophy of Freemasonry, however, has always and must always transcend the variances with which it will be confronted in the environment in which it exists. Because of the universality of its purpose, coupled with the constancy of its zeal, it has risen above those restrictive barriers that have hindered societal evolution for several hundred years. The very fact that it continues to thrive throughout the free world is undeniable evidence that its purpose is universal and undying.

None of us, however, can be unaware of the decreasing interest in our Craft and decline in our influence that North American Freemasonry has experienced over the last thirty years. I have become far more concerned in recent years, with the decreasing quality of the membership than with the quantity. The decreasing quality is a major factor in the decreasing quantity through losing our attractiveness to the professional class of men who creates a more positive image in society.

For most of our existence, even though there was that "Mystic Tie" binding us together in a universal brotherhood, there was a great tendency toward a provincial attitude of our Grand Lodges. Today, however, modern technology has driven us to become a more visible organization, forcing us away from our isolationism and causing us to be more exposed and subject to more external examination.

What it means is that we must face reality, confront the complexities it brings with it and adapt to using the technologies to further our goals which in turn must contribute to the betterment of mankind. We first, however, must understand ourselves and our goals.

If it is the intent of Freemasonry to remain a driving intellectual force in the evolution of civil society, if we wish for future historians to acknowledge our contributions in the developing world for the betterment of mankind, if we want to continue toward our goal of taking good men and making them better, then whatever style of the Craft we choose must lead us on a pathway to that end.

There can be no doubt that its impact on the creation of the United States of America and Canada was extraordinary. The intellectual stimulus of the Enlightenment played a vital role in the idealistic structuring of our countries and more than a few of the enlightened thinkers who played a role in this structuring were Freemasons.

Now however, it has changed in both the United States and Canada. As a result of never having to face the great challenges to be a Freemason that most of the world has faced, it has not only failed to become stronger, but as a result of complacency, it has become weaker and has now evolved into apathy. Much of the present-day leadership lacks the vision of our forefathers who structured our great society. Today our goal is not to change society but simply to become visible to society. In the name of political correctness we have bought into the concept of the equality of men regardless of initiative or ability. We were an organization respected beyond any other in North America and one whose members were responsible for structuring a society that has been emulated by many others throughout the world.

Numbers of members and financial wealth are not visible signs of success in Freemasonry. We have had both and now are rapidly losing both. So in studying the styles of Freemasonry, we must not become blinded by the number of members or by the magnificence of structures. Freemasonry changed the world by improving good men one man at a time.

In reviewing the history of World Freemasonry, it doesn't take long to realize that it had its detractors and enemies from the beginning of its existence. Almost universally, dictatorial and despotic governments and many religious leaders have opposed the Craft. The major objection they indicate is that we accept membership from all monotheistic believers while requiring only a belief in a Supreme Being. Even though this opposition from both groups continues to exist today, Freemasonry has never been destroyed by the forces of either.

Looking at the condition of Freemasonry on a world level today in general, we find a thriving organization continuing to exert influence in evolving societies. There appear greater problems in some Grand Lodges especially in number loss. There seems to be willingness in these Grand Lodges to lower standards and to adopt a more charitable style of the Craft that has resulted in the decline and loss of influence in society.

I have been greatly impressed almost everywhere I travel, not only with the quality of the men I have found comprising the Craft but also in the positions of influence that they hold in their societies.

Now, however, Freemasonry is being confronted with challenges unlike any that we have faced in the past and will require a continuing re-examination of our methods of operation. The greatest enemies threatening us today lie not in the leadership of governments or religious institutions although some remain enemies of the Craft. Our greatest enemy today is ourselves.

The three greatest challenges that I see confronting Freemasonry today are expansion of Irregular Freemasonry, development of modern technology and ignorance of our membership.

Of course, Irregular Freemasonry is nothing new in the Masonic world. It has become a major obstacle in stabilizing Freemasonry in Eastern Europe and is making its appearance felt in Africa. This is an issue that we cannot choose to ignore because it presents a different face of the Craft to society, one not bound by the protocols that define the Freemasonry we know.

What is of an even greater concern and is something totally new is the impact that is being felt via the use of the World Wide Web. The Internet has created a new atmosphere that is causing considerable problems for us and is one that is not going to go away or one that we can eliminate.

In addition to the damage that is being caused by our own membership on the web, whose voices are accepted as fact by the non-Mason as well as our own members because they are Freemasons, more damage is caused by those who would destroy us. Our enemies have found fertile ground on the web to dissipate their vitriolic hate of our fraternity. This we cannot contain any more than we could contain it in the past, but we must understand that it is there and educate our membership concerning it.

One of our glaring weaknesses as leaders today has been our inability to see the big picture of the Craft. We have a tendency to lose sight of the great accomplishments for which Freemasonry has been known, and concentrate our efforts on issues not paramount to our existence and of little consequence to society. This is not a viable option. We simply cannot afford to fail to understand the diverse impacts that we have created and continue to create on human society.

For 300 years, our past brothers have worked to develop an unparalleled organization whose philosophical purpose could easily be used as a guide for world peace. There has probably been no time in our existence that the influence of that philosophy was anymore needed in the world than it is today.

As we acknowledge and recognize our place in the world as Freemasons we must also acknowledge and recognize our responsibility to the world as Freemasons. Our brothers of the past have done their job exceedingly well. They have placed it in the forefront as an elite organization, one respected highly for its contribution in developing world society. It is now up to us to continue to build upon what they established. The very least we must do as Freemasons to contribute to a better world is to live as Freemasons and so mote it ever be.

[17]

What Do We Want to Be?

Given at the Rubicon Masonic Dinner Club

I regard it a very distinct privilege to have been invited to speak, as a participant in the Masonic Education Series for this distinguished organization. I consider Masonic education to be a very vital and integral component in the process of the re-establishment of influence of Freemasonry into American society. Therefore, I regard any opportunity presented to me to be involved relative to Masonic education as an opportunity and an honor.

I recall reading many years ago, "It is only Masonic education that will assure us that the brothers shall be more knowledgeable, conscious, and concerned with the canons of Freemasonry. To do otherwise is to fail in our mission to filter and purify the brother with the romance and beauty of Freemasonry."

I never expect everyone to agree with my thoughts and observations and indeed for many years there were far more dissidents than adherents to what I had to say. However, the pendulum is starting to swing the other way. There are those in leadership positions today realizing that we cannot continue to practice failed procedures and expect them to succeed. There is a beginning of acknowledgment that what we have been doing for the past 30 to 35 years has been a failure. What we have actually succeeded in doing has been devastating to our image in society and destructive to the magnanimous influence we once had.

I will be very candid with some of my comments this evening but I want it understood that I am not issuing a condemnation against our present day leadership. We are the current product of an ongoing deterioration of commitment to the philosophical idealism of a great fraternity. It is, however, essential that our present day leadership comprehend that it is their responsibility to reverse that deterioration. It is also important that we all realize that we cannot depend upon our past to support our present or our future. That ongoing parasitization has led us into a complacency that is now evolving into apathy. When we became leaders, we assumed the responsibility of committing ourselves to supporting and restoring the fraternity to its former greatness. If any leader today feels that he has not assumed that responsibility, he does not belong in the position he holds.

I have also become increasingly cognizant of my mortality and recognize that the time that I have left is rapidly shrinking. For that reason I express my concern more forcefully than I have in the past.

Let me also emphasize that tonight I am referring, principally to the Freemasonry of North America and several other countries, not to Freemasonry in most of the world. It is interesting and probably significant that the greatest failing of Freemasonry today has been in English-speaking countries, if measured in terms of decreasing membership numbers and influence in society. This is not in consequence of the language but of an adoption of a similarity in style of Freemasonry. The Craft however, is thriving in a large portion of the world and continuing to impact the evolution of the societies in which it exists.

There have been twenty-seven new grand lodges consecrated since the beginning of this century. That represents perhaps, the greatest and most rapid rate of growth that

Freemasonry has experienced since its inception in the 1700s. These grand lodges are already, playing a significant role in the societies in which they now exist.

We in North America, however, have been approaching the day of reckoning and have failed to find a solution to prevent it. We now have some serious decisions that must be made if we are to survive as a significant and influential organization. Decisions, such as; are we willing to accept what we have become, or do we fulfill our obligation to our brothers of the past and to society, to restore Freemasonry to the prominence bequeathed to us? Do we continue to dwell upon the greatness of our past, ignoring the significance of our present, and measure our success by the quantity of members that we deem necessary to support the great material structures we have built, or do we begin again to concentrate on the quality of our members to support the great mystical and intellectual structures that our brothers of the past built for us? Is it our intent to persist in ignoring the intellectual qualities for which Freemasonry has been historically known, to violate the protocols upon which we have thrived for centuries and surrender our ethics to the demands of the present-day world or do we restore those qualities through a commitment to succeed and to a re-vamped educational process?

It is no great mystery as to where, when and why we have failed. However, there is no one mitigating factor that has caused the dramatic loss in numbers. Multiple factors certainly played a role, such as increased number of deaths, sociological changes in the environment, and self-centeredness of the populace.

But, I would suggest that a major dramatic cause for our loss of significance and influence in society has been our response to the loss in numbers. The most visible challenge each brother assuming a leadership role faced, was a declining membership, and herein begins our decline, and herein it continues in both numbers and prestige. Our leadership has simply failed to retain the vision of our purpose. That response not only impacted our influence in society but actually accelerated the decrease in numbers. We need look back no farther than 30 to 35 years to observe the beginning of the staggering decrease in membership numbers along with our impact on American society.

In North America we have recognized that our numbers have been on the decline since our peak membership in 1959. At that time we had 4,103,161 members. However, I observed with increasing concern, starting in 1980 as a Grand Secretary, the rapid decrease in numbers that was occurring. This rate of decrease has continued through the past 30 to 35 years.

I did some research in preparation for a paper that I delivered to the Masonic Restoration Foundation two years ago. It supported the observation I made back in the early 80s, "that if we continue to destroy the perceived value for a man to say 'I am a Freemason,' we ran the risk of losing the 90% of our members who we acknowledged are not active participants in the Craft, yet pay their dues annually for that perceived value. That is exactly what has been taking place for the past three decades.

From 1959 to 1979, the twenty-year period following our peak, the loss in numbers was 18.10%. The loss from 1979 to 1999, the next twenty years was 42.16% and the loss from 1979 to 2009 was 41.45%. Our total decline in membership over the fifty years from 1959 to 2009 is 64.78%. Our loss to the present time is now three quarters of our peak membership.

Suspension from the Craft for nonpayment of dues 35 years ago was almost unthinkable. Now it takes place in the thousands annually. We continue to make excuses, blaming the increased rate of deaths of our members as the principle cause for the decrease in numbers but discount the marked increase in suspensions and resignations. The suspensions and resignations must be in consequence of our own members losing respect for the Craft. The time is long overdue for us to stop making excuses for failure and begin seeking a foundation for success.

However, the catastrophic loss of our image in society is both a cause and the result of our continuing emphasis of the need for quantity of members instead of the quality of the member. As our numbers declined we have been willing to sacrifice the prestige of the fraternity to regain the numbers. Along with the prestige, our influence in society diminished. With the loss of prestige, the perceived value of membership was lost with it and the numbers plummeted.

This observation is not to be taken as a disapproval of those members accepted over the last thirty years who have become deserving brothers. One of the major factors for the success of the Craft has been its willingness to accept men from all social strata of society. However, we cannot ignore the marked increase in Masonic trials that has taken place over that span of time for un-Masonic conduct. All "social strata" does not mean all "classes" of man.

During my first years as a Grand Secretary, Masonic trials were an extreme rarity. Now they are a routine occurrence. I recall a quotation I once read, "The Craft can do much in the transformation of character, but it cannot transform material." Our failure to guard the west gate has impacted us far more than we would like to admit. We have simply failed to use enough black balls and now we are paying the price.

Nor can we fail to note the decrease in the number of professional men who have affiliated during that same span of time. Both of these factors must be accepted as having an impact on our numbers and our image, reducing the attraction to Freemasonry. Society will always judge on the worst, never on the best, nor even on the average.

We are the most unique fraternal organization that has ever existed. We are also the oldest and most successful. We should not be imitating other organizations. We should be building upon the uniqueness of our own. Many fraternal organizations were created and structured on the Masonic fraternity. Today most of them no longer exist and if we study these fraternities and the road they took to their demise, we will find great similarities on the road that we are currently traveling.

And why do we continue in our attempts to buy back our prestige by raising large sums of money and contributing it to public charities. We cannot hope to achieve the success of those charities whose entire goal is for the specific purpose of the charity. The charities will get the credit for the use of the money and we become regarded as a collection agency for them.

Many North American Masonic leaders have unfortunately bought into the political correctness attitude that permeates our society. This attitude supports our willingness to lower our standards of acceptance and has proven a disaster for our Craft. My Brothers, Freemasonry is not for every man. For those who have ears to hear, let it be known; not every man deserves to be a Freemason. Again, I recall reading more than twenty years ago, "We should tilt the balance of admission in favor of the quality of a few than the quantity of the undeserving."

Freemasonry has always been an elite organization. Yet, there are leaders today who feel that elitism is a dirty word when applied to the Craft. We must acknowledge that one of the reasons we became as great as we have was a result of our acceptance of good men, regardless of their occupation or status in society. This was a highly radical move considering the class structure of society of that day.

We must also recognize, however, that an even more important reason for our greatness was that we attracted some of the most prominent and greatest men from those societies. These men were the ones who structured the most significant fraternal organization ever conceived. These men represented an elite segment of society, elite in the sense of their intellectualism, visibility and influence. Without these men, we would not be what we are today. We are the beneficiaries of what those men created.

We have been failing to attract men of this caliber for the last three to four decades. My Brothers, every man wants to belong to an elite organization and were we to permanently lose that quality of "elitness," we lose our greatest visible image to society. When the decision was made that we would accept only good men, we became elitist and we must remain elitist.

Let's face it, you and I could never have structured what we have inherited. These early brothers crafted the foundation of Freemasonry and what they have created; we have no right to destroy. The men who created the early visual image of our Craft were of a superior intellectual level than are most of us and they were highly visible in their societies. But, it took more than their intellectualism. It took a dedication to creating something that never had existed in the past. It took a vision to see beyond the mundane. It took a vision that in essence, created the concept of a democratic society during the age of Enlightenment. I quote Margaret Jacob from her book, *Living the Enlightenment*, "Modern civil society was invented during the Enlightenment in the new enclaves of sociability of which Freemasonry was the most avowedly constitutional and aggressively civic." It was these visionary men, in the ideological enclaves of

Freemasonry, who fomented the foundation of the United States of America. These men created an ideal and we must remain idealistic in our goals.

The most idealistic style of Freemasonry that I have found in the world today exists in Latin America. They have retained much of the idealistic thinking of the past. It is impressive what they continue to achieve in that area of the world. They continue to express much of the character we had developed in our past. In some countries they operate universities. They feed and school significant segments of the population. They operate hospitals and health centers and provide much care for the widows of their members and their expression of the brotherhood of man far exceeds what we know today in North America.

We may rebut with the observation that we do much of the same in North America, and indeed we do but on a totally different scale. Recognize the environment in which they must operate; a far more hostile environment with much more poverty than we have ever known. Yet, they have not lost their commitment to the principles and precepts of Freemasonry. They have not surrendered the soul of the Craft for the sake of impressive numbers. They continue to attract the segment of society that we are failing to attract and they continue to carry the image that we once had.

I suspect that they have thrived with that idealism intact as a result of the ongoing challenges continually faced for their very existence. The prevailing religion of Latin America is Catholicism, a religion that has not looked favorably upon Freemasonry since the 1700s. They also have struggled against oppressive forms of governments and radical societal elements. A Grand Master in Latin America was assassinated just a few years ago.

Freemasonry in America has never been confronted with

these challenges and that perhaps, is a major cause for its ongoing success in much of the world while declining in North America. The only major challenge that American Freemasonry has known, followed the Morgan affair and we survived it as a far stronger fraternity. Now, lacking challenges, we have changed from a hugely successful fraternal structure into one of invisibility, complacency and perhaps apathy.

There can be little doubt that the public image of Freemasonry has eroded considerably, one of going from a highly sought after organization to one of public solicitation for whomever we can convince to join. We have gone from an organization selective of its members to one of almost begging for numbers.

It is vitally important to the future of Freemasonry, and frankly to the world, that we once again become an attractive force to the segment of society, that has the potential to provide the visionary leadership to restore Freemasonry to its past prominence; men with not only the vision but with the determination and commitment to something other than for themselves.

The greatest challenges with which Freemasonry was confronted in its past has been external to the Craft. The greatest challenges confronting us today and in our foreseeable future are internal. They are from a leadership with limited vision and with an ego-driven need for self aggrandizement. The National Grand Lodge of France was almost totally destroyed recently by the actions of a single ego-driven Grand Master.

Our leadership today must be able to extend their vision beyond projects that are of little or no consequence to the future of Freemasonry. They must be capable of divesting themselves of any ego dedicated to self-satisfaction and accept the responsibilities they assumed in accepting a leadership position in Freemasonry.

In my travels over thirty years, I was able to observe much of the difference between the Freemasonry as practiced in North America and the Freemasonry practiced in most of the world. Our requirements to become a Freemason and to remain a Freemason pales to what the rest of the world requires. While we continue to insist upon low initiation fees and dues (in the hundreds of dollars), most of the world measures their membership requirements in the thousands of dollars. While we eliminate or reduce the requirements for learning, it is part of the required progression to secure membership in much of the world. While we are satisfied to have 10% of our members attend our meetings, attendance is required at all meetings in much of the world. Several years ago I reviewed the Constitution of the Grand Lodge of Paraguay. Written in the Constitution is a requirement of attendance at all meetings and if two successive meetings are missed without a justifiable cause, the brother is subject to suspension.

In preparation for a paper I delivered at a Masonic symposium held at UCLA, twenty years ago, I learned from *The Master Builders* by Dr. Wayne A. Huss that the "the admission fee in these early (Pennsylvania) lodges was equivalent to 30 days' wages and over half the estimated annual food budget for an unskilled laborer." In addition the brother was expected to pay his share of the food, drink, and charitable contributions.

I read recently in the publication, *Laudable Pursuit: A 21st Century Response to Dwight Smith*, that in 1897, the average Lodge dues were $50 and the initiation fee was $200. That would equate to $1037 for annual dues and $4151 for initiation fees in 2002.

A research paper written by Mohamad Yatim, was published in the fall issue of *The Journal of the Masonic*

Society with the title, "Freemasonry and Your Return on Investment." He introduced the paper with a question asked frequently by our membership, "Have we cheapened our fraternity?" This is not a new question. I was asking the same one over 35 years ago. There is no doubt as to the answer to that question and there was no doubt 35 years ago. And yet, we have done precious little, other than to continue to acknowledge the answer. Whenever proposals are made to increase dues and fees our members act as though we were trying to impoverish them, the same members who would think nothing about paying much more for an evening for food, drink or entertainment or even a carton of cigarettes. There is a North American Grand Lodge that for two consecutive years voted down a twenty five cent increase in grand lodge dues. It is simply a matter of priority. With the perceived value gone, it became no longer, a priority.

Brother Yatim revealed in his research paper a chart showing Lodge fees and dues in eight lodges in the United States and Canada dating back as far as 1854 and continuing to 1955. The highest initiation fee was $100.00 in 1904. Considering inflation and labor prices, the equivalent in today's money is $11,500. Eliminating that Lodge as perhaps an anomaly, the average fee in today's currency, for the other seven lodges was $3282 and the average per annum dues were $286.

Of course, the small number of lodges involved in the random sampling creates a greater margin of error but even assuming the worst sampling error, it is quite evident that the cost to be a Freemason was considerably higher in our past than it is today.

A week and a half ago I was attending a communication of the Grand Lodge of Spain in Barcelona, when they voted to raise the grand lodge dues from €8 to €9. That evening I expressed to the Grand Master, that I was amazed that grand lodge dues were only €9 per annum. He told me that was monthly dues, not annual. Also they had a €30 per year assessment for charitable purposes plus a fee for a building fund.

So today, we sit and lament that our past was much greater than our present. We watch those great material structures that we built on the quantity of the membership, being traded for something with far less grandeur and for which we surrendered our intellectual and mystical structures built on the quality of the member of the past. As our subordinate lodge buildings are crumbling and becoming eyesores to the public, we continue to concentrate much of our efforts in raising funds to give away, in an ill-fated attempt to buy back the respect and admiration that we surrendered along with the quality of the Craft.

We continue to place the blame for our failings, on everything and everyone but ourselves. We refuse to alter our approach to solving the dilemma. We continue to emphasize the need for numbers and reject attempts to change our antiquated dues and fees structures because of a concern of losing members.

Let me give you a possible case scenario. If a lodge is charging $50 a year dues and they increase it to $200, resulting in a loss of three quarters of their membership; they would be receiving the same amount of dues income, they would reduce their operating costs and the remaining brothers are those who truly placed a value of membership in Freemasonry.

Much resistance has been offered by some of our leadership to the concept of Traditional Observance Freemasonry, because, they claim, we are trying to change into some new form of Freemasonry foreign to America, when actually it is simply an intent to change back into something American Freemasonry once was. At the present time, it is possibly the greatest hope that we have for survival as an influential and respected organization.

In Dwight Smith's book, *Whither Are We Traveling?*, published in the 1960s, the answers to his first three questions reveal powerful reasons for the failing of North American Freemasonry. 1. "Can we expect Freemasonry to retain its past glory and prestige unless the level of leadership is raised above its present position?" 2. "How well are we guarding the West Gate?" 3. "Has Freemasonry become too easy to obtain?" My brothers, we are failing on all points.

Dwight Smith, a Past Grand Master and a Past Grand Secretary, was indeed, a visionary. His observations made over fifty years ago, are no less applicable today as they were then.

I spoke last Saturday at our Academy of Masonic Knowledge, when a brother pointed out to me that it wasn't only Freemasonry that was suffering in our present climate. Most organizations are encountering the same dramatic loss. I readily agreed with him. This decline was being abetted by a societal change in our environment. For several generations, interest in any organization dedicated to helping others had become passé in American society. Thus all organizations with a similar character were facing a similar fate. Interestingly, their solutions to these challenges were the same as we are following today: aggressively seek numbers, reduce admission requirements and grant more recognition for less effort.

However, the loss of most of these organizations was of little consequence to society. Hundreds of fraternal organizations have ceased to exist without a whimper but most were little known to begin with. However, as a result of the impact that Freemasonry has had upon society, its loss will be far more pronounced than any of the other organizations. We were the largest, the most visible, via impact and prestigious, via composition. We will also be the most missed.

There is much being written by historians today concerning Freemasonry but you will find very little written about other fraternal organizations simply because of the significance to the world forged by our Craft. This significance provides for us a far greater potential for recovery, simply because of the respect that remains from our past. But that recovery is in our hands.

Now, we must decide what we want to be. If we want to remain a little respected and declining organization, almost invisible in modern-day society, all we need do is continue to travel on the same road we have been traveling for over three decades, a road to oblivion. It assures our extinction.

If we want to recapture the vast influence we once had. If we want to again become a highly visible and respected organization in society, if we want to once again become the movers and shakers that helped shape the United States of America and the world, then we must change the road that we are traveling. Our future lies not, in what we once were. Our future lies in each one of us and what we can be.

If the Freemasonry of today was the Freemasonry of fifty years ago, I doubt that I would be a Freemason today. The mystique of the Craft and the men of the quality that I knew then, are gone.

A very proud Filipino Freemason once wrote, "And when the Great Architect of the Universe shall call my number and I shall stand naked and alone, before the Great White Throne and He shall ask about my nation and my organization, with my head held high, looking straight into HIS eyes, I would with humility be proud to respond, FILIPINO, sir and a FREEMASON.

Could we do the same? My brothers, what do we want to be?

[18]

Where We Are, Where We Are Going, and Where We Want to Go

Given at a Traditional Observance Lodge in California

S everal years ago I was asked to speak at a symposium here in California, to which I readily agreed. Only then did I inquire on what subject I would speak. I was told that the preferred topic would be the American Enlightenment and Benjamin Franklin's involvement with it.

My knowledge of the American Enlightenment at the time might have been described, at best, as minuscule. The required research served to remind me of how much I disliked sitting in a library studying in preparation to write a paper. It also reminded me, however, of my passion for learning a new subject. I don't know if the audience benefited that day from my presence but I certainly benefited from the required preparation.

This time, when I was asked to come to California to speak I inquired first concerning the subject on which I would be speaking and was told that the preferred subject would involve world Freemasonry. Now, that is a subject about which I do know a little about and I am fairly well known for my knowledge and opinions concerning it. What you hear from me tonight, therefore, will concern far less what I have read to prepare and far more what I have seen, what I have learned and my opinions from those observations.

About eight years ago, I was introduced to the President of Portugal as a "noted Masonic philosopher" and I stood there at that time thinking, "Why would anyone call me a philosopher?" In thinking about this introduction later on, I realized that the one thing that I cannot debate about myself is that I have opinions. Indeed, I am probably most known for my opinions, and since it is the opinions of philosophers for which they are known, I guess I fit into that category as well as any other. I don't think it is all that important that we be categorized in life, anyway. Regardless of the category into which I may be placed, I well know that no matter how important I may ever think I am to this world, a year after I'm dead the world will ask, "Tom who?"

Rest assured that what I say to you tonight is totally dedicated to my firm conviction of what is best for Freemasonry and in turn, for the world today. I am also just as firmly convinced that Freemasonry's role in the world today is no less important than it was at any other period in history.

I noted in the flier that was sent out for this meeting that the subject title was: "Where we were, where we are and where we want to go?" Actually, I will not speak on where we were. Historians have been writing on this subject for a considerable number of years and it would certainly be presumptuous of me to venture into their realm. I will note, however, that it is significant that in the last decade and a half, historians have become far more prolific in analyzing and writing about the influence of the Masonic Fraternity on the evolution of civil society. It is also significant that many of these historians are not members of the Craft. UCLA's own Margaret Jacob has become one of the most visible and astute of these historians. My subject will be: where we are, where we are going and where we want to go.

In order for us to understand the significance of this subject, it is necessary that we understand something about the characteristics of Freemasonry on a world level. I have had the great privilege to be able to travel over a considerable part of the globe. During these travels, I began to comprehend that the structural philosophy of Freemasonry is universal.

I wish I would be able to look back fifty years from now to see how these new Grand Lodges in Africa impact their developing societies and to see how those societies influence the development of Freemasonry. It is also going to be very interesting to watch the newly developing Grand Lodges in Eastern Europe. They are currently adopting the philosophical style but are unfortunately, being influenced by outside forces that may compel them to become something else. In addition, there are challenges existing there that are going to be unique in the evolution of their societies.

One interesting observation I have also made, is that the development of early Freemasonry in Russia played an almost opposite role in its relationship to society. As I have indicated, Freemasonry in the world was greatly influenced and probably even driven by the needs of the society in which it existed. In the case of Russia, instead of society driving the development of style of Freemasonry, Freemasonry played a far greater role in driving the development of Russian society. I have found no other country in which this phenomenon has so clearly occurred. The character of Russian society, to a great extent, was developed in emulation of the enlightened characteristics and leadership of Freemasonry. This period in Russia Freemasonry came to a close with Catherine the Great.

With this brief background, we can more easily understand where we are, where we are going and where we want to go. Hopefully, we may also comprehend why we are failing in some areas of the world, while thriving in most others. Although we will be looking at Freemasonry on a world level, I will deal more specifically with the Freemasonry of the United States. I will also make some candid observations that tend to run against mainstream thought of American leadership. Again, I remind you that these are my opinions and anyone is free to disagree with me.

Prior to the creation of the World Conference of Masonic Grand Lodges, American Masonic leaders rarely visited beyond the borders of the United States. Today, a number of our leaders are beginning to see that the Freemasonry of the world can be distinctively different in its operation from what they know. For us to understand where we are in the United States, it is important for us to see where Freemasonry is in other areas of the world.

In almost every Grand Lodge in the world outside of the English-speaking countries, Freemasonry continues to increase in membership numbers and its influence continues to be exerted in their respective societies. Although there are several factors influencing the decline of the Craft in English speaking societies, the direction in style must be a major component. Challenges by religious institutions and governments have played a role in the decline but the trend toward a public charitable-like institution can be found in each one.

If we look at Freemasonry in the world in general, we find it is not only growing in membership numbers, but it is spreading over wider areas of the world than perhaps since its beginning.

It would be extremely prudent for us, here in America, to take a very close look at those Grand Lodges experiencing the greatest success and begin to consider the logic in trying to emulate their blueprint for succeeding.

In almost every case, the requirement for membership

is far more rigid than anything we know here. The cost to become a Freemason and the cost to remain a Freemason in many Grand Lodges can run into the thousands of dollars.

The requirement for members to study and to learn in most Grand Lodges of the world would put to shame the most stringent requirements of any Grand Lodge in United States. In Brazil and Argentina, for example, prior to a man's being considered for crafting or raising, he will have given several learned papers on Freemasonry and pass an examination questioning his knowledge of the Craft. In addition, in most Grand Lodges of the world, investigation on a petitioner and advancement through the degrees may run many months and, in some cases, years.

The result is a waiting list for men who want to become part of Freemasonry. I learned when visiting the Grand Lodge of Iceland, that they had a waiting list of six years for anyone wishing to become a member. Whether we consider all or any of these requirements right or wrong, relevant or irrelevant to us, the fact remains that they are thriving and we are not.

Much of the American Masonic leadership for years has stated that Freemasonry in America must be open to everyone. Any restrictions, either financial or intellectual, should not be part of Freemasonry in America. Elitism has almost been made into a dirty word for Freemasonry. When we defined our position to accept only good men, we became elitist—and, like it or not, that is a major cause for our greatness.

If we judge the position of where World Freemasonry is today and exclude the United States and several other English-speaking countries we must recognize that its position is quite secure and its future positive.

Where we are going on a world level, becomes a little more complex. Because of the challenges of religious institutions and in some cases governments interfering with the freedom of operation of the Craft, where we are going is somewhat more clouded.

I suspect that you are all familiar with the challenges that have faced the Grand Lodges of England, Ireland and Scotland recently by several different religious denominations as well as the confrontation by the government of Great Britain with members of the constabulary for being members of the Masonic Fraternity. This is not something new. It has occurred sporadically over the history of Freemasonry. However, no religious leadership or despotic government politicians have been able to destroy it. I find it symbolic, in a sense, that some of the strongest and most active grand lodges operate in predominately Catholic countries and that denomination's leaders have historically been Freemasonry's most ardent adversaries.

There must be a concern with the instability of some of the newly constituted or reconstituted Grand Lodges in Eastern Europe. As a result of a different mindset that existed under communist rule, there now exists almost an inherent distrust of organizations. Masonic leadership, in many cases, must struggle with the need to stabilize Grand Lodge operation while facing challenges of opposing factions as well as the need to, in some cases, rein in their own great egos. In addition, the development of appendant bodies in these jurisdictions has created opposition to the Masonic authority of the Grand Lodge. This has resulted in schisms occurring, creating competing Grand Lodges in the same jurisdiction.

The potential to influence in the development of civil society by the Eastern European Grand Lodges cannot be overstated. Participation in this development, however, will depend upon commitment of the leadership to the Craft and not to their own ambitions along with restraint of interfering appendant bodies.

Some African Grand Lodges have also been faced with this interference of appendant bodies in Grand Lodge operations. The result has been that in more than one African jurisdiction, there are now two Grand Lodges. Issues like this can never benefit the Craft or the society.

An even greater concern in Africa may be that there is such a respect for the potential influence of Freemasonry, that it may become desirable for leaders to use it for political purposes. The presidents of two African countries are also Grand Masters of their Grand Lodges. In addition, other African presidents, although not Grand Masters are active Freemasons. This is not necessarily a bad situation, nor am I implying that it is used today for political purposes. Indeed, it is desirable to see Freemasons active in the operation of their respective countries so long as the Craft is not used as a base for power in politics.

Another point of concern for Freemasonry today is that some Regular Grand Lodges are granting recognition to competing Grand Lodges in the same jurisdictions that Regular Freemasonry exists. The result is a dilution of the potential influence of the Craft in that jurisdiction. This not only weakens Regular Freemasonry but it damages the image of the Craft in general, to the public.

All of these issues will seriously challenge where Freemasonry is going at the present time. It is important not to forget, however, that Freemasonry has been faced with these types of challenges almost since its inception. In spite of them, the philosophy of the Craft and the strength and significance of the membership has carried it beyond all challenges. Consider the Morgan affair. Freemasonry came close to dying out in some jurisdictions, but it not only survived, it eventually flourished. These challenges, however, came from without, not from within, as is happening now.

The greatest questions facing Freemasonry about where it is going today, is in the United States of America. We have been highly regarded for many years, because we represented the largest number of Freemasons in any area the world as well as the wealthiest. Freemasonry, however, is declining here at an alarming rate and not only declining in numbers but our image in society has been plummeting over the last thirty years. We will look at this phenomenon more closely shortly.

The greatest uncertainty that needs to be seriously considered today is: Where do we want to go? Freemasons historically have played a vital role not only in the evolution of civil society but in leading in the struggle for freedom and equality in many parts of the world for generations. It has been one of the best-known organizations in existence for 300 years and in spite of its detractors and its enemies has become one of the most admired and respected. We would expect that our decision of where we want to go is therefore to retain or return to that status.

Fortunately, in most parts of the world, this admiration and respect remains, so the goal for them should be to retain them. Freemasons continue to lead in the evolution of civil societies as well as in the struggle for the rights of man. They continue to hold positions of prominence in the development and operation of their respective countries as well as eminence in diverse fields of endeavor. I am constantly impressed with the significance of our Masonic brothers that I continue to meet in other countries. There should be little concern on our part as to where Freemasonry is, where it is going or where it wants to go in most of the world.

Now, however, we must take a look at these issues in this country. It must be our greatest concern, not only because we represent the Freemasonry here, but because we are representing one of its greatest potential failures.

Nowhere else in the world, with the possible exception of the Grand Lodges of Australia, is the threat to extinction more visible.

If we survey our past membership along with the worlds past membership, it is like a study of Who's Who in the history of the world of great men. No other organization can even come close in imitating what we were. Our brothers were men with vision, vision to see far beyond those mundane exercises that we here attribute to Freemasonry today.

We in the United States of America have inherited from our past brothers not only one of the greatest examples of Masonic influence in the development of a civil society, but also in the development of a system of government that has served as a template of idealism of what can be, to the rest of the world. Freemasonry in the United States served our society admirably for close to 250 years, and if we must consider it today as failing we need look back no further than fifty years and probably closer to thirty and that, my Brothers, must include many of us.

I would propose that it was at this time in our history, that our leadership began to lose its vision of the purpose of the Craft. It is the time when we became more engrossed in the need for large numbers and geared our efforts to securing those numbers. In addition, it was also the time that in order to regain the respect and admiration of society we once had, we tried to buy it back by concentrating much of our energy and efforts in raising and giving large sums of money away to charities. Very few of our leaders in recent years have applied any effort during their term of office to any other projects than increasing numbers or raising money for charity. My brothers, this was not ever and is not now, the purpose of Freemasonry. If we have any hope of survival, we must become more introverted for our own preservation and realize that respect is earned, not bought.

First, let's take a look at where we are. In less than fifty years, we have lost over half of our membership. In that same span of time we have gone from being a highly respected and admired fraternity that attracted the greatest leaders in our communities, to becoming almost invisible and ignored. We have, in that same span of time, concocted various theories on why this is happening and developed numerous programs to try to stop it. We have placed far too much effort in trying to justify our failure and not nearly enough in understanding our past and building for our future.

The result is that in almost every case, we have not only failed, but we have seriously abetted its demise by contributing to the destruction of its image. The quality of the membership has become less important to most Masonic leaders in North America than the quantity of the members. Now, in spite of any camouflage we wish to spread across the face of Craft, we are, in the United States, in the process of dying.

Our image and influence have not waned as a result of the decrease in numbers; they have plummeted as a result of our response to it. Our willingness to accept those who, not too many years ago, could never have hoped to become members, will continue to serve to keep the quality man away in the future. This observation is not meant to be a condemnation of American leadership. We have inherited a failing style that has characterized the sociological condition of the times, but they have not changed it. We are simply a present end product of a system that has been eroding our Freemasonry for years. But, we must be greater than the system. We cannot afford to allow the sociological condition of the time to dictate our future.

Many North American Grand Lodges have jumped on the one-day-class bandwagon, looking at it as a panacea for all their woes. However, it is my firm conviction, and I hope that I will be proven wrong, for we cannot reverse the impact, that it is perhaps the greatest tragedy to befall Freemasonry in America.

I know that statistics will support the fact that some Grand Lodges have possibly curtailed, at least temporarily, the rate of decline with them. I know that statistics will indicate the some of the subordinate lodges have gained some leadership from one-day-class members, and I know that statistically, we can claim some quality membership from them. These results, however, are evidence of treating a symptom, not the disease; we are placing a band aid on a hemorrhage. There is no way to measure the negative impact that it has had on the attractive force of the professional man. One grand lodge took in at least two convicted felons in a one day class. What type of an image do we therefore, present to the community? Unfortunately, there is no way to compile a statistic of how much damage was done by those who should never have been admitted.

There can be little doubt that the public image of Freemasonry has suffered considerably by going from an elite and highly sought after organization to one of public solicitation for almost whomever we can convince to join. We have gone from an organization selective of its members to one almost begging for numbers. At least, that has become our public image. Unless we become capable of visualizing our Craft and its potential much farther into the future and on a much higher plane than we are now, we will continue to dilute any capability of being an impact in that future.

A noted Masonic author once wrote, "One bad man in your Craft will do you far more damage than any ten good men can ever do you good." My Brothers, we will always be judged by our worst, never by our best. There are probably far more peoples in the world looking for us to fail, then to succeed.

How can we possibly justify the amount of effort and the amount of money that we continue to put into the raising of funds to give away to charities? Even as our numbers are plummeting, even as our buildings are crumbling, even as the quality of our membership is waning, we continue applying the same emphasis on trying to buy respect.

The uniqueness of Freemasonry promoted its survival, when hundreds of other organizations ceased to exist. Now, our leadership seems to think that our survival depends upon emulating the characteristics of organizations that are dying more rapidly today than are we. For almost three decades, we have tried to imitate civic organizations and social clubs and we continue to do so. What has that accomplished other than making us less unique? If we must die, at least let us die as an organization that historians will acknowledge as one that played a vital role in history and died doing the same.

Where we are and where we are going requires little debate on our part. Now, our leadership must decide where we want to go. If it is our intent to sacrifice any potential influence on society in the future, all we must do is continue along the path that we are currently following. But, if it is our intent to restore North American Freemasonry as a top quality organization possessing the capabilities of continuing to influence the evolution of our civil society, if we wish to fulfill our obligation to generations of our past brothers, if we truly want to be more than a collection agency for charities, or just an organization with the name "Freemasonry," then we must re-examine the direction we are going and decide where we want to go.

We know where we are, but we cannot continue with our head in the sand, denying that our future may be greatly limited. We must stop parasitizing the greatness of our past and start programming for the future. It must, however, be a future that encompasses the need to restore our quality and to attract great men. We must also restore the elitism that characterized our past. If we continue on the pathway we are currently following, it is highly doubtful that Freemasonry will be in existence in North America in the next 25 years, at least not in the form that we have known it.

Ask yourselves this question. "Would I have joined Freemasonry when I did, if it was then what it is now?" Freemasonry has been my life for forty-five years. I gave up my profession to dedicate myself to it, but when I ask myself this question, knowing what I know now, I seriously question whether I would have. And yet, Freemasonry is far too significant to the world to give up on it.

Now the future of the Craft is in our hands, my brothers. We are in the position of decision to impact where we will go in the future. We know where we are, we know where we are going and now we must decide where is it that we want to go.

[19]

Crafting the Mason

I have been asked to speak to the application of change as it can apply to North American Freemasonry in making the initiatic experience one of value when introducing a man into the Craft. Brothers Robert G. Davis and W. Kirk MacNulty are far more qualified to address the idealism of the historical application of Masonic philosophy than am I. However, with twenty years' experience as a Grand Secretary, I suspect that I am as qualified as anyone else to analyze the obstacles we must face in Crafting the Mason in the future of North American Freemasonry.

It is important that you understand that when I speak, I speak as one who has spent the last twenty-six years of his life working full-time in Freemasonry. Twenty-two of those years were spent as an officer of the Grand Lodge. Therefore, you must realize that I have full commitment to the structure of Grand Lodge operation. What I have to say, therefore, is not a criticism of the system but of the direction that we have taken with Freemasonry in North America.

It is a sad commentary, that North American Free-masonry has been de-emphasizing the significance of the initiation ritual as the foundation of the candidate's first exposure into a new dimension of life. Indeed we have been de-emphasizing the significance of all of our ritual. So why should we be surprised when we see the lack of quality in the ritual that exists today. It would pay us not to forget the old adage that says, "You have only one chance to make a first impression."

For more than thirty years, I have been expressing a great concern about the future of North American Freemasonry. For many of those years, there were very few of the North American leadership who wanted to listen to anything I had to say concerning that subject. Today, it has become the dominant subject of Masonic discussion. Now, the future of North American Freemasonry is seriously clouded and even its survival must be brought into question.

An observation I made several years ago was that if we continued on the pathway we are following and fail to recognize a need to adapt to what society needs, that we would probably not exist in North America in 25 years, at least not in any form that we recognize today. Please note that the adaptation must be for what society needs, not what society wants. I suspect that this character of the Craft might well be the paramount reason for our past success. However, our efforts at adaptation in the recent past have been to change into what we feel society wants rather than what society needs. The practice of the philosophy of Freemasonry should always direct that we bring others up to our standards not go down to theirs.

Very few, if any, Grand Lodges in recent years have failed to institute some type of a program designed for any purpose other than increasing membership. Indeed, very few Grand Lodges have any other type of major program other than raising money to give away to charities. If other types of programs do exist, even they have the ultimate end of increasing membership, even in the raising of money to give to charity. My Brothers, that is not the purpose of Freemasonry. This Craft did not impact the world by crushing it with large numbers or through supporting charities, even though much of our leadership seems to think that to be the case, or at least necessary today to be successful.

Even with all of these programs, however, we have failed in almost every way to even slow the rate of decline in membership numbers. And yet, we continue year after year to beat the same dead horse. Unless we begin to realize and acknowledge that we are failing to succeed, you can bet that we are going to fail.

One of our glaring weaknesses as leaders today is our inability to see the big picture of the Craft. We have become so enmeshed in issues of lesser magnitudes that we ignore the great ones for which the Craft is known and we have become so engrossed with issues that are not paramount to the purpose of Freemasonry that we have ignored those that are.

It is imperative, if we have any hope of succeeding, that we once again develop a long-range vision of where we are going and where we want to go. If we are going to develop that vision, then our leadership must once again begin to comprehend the philosophical purpose of Freemasonry. We must decide whether we wish to remain simply as a funnel for monies into charities or to once again participate in the evolution of civil society. We participated in that evolution in the past by accomplishing our goal of making a good man better.

Please do not feel that my evaluations amount to a condemnation of our present-day leadership. They are simply representative of what amounts to the culmination of an evolutionary process that changed North American Freemasonry from an elite, philosophical, learned, highly respected society into a less than elite, almost ignored organization devoted to charitable objectives.

More than fifteen years ago, I began looking at what was taking place in Australia and suggesting that we should seriously consider a similar program in North America. I made an observation at a Landmarks committee meeting, "that we will never change our old lodges, and if we cannot change the old, there is only one thing left to do, and that is to create new." I am convinced today that creating new lodges of a different style is perhaps our best hope for survival and that is the intent of an organization that has been created for the purpose. Both Brother Davis and I serve on the council of the Masonic Restoration Foundation."The MRF is structured to promote the study and understanding of traditional Freemasonry and to provide education and support for Traditional Observance Lodges in recognized jurisdictions in North America.

When discussions first began several years ago regarding a "Foundation for Masonic Reconstruction," we were referring to adopting a European Concept style of Freemasonry. We found, however, that there were those within the leadership of North American Freemasonry who opposed this change, using the rationale that North America had its own style of Freemasonry and that we should not change to the style of somewhere else.

We can argue all we wish against changing to a different style of Freemasonry but like it or not, we are rapidly showing the characteristics of a dying organization while most of the world's Grand Lodges are continuing to thrive. Is it not time that we begin to recognize that all of the programs that we have instituted in the last twenty years to solve our membership issues have shown no major significance in the direction that we are going, and begin to study and emulate a style of the Craft that is succeeding?

I have made the observation during my many years of travel to Masonic jurisdictions around the world, that even though the philosophical purposes of Freemasonry are universally the same, the operational philosophy varies depending upon the environment in which it exists. What is significant, however, is that only in the charitable style found in North America has the leadership lost its vision of the purpose of Freemasonry and its obligation to its roots of taking good men and making them better, via a stimulus to learn and a commitment of time to the Craft. We continue to lower requirements to become a member, requirements to remain a member and almost any requirement to improve a member.

As a result, we have evolved into a form of Freemasonry ignorant of its heritage, its purpose and its potential. As this self-perpetuating ignorance has increased, it has been followed by an ongoing erosion of the general quality of the membership, followed by an increasing rate of decline of not only an interest in membership, but of our image in society, a phenomenon that was highly predictable.

I have spent a considerable amount of time over the last dozen years visiting grand lodges as well as subordinate lodges throughout the world and I am greatly impressed with how much influence they continue to have in the societies in which they exist. Freemasonry is probably growing and expanding into new territories at a more rapid rate than it has in over the last 100 years, while we here in North America struggle to sustain its life, and we, my Brothers, must shoulder the responsibility.

I speak now to what I consider our greatest hope not only of regaining our rightful place in society, but of survival as a viable institution. We can continue to de-emphasize the significance of the initiatic experience of the new candidate and ignore our greatest opportunity of impacting him in his introduction to what could very well become his way of life, or we can examine its significance in our past or where it retains its significance in the present, and change. I know, without the shadow of a doubt, that without it,

I would not be speaking now. Think back to the impact you felt on that first night when you walked through the preparing room door.

When I began contemplating this presentation, even though I am on the foundation council, I found that I did not fully understand the difference between what we referred to as a European Concept Lodge and a Traditional Observance (TO) Lodge. I presented this question to the president of the foundation, and his response was that "it is so named because of an observance of the traditional initiatic elements of Continental European Freemasonry." He went on to write that "this means the lodges have a very solemn approach to holding meetings and conferring degrees: the Chamber of Reflection is used as part of the initiation ceremony, they incorporate higher dues and fees, include festive boards and require a strict dress code, have longer time frames between degrees and required learning, along with other nuances." Most European grand lodges incorporate these characteristics into their operations. It is perhaps the other nuances that make the greatest difference. A significant goal of the foundation is to create an atmosphere where the members can learn the lessons of Freemasonry and incorporate them into their daily lives.

Very frankly, I find that the definition and practice of a Continental, European Concept Lodge and a Traditional Observance Lodge to be very similar. Much of what is to be found in a Traditional Observance Lodge will also be found in a European Concept lodge. The most significant difference is the emphasis placed upon the initiatic process of the individual.

The foundation also recognized early on, that what we were trying to create must operate in full accordance with Grand Lodge regulations in all jurisdictions. The Masonic Restoration Foundation readily acknowledges the supremacy of Grand Lodge authority in any given jurisdiction. For that reason, these new lodges must conform to the operating requirements of Grand Lodge law in each jurisdiction. Out of necessity, this will mean that flexibility must be an integral part of the goals of the foundation. Each Grand Jurisdiction may show variation in the new lodges created but in order to be termed "Traditional Observance," they will have to meet certain criteria as established by the foundation.

This is not an attempt to subvert Freemasonry, but rather, it is an attempt to restore Freemasonry to its age of grandeur. Perhaps, in the long run, the greatest contribution that Freemasonry has made to the evolution of civil society was in providing an environment wherein great minds were stimulated. It was through that environment that it played such an integral role in the age of Enlightenment. Traditional Observance Lodges should be far more suited for that environment.

I have no delusion that I will live to see the impact of what this approach may produce in North American Freemasonry, but I am convinced, that it offers our greatest potential to reclaim what our past brothers bequeathed to us.

The greatest challenge that will confront us is that it represents change. We are all familiar with the phrase, "we never did it that way, before." Well, my Brothers, we did. What we have ended up with today is a result of change. What the foundation is looking to do is restoration.

We in North America have excised from the Craft, those intellectual and philosophical standards for which it was known throughout most of its existence. The goal of the foundation is to restore those standards. We have made elitism a dirty word when applied to the Craft. The foundation hopes to restore elitism to the Craft. If we enforce our goal of accepting only good men, then we restore elitism.

We have spent far too much time in recent years seeking excuses to justify failure. It is far past time that we recognize that our failures are our fault. We are the ones responsible for converting North American Freemasonry into something it was never meant to be, and now we are the ones who must shoulder the responsibility of restoring it. Ask yourselves, my Brothers, this question; would I have joined Freemasonry when I did, if it were then, what it is today? I doubt whether I would have, and that is not so long ago.

Now we are being given the opportunity to participate in the reconstruction of the Craft and its restoration to its deserved greatness. We can restore our influence to impact the ongoing evolution of civil society. It is going to require change and it is going to require visionary leadership with a commitment to a higher standard for Freemasonry. We have it within our power, to change the ultimate destiny of our Craft. I would not want our generation to become a footnote in some future historian's book that it was our generation that destroyed Freemasonry in North America.

[20]

The Grand Lodge of Iran in Exile

Given to that Grand Lodge in 2011

Once again it is my privilege and great pleasure to be able to address this distinguished Grand Lodge. I have so many good friends here that for me it is like returning home. Certainly, those of you who have known me for some time, know the great respect I hold for this Grand Lodge, the Grand Officers and the brothers that I have been privileged to know. I sincerely appreciate all the kindness and hospitality that you have shown me over the years and also the ongoing support that you have given to the World Conference of Masonic Grand Lodges.

There is a great need today for the influence of Masonic philosophy to serve as a guiding light in man's relationship to man. In order for this to occur, however, it is necessary for Freemasons to know and understand Freemasonry not only within the confines of their own Grand Jurisdictions or even within regional jurisdictions but on a world level. The World Conference of Masonic Grand Lodges has been serving as an environment to bring together Masonic leaders from around the world and to encourage them to develop a better understanding and appreciation of Masonic philosophy. The Grand Lodge of Iran in Exile has been a constant supporter of the World Conference since its formal structuring. I suspect that most of you have acquired a far greater appreciation for the need of a stabilizing philosophy as a result of your firsthand experience with tyrannical suppression than those of us who have not had that experience.

Unfortunately the conditions in the world that caused your Grand Lodge to operate in exile from your homeland have changed little over the ensuing years. Even as we can note progress in some areas of the world we see deterioration of conditions in others. Certainly, the conditions in your native country continue to provide a barrier for most of you to even return to visit. One of my great personal hopes is to live long enough to see that happen; to see you; my brothers have the opportunity to return.

It is comforting on one hand to recognize that Freemasonry is continuing to expand and develop in some areas of the world. Freemasonry in much of Eastern Europe is maturing in spite of great odds with which they have been faced. Freemasonry in Africa is expanding into countries where it has not existed with new Grand Lodges being consecrated offering for many their first exposure to a concept of the Brotherhood of Man under the Fatherhood of God.

On the other hand, the Craft is being confronted with challenges unprecedented in our past. Never before have we had so many "experts" on the subject of Freemasonry expounding their knowledge on the scale provided through the World Wide Web. Never before have irregular forms of Freemasonry actively challenged the stability of our Craft. Never before have Masonic leaders questioned the protocols that has sustained us for three centuries.

One advantage afforded to irregular forms of the Craft is that they are not subject to operating within the parameters of the protocols and landmarks that have created the image for which regular Freemasonry is historically known. The World Wide Web has provided them with a medium through which they can extend their influence to those who are unaware of the difference and unfortunately, there are leaders within regular Freemasonry today who through lack of knowledge support that influence.

Freemasonry has thrived as the premier fraternal organization in the world much longer than has any other. It has thrived because it attracted some of the greatest men this world has ever known while at the same time remaining steadfast in its purpose for existence. Its philosophy impacted the development of every country in which it was found and it did so by taking good men and making them better men. These men became better men by being shown that they were much more capable than they ever thought possible through the Masonic emphasis on the need to become more knowledgeable and more dedicated to society's needs.

The Grand Lodge of Iran in Exile sits in the unique position today by not only serving as a living example of the impact that can be created by religious radicalism through evil in men, but as an even more important example of the survivability of an organization based upon the good in mankind. Religious radicalism in any guise becomes a colossal threat to man's inherent right to be free. This threat becomes even more pronounced when those radical religious leaders come in control of the government of their countries. Realistically, many of you are sitting here today for both of these reasons: the impact of evil and the survivability of good.

Historically the greatness of Freemasonry and its contribution to society have left its greatest impression on societies with the greatest need for its philosophical purposes. This knowledge may provide little consolation for those who have felt the sting of tyranny but it should provide solace to all of us looking at the big picture of its accomplishments. When and I will not say if, Iranian citizens regain their rights and freedoms, the challenge to our Craft will be reinstituted in Iran by the need for Masonic philosophy as a stabilizing force even as it has it has done so in other countries, for centuries.

My brothers, we—you and I—can live in hope with the realization that evil perpetuated by man has always had a temporary lifespan. Freemasonry will again operate with freedom in Iran and my brothers, your steadfast dedication to the philosophical principles of Freemasonry will provide the desperately needed material to fill that vacated niche. May the Grand Architect of the Universe be your guide. This Grand Lodge serves as an inspiration to me.

[21]

The College of Freemasonry

Scottish Rite Valley of Rochester, New York

I consider it a great privilege to be present at the College of Freemasonry. I regard the recognition of having an award for scholarship named for me as one of the greatest honors I have ever received and I remain totally humbled and appreciative to the Valley of Rochester for choosing to do so.

At the request of the chairman for this program, I will speak to you for a short time of the need in American Freemasonry for returning to an emphasis on Masonic education. I have frequently acknowledged the deficiency of educational programs in North American Freemasonry.

This was not always so, however. It is only in the last 30 or 35 years that we began to lose sight of that precept of Freemasonry of an emphasis on the acquisition of knowledge. We continue to express it in our rituals but have forgotten it in our practice. We have become so concerned over that period of time with the decline in quantity of the membership that we have forgotten the need for the quality of the membership and thus have neglected the need to educate our members.

The result is quite evident when we observe the decline in our lodges of the more prominent members of our society. It is also quite evident when we observe the ignorance of our members concerning the fundamental principles of

Freemasonry and the lack of intellectualism that was at one time a driving force for the Craft.

We must never forget, however that one of the principal reasons that Freemasonry rose to heights above all other organizations was because we accepted men from all social strata and set them in a lodge environment as equals. However, there is no denying that the visual image of Freemasonry to society was created by those great men and leaders who were our members in the past. Had either of these two factors been lacking, we could not have become what we did nor remain what we have.

It was our emphasis on the precept of continuing to acquire knowledge, however, that projected an image of an elite organization in American society, dedicated to making better men from good men. Freemasonry in North America has lost sight of that goal with the result that we have seriously damaged our image in society and deleted much of our influence to impact its ongoing evolution. It has also contributed to a loss of close to 75% of our membership in the United States.

In spite of all of the attempts that we have made to change North American Freemasonry, we have done little to educate our membership concerning our contributions to world societies and our impact on the world. How can we possibly expect there to be an interest in an organization in which so few of the members themselves even know what we are or our purpose for existence. It is quite evident that all of the changes that we have made to North American Freemasonry over the last thirty years, in our practices and our policies have not only failed to provide a solution but have proven detrimental to our future success.

I have found in recent years, however, an increasing realization by some of our leaders of the need of Masonic education. This realization was probably stimulated by some of the good young men who have been affiliating with us and who are seeking that intellectual presence that we promised. They have seen potential in the Craft that has been almost invisible for decades. Our great hope should be that we continue to find a leadership that can satisfy their quest.

We have acknowledged for decades the ongoing decline of interest in Freemasonry in North America and there is no one factor on which it to place the blame for this decline. But certainly the lack of knowledge by our members has to be a mitigating cause.

Perhaps our greatest hope for future success is that some of these good and I emphasize good young men can wrest control away from we old men, but they also must realize that they do not have all the answers.

I give much credit to the writings of Dan Brown in creating this increased interest if for no other reason than that he restored some of the mystique to Freemasonry that has been lost over the past thirty years. The mystique and the unknown of the Craft has been an attractive force to many men, providing a stimulus for them to want to become part of us. For some reason our leadership over the last quarter century or more have found it prudent to expose to the public most of what we have concealed or attempted to keep concealed for centuries, with the concomitant decrease of interest to that segment of society. This mystique surrounded us with an aura that tended to lift us to a higher plane than other fraternal organizations.

Many of you know that I have been afforded the great privilege of traveling over much of the world for the last twenty years simply for the purpose of Freemasonry. In these travels I learned that what we have lost in North America regarding an emphasis on learning has been retained and emphasized in a greater part of the world. It is therefore;

not surprising that Freemasonry is surviving, and indeed thriving in most of the world.

We are living in a stimulating age for world Freemasonry. When traveling to other countries, I have been honored to address members of the Senates, other government leaders and top military personnel. I have been received by the presidents of six countries and several prime ministers because of their interest in what Freemasonry can contribute to their societies. I have been privileged to speak in over thirty countries and been on numerous radio programs and television stations and given many press interviews. The United States experienced the same characteristic in our colonial days. It is important that you understand that this was done because I represent an organization that is significant to their societies.

Unfortunately, Masonic leadership has bought into the political correctness concept and as a result we have seriously reduced our effectiveness to make future contributions. We need more than ever, a leadership with a vision to see beyond self-satisfaction and a dedication to rising above the mediocrity of today's social structure. The future of Freemasonry in North America may very well be dependent upon the leadership's realization that Masonic education is a vital component for our survival.

I could stand here and tell you some fascinating stories of the respect I receive simply because of what I represent but this is not why I am here. I am here to convey the importance of educating our membership of the significance of Freemasonry in the world today. I am not implying that Masonic education is the definitive answer to solving all the problems that we are experiencing but I am absolutely convinced that without it, we have little hope of ever recapturing that significance we once had in our influence in society.

Freemasonry continues to be held in highest esteem in

most countries of the world, even in environments where they have had to struggle far beyond anything we have ever known to even exist as a fraternity. I have also observed that the acquisition of knowledge as has been universally professed in our Craft has not become a lost art as we have made it in North America.

I find nothing in our Freemasonry to compare with the stimulus for intellectual discussion that tends to permeate Freemasonry in most of the world. Sadly, this lack of challenge to our members tends to diminish the intellectual quality for which Freemasonry has been historically known. As a result, we have lost much of our allure to a segment of society that structured and gave Freemasonry its societal image.

Historians are finally acknowledging the influence that our Craft has had on some of the greatest leaders that the world has ever known at a time when we are failing to educate our own membership of this influence.

Freemasonry played a vital role during the age of Enlightenment as one of the principal organizations in America that provided an enclave wherein great thinking minds from different social strata met and created the concept of a democratic society based upon the structure they found in Masonic lodges. Is it not incomprehensible that an organization of the likes of Freemasonry with the avowed purpose of improving the man and in stimulating a desire for him to seek to acquire knowledge should lack any major system for substantial education like we do here in America?

Freemasonry impacted this world by improving good men, by taking one good man at a time and making him a better man and we made him better by infusing into him the realization that he was far more capable than he himself considered possible. We stimulated him to want to be better and incited his intellect to want to become more knowledgeable, and more capable. Freemasonry became the educational tool that provided an environment wherein men like Washington, Franklin, Wren, Newton and many others like them crafted the ideas that created the ideals of a democratic society.

This world is as it is today because Freemasonry lived and Freemasonry lived because it undertook the responsibility of taking the good man and making him a better man by teaching him the precepts and philosophies of Freemasonry through a process of Masonic education. These better men then became the leaders that created modern-day civil society and also the image we live by.

These young men that are showing an interest today are seeking much more than we are providing. They are on a quest searching for something that society is not providing to them. They are searching for a quality organization far above the mediocrity of present-day society. They are searching for knowledge and a system that will provide it for them. It is now up to us to make available to them, that for what they search.

Freemasonry is being given an opportunity that it may never see again. This interest has created a potential to recreate an image of Freemasonry that has been lost to America. It will, however, require that the leadership uses it as a potential to improve the quality of the Craft and not simply as a recruitment tool to improve the quantity of the Craft. This regenerated interest in Freemasonry is giving us that opportunity.

If we are deserving of our heritage then we must undertake a program of educating ourselves and our membership. The legacy of our past brethren deserves that respect and respect given to the Craft will be proportional to the educational requirements of the Craft.

[22]

The Way of Leaders

Dallas historian A.C. Green stated, "Freemasonry was once like owning an American Express Card, it showed a level of class, but now that's all over." There was a time in our past when membership in Freemasonry was ardently sought. It was a goal of many young men to become members of our great fraternity. They understood it by the composition they saw in it.

We no longer are attracting the young man of this segment of our society and it is evident by the decline of our image. It is nothing short of a major tragedy to North America if indeed; we are now conceived as an organization of old men clinging to the past. Organizations are built and organizations succeed by those in positions of leadership and if they fail, most fail for the same cause.

Very few organizations, if any, have existed in this world that have contributed as much to the betterment of mankind than has Freemasonry. Indeed, Freemasonry has been in itself a history of phenomenal achievement. It is not possible to measure the impact that our Craft has had on the evolution of civil society but outside of organized religion, it is doubtful that any organization can match it. Perhaps its greatest success has been in nurturing a whole new concept of the rights of the individual man while structuring the man to respect those rights.

For most of its history, Freemasonry's success was

measured by the societal image of admiration and respect it generated and in America (with the exception of the period following the Morgan affair) this image can be traced from its origin in the eighteenth century until approximately 35 years ago. It was then that we began to measure our success in terms of the quantity of the members rather than the quality of the membership.

Freemasonry faced numerous challenges during its history in America especially during the Morgan affair when its numbers were reduced catastrophically. It not only survived but emerged like a phoenix from the ashes stronger than it was before. Every challenge large or small was temporary because its philosophical purpose was never questioned and the leadership of the Craft never lost its vision.

The credit for this success lay in the hands of the leadership at every period in history. Indeed, credit for the success of Freemasonry worldwide must be given to some of the greatest leaders this world and our Craft have ever known. When the challenges have been the greatest, visionary leadership was there to accept the challenges. A listing of those who have led this Craft around the world and indeed whose members have led their societies would read like a listing of Who's Who in the World over several hundred years. If, however, their names did not appear in a Who's Who in the World they would certainly appear in a listing of Who's Who in Freemasonry.

Freemasonry continues today to be in the forefront of many developing societies around the globe. The Craft is expanding at a more rapid rate with new grand lodges being created than perhaps since the eighteenth century.

I have been most fortunate to have been in a position to observe our Craft functioning on a worldwide level for a number of years. It is impressive to see the interest being shown by the leaders of the governments of these newly emerging societies in Freemasonry's potential to be a contributory influence in their development. It is impressive to see the respect Freemasonry receives due to the results of the performance of our leaders of the past and the Craft's impact on their societies.

It is not only in the newly created grand lodges, however, that membership numbers are increasing. Grand lodges hundreds of years old continue not only to increase in numbers of members but to attract some of their societies' most capable and educated citizens.

The Grand Orient of Italy, for example, has existed for more than 200 years. Even though they operate in one of the more difficult environments in the world along with the fact that there have been numerous grand lodges operating in Italy, they have tripled their membership over the last decade and a half and are attracting some of the most prominent members of Italian society. Credit for this evident success must be given to the visionary leadership of the Grand Orient.

Many claim that our failures today are due to the different world in which we live. Yet, the Craft has thrived for almost 300 years. Does this imply that world societies have been stagnant and unchanged for 300 years and does it mean that the world has not changed where Freemasonry continues to succeed or is it an excuse to justify our failings?

We need to concentrate more on solving our problems than on justifying our failures! The challenges that are confronting us today are different only in style and form from the challenges that confronted us in the past and we rose above those challenges. Instead of measuring our success by societal image and respect, we are measuring our failings by the decreasing number of members on our rolls and we are not rising above the challenges. The result has been a willingness to lower our standards to support the numbers which in turn have reduced our image and lessened the respect along with the attractiveness to potentially great leaders.

It would be well for us to remember that the challenges for Freemasonry to succeed in most of the world are far beyond anything we have ever known in North America: tens of thousands have given their lives to say, "I am a Freemason." In North America our lack of serious challenges is perhaps the major contributory factor to the complacency we have experienced in Freemasonry. This complacency has now evolved into apathy and the apathy has made us an almost invisible entity in modern American society. Few in America comprehend the ongoing influence that Freemasonry has on the present-day world. Indeed, few in America truly comprehend the impact that Freemasonry has had on the development of world societies in the past.

An adage states that leaders are born not made and indeed this is partially true. There can be no question that some are born with greater psychological and physiological advantages for greatness. The great personages in any field of endeavor must have the genetic potential to become great. Da Vinci, van Gogh and Michelangelo certainly had the genetic potential to be great artists; Mozart and Beethoven great musicians and Babe Ruth, Arnold Palmer, and Cal Ripken great athletes.

I well know that no matter how I may have tried, I could never have become a da Vinci, a van Gogh, a Michelangelo or a Mozart, or a Babe Ruth, Arnold Palmer, or Cal Ripken simply because the genetic potential was not there. However, there is another requirement to reach our genetic potential. These men, known for their greatness, lived in the right environment and took the opportunity to excel.

What if da Vinci, van Gogh, or Michelangelo had never

been exposed to art? What if Mozart or Beethoven had never been stimulated by music or Palmer or Ripken by sports? Would we have known them now? Would we have ever heard the name of Babe Ruth had he not become a great baseball player? The environment to which they were exposed was vital for their greatness as was their initiative to take advantage of the environment offered them.

The environment plays an equally significant role in the development of greatness of leaders as does the genetics. The potential is born from within, but the result is made from without. The genetic potential must still be present in the world's population today. Indeed, with millions more living today than there were 300 years ago, there must be many more potentially great leaders in today's world. So where are the Visionary Masonic leaders today? If the genetic potential is here, the environmental stimulus must be lacking and if the environmental stimulus is lacking where does the responsibility lie?

Unfortunately, the country in which we live is now a country where political correctness dominates. We now are being forced to accept that everyone is entitled to the same as everyone else. We reward mediocrity so well that there is little incentive to excel and there is no way any organization built on the quality of its membership can continue to be a positive influence by adherence to that concept. Freemasonry has now bought into it or perhaps it would be more accurate to say our leaders have led us into it.

It is not the intent of this essay to serve as a criticism or condemnation of our present-day leaders. It would be wrong for us to blame the current leadership of the Craft for the crisis we are facing today. They have simply inherited a product of change that has been going on for decades. They however, must now be willing to shoulder the responsibility of trying to reverse the crisis they have inherited.

Our leaders today must be willing to admit that what we've been doing for decades is not succeeding. We cannot continue to permit our societal image to deteriorate though a willingness to lower our standards. One of the reasons for our success for nearly three centuries was our commitment to stand firm on the quality of the men that we would permit to become part of us. Now we are willing to accept almost anyone simply to add another number to our membership roll. Like attracts like and Freemasonry was composed of a quality of men who readily attracted men of quality who wanted to be associated with them. Our failure to guard the west gate has resulted in not only the declining quality of the Craft but the loss of quantity of the Craft as well.

Even when we take in men of quality, however, we no longer put emphasis upon making them better men. Herein we are failing in one of the fundamental purposes of the Craft. We cannot continue to fail in this basic precept and expect society to respect and honor us for it. We cannot continue to ignore the requirement of the acquisition of knowledge by eliminating those requirements to learn. There are grand lodges in North America today that require absolutely nothing in the way of learning nor do they even encourage it.

Our leaders must also come to realize that admiration and respect cannot be bought; they must be earned. Freemasonry has always been an organization with a charitable concern with a concentration on the needs of our brothers. Over the past 35 years, however, we have almost evolved into a collection agency for public charities. While our membership is declining, our buildings are deteriorating and our image is eroding, we continue to concentrate massive amounts of energy to raise funds for other organizations. We will never regain our prominence in society by raising funds for public charities.

How do we change what we are now? How do we alter the direction we have been traveling for 35 years? The answer of course is going to depend upon the vision of the leaders of the Craft today.

We need leaders with vision to look farther into our future than we have been looking for many years. We have been considering long-range planning in terms of time spans that are far too short.

There was a time when suspension for non-payment of dues in a Masonic Lodge would be regarded as a definitive disgrace to the individual. No man wanted to place himself in that position. Today non-payment of dues suspensions occur in the thousands annually.

It is vitally important to the future of Freemasonry that we diligently seek out those men in society with the potential to provide the leadership to restore Freemasonry to its past prominence; men with vision and men with determination and commitment to something other than themselves. I am not talking about solicitation. Indeed, solicitation is simply another stepping stone in our failure to maintain or to regain the quality of the Craft. The most highly qualified members of the Lodge will be the ones who will solicit the least. There is nothing wrong, however, in telling a good man that he should be a Mason.

How do we recognize potential leaders for Masonic lodges and generate their interest in Freemasonry? There are those who are readily recognized as dynamic leaders by their actions. These men stand out in the community and are seen as leaders before they consider Freemasonry.

There are those who develop into leaders after joining the Craft and probably are a result of Freemasonry's claim to making good men better. These men are active leaders.

But there are also those who are leaders by their willingness to follow and assist. These men lead by setting an example and inspiring others. They may be regarded as passive leaders. After all, of what value would be the greatest leader in the world if there were no one to follow?

Even as the challenges to Freemasonry today differ only in form and style from those in the past there is a major difference from those in the past. The major challenges in the past came from outside the Craft. These objections were generally related to ritual and practice with religious and political powers being the greatest obstacles to the success of the Craft.

Today, with some exceptions our major challenges come from within. The greatest obstacles to our continuing ability to influence society and to retain our image are those created by ourselves.

Those who accomplish anything in life do so because they have an ego driving them. Without that ego, they would have accomplished little. Without that ego, there could not have been Freemasonry. Today however, perhaps the greatest threat to our success is the uncontrolled ego of some of the leadership. Far too many leaders today use their egos to build their own image without comprehending that the legacy they will leave behind will be a decidedly negative one. Many great leaders have sacrificed their legacies by an excessive need to inflate their own images.

There are few organizations where there is as much power given to the leaders as there is in Freemasonry and there are probably few organizations where as much ego can be found within the leadership. This is perhaps one of the greatest threats to our continued success today. Without ego there can be no accomplishment but how many of us will be remembered for our pomposity rather than our contributions? Until the time comes when the leadership begins to think more of the Craft and less about their own image, we will continue to struggle to survive.

There is always that tendency to give our leaders' sizable credit for our successes so does it not naturally follow that we should qualify our failures by the same standard? If Freemasonry is failing anywhere, it is not the failure of Masonic philosophy it is a failure of Masonic leadership.

So, are we really old men clinging to the past or are we what we think and say we are and as Daniel Poling described us, "a vital force for everything high and worthy?"

The future of Freemasonry is now in the hands of the leaders of the present. The leaders of the past have served the world well. History will judge how well we have served the world today.

[23]

A History of the Future of Freemasonry

Given to the Masonic Society

My brothers, It is a great privilege for me to participate in this conference of the Masonic Society.
I stand before you now in the unique position of
representing some of the last who were privileged to know
a number of the brothers of a class of visionary leaders of
Freemasonry in North America; brothers who were leaders
of the Craft 50, 60, 70 even 80 years ago, brothers whose
names continue to reverberate in the Masonic world. I recall
going to Washington each year for Masonic Week close
to fifty years ago and sitting in awe and listening to some
of these brothers speak on Freemasonry. It was a privilege
just to meet them. It is sad that so many of you here will
never have that opportunity.

I may not be the oldest brother attending this conference but I am the oldest participating as a presenter in
the program. I will be 83 years old in six days, and I am
participating with the realization that most of what will
be my life's history is behind me and my future is limited,
along with any opportunities that I may have to cause you
to think.

It is important that you understand that I speak for no
grand lodge or any Masonic body. What I express are my
thoughts and opinions that I have developed over 54 years
as a Freemason.

This paper I deliver today is not presented as projecting an actual history of our future but as a prediction of what it might well be if we continue to follow the same pathway that we have been following in North America for the past 40 years, along with my observations and thoughts concerning the cause and what is needed to alter the pathway.

I have had the privilege of traveling over a large portion of the world and seeing Freemasonry as it operates in various environments. I have observed it where it continues to be an extremely successful influence on the society in which it exists. I have also experienced its struggles to present itself in newly emerging societies where it faces obstacles of a magnitude that we have never experienced in our country. Even in those environments, however, it continues to have its influence felt and to serve as an attractive force to leaders in their societies.

Last year, I traveled to eighteen countries, for the purpose of Freemasonry. I've spoken in over forty countries and have had my papers published in more than thirty. I have met with the presidents of eight countries and several prime ministers. I have addressed senates, military officers and other political and public personalities. I have participated in numerous television, radio and press interviews. I tell you this, not to inflate my significance but to justify my qualification to speak on the subject.

My brothers, there are few countries in the world in which the Masonic fraternity is struggling more than in the United States, simply to remain a viable institution. And yet, there are very few countries in the world, using any measuring criterion, in which the Masonic fraternity showed a greater degree of success than it did in our past. It is a monumental tragedy that the Freemasonry in North America is going through what is perhaps the greatest threat to its survival that we have ever experienced, while

Freemasonry in much of the rest of the world is showing the greatest success that it has experienced since shortly after its creation. Consider that there were thirty new regular grand lodges consecrated since the turn-of-the-century, while many of the older grand lodges continue to grow in numbers and influence.

We in America have been extremely fortunate. We did not have to deal with an already well established form of government with its opressive laws to restrict it, to become organized. We were therefore able to construct Freemasonry with contributions from citizens of numerous world societies with different thoughts concerning the rights of man. We have also, been able to practice the Craft since its beginning without serious confrontation as a result of having no powerful monarchs, pontiffs or dictators challenging that existence. American Freemasons have never had to live with the realization, that simply being a Freemason carried with it the potential of death. However, many thousands of our brothers in other countries died for that very reason.

When I joined this Craft, I was a consummate idealist. However, my idealism has been tempered by pragmatism during those 54 years. I do not know now whether I am a pragmatic idealist or an idealistic pragmatist but I do know that I think much differently today concerning the Craft than I did when I joined. Frankly, my brothers, if the Craft was then as it is now, I seriously doubt that I would be a Freemason today.

I was privileged to be a Freemason during a time when the general public looked upon us individually with respect, simply because we were a Freemason. It was the period I recall, when almost every professional man in my small town was a member of our Craft. Today, only a very small percentage of these men are members.

Little rationalization is required on our part to recognize

that unless there is a major change in the thinking of our leadership, our future is bleak and the demise of Freemasonry is almost inevitable in North America, at least in any form for which it has been known historically.

Although our numbers have been in decline for almost 6 decades, it has been in freefall over the last 35 years. This was a time when we weakened the guard at the west gate to gain numbers and we have now lost 75% of our membership. It is not my intent to be a harbinger of doom but nor is it my intent to paint a rosy picture based upon the greatness of our past as many are intent to do. We have been parasitizing our past far too long to inflate its significance in the present.

We must credit the phenomenal achievements of Freemasonry and its contributions to society to the visionary leadership that structured and led it. At the same time, however, on the shoulders of those leaders who have abetted its failing and reduced its success, must be placed the blame.

For the past 35 to 40 years we have continued to think that our survival depended upon large quantities of members instead of the quality the individual member. Now, even though membership numbers have not declined significantly in my Lodge, there are few professional men who are members and the visual image of Freemasonry in that town has declined significantly along with the respect. This image now serves as a deterrent and continues to discourage membership by professional men. I do not mean by this observation, to imply that we do not have good men but we do not have the membership of the professional men to serve as a visual image in the community. Please note, when I speak of quality professional men, I am referring to the professional men with high moral and ethical standards, not necessarily those with the highest visibility in present day society.

For most of its history, Freemasonry's success was measured by the societal image of admiration and respect it generated. This image can be traced from its origin in the eighteenth century until approximately 35 years ago. The credit for this success lay in the hands of the leadership at every period in history. Indeed, credit for the success of Freemasonry worldwide must be given to some of the greatest visionary leaders our world has ever known. Today instead of measuring our success by societal image and respect, we are measuring our failings by the decreasing numbers of members on our rolls.

Unfortunately, in North America, in light of political correctness, too many leaders have determined that elitism is a dirty word. Yet, when Freemasonry stated that its goal was to take good men and make them better, we became elitist and my brothers there is nothing wrong with elitism. Elitism played a major role in bringing together the great minds in the age of Enlightenment. It was these men, capable of great thinking that made Freemasonry an influential segment of society. Freemasonry was, is and should always remain elitist; not in a sense of implying superiority over nonmembers but a sense of being capable of performing a superior purpose.

When I first traveled to the Conferences of Grand Masters and Grand Secretaries of North America, there would be more than twenty members of the Senate and House attending. Today there are none. Where at one time, there was a distinct value for these men to say, "I am a Freemason" now they avoid it.

We have also dedicated far too much of our efforts in trying to buy back the respect we surrendered, through support of public charities. Where we were once looked upon as an organization of successful men, dedicated to the good of society, today there is a greater tendency for us to be looked upon as a collection agency for public charities. If this remains our vision, there is little challenge in writing the history of the future of Freemasonry, today.

It is truly distressing when we look at the condition of some of our buildings and at lodges who had to give up their temples due to lack of a financial ability to sustain them, and then acknowledge the millions of dollars we have given away to other organizations. What is even sadder is that those other organizations received the credit for the use of the funds that might have been used to maintain the temples.

Very few with the knowledge of the history of Freemasonry could fail to concede that the leadership that created and sustained it in the past was of a visionary level greater than that of the general leadership of Freemasonry today. Many of the men who developed the concept of Freemasonry were members of the Royal Society, the then and now, premier scientific organization in the world. Many of those men were the great thinkers of their day and certainly the most visible.

These brothers were followed by men like Benjamin Franklin, George Washington, Amadeus Mozart, Harry Truman, Alexander Fleming, Rudyard Kipling, Robert Burns, John Philip Sousa and I could continue naming brothers whose names would be readily recognized. Certainly, not all of these men were active participants in leadership positions within the Craft but their very membership and visibility in society stimulated others to become members and leaders. Today it would be a challenge for any of us to name within the membership of the Craft in North America, many brothers of this caliber and yet, they must exist. Why are we not attracting them and why do we not utilize the abilities of those who do belong?

I realize and acknowledge, that those to whom I address

today, are some of the more astute thinking brothers we have in the Craft. I do not mean in any way, to demean your abilities or your contributions to Freemasonry. However, I have absolutely no misconception concerning my position in Freemasonry. I recognize that I do not think on the same level as many of my predecessors. I realize that I do not serve as an attractive force to stimulate great men to want to join with us. I know and accept that I probably could not have been elected as Grand Secretary of my grand lodge a hundred years ago. For those reasons, I look upon my responsibility to Freemasonry is to work to preserve it until leadership with a vision comparable to those of our past leaders come along again to lead it.

My brothers, when we consider Freemasonry, we are not examining another world under a microscope. We are not a different organism, immune to the vicissitudes of the environment that impacted other fraternal organizations. It would be a serious mistake were we to develop the attitude that we are exempt from their fate.

During the great age of fraternalism in North America there were hundreds of fraternal organizations whose names are not even remembered today and the ones that continue to exist are in a death spiral worse than ours. Interestingly, many of them were patterned after the structure of Freemasonry, so what makes us think that we are any different. We might benefit greatly by studying the pathways they took to their ultimate demise. In that study, we would probably find that we are traveling along parallel pathways today.

We must all, individually, recognize and be willing to acknowledge that we may not be as great as we may think we are, or as were many of our past leaders. We must also recognize, however, that we do have much to offer to our societies. I do not wish to imply that we do not have brothers with vision but many with that vision never have the opportunity to put it into action. I have been amazed, in recent years, with the abilities of some of the brothers that I have seen in our subordinate lodges who will never have the possibility to lead. Our leaders must be willing to seek them out and make use of these abilities.

At the same time, I have observed brothers sitting in chairs that not too many years ago would have been beyond their wildest dreams. Just because we are given the title, does not inoculate us with the wisdom of former leaders or the knowledge of the past. There must be an effort exerted to learn and programs to teach. Therein has become one of the great failures of North American Freemasonry. There is very little effort required to reach "exalted" positions in Freemasonry today and there exists almost a total failure to teach. There are Past Masters today who reached that lofty position with just a few years of membership and though they may possess the ability to lead, most lack the knowledge of what they are leading and there are very few grand lodges in North America today, supporting any viable educational program to teach them. That is unfair to them and possibly destructive to their future. My brothers, there has never been an osmotic process developed whereby we could sit and absorb knowledge as too many tend to rely upon in our lodges today.

Granted, external factors played a role during periods of adversity, i.e. the Morgan affair in North America but Freemasonry has always been challenged by external factors, many far greater and far more devastating than the Morgan affair. It was the leadership that was responsible for successfully confronting those challenges for maintaining or for resurrection of the Craft, including the American leadership following the Morgan affair. Visionary leadership was always responsible to supplant the external challenges that have consistently confronted Freemasonry for 300 years. The question that we must now ask is, "Do we have the leadership with the vision to restore American Freemasonry to its greatness?"

Today, external factors although continuing to exist, are not the greatest challenges facing us. The factors that are offering the greatest challenge to our survival today are internal. There are far more divisive issues for Freemasonry today existing within inflated egos of the leadership and liberal attitudes of the membership than from challenges and forces outside of it.

My brothers, have we as a Craft become nothing more than a reflection of present day society in general? Is it possible that the visionary leadership of our past was drawn from a better pool of potential brothers that is available today? Is what we are today, the best of what society can provide? I don't think so? The average intelligence of society in general has not declined. We are simply not an attractive organization to those men who might've been the visionary leaders and who may have sidestepped the pitfalls which we could not see.

What I say is not meant to be a criticism of present day leaders. We cannot blame the current leadership for the crisis we are facing today. I am convinced that each leader thinks that what he is doing is best for the Craft. Now however, we depend on leadership with a limited knowledge of the Craft and its purpose, and what is an even greater problem, they don't know that they don't know. Upon their shoulders, however, rests the responsibility and hope for our future.

Too many of our leaders have bought into the "political correctness" attitude permeating our society, that almost any male member of society has a right to be a Freemason if he can pay the required fees. They have forgotten the sustaining protocols that made America great, protocols that provided its citizens with the opportunity and stimulus to rise above the ordinary and to excel in their lives. This political correctness attitude has resulted in the conversion of many citizens of America to living as parasites upon society. Now, we wonder why we cannot attract the professional man, the thinking man, the visionary man who we need to pull us from this quagmire that is rapidly becoming, American Freemasonry.

In North America we have surrendered Freemasonry to the financial demands to sustain what we have created and yet, these financial demands should never have existed. Our failure to recognize and adjust to the changes of a progressing society has resulted in a willingness to accept less, simply for the dollars they could provide.

I suggest that Freemasonry became and remained the premier organization that it did due to three primary factors; one, it was the first organization created in a "class" society that accepted men from all social strata. Two, it attracted some of the greatest minds that ever lived and three, it remained selective on who it would accept. This last factor perhaps represents the greatest failure of North American Freemasonry; our failure to guard well enough, the west gate. That would explain the loss of attractiveness to the professional man. It probably also explains the increase in Masonic trials in our grand lodges.

From the beginning of the 1980s our concern with the quantity of the membership has caused our leadership to implement numerous approaches to stem the loss, even changing accepted protocols and violating ancient landmarks of Freemasonry by, in some form, soliciting membership and/or accelerating conferral of degrees. The most dramatic transformation was the implementation of one day class conferrals. This concept began in the Grand Lodge of District of Columbia in 1992 and has since spread to over thirty other North American Grand Lodges.

Since that time there have been mixed opinions as to their success or as a benefit to Freemasonry. The long range value of one day classes might be judged by comparing the Grand Lodge of Ohio's membership changes with the Grand Lodge of Pennsylvania's. These two grand lodges have represented the two largest grand lodges in North America for much of our history and the Grand Lodge of Ohio has taken in more members through one day conferrals than any other grand lodge in North America. The Grand Lodge of Pennsylvania has also held one day classes but on a much smaller scale.

In 1987 the Grand Lodge of Ohio had 13,413 more members than did the Grand Lodge of Pennsylvania. Their net member loss that year was just 455 greater than the Grand Lodge of Pennsylvania. They remained the largest Grand Lodge in North America until 1997.

Pennsylvania then grew steadily larger and in 2001 the Grand Lodge of Pennsylvania had 9330 more members than the Grand Lodge of Ohio.

In 2002 the Grand Lodge of Ohio held a one day conferral taking in 7,700 new members that year. Pennsylvania then had only 2119 more members than the Grand Lodge of Ohio. By 2015 however, The Grand Lodge of Pennsylvania had 15,012 more members than the Grand Lodge of Ohio and their net loss that year was 825 higher than the Grand Lodge of Pennsylvania.

The net losses of members following that one day class in Ohio has remained consistently higher and in 2004 their net loss was 4,090 greater than the Grand Lodge of Pennsylvania.

For that same period of time 1987 until 2015 the membership in the District of Columbia, where one day classes began in 1992, the membership has decreased from 8,120 to 4,215.

There is no question that there have been brothers created in one day classes who have become an asset to their lodge, sitting in positions of leadership and progressing though the chairs. However, what cannot be measured is the loss of our visual image in our communities and our attraction to professional men as a result of that loss. Also, what has not been determined is how many of these brothers who became leaders would have joined through the regular process.

I was watching a documentary on television recently on Freemasonry. In it they implied, as I have heard many times in the past that the true purpose of Freemasonry along with other esoteric organizations such as the illuminati the Bilderbergers, and the Trilateral Commission, was to rule the world. If this indeed was the intent of Freemasonry, after 300 years of organized existence, we would have to represent one of the greatest failures of any organized intent in history.

We must now decide whether our responsibility and our legacy will depend upon the great physical structures that we have built or upon the great philosophical and intellectual structures that our brothers of the past built for us.

I suspect that there are of those sitting here today who disagree with my evaluation of North American Freemasonry, the direction we are going and what is needed to alter the course and I have absolutely no problem with that. As I have indicated many times, when I speak, I want to stimulate thinking. If I have achieved that, then I have accomplished my intent. If you disagree, you must've thought about what I said.

However, if we are to change the pathway, we must:

1. Consider seriously a change in how we measure what we consider success. Our leadership must acknowledge that the capability to influence society is more important than

having a large number of members who cannot.

2. Totally comprehend that respect cannot be bought through large contributions to public charities. All of our millions in contributions have solved nothing for our future or for our purpose.

3. Practice the premise of making good men better through a viable educational process so that at least our membership comprehends our purpose.

Regardless of whatever excuses we garner for our failings, we cannot avoid the realization that unless we can reverse it, the history that could be written today, of our future will be, of a once great and significant organization that contributed to the development of many societies but failed to find the vision to avoid their own demise.

THREE

Ladies Present

Why A Freemason?

Given at a ladies' night banquet

I learned many years ago that my wife tended to get bored sitting listening to Masonic talks. Therefore, tonight I will try to avoid talking of problems and issues with which we deal. I am going to try to cause you, ladies, to understand a little of the meaning and the impact of Freemasonry.

I am sure that many of you have wondered why your man became a Freemason. What is it that brought us together? What is it that keeps us together? What is it that makes us work so hard to keep what we have? What is this amalgam of the great and the not so great—where all men are brothers, nothing more, nothing less.

My good friend, Brother Stewart M.L. Pollard told me this story: "After the battle of Leyte Gulf and the liberation of Manila he was visiting a small lodge in Cavite that was holding its first communication in four years. When word got around, a large contingent of American Masons showed up. Sitting two seats away from bother Pollard was General Douglas MacArthur. The master proudly acknowledged the presence of the Supreme Allied Commander. When MacArthur stood, he said these words: 'When I walked through the portals of this lodge room, I dropped my cloak of authority as Supreme Allied Commander and assumed the title of Brother. I would appreciate being treated as such'." What a lesson on Freemasonry.

Brother Burl Ives — who played in every major concert hall in the world, received every prestigious award that can be given to an entertainer including the coveted Oscar for his performance in *The Big Valley*, and who gave command performances before royalty and the president — was asked by Robert Schuller on national television what he regarded as the greatest honor he had ever received, and he replied: "When I was made a Mason."

I'm not sure whether this doesn't say it all; that I could stop here and perhaps you would understand but that doesn't say it all. We can list an impressive diversity of great men who were united into this common band of brothers, men from all categories of life.

Although I continue to advise our members not to dwell upon what we were or upon the great brothers of our past, it is probably worth noting to you ladies, the men who found within the bonds of our brotherhood a stimulating influence in their lives.

MUSICIANS: Franz Liszt, Paul Whiteman, John Philip Sousa, Amadeus Mozart, the last two of whom composed Masonic music.

MILITARY MEN: Jimmy Doolittle, Eddie Ricken-backer, Audie Murphy and Generals George McClelland, Mark Clark, Black Jack Pershing, Omar Bradley, Douglas MacArthur.

WRITERS AND POETS: Robert Burns, Charles Dickens, Sir Arthur Conan Doyle, Johann Wolfgang von Goethe, Mark Twain, and Rudyard Kipling whose writings frequently referred to the Craft.

ROYALTY: Kings George I through VI, Frederick I, III, VII, VIII, Alexander I, Peter the Great, Constantine I, Edward VIII, and Kamehameha IV, V.

SCIENTISTS: Luther Burbank, Francis Bacon, Sir Alexander Fleming.

ATHLETES: Rogers Hornsby, Ty Cobb, Cy Young, Arnold Palmer.

THEOLOGIANS: Joseph Fort Newton, Brigham Young, Norman Vincent Peale.

STATESMEN: Stephen Douglas, Jefferson Davis, Winston Churchill, Thurgood Marshall, Daniel Webster, Thomas Paine, Williams Jennings Bryan.

EXPLORERS: Richard E. Byrd, Robert E. Perry, George Rogers Clark, John Fremont.

INVENTORS: Robert Fulton, DeWitt Clinton.

PHILOSOPHERS: François Voltaire, Gotthold Lessing.

ENTERTAINERS: John Wayne, Roy Rogers, Arthur Godfrey, Ernest Borgnine, Will Rogers, Gene Autry, Douglas Fairbanks, Nat King Cole, Danny Thomas, Red Skeleton, Cecil B. DeMille, Harry Houdini.

OTHERS: John Wanamaker, Kit Carson, Sam Houston, Charles Lindbergh, Buffalo Bill Cody, Davy Crockett.

This list touches only a small number of readily recognizable names who have been united by this Masonic fraternity. It also includes fourteen U.S. presidents and a multitude of other government personalities, both foreign and from the United States.

You have probably noted that I mentioned none from early America. This I did purposely because I want you to dwell upon how greatly the Masonic fraternity has affected you.

Let us look back in history to the eighteenth century and observe how many men of significance were Freemasons; men like George Washington, Marquis de Lafayette, Paul Revere, John Hancock, Benjamin Franklin, Baron von Steuben, Israel Portman, Henry Knox, John Adams, Sam Adams, Patrick Henry, and I could go on and on. 29 signers of the Declaration of Independence, 10 signers of the articles of Association, 9 signers of the articles of Confederation, 13 signers of the Constitution of the United States, 33 generals of the Continental Army and 8 of Washington's aides were members of the Craft. Without these men it is highly unlikely that we would be an independent nation.

Brother George Washington is still regarded as one of the greatest leaders this world has ever seen and the greatest Freemason and it was Freemasonry that contributed to making him acceptable to the leading patriots with the divided ideals of the time and it was Masonry that guided his judgment.

Historians have chosen to ignore Freemasonry but they could not ignore Washington. Edward Everett wrote that "Washington was the greatest of good men, and the best of great men," and Washington said of Masonry, "I shall always be happy to advance the interest of the society and to be considered by them a deserving brother." Daniel Webster wrote, "America has furnished to the world the character of Washington and if our American institution has done nothing else that alone would have entitled them to the respect of mankind."

So ladies you can readily see the effect that Masonry had on Washington and through this, the effect Washington had on others and through that effect on others, what we have today.

One historian did acknowledge Freemasonry although you rarely see it written. C. T. Brady wrote:

The United States of America was conceived at Lexington, quickened at Bunker Hill and born at Philadelphia. It was baptized in the blood and snow at Trenton. It spoke stern words from the cannon's mouth at Saratoga. It struggled desperately for life amid the snows at Valley Forge. It finally assumed the Toga

Virilis of independence at Yorktown. On all occasions the will to victory was the will of Washington and his Masonic generals.

So it is highly doubtful that were it not for the influence of these men that we would even be here today, in fact we would probably not even be or our lives would be vastly different. Remember that we are, because of the genetics of our parents, so unless you were conceived in a different country, you were probably born because of the influence of the Craft.

Norman Vincent Peale, Grand Chaplain of the Grand Lodge of New York wrote, "I can think of no greater thing that can happen in the life of any man than to have the experience in his young manhood and across the years of being a member of this great fellowship and of learning to know in the intimacies of brotherhood some of the greatest men you will ever meet."

So what is it that brought us together, that keeps us together? I don't know, but I do know that it had an attraction and holding force for those much greater than me. Perhaps it is an inherent desire to associate with any organization with the potential for so much good.

Whatever it is my brothers, be proud that you are Freemasons. And ladies, be proud that Freemasonry thought enough of your man to make him a Freemason.

[2]

You Are Because — A Biology Lesson

*Given at a ladies night banquet
where young people were present*

I have devoted much thought on what subject I could speak on tonight that would be of interest to all of you; men, ladies and young people. Well, my friends, I am a biologist and I spent a big part of my life as a biologist. So, tonight I am going to give you a biology lesson.

The increase in attacks against us has recently become a great concern for our fraternity. Freemasonry has always had its detractors but recently we have been attacked more frequently and more viciously than has been true in the recent past. These attacks have been led by a few pious bigots like Pat Robertson, John Ankerberg, and James Holly.

Last year I attended a meeting in Guthrie, Oklahoma, concerning the Southern Baptist Convention's developing attitude on Freemasonry. Dr. Holly from Beaumont, Texas, is heading up a committee to investigate Freemasonry. No Freemason will be permitted to serve on the committee whose goal is to condemn the fraternity. They are demanding that all Freemasons publicly resign from the Craft and that the churches then be exorcised to cleanse them from whatever Masonic influence might be present. I recall one pastor standing at that meeting and stating that, "My father did not battle fascism in the 40s to have it thrust upon me in the 90s by my church."

My friends, it is time that we began to realize how significant we are. It is time that we began to recognize the impact that we have had on society. I am not sure what it was that brought us together. I am not sure what it is that keeps us together and I am not sure that it is all that important that I know. What is important is that we were brought together and kept together and because of whatever that force is, the world will never be the same.

I consistently tell our members to stop dwelling upon the past and lamenting that we may not be as great as we once were. We must live for today and work to build tomorrow. We must not fail to acknowledge however, those great men who found within the Fellowship of Freemasonry, a unifying bond of brotherhood.

Any list comprised would include a host of readily recognizable names of those who contributed in diverse ways to our society. Fourteen presidents of the United States and a multitude other personalities, both foreign and native to the United States have found within the fellowship of Freemasonry a unifying bond of brotherhood.

The radical fundamentalist's accusations today imply that only a very few of the top Masonic leaders know what they say is "the true Satanic purpose of Freemasonry." Yet, in our ranks have walked some of the greatest humanitarians who have ever lived; indeed some of the greatest minds and most devoted theologians have been members of our Craft. To condemn the Craft is to condemn them.

I want you to know and to consider how greatly the Masonic fraternity has probably affected you, even more than you ever dreamed.

Let us look back to the men of note in the 1700s, men like Washington, Revere, Lafayette, Hancock, Von Steuben, Putman, Knox, Franklin, Henry, and I could go on and on. These men represent the founding force of early America and they were Freemasons all. Freemasonry was one common thread uniting divided ideals, classes and ranks.

Without these men it is highly unlikely that we would be the independent nation that we are today. Without these Masons whose names are forever imprinted in the minds of freedom loving people, not only would we probably not be living in a free nation, we would probably not even be.

Now, I know you have all been sitting here in anticipation of your biology lesson. So, here it comes. Those who know simple genetics know that all that you are came at conception from chromosomes, 50% of which came from your mother, and 50% from your father. If your father had not met your mother, you could not be. If your grandfather had not met your grandmother, you could not be. If your great-grandfather had not met your great-grandmother you could not be and so on back through the generations.

Therefore, unless your parents were both born and met in some other country, chances are you exist today because of the character of the United States of America and that character was forged by Freemasons. Immigrants came to America because of what it was, and what it was, was determined to a great extent by Freemasons. There are writers today who are not Freemasons, who suggest that the development of the Lodge structure of Freemasonry was a concept that led to modern-day democracy.

So, biologically we quite probably exist today because of Freemasonry and that includes Robinson, Ankerberg, and Holly. Do not, however, expect any acknowledgment from them.

As for me—the experience of being able to sit with my brothers and to be regarded by them, as such, is the greatest privilege I can ever expect to receive other than being accepted by my God.

[3]

Does the World Need Us?

The last time I spoke here, I tried to impress upon the ladies the significance of Freemasonry by making them more aware of the great men who were members of the Craft. I also emphasized the significant role that the ladies play in the lives of the men who are Freemasons. In addition, I tried to give you a biology lesson, pointing out that we are what we are because of our genetic inheritance and the significant role that Freemasonry played in bringing that inheritance together.

Many of the greatest men and greatest humanitarians who ever lived have chosen to become a member of the Masonic fraternity. I guess not very many take the time to wonder why, but I have and I do. Much more recently I have begun to wonder a great deal more so.

I have known for a long time that if Freemasonry were nothing else, it is a journey through knowledge. Several years ago I became book reviewer for *The Northern Light* of the Ancient Accepted Scottish Rite. In that position I have been stimulated to think a great deal more about all aspects of Freemasonry. As a result, I have delved more deeply into the forces that have attracted men of this caliber.

In the last ten years we have seen an upsurge in the amount of anti-Masonic propaganda being written and spoken. Anti-masonry is nothing new to the world. It began shortly after the establishment of the first Grand Lodge and 1717 and Freemasonry has always had its detractors.

Much of this opposition is due to ignorance of what we are and what our purpose is. Some religious leaders will always oppose us due to our acceptance of members who are not believers specifically in their faith. Their attitude is if you're not for me, you are against me and there will always be those who try to destroy what they do not understand.

There is also opposition to the Craft due to jealousy of what we have been able to accomplish. I suspect that any organization that has accomplished much will generate its enemies. Unfortunately, a considerable amount of the opposition that confronts us is from some Christian theologians who want 100% from their members and will always oppose that which they perceive as competition. I sometimes think that our greatest crime in the minds of some is our requirement for the belief in God. Without this requirement we would probably be ignored. Interestingly, Father Robert Flores, a Catholic priest from Houston, Texas, said, "If it takes our gentle fraternity to teach brotherly love and tolerance to the churches of the world, then so be it."

Finally, much opposition confronting us today is due to hate, pure hate. This is readily seen in men like Pat Robertson, John Ankerberg, and Dr. Holly. Again, we have always dealt with hatemongers like these men, but nothing I have read of in the past compares with the hate of the present.

We must not forget, however, that big men like big organizations, build. Small men tear down and their organizations diminish with them. Freemasonry and Freemasons have always been builders and we must continue to build but times change and we must deal with the change. We must adjust to the environment in which we operate. We must be seen for what we are; a viable force for all that is good and great. For even as the environment changed this force for good has not and I sincerely hope, never will. We must never let the changing environment cause us to lose sight of our purpose.

Freemasonry has been an attractive force for some of the greatest men this world has ever produced because it not only embraced high ideals and principles but because it nurtured those ideals and principles. It developed the minds of the members and stimulated aspirations to greatness.

I have often thought and wondered why we became so great. Perhaps, Margaret Jacob hit upon the answer to my wondering when she wrote, "More so than any other forms of private sociability, Freemasonry wove enlightened ideas into a tapestry of rituals and oaths, rules of conduct intended to induce loyalty and civility, in short, into a way of life for most of its dedicated followers."

There are historians today suggesting that the very concept of modern democracy had its embryologic development in a Masonic lodge, and I'm not sure they are not right. Can you see the importance of this concept? We owe so much to the members of our past and not only masonically. We must continue to nurture those ideals, develop the minds and stimulate the aspirations. In short, we must continue to be Freemasonry.

As Freemasons, we must always continue to strive for excellence in everything we do, in everything we are and most of all in the image we project. Because of it, others want to be part of us. Each one of us individually is part of our future.

Am I concerned about the anti-Masons? Am I concerned about our future? You bet I'm concerned, but I am not pessimistic. Freemasonry has been too great for too long not to be needed. I read in a newspaper yesterday of a British headmistress in a private school referencing Shakespeare's great work Romeo and Juliet. "She considered it a politically incorrect heterosexual love story and said that until books, films and theater reflected all forms of sexuality, it was inappropriate to expose her pupils to the tale of the ill-fated lovers."

When I see issues like this appearing, I am glad that I am as old as I am. Does the world need us? There are times when I think that we are an island of hope in a world gone mad. I am extremely proud to be part of us. I can only hope that in some small way I can pass on the understanding of how important Freemasonry has been in the formation and operation of this world. Others have passed it on to us we are here because of them. It is now our turn.

[4]

What Is Freemasonry?

*Presented to Grand Lodge of British Columbia
and Yukon Biennial Leadership Conference
Ladies Banquet*

As you might expect, most of my speeches and papers are prepared for and presented to male audiences. However, I have become more acutely aware that most of the ladies are far more astute than I was giving them credit for, even though I spent fourteen years of my life teaching in a private girls college and believe me, those girls were astute. Indeed, I have found that many of the ladies understand more about us than we do about ourselves. So, tonight I hope to bring a little more information concerning Freemasonry to the ladies as well as to the brothers.

Interest in Freemasonry in North America has been waning over the past several decades but there has been a rejuvenated curiosity by the general public as a result of Dan Brown's books *The Da Vinci Code* and *Angels and Demons*. The movie *National Treasure* and its sequel have also stimulated an upsurge of interest in the Masonic organization and as a result, I have been requested to speak to a number of different organizations recently regarding it. It is my hope here today that I might provide you with a greater understanding of "What Is Freemasonry?"

To understand it, it is helpful to know a little of its history. Freemasonry as a fraternal organization dates its heritage back at least to the seventeenth century and possibly a couple of centuries before that. In the organized form for which it is known today, it dates its origin to the year 1717 when four London lodges came together to form what today is known as the United Grand Lodge of England. Following the creation of this Grand Lodge, Freemasonry spread quite rapidly over the face of the globe and has been found in most countries that experience some form of freedom. Although Freemasonry is generally regarded as a male bastion, there are also lodges composed of only females and some that include both male and female members. To be regarded as Regular Lodges, however, they must have descended from the first Grand Lodge formed in England and comply with required protocols and these are all composed of male members.

In spite of this worldwide distribution, Freemasonry has proven to be an enigma to most outside of it and indeed, to many members who fail to understand its true philosophical purpose. In spite of its massive contribution to the evolution of civil society it has remained a mystery to most, feared by many and indeed, hated by some. As a result, it has experienced highs and lows in its membership numbers and influence on evolving civilization over the centuries.

Freemasonry has been defined in many terms throughout its existence. Perhaps the most descriptive is that it is, "a beautiful system of morality, veiled in allegory and illustrated by symbols." We look at ourselves as a "brotherhood of man under the fatherhood of God," and as a "way of life." The simplest and most definitive expression is that we are an organization with a purpose to "take good men and make them better." All of these definitions, however, are at best, somewhat ambiguous. As a result, it is difficult even for our own members to define it to those outside of the organization.

We, in actuality, do not know our own origin. There have been a number of theories proposed over the years concerning this issue, but we really do not know. And yet, it is almost incomprehensible that an organization that has existed for at least 300 years and has created the impact on society that Freemasonry has, for even the membership not to know where and how we began.

The most widely accepted theory is that Freemasonry descended from the early building guilds that were responsible for the erection of the great cathedrals and other structures in Europe during the Renaissance. There is, however, no conclusive evidence to prove this theory to be true. Indeed, it is confounding to think that an organization that has attracted some of the greatest minds that ever lived could be the result of simple stonemasons accepting into their membership those from the highest echelons of society.

A second theory advocated by some Masonic authors, is that Freemasonry is either a direct descendent from the remnants of the Knights Templar or that the Knights Templar joined forces with the early Freemasons to produce the foundation of what exists today. This has not been widely accepted and has passed in and out of favor over the years in the minds of most scholars. Again there is no proof for its accuracy.

I recently wrote a review of a book with the title, *Isaac Newton's Freemasonry: The Alchemy of Science and Mysticism.* It is the author's conclusion that Freemasonry had an indelible relationship with the Royal Society through which Isaac Newton was a significant player when "Freemasonry emerged as the incestuous child of research, theology, and freedom." This theory is far too new to have been examined or debated by scholars of the Craft but it is an intriguing concept. It carries much logic when trying to piece together a stimulating force within the parameters of the Masonic fraternity that proved attractive to so many great men. (Two books have been written recently by Robert Lomas giving support to this theory that you might be interested in reading: *Freemasonry and the Birth of Modern Science* and *The Invisible College*).

Regardless of how Freemasonry came into being, however, it was one of the principal organizations that provided an environment during the Age of Enlightenment for great minds to gather together and share their thoughts and ideas. This environment was especially significant in colonial America, for it contributed to the development of a whole new concept of what a nation should be. This new concept has served as a pattern for developing democratic societies even to the present time.

Many of the leaders of early America were members of the Fraternity including George Washington, who served as master of his lodge, and Benjamin Franklin, who twice served as Grand Master of the Grand Lodge of Pennsylvania. It remains debatable, as to whether Freemasonry attracted great men or contributed to making men great but it is inconceivable that so many of the historically significant figures who led their countries' struggles for freedom, liberty and equality were not influenced by the philosophy of the Craft.

To list these great men would be like a listing of Who's Who of the liberators of the world. This list would include men universally revered in their countries for providing the leadership to rise above the tyrannical suppression that dominated the freedom of thought in the minds of its citizens. It is significant that where freedom does not exist, Freemasonry cannot exist.

Unfortunately, the philosophical precepts espoused by Freemasonry carry with them a price. An estimated

100,000 Freemasons died in the same prison camps as the Jews during the Holocaust. Some of the greatest enemies of Freemasonry over the years have been Hitler, Mussolini, Stalin, Tito, Mao, Franco, and others who sought to control the minds and bodies of their citizens. The Japanese, during World War II, executed all known Freemasons and Franco, in Spain, sentenced all Freemasons to ten years' imprisonment. When Khomeini returned to Iran, those members who were not out of the country at the time or were unable to escape were either imprisoned and/or had their properties confiscated. This persecution continues even to the present time. The Grand Master of Venezuela was assassinated just several years ago.

These men were all enemies of Freemasonry, and they all opposed the Craft for the same reason that others embraced it; the Masonic precept of the right of man to be free and equal and the practice of acceptance of all men's right to believe in and worship their God as their consciences dictate.

Regretfully, Freemasonry has also been attacked extensively by some spiritual leaders who look upon it as a form of competition since we require a belief in a Supreme Being as a qualification for membership along with our support of other theologies. They have great objection to the fact that Freemasonry promotes toleration and freedom of thought, embracing all people of all religious dogmas, testifying to a belief in a Supreme Power. This attack against Freemasonry by various religious institutions has been ongoing since Pope Clement XII issued the first papal bull against the Craft in 1738. Today, the greatest challenges we face from religious leaders are from the fundamental radical elements of the leadership and, as evidenced in today's world, fundamentalism and radicalism in any form of religion is a threat to those who accept the freedom of religion for all people.

It is a tragic commentary that the enemies of the Craft have been the world's greatest tyrants and some of the world's prominent spiritual leaders, major antagonists to each other. It is even more tragic that they oppose us for the very same reason, our support of the freedom of thought and the philosophical principle that man should not only have the right to worship God but the right to worship God as he sees fit.

Freemasonry's only religious requirement for membership is the belief in a Supreme Being, but it is not a religion. We reject all claims to being a religion and we lack all the basic criteria to be one, such as a theological dogma or doctrine, or a means to salvation. As a result, Freemasonry lacks the built in bigotry of religions and provides an environment where religious bias does not hinder the meaning of the brotherhood of man. Therefore, it serves not as a barrier to bringing men together but rather as an attractive force. The seal of the Grand Lodge of Israel for example, includes the Christian cross, the Muslim crescent and the Jewish Star of David. I have been in Grand Lodges in the world where there were five volumes of the sacred Law upon the altar; one for each major religion in that environment.

I have just finished writing a review of the book Founding Faith, in which the author emphasized that our early North American leadership's concern was not only freedom of religion but freedom from religion. This is one of the reasons Freemasonry played a significant role in early America and Canada during the Age of Enlightenment for it brought together men from different religions that tended to dominate in the colonies.

Freemasonry's philosophy, however, not only requires a commitment to religious freedom but also to intellectual improvement as well as a committed patriotism to one's country. Part of our ritual states: "You are to be a lover the arts and sciences and take every opportunity to improve yourself therein." By this admonition, we encourage our membership to rise above the mediocrity imposed by society. Where freedom exists, the Masonic mandate is to submit to the laws of the country in which one lives. Part of our ritual also states, "You are to be a peaceful and dutiful citizen and support the laws of the government under which you live."

The practice of these admonitions should prepare a man not only to improve his own self worth but also to support the rights of all mankind as well as to promote the stability of the environment in which he lives. This philosophy has served as an attractive force to bring together some of the greatest leaders who have lived over the past 300 years. In addition, it has brought together a multitude of prominent men whose names are readily recognizable in many diverse fields of endeavor. Indeed, the practice of the philosophical principles of Freemasonry could resolve most world issues that lead to conflict.

Since the fall of communism, Freemasonry has re-emerged in most of the Eastern European countries and I am impressed with the quality and influence that these men are having in the development of their societies. Also, the Craft is expanding rapidly on the African continent where two of the presidents of their respective countries are also the Grand Masters of their Grand Lodges.

So, where does that take us on the subject, what is Freemasonry? We return to the simple definition that it is a fraternity with a purpose to take good men and make them better. Do we always succeed? Of course not! We do not always succeed in accepting only good men and we do not always succeed in making good men better.

It remains the oldest and largest fraternal organization

in existence. Outside of organized religion, it has probably created a greater influence on the evolution of civil society than any organization that has ever existed, and it retains the potential in much of the world to be a major player in the ongoing development of civil society. In North America, our numbers continue to decline, but as I emphasized in Moscow several years ago, the Craft changed the world by maintaining its significant qualities and in making good men better, one man at a time. With the renewed interest being generated in North America, it will be interesting to see where we are in the next fifty years.

FOUR

Non-Masonic Audiences

[1]

Cathedral in the Pines

Given at an annual New Hampshire program

I t is a tremendous honor for me to be with you here today. I oftentimes wonder when I am asked to speak why this privilege has been given to me. I have not yet found an answer but I do thank you for your kindness. Generally when I speak at a church service, I take my topic from the Scripture lesson for that day. However, when I asked what I should speak about here, I was told it was my choice. It is always more difficult for me when it is my choice.

It is easier today, however, because this site and its purpose is based upon commitments that I have been raised on and taught all my life, to God and to country. This site is a living memorial to that commitment and to one who died for his country and that is used to honor God. These are probably two of the subjects that I appreciate speaking on the most. As an Eagle Scout these precepts of God and country were ingrained into me. As a Freemason for me they are constantly being reinforced.

My short message today is also impacted by a panel on which I served last weekend where I was defending the precepts of toleration and brotherly love. I probably did not win during the discussion because those who disagreed thought it was in opposition to Christian principles to associate with non-Christians. And so hate goes on and on.

Toleration of others belief is a mandatory requirement

for peace and yet the killing continues in Bosnia, in Ireland, in Israel, and in so many other places in the world today. We are fortunate to live in America where toleration and peace is exceptional.

I was asked to speak here today by Jack Marden, the Grand Secretary of the Masonic Grand Lodge of New Hampshire. He told me that many of you here today would be members of the Masonic fraternity and so I greet you as my brothers.

For those of you, who may not be familiar with Freemasonry, permit me to briefly comment on it. Freemasonry is a unique organization when compared with most others in that a prerequisite for membership is a belief in a Supreme Being. When one walks into a Masonic Lodge, the most visible symbol reveals our commitment to God; the Volume of the Sacred Law lying open upon the altar. This is a required landmark in all regular Freemasonry.

However, we are not dogmatic. So believers in any monotheistic theology are eligible to join with us. As a result, issues which might divide others are not significant factors to us.

Several years ago in London while attending the 275th anniversary of the Grand Lodge of England, I met a young attorney from Malaysia. He told me that with all the diverse political and religious factions in Malaysia, the only place where men could meet as equals and at peace was in the Lodge room. Isn't that a sad commentary? Even to this day man is still killing man in the name of God. I cannot convince myself that this is the will of God.

It is the intent of Freemasonry to provide an environment wherein differences in the way a man worships his God are not dividing issues.

Patriotism is another great teaching of Freemasonry and New Hampshire is irrevocably linked to our forefathers struggle for liberty including the right to worship God as they pleased. This hallowed site serves as a constant reminder that this is a freedom that cannot be taken for granted.

Not one of us feared walking into this cathedral today to worship our God as we wished. None of us were forced to acknowledge God in a form others conceived. Yet even to this day, this freedom does not exist everywhere in the world and we are here today from different faiths committing ourselves to our God as our consciences direct because of those who preceded us. I have a profound respect for what they did and a great concern for the indifference shown by many Americans today.

In the mid-1700s a fledgling nation was in an embryonic stage, developing a different philosophy and a different set of principles. That nation survived and became the United States of America.

At the same time and developing parallel with this nation was a group of people setting those principles and establishing that philosophy. They also survived and are known as Americans.

Both survive today because there has always been those dedicated Americans willing to give their all, if needed, from the American Revolution to the Persian Gulf and now in Bosnia, that this philosophy and these principles might live on.

These ideals were born in conflict and were tempered in conflict, and if they are to remain as a fundamental basis to this nation and conflict is required for that to occur, we can only pray that this same character will be present in the time of need in the future, but I wonder today.

My friends, there is nothing glorious about war but if it is necessary to remain free and retain that philosophy and those principles then we must be eternally grateful to those whom we honor today and pray that there will always be those ready to replace them.

No, war is never glorious. It can never be the moral answer, never the right way. But there are times because of tyranny and tyrants that it may again become the only way. We must hope and pray that the indifference shown by so many today may not become an etching on the tombstone of American freedom. No other country has ever given a greater definition of the word freedom, including the freedom to worship God.

Our forefathers committed themselves, risked their lives and many gave their lives so that we could have these rights that we have today, rights that we tend to take for granted. No other country ever had from its beginning, this degree of freedom. My friends, I wonder if we truly appreciate it.

George Mardikian, an immigrant to America and a successful businessman, wrote:

> You who have been born in America, I wish I could make you understand what it is like not to be an American, not to have been an American all your life and then suddenly with the words of a man in flowing robes, be one, for that moment and forever after. One moment you belong with your fathers in a million dead yesterday's, the next you belong to a million unborn tomorrows.

I suspect that this type of individual truly appreciates the meaning of freedom much more than do we. Lack of total commitment must never be an option for an American.

These forefathers placed a great emphasis upon faith that is evident in their frequent references to God. An example, "in God we trust." I seriously doubt that this could occur in America today. We even have a restriction imposed upon us where we can pray.

My friends, we are free. We know liberty and we practice equality on a scale this world has rarely seen because of a young man whom this site memorializes and hundreds of thousands like him. Thank God they lived.

In the name of political correctness today we seem more intent on denying God for the sake of the minority than of thanking God for the gratitude of the majority. We live in a country founded upon a faith in a Supreme Being and we act like we are afraid to admit it. Indeed, we at times even seem intent in forgetting those who gave their lives to give us that right.

And yet, history is replete with the names of men whose commitment to God and country, to liberty and equality, to freedom for man gives us the privilege to sit here today, men whose commitment was to liberty, to live to think and to worship without fear. To them it was life and Freemasonry helped prepare many of them.

American history is filled with their names; Washington, Revere, Lafayette, Franklin, von Steuben, Hancock, MacArthur, Pershing, and on and on. But the world has also been changed by other brothers whose commitment to religious and political freedom rings like a bell peeling out their names; Bolivar, Kossuth, Juarez, Garibaldi, Ataturk, and Kokolotronis, to name but a few.

All of these men, Americans and others left names forever enshrined in the enclaves of liberty—all with a commonality of a commitment to God

[2]

Constitutional Convention

Given in a church, for a national holiday

"Keep ancient lands, your storied pomp, cries she with silent lips. Give me your tired, your poor, your huddled masses yearning to breathe free. The wretched refuse of your teeming shore. Send these, the homeless, tempest tossed to me. I lift my lamp beside the golden door."

I know that most of you will recognize this as Emma Lazarus' poem, "The New Colossus" quoted on the base of the statue of liberty but none of us, not one, can truly appreciate its meaning. None of us has known what it is to lack the freedom of what America gives. We cannot even conceptualize what it is to live with the lack of freedom. Those who immigrated to this country undoubtedly appreciate it more than those of us who were born here and who take it for granted.

200 years ago in 1787 in Philadelphia, God's wisdom put together men and events which would forever change the direction of the world and the meaning of the word freedom. It was here that they drew up the constitution.

The eighteenth century British statesmen and premier William Gladstone said of America's Constitution, "it is the greatest work ever struck off at one time by the brain and purpose of man." The median of all national charters today, is fifteen years; fifteen years including all nations.

Yet, here is ours at more than 200 years and continuing and none other recognizes so clearly that all legitimate political power flows from the people.

With all that our Constitution has given to us, with all it means to so many, so very few understand it. Why does the oath for the United States officials state, "I will defend the Constitution"? Why not old glory? Why not our people? Why not our coast lines and borders? Why defend a piece of parchment?

After all, it is not the Constitution that spells out our rights and freedoms. Many, even most of our forefathers were reluctant to support it and many even refused. Few favored the concept of democracy, a type of government often equated with anarchy, but to defend the Constitution was to preserve our heritage, a nation of law, not just the flag, not just people, not borders but to defend our right to live in peace as a free people.

Most Americans look at the Constitution as granting their right of freedom of religion. Yet, the Constitution contained only one reference to religion. Article VI reads, "But no religious test shall even be required as a qualification to any office or public trust under the United States." To satisfy many to support the Constitution an agreement was reached to draft a Bill of Rights that was not ratified until four years later.

These freedoms which we view as part of the Constitution were not in actuality, part of the original Constitution but the very first amendment of the Bill of Rights granted us freedom to worship God as we pleased. It states, "Congress shall make no law respecting an establishment of religion, or prohibiting the free exercise thereof." This clause has given us the greatest of all freedoms, the freedom to worship our God in our own way.

In drafting the Bill of Rights, George Mason of Pennsylvania proposed, "full toleration in the exercise of religion." James Madison disagreed saying, "toleration is not enough; it implied that some religion or government was in a position to be tolerant." Nothing in one's life is more personal than his belief in God as he or she sees God.

At the same time, nothing has been more brutal, more vicious, and more inhumane, than man's intolerance in his attempts to force his beliefs upon others and Christians are not exempt. Ah, the wisdom of our founding fathers. This conviction of strict neutrality between church and state grew out of recognition of historical abuses that resulted from church domination of state and state domination of church or a corrupt alliance between the two. Because of this clause, you do not see in America, Jew fighting Jew, Christian fighting Christian, Muslim fighting Muslim and all fighting each other as is found in much of the rest of the world today.

We can worship here today because our forefathers said that the government cannot force or influence a person to go to or remain away from church against his will. No person can be punished for entertaining or professing religious beliefs or disbeliefs or for church attendance or non-attendance.

Still, well-meaning religionists continue to attack, misinterpret or attempt to erode the vitality of these cornerstones of liberty. They fail to recognize that majorities are transient. Those who are part of the majority today may be part of the minority tomorrow. When we contribute to the erosion of any man's liberty, we diminish our own.

Liberty of conscience is inherent in the nature of a man and is an incalculable gift from God. It is therefore appropriate for us this day, to thank our God for the wisdom of our forefathers. After all, in the end the real question that man will have to face is not what did men think of this but what is God going to think. It is not the verdict of public opinion but the verdict of God that settles our destiny.

Our ancestors in America worshiped the way they pleased and because of them, we are worshiping here today. As long as the Constitution remains intact we can relax in the knowledge that our children's and their children's future to worship God in their way is secure. This is why we must protect the Constitution. We owe so much gratitude to God, just for making us Americans.

Daniel Webster has expressed in part what we all owe our God and our forefathers. "I was born an American, I live as an American and I intend to perform the duties incumbent upon me in that character to the end of my career. No man can suffer too much and no man can fall too soon, if he suffer or if he fall in defense of the liberties and Constitution of his country."

My friends, we have so much in life to be thankful for, not the least of which is to be an American and to have the American Constitution.

[3]

Where Have Our Heroes Gone?

*Given at a banquet for the descendants
of Washington's Army at Valley Forge*

For the purpose of this paper, let us first qualify that heroes must meet a basic criteria of being great and that their hero status exists in the minds of those whom they influence. There are no 'un-great' heroes. Secondly, let us establish that we are referring only to a positive hero status and thirdly, that status is of such a level that it has impacted the world. In the thirty-four years of my Masonic membership, probably the most impressive characteristic of the Craft to me was the number of great men who were Freemasons. Men from such diverse backgrounds, that to find any force to bring them together let alone hold them together, would be unique in it. Other organizations attracted members with similar backgrounds, interests or social status, but Freemasonry transcended class distinction, occupational restriction and educational categorization.

For a great portion of my life, I have been looking at changes in society almost as a detached observer. I analyzed it, thinking it to be a temporary phenomenon, a reversible transition into a world that I did not want to accept. It has only been in recent years that reality has sunk in and I finally acknowledged that we are traveling on a one way track that leads into a world in which I must live whether I want to accept it or not. It will not, it cannot go back to what it once was.

Yet, I find myself longing for the days when our children's heroes were committed to setting a desirable example for them to follow and when it was important to do right just for the moral and ethical principle of it being right.

I continue to search for remnants of those days of respect for our country's flag and all the principles it represents, when one stood and saluted when it was passing by, for the display of patriotism which was expressed in, "my country right or wrong," for that commitment to service to helping others which permeated what I remember. Those are the same qualities that were emphasized to me in the teachings of Freemasonry. This is probably one of the reasons Freemasonry is so attractive to me and why it may be less attractive to current generations. One cannot miss what one is never known. If we fail to teach the young what is important in our lives, we cannot expect them to share in our values.

I do not mean to imply that these qualities are non-existent today but they are surely diminished. Nor would I seek a blind commitment, ignoring what may not be right with no inclination to correct it but I do look back with a feeling that something has been lost. *Where have all our heroes gone?*

We may debate the issue that we are not producing heroes today by pointing to generals Norman Schwarz-kopf and Colin Powell and the service they performed. I in no way wish to detract from the significance of their contributions. They are both great examples to our youth of what can be, but their rise to hero status was almost a spontaneous reaction to a short lived occurrence. I am seeking more the hero of long term commitment, those whose very lives were of heroic stature, a man like George Washington.

Heroes are necessary building blocks in an operational society but they must create a positive influence or they become worse than none at all. History is rife with the tyrant "heroes." However, humaneness in the profile of the individual is a requirement if he is to be a positive influence to the world. It was the humaneness of Washington that helped set him apart from the average.

It is a tragedy of monumental proportions that our society of today is not only, not developing that stature of a man but also seems to be committed to destroying the image of those who were. It seems of importance to search for flaws in the character of those who we learn were of significance in the development of our nation and of all civil society. It is incomprehensible that anything tangible can be gained by any society which seeks to destroy the image of its positive heroes. I am not aware of any historically that found a need to seek out the negatives of the great as we have become so inclined to do.

Isn't it sad that we must search for the few who remain positive role models among the prevalent negatives? Thank God for the Cal Ripkens and the Julius Ervings scattered through the overpaid, ego bloated, self-centered athletes of today and for the Ernest Borgnines, Bob Hopes, and Red Skeletons whose own images help bolster the image of the entertainment industry. Regretfully they are the exception to the norm. When I asked the employees of the Grand Lodge to name some positive examples of the present-day entertainment industry that I could use for illustration, I received none.

It is perhaps in this context that Freemasonry made its greatest contribution to the world. It did bring together great men, and it did influence the development of these men while making most men better than they were. Toleration is a premise of the Craft, and therefore those heroes it helped to develop had to be positive heroes. At the same time it is probably that characteristic of toleration that sets the intent of dictators and tyrants to destroy it where they rule. For where there is tyranny and despotism, there is no toleration and where there is no toleration there is no Freemasonry.

Even amongst the greatest, however, George Washington stands tall. His presence will be noted with the great patriots of the world whose contributions to their country caused their name to be etched upon its very foundation. His name will rank in history with the great military leaders, such as Alexander the Great and Genghis Khan even though he lacked the dictatorial power of Alexander and the demonic nature of Khan. As a statesman, his influence on the creation of this nation cannot be overstated. And yet, it was his humanness, his commitment to his men and to his God which causes him to be a great man among great men.

Noted historian, Edward Everett, described Washington as the greatest of good men and the best of great men. Lafayette once exclaimed "Never did I behold such a superb man," and Gladstone said of him, "Washington was the purest figure in history." There have been few great leaders in any field who could be so described.

George Washington stands alone in respect granted by other nations which is reflected by the comparing of their great heroes to him. Simón Bolivar is referred to as the George Washington of South America and Lajos Kossuth as Hungary's George Washington, to name just two. Yet, sadly many of today's Americans have lost touch with his character. How many of us today take time to reflect upon him, even on his birthday.

Isn't it ironic that we as a nation are losing this contact when so many other countries are using him and his contributions as an ideal to emulate? But then those who struggle to gain have a greater appreciation of the gain, and it has been a long time since the average American has had to truly struggle. Prosperity has a way of dulling appreciation for those whose sacrifices and commitments gave us that prosperity. That is a tragic commentary, for when we fail to remember the great personages of the past, we fail to remember why they were great and this paves the way for failure to produce greatness for the future. Maybe this is where our heroes have gone. It would be well for us to impress upon the young the meaning of the struggle and an appreciation of the hero.

One of our societies glaring ongoing errors is in its constant giving while requiring so little in return. How can we expect to develop responsibility when we require none? We live in an environment today which seems to thrive on self-centeredness and the promotion of mediocrity. With a concentration on oneself, there can be little time for an interest in others. Why should one try to reach a stature of greatness when mediocrity is so well rewarded? And without greatness there can be no heroes.

In a world population so many times larger than it was 300 to 500 years ago, where are the Michelangelos, the Beethovens, the Rembrandts, the da Vincis, the Mozarts of today? With so much greater a population base, one would expect more greats in each field, not fewer. And where are those notable patriots whose lives are synonymous with service.

I would suspect all of you here know more about George Washington then do I. It would therefore be presumptuous of me to dwell totally upon his character, so I will take a few minutes to point out a little about Washington the Freemason.

Washington was initiated into Fredericksburg Lodge in 1752. He was admitted before his 21st birthday, the required age. One must assume, therefore, that his character was obvious at an early age. Of the fourteen United States presidents who were members of the Craft, he is the only one to serve in that capacity and master of his lodge at the same time. He was proposed as Grand Master of Virginia in 1777 and as General Grand Master of the United States of America in 1779, both of which he declined and to this day there is no General Grand Master of the United States. He officiated Masonically at the laying of the cornerstone of the US Capitol in 1793 and he was buried with Masonic honors in 1799. We as Freemasons point with pride to him as a glowing example of the spirit of the Craft.

There are enemies of Freemasonry who have worked to deny Washington's commitment to our Craft and there are those who even wish to deny his commitment to God. We oppose all who attempt to destroy the image of our heroes. What can possibly be gained by destroying a positive image? In spite of all their efforts, there is too much evidence in the positive to be denied.

One day while walking along a creek near his home, Isaac Potts, a Quaker, found Washington on his knees in prayer his eyes suffused with tears. This peaceful Quaker later declared "that he could no longer regard it inconsistent to bear arms." If Washington could have this influence on a casual observer think of his influence upon those who knew him well.

It is interesting that the Assistant Director of Mount Vernon said, "I never met a Mason who was not able to offer at least one new story or fact about the father of our country." It is not that we are any more knowledgeable than others we just have a greater interest than most.

Daniel Webster said of him, "America has furnished to the world the character of Washington and if our American institution has done nothing else that alone would have entitled it to the respect of mankind."

This is the Washington about whom I learned. Few men and no American have ever been revered to the extent of this man. And in spite of those who would try to deny his feelings about our Craft he said, "I shall always be happy to advance the interests of the society and to be considered by them, a deserving brother."

Our feelings about our brother stand on Shuters Hill in Alexandria Virginia. The George Washington Masonic National Memorial, one of the most expensive, elaborate, and enduring memorials ever erected to the memory of one man. It was not erected to George Washington the public servant, not the George Washington the hero, but to George Washington the Mason—and it was not paid for with taxes, nor by a nationwide solicitation, but as a mark of undying brotherly love and appreciation by the Freemasons of the United States.

Those who cannot be great, try to destroy the great. Those who cannot build, tear down. It must be the commitment of those who care, to cause others not to forget these heroes of our past or we shall surely lose those of the future.

[4]

Our Patriots and Their God

Given at All Saints Episcopal Church in Philadelphia

It is a great privilege for me to speak here tonight at All Saints Episcopal Church. I was baptized in an Episcopal church a considerable few years ago and I think this is the first opportunity I have had to speak in a church of this denomination. I thank you so much for your kindness. I also wish to acknowledge the presence of those from the police and fire departments of Philadelphia who are worshiping with us here tonight.

Generally when I speak at a church service, I take my topic from the Scripture lesson that is selected for that day. However, when I asked what I should speak about here tonight, it was suggested that I speak on "The Colonial Period" because of the history of this church and also of Freemasonry.

I am aware that All Saints Church is celebrating the 225th anniversary of its founding this year and thus predates the Revolutionary war. I am speaking here tonight as a representative of the Masonic fraternity that also predates the Revolutionary war having its formal beginnings in London in 1717 and in Pennsylvania in 1731 making it the oldest Grand Lodge in North America.

Freemasonry is a unique organization when compared with most others in that a prerequisite for membership is a belief in a Supreme Being. When one walks into a

427

Masonic Lodge the most visible symbol seen reveals our commitment to God: the Volume of the Sacred Law lying open upon the altar. This is a required landmark in all of regular Freemasonry.

We are not dogmatic. Believers in any monotheistic theology are eligible to join with us. Therefore issues which might divide other organizations are not significant factors with us.

I just read in a newspaper this week of the pope's appeal in Lebanon for Christians and Muslims to find peace. Tolerance of others is a requirement for peace and tolerance is a byword of Freemasonry.

As the members of All Saints Church are proud of their heritage, as well they should be so too are Freemasons proud of ours. Much of our pride is the result of our member's commitment to the precept of liberty and equality of man.

My friends, our predecessors in the 1700s committed themselves, risked their lives and many gave their lives for these rights that we tend to take for granted. Not one of us feared walking into this church tonight to worship our God as we wished. We were free to do so. We know liberty and we practice equality on a scale this world has rarely seen because of them. Thank God they lived. We cannot afford to forget.

Even today, however, this freedom does not exist everywhere in the world and we are here tonight from different faiths committing ourselves to our God as our consciences dictates because of those who preceded us.

A young man from Russia walked into my office recently who told me that even though Freemasonry continues to exist in Russia it has been underground since the time of Catherine the Great. To come out into the open for them, possibly means death. How fortunate we are to live in America.

History has preserved the names of men whose commitment was to the liberty of man to live, to think and to worship without fear. To them this was life. Men like Simon Bolivar in South America, Giuseppe Garibaldi in Italy, Benito Juarez in Mexico, Ataturk in Turkey, and Theodore Kokolotronis in Greece, to name just a few are some of the greatest names in their respective countries. The commonality to be found in all of them is that they were all Freemasons.

Our interest tonight, however, is to our American forbearers who made this night possible by advancing the cause of freedom in the United States of America. They have given us this opportunity to sit here tonight. It is to them that our commitment to protect this right is pledged, men whose names are forever enshrined in the enclave to American freedom. Just listen my friends, Benjamin Franklin, Paul Revere, John Adams, Baron von Steuben, John Hancock, Patrick Henry, Marquis de Lafayette, Israel Putman and of course George Washington, again but to name a few. What feelings these names should conjure in all of us. The commonality: Freemasons all.

George Washington an Episcopalian, as you probably all know, was deeply committed to his God. In spite of those who would deny this commitment his life exemplified his belief. The example set by Washington must have impacted those who served with him. His commitment to his faith is revealed in the frequent references to God in our early history. But, I seriously doubt that in this age of political correctness that this could occur today.

So, as we celebrate our anniversaries dating back so far, let us express our gratitude for our early patriots, and for their commitment to the cause of liberty. I wish for you that this period of time will represent just the beginning of your history and your commitment to God and to the freedom of man.

[5]

The Potential Contribution
of Freemasonry to Global Dialogue

Given at the International Theosophy Conference

W hen I was first contacted regarding my addressing
this conference on the subject of Freemasonry's
relationship with religion, science and philosophy
and its potential contribution to global dialogue, I must
admit that I had serious reservations concerning my qualifications to do so and I still do. First of all, even though
Freemasonry has mystical and esoteric elements that are
attractive to many adherents, my relationship to the "Craft"
is in a far more practical sense as its practice relates to its
philosophical purpose and its contribution to the evolution
of civil society. Secondly, I was totally ignorant with the
subject of and practice of theosophy.

Dr. Levy alleviated some of my concerns when I talked
with him in a telephone conversation. He pointed out that
my professional training, interests and occupations might
offer a unique perspective especially as the world looks
hopefully forward to a more stable environment than the
one in which we presently live.

I grew up with a great interest in religion and religious studies and when I entered college, it was to prepare
myself to enter into the ministry. Before I finished, however, I changed my major studies to the field of science.
I graduated from undergraduate school with a Bachelor of

Science degree in chemistry and biology and finished my graduate studies in the field of zoology with a minor in botany. I entered the teaching profession on a secondary school level teaching biology, chemistry and physics and finished with fourteen years on a collegiate level teaching biology, anatomy and physiology.

I eventually left the field of science and after a short time in the business world became a full-time participant in Freemasonry. I served for twenty years as the Grand Secretary of the Masonic Grand Lodge of Pennsylvania, two additional years as Grand Secretary for foreign relations and am now in my tenth year as Executive Secretary of the World Conference of Masonic Grand Lodges where I am now generally looked upon as a Masonic philosopher. When I was introduced to the president of Portugal about 12 years ago as a noted Masonic philosopher I questioned in my mind, how I could be considered a philosopher. I then began to recognize that a philosopher was an individual with opinions and I do have opinions, especially as they relate to the philosophical purpose and the practice of Freemasonry. In essence, therefore, my life did indeed relate to the elements of science, religion, philosophy, and Freemasonry.

In researching the subject of Theosophy I found that according to Webster it relates to the knowledge of divine things and wisdom in divine matters. It also involves the study of various philosophies or religious systems that propose to establish direct mystical contact with divine principle to contemplation, revelation, etc. I found on the Internet that it is a nonsectarian worldwide organization devoted to human solidarity, culture, understanding and self-development. This definition could very well be applied to Freemasonry.

Before I continue, let me point out that my references to men in this paper are in a generic sense. Freemasonry is generally thought of as a male bastion and what we refer to as "Regular Freemasonry" does indeed limit itself to male only membership. However, there are lodges of female only membership and lodges that accept both men and women. These lodges are also ancient, originating in the mid 1700's.

Although Freemasonry lacks the basic criteria of a religion, i.e. a dogma, a theological doctrine or a means to salvation, it does require its adherents to the belief in God's existence as the creator and architect of the universe as a precondition for admission and it encourages its members to become active participants in the religion of their choice. There is no special God of Freemasonry. Each Mason's God remains the one of his religion. It respects all religions and accepts only those who have faith in what they believe. It stimulates all to be a lover of the arts and sciences and to make every effort to improve themselves therein. This encouragement also applies to the studies of their religious commitments so that they might understand more fully the meaning of their belief in a power greater than themselves. In this sense there seems to be some relationship between the philosophical purposes of Freemasonry and that of the Theosophical Movement.

I noted in your program that the keynote address was titled, Global Dialogue: Universal Communication of Wisdom in the 21st Century. I would think that the title of this address would be applicable to a major purpose of Freemasonry throughout the centuries of its existence. It certainly is one of the defined goals of the World Conference of Masonic Grand Lodges. This purpose has not changed over time although the application of its methodologies has been greatly altered in some areas of the world since the age of Enlightenment. However, this evolution of its commitment is not totally unlike that of any other organization that played a vital role during this period in human history.

Freemasonry has been defined in many ways throughout its existence. Perhaps the most descriptive is that it is a "beautiful system of morality, veiled in allegory and illustrated by symbols." We look at ourselves as a "Brotherhood of Man under the Fatherhood of God" and as "a way of life." The simplest and most complete definition is that it is an organization designed, "to take good men and make them better." Unfortunately most of the definitions are ambiguous enough so that few understand them. It is extremely difficult for most Freemasons to define it in such a way as to make it understandable to those outside of the membership. Indeed, today only a relative small percentage of the members themselves truly understand the significance of the purpose of the Craft. Words are simply words. Understanding must transcend words.

To understand the potential for Freemasonry to create a global impact through global dialogue and therefore to impact the ongoing evolution of civil society, we must first understand the proposed origins and history of an organization that did undeniably contribute to this evolution in the past and therefore to its potential contribution in the future.

It is almost incomprehensible that any organization that has existed for as long as has Freemasonry to have no true knowledge of its origin. The generally accepted theory is that Freemasonry descended from the early building guilds that were responsible for the erection of the great cathedrals and other structures in Europe during the Renaissance. There is, however, no conclusive evidence to prove that this theory is true. Indeed, it is confounding to think that an organization that has attracted some of the greatest minds that ever lived could be the result of simple stonemasons accepting into their membership those from the highest echelons of society.

A second theory that has been advocated by some

433

Masonic authors and that has passed in and out of favor in the minds of most, is that Freemasonry is either a direct descendent from the remnants of the Knights Templar or that the Knights Templar joined forces with the early Freemasons to produce the foundation of what exists today. This is not a widely accepted theory and again there is no proof for its accuracy.

I have just finished writing a review on a book entitled, *Isaac Newton's Freemasonry: The Alchemy of Science and Mysticism*. In this book it is the author's conclusion that Freemasonry had an indelible relationship with the Royal Society through which Isaac Newton was the significant player when Freemasonry emerged as the "incestuous child of research, theology, and freedom!" This theory is far too new to have been examined or debated by scholars of the Craft but it is an intriguing concept and frankly stimulates my interest. It carries much logic when trying to piece together a stimulating force within the parameters of the Masonic fraternity that was attractive to so many great men.

I also recently wrote a review on a book with the title, *The Knights Templar of the Middle East: The Hidden Mystery of the Islamic Origins of Freemasonry*. The authors of this text trace the origins of Freemasonry from the pre-Christian era through the Egyptians, the Mediterranean mystery religions, Islam, and finally the Templars and their influence in structuring Freemasonry. It is therefore their conclusion that Freemasonry's development was directly through the Knights Templar and into its present form but with its embryonic roots in Islam. This is also a new theory that remains to be analyzed and debated.

The principal author of this book claimed to be "Prince Michael of Albany" a legal descendent of the Stewart House of Great Britain and head of Scotland's legitimate Royal House of Stewart. Two days ago I received a communication from a good friend who suggested I might want to take a look at the Internet regarding "Prince Michael." In doing so I find that there is much evidence to indicate that he is a fraud and a forger.

However, I take solace knowing that I was not alone in spreading his claim. He has been doing so with support from many more knowledgeable people than me for thirty years. I do not know where this places the information in the book. It was still an interesting concept but has now a seriously damaged credibility.

There have been literally tens of thousands of books written on the subject of Freemasonry throughout its several hundred years of existence in an organized form that began in London in 1717, and yet no one knows for sure where we came from. The principal cause of this lack of knowledge of our own heritage is that very little was ever recorded in written form and most of what was written has either been lost or destroyed. Even to this day the ritual of the Grand Lodge of Pennsylvania has no written form. It has been transmitted via word-of-mouth for more than 275 years.

Regardless of how Freemasonry came into being the significance of it is in the impact that it created on the evolution of civil society for several hundred years. It was one of the principal organizations that provided an environment during the age of Enlightenment for great minds to gather and share their thoughts and ideas with limited fear of governmental suppression or religious restraint. (I would point out that this limited fear depended upon the rule of the country in which it existed.) This environment was especially significant in colonial America for it contributed to the development of a whole new concept of what a nation should be.

Many of the leaders of early America such as George Washington, Benjamin Franklin, Paul Revere, John Paul

Jones, John Hancock, the Marquis de Lafayette, along with many others, were members of the fraternity. Of course, it remains debatable as to whether Freemasonry attracted great men or contributed to making men great but it is inconceivable that so many of the historically significant figures who lead their countries struggles for freedom, liberty and equality were not influenced by the philosophy of the Craft. To list these great men would be like a listing of a Who's Who of the liberators of the world. This list would include names like Simon Bolivar in South America, San Martin in Argentina, Benito Juarez in Mexico, Giuseppe Garibaldi in Italy, Theodore Kolokotronis in Greece, Ataturk in Turkey, Lajos Kossuth in Hungry, to name but a few. These men are universally revered in their countries for providing the leadership to rise above the tyrannical suppression that dominated the freedom of thought in the minds and bodies of the citizens. There are few countries in the world today that enjoy freedom, liberty and equality that do not do so as a result of the philosophical precepts of Freemasonry or the influence of Freemasons. Even to this day where freedom does not exist, Freemasonry cannot exist, and where Freemasonry cannot exist, the environment is not conducive to Global Dialogue.

The Masonic fraternity has, however, exhibited a phenomenal capability of survival. With the exception of the continued operation of Freemasonry in Cuba, dictatorial and repressive forms of government have worked to destroy it. Up to an estimated 100,000 Freemasons died in the same prison camps along with the Jews during the Holocaust. In Austria during the Nazi domination, all Worshipful Masters of lodges were imprisoned in those infamous concentration camps. Those in Japan suffered the same fate simply because they were Freemasons. Many more thousands died under the repressive regimes of Mussolini,

Stalin, Tito, Mao, Franco (who sentenced all Freemasons in the country to ten years imprisonment), and others. Freemasons who were present when Khomeini returned to Iran and could not escape were imprisoned and had their properties confiscated, and it continues into present times. The Grand Master of Venezuela was assassinated just this past summer.

These men all were enemies of Freemasonry and they all opposed the Craft for the same reasons that others embraced it, the Masonic precept of the right of men to be free and equal and the practice of tolerance of all men's right to believe in and worship their God as their conscience dictates. This belief is an antithesis to their type of rule.

During the early days of Freemasonry, persecution in many countries was a way of life. Lodges and Grand Lodges were forced to close in numerous European countries as a result of both religious and civil persecution. When Catherine the Great came into power in Russia she shut down all Masonic lodges even though it was through their efforts that Russia gained its greatest introduction to civility. Indeed, in most countries, the society influenced the structuring of the style of Freemasonry based upon the sociological needs of that environment. In Russia, however, Freemasonry contributed more to the structuring of the society. And yet, there will rarely be a reference to any of this impact in history books.

For many years I questioned why historians chose to ignore the organizations of history until I began to comprehend that historians wrote about men and women not organizations that may have influenced them. Today, however, historians are taking more note of the influence that organizations have had upon the minds of those who were creating the history. Freemasonry is one of the most significant of these organizations due to the lasting influence it has had on the evolution of civil society, especially during the age of Enlightenment.

The Lodge of the Nine Sisters in Paris included in their constitution that the brethren were to devote their attention to studying the arts and sciences: "The Lodge of the Nine Sisters in making virtue its base has dedicated itself to fostering the arts and sciences. The aim of the lodge is to restore them to their place of dignity. Did not the arts and sciences serve as the foundations of great civilizations and nations? Work then with zeal to preserve and to advance civilization and our fraternity."

Regretfully, our Craft has also been persecuted extensively by misguided spiritual leaders who looked upon it as a form of competition since we require the belief in a Supreme Being and as a barrier to their desire for mastery over the minds of their followers. This attack against Freemasonry by various religious institutions has been ongoing since Pope Clement XII issued the first papal bull against the Craft in 1738. Today the greatest challenges are from the fundamental and radical elements of religious leadership. Fundamentalism and radicalism in any form of religion is a threat to those who accept freedom of religion for all people.

This objection is the result of the attitude that if you are not totally supportive of us, you are against us—i.e., if you are not Christian, you are antichrist. They find great objection to the fact that Freemasonry promotes toleration and freedom of thought, embracing all people and all religious dogmas testifying to a belief in a Supreme Being. In spite of the efforts of those who would destroy it, however, it has not only survived, it has flourished. It is a tragic commentary that the enemies of the Craft have been the world's greatest tyrants and some of the world's prominent religious leaders, both major antagonists of each other. It is probably even more tragic that they oppose us for the very same reason, the philosophical principle that man should not only have the right to worship God but the right to worship God as he sees fit.

This propensity for survival along with a steadfast dedication to the philosophy of the Craft also increases the potential that Freemasonry can play a vital role in an ethical, moral and even a spiritual awakening in society through stimulating global dialogue. If this development of a new age of Enlightenment is to be achieved, survivability will be mandatory. It is going to require dedicated and committed individuals and organizations with the vision to look far into the future and possessing the capacity to survive.

I have looked upon the influence of Freemasonry along with its survivability primarily as a result of three factors. Firstly, it was one of the first associations to accept men of all walks of life as equals, or as the prominent Masonic historian Margaret Jacob expresses it, "it was the first leveler of society." It became an organization of like-minded men wherein one could experience an environment of order, harmony and charity with limited fear of suppression. Secondly, it attracted some of the greatest minds that ever lived. Very few, if any, organization can boast of as many great men in its membership over several hundred years as can Freemasonry. Thirdly, it remained selective on the quality of the man that it would accept. Elimination of any one of these three factors would have resulted in an inability to create a lasting influence on society.

In addition, Freemasonry lacks the built in bigotry of religion. Freemasonry's one requirement which causes it not only to be linked to religion but to be opposed by some religious leaders is the requirement of a belief in a Supreme Being that Freemasons refer to as the Supreme Architect of the Universe. There is no religious line drawn in the sand to prevent great thinking minds from working together toward a common goal. Therefore Freemasonry serves not as a barrier to bringing men together but rather as an attractive force. The seal of the Grand Lodge of Israel, operating in one of the more unstable environments in the world today for example, contains the Cross for the Christian, the Crescent for the Moslem and the Star of David for the Jew. I have been in lodges in areas of the world that had as many as five volumes of the Sacred Law upon the altar. Freemasonry truly is a brotherhood of man under the fatherhood of God. This in itself provides a solid foundation upon which to structure global dialogue.

However, it was not the intent of early Freemasonry to create a global dialogue. Indeed, early Freemasonry tended to express an attitude of provincialism and continues to some extent to do so today. In spite of itself, however, it became a global phenomenon and its commitment to enlightened ideals caused it to become a major factor in the development of freedom seeking societies. It is impressive to see the number of countries that have consecrated or re-consecrated Masonic lodges in Eastern Europe since the collapse of communism. It is just as impressive to observe their dedication not only to the principles that created the greatness of the Craft but also to the intent of the leadership to a global understanding.

I have had the privilege of speaking in most of these Eastern European countries since the fall of communism and have encouraged them to study the past and to structure themselves upon the successes of Freemasonry and to avoid the failures. I also emphasized the need to participate in worldwide networking of ideas and in setting and achieving universal goals. This is where Freemasonry has the added potential to contribute to global dialogue. The network already exists and has for several hundred years. I have traveled over much of the world during the past 25 years and never cease to be impressed with the quality of the men that I find within the fraternity. These are the men who are the leaders in their respective societies and countries and are therefore the men who must assume the principle responsibility for global dialogue.

When I was still in the teaching profession and that was over 35 years ago, I was cautioning my students that with the rapidly advancing technology of today, the world will find it impossible to keep up with the legal, ethical and moral requirements of a moral and ethical Society. How true that possibility has become! Unfortunately it appears to be worsening. The need for committed organizations to these fundamental principles of a stable society will continue to increase.

I also challenged my students to locate in today's world with so many more inhabitants the da Vincis, the Beethoven's, the Michelangelos, the Mozarts, the Rembrandts, the Haydns, the von Goethes of the arts, the Voltares of philosophy the Washingtons, Jeffersons and Garibaldi's from the world of government and from the world of science the Newtons and Galileos who contributed so greatly to the development of a true civil society. Theirs became more than an isolated contribution in a field of expertise. Their contributions tended to unite societies and stimulate enlightenment where they were accepted. Jean Roucher in 1779 wrote regarding Isaac Newton, "Newton made the heavens his domain and through his discoveries made the world humane." What a great legacy from the age of Enlightenment. What a great goal for a new age of Enlightenment; to make the world more humane.

Regretfully today, we live in an environment that rewards mediocrity so well that there is little incentive to rise above it. We live, however, in a society that desperately needs an infusion of civility into civil society, a development of a leadership with vision to see beyond self-satisfaction, and a character of life dedicated to rising above the mediocrity of today's social structure. We really do need an organization dedicated to taking good men and making them better; making them better by injecting ethical and moral principles into whatever their profession along with proving to them that they really are greater than they thought they could be. It is a tragedy of no small proportion when we find religious, business and political leaders upon whom we tend to place our greatest trust, functioning as if they are beyond the laws that govern our societies.

What a great goal the Theosophical Movement has assumed to in essence, advance us into a new Age of Enlightenment. It matters not; the name or structure of the organization as long as its dedication is for the uplifting of mankind. Up until a few weeks ago I was unfamiliar with Theosophy and the Theosophical Movement and yet I have come to respect your motives and goals, probably because of the similarity to many of the goals of Freemasonry.

Several years ago I presented a paper to a symposium meeting at UCLA on the subject of the American Enlightenment. During my research for this paper I discovered how illogical it is to consider the creation of the United States of America and fail to comprehend the influence that enlightened minds must have had upon its establishment. I also became more acutely aware of the impact on the development of our society that Freemasonry has created through its environment for enlightened thought. The attributes of the Enlightenment became manifest in principle and in almost every direction early American leaders took in the creation of this country. Indeed, it might not be far-fetched to say that the United States of America is a living manifestation of the Enlightenment or that it precipitated a movement that resulted in what we know today as modern civil society. It can in truth be said to be an invention of the Enlightenment. Margaret Jacob in her book *Living the Enlightenment* stated that "Modern civil society was invented during the Enlightenment in the new enclaves of sociability of which Freemasonry was the most avowedly constitutional and aggressively civic."

The Masonic lodge in early America found itself in a unique position to develop enlightened thought by gathering together men from different countries, with different ideologies, opinions and religious backgrounds and fusing them into a common band of brothers with diverse approaches toward a common goal. The result was New World idealism with an entirely new concept of what a nation could and should be with respect to the rights and freedom of humankind.

Today we find ourselves in an environment not dissimilar from those who contributed to the breaking of the bonds of suppression and restraint on the minds of men 250 years ago. The binding forces and restraining elements may be different but they are nonetheless, just as real. There are certainly those societies today that are experiencing similar types of oppressive rule that was experienced at that time; just the systematics and methodologies have changed. This condition offers organizations dedicated to philosophical precepts that promotes the rights and freedoms that all peoples deserve, the opportunity to exert their influence on a global scale.

Of an even greater challenge, however, may well be the need to generate within the leadership of our Western societies the ethical and moral values that will permit them to rise above their self-imposed limitations and clouded vision that have hindered the achievement of the full potential of democratic society. The need for enlightened minds may today be greater than at any time in history since similar minds developed the new concept that resulted in the birth of the United States of America that in turn served as a template in structuring future democratic societies.

Political correctness today places great restraint on freedom of action if not on freedom of thought. The democracy experienced today is not the democracy created by the enlightened minds of our forefathers. If there is to be continued evolution of positive progression of human development characterized by a moral and ethical commitment, it is going to require organizations with the philosophical purposes of Freemasonry and of the Theosophical Movement, to become more influential in that development. We must always aim to pull others up to meet at our level, not climb down to meet on their level.

Unfortunately for North American Freemasonry and probably for Theosophy as well, the environment in which we operate in America is the great equalizer. It is extremely difficult to produce greatness in a society dedicated to an equality regardless of the efforts or capabilities of the individual.

More than thirty years ago, I wrote a paper for a Flag Day observance which I titled, "What My Flag Means to Me." In it, I made these observations:

> My flag guarantees me the right to an education but it does not guarantee me an education. My flag assures me protection under the law but my flag does not give me the prerogative to violate the law. My flag gives me the freedom to practice my own religious beliefs, but this freedom does not include the right to force my beliefs on others through our political process. My flag gives me the privilege to stand with the decisions of the majority, but my flag does not give me, if I so choose, minority opinion, to dictate my beliefs to the majority.

The equality professed by Freemasonry provides the opportunity for acceptance of men of different religions, social strata and occupations to sit together and act together on equal grounds. It provides the encouragement for men to rise above the limitations that are self-imposed or even societally-imposed. It does not, however, imply that all men are equals genetically, intellectually or physically.

Elitism is not a dirty word. Freemasonry became elitist when they decided to take good men and make them better. Elitism played a major role in bringing together the great minds of the age of Enlightenment and even though one of the fundamental premises upon which Freemasonry is founded is accepting men from all walks of life, it was the men with great minds and capable of great thoughts that made it an influential segment of society.

In America today, the attractiveness of Freemasonry to the influential leaders of society and as a result its potential to influence evolving society has waned considerably. The decreasing vision of the leadership is certainly partly responsible for this decline but the sociological clime in which we operate must assume a major responsibility. We simply live in a society where organizations dedicated to helping others are no longer a dominant factor in our social structure. We are struggling against a sociological apathy for which we have found no cure and until this cure is found our capability of stimulating and advancing into a new age of Enlightenment is improbable.

The failure to maintain the third factor that I mentioned, selectivity, has resulted in a dramatic decline in its ability to attract prominent thinking individuals. Any organization tending to place responsibility on its members is not readily received in this day and age. Hundreds of fraternal, beneficent, civic and social organizations have become extinct in the past fifty years and many more are on the brink of extinction for that very reason. Our government has assumed at the expense of the taxpayer many of the functions that these organizations provided without this expense in the past but even as Freemasonry is not a religion it is also not a political lobbying organization for governmental reform nor is it a forum for political discussion. Indeed, two subjects that are never permitted to be discussed in a lodge are religion and politics. This is enforced to maintain harmony and good order in the lodge room.

It is the function of Freemasonry to build the man; it is the function of the man then to build the society. Freemasonry for several hundred years has proven its potential to stimulate men to excel. However, of an even greater importance is its potential to instill in their consciences those philosophical precepts that will stimulate them to strive toward improving the world for all of its citizens. Our Craft has served as a classic example of how an organization with dedicated purpose can rise above almost insurmountable resistance and intractable odds to remain a leader in a cause to resist those who would seek to destroy the freedoms and rights of man.

It is going to require for North America to internally generate a new long range vision along with a regeneration of enlightened thought to inspire the membership and to cause them to comprehend the potential that they possess to make this world a fit abiding place for all mankind as well as for the Supreme Architect of the universe.

The need for a new Age of Enlightenment is paramount. Great thinking minds must be out there. Kant defined the Enlightenment as, "a search for truth and the freeing of human knowledge from the chains of suppression and superstition with which it has long been bound" but does not sociological apathy, result in a decline of effort in the search for truth, the loss of ethical standards and the failure to maintain moral principles and is not that, just as binding on enlightened thought?

So where in this age of rapidly advancing technology inhabited by citizens with a "me now" mindset and a commitment of their time to self-satisfaction allowing little time for concern of the need for enlightened thought leave organizations that tend to appear archaic, with commitments such as the fraternity of Freemasonry or the Theosophical movement? Have our organizations with our philosophies really become an anachronism in present-day society?

If we are not an anachronism then we must become more active participants in structuring an ethical and moral global society. This cannot happen unless it is preceded by global dialogue. We may not resolve our issues through global dialogue but we definitely will not resolve them by failure to have a dialogue. This knowledge opens wide the door to organizations based upon the fundamental commitments such as Freemasonry, that has a perspective to do so, a history that has done so and a survival capability to outlast the opponents of a civilized world.

There can never be a time when our principles are not applicable to any society. The path we are on today is not proving successful if we analyze it with a measuring standard grading on ethics morality, honesty and integrity. Somewhere out there in this world's vast population are minds just as capable of enlightened thought as were present during that last great age. The demand for organizations to attract these minds and stimulate them with philosophical fundamentals for the benefit of human social structure may be our greatest hope for survival as a civilized society. We simply cannot afford to fail in our quest, for if we do, the world will be the poorer for it.

[6]

Leader of Leaders

Written for a conference of the same name

When I was requested to speak here today, I asked how long I was to speak. Well, I'll tell you now, I will not take all the time that was so graciously granted me. I used to teach in a private girls' college, and I had one-hour lectures. One thing I learned from that experience is that the students quit listening before I quit speaking, and they were a captive audience.

Frankly, I'm not quite sure what I am even doing here speaking to you about leadership in the first place. Each of you is more astute and more qualified in this realm than am I. After all, this is a leader of leaders' celebration.

I am not presumptuous enough to think that I can coach anyone here in leadership. All of you are here because you have risen to a level of leadership beyond mine. You have positioned yourselves to be regarded as leaders in today's world, and you have succeeded well in that regard.

It is always my intent, however, when I speak, to stimulate those listening to think. This probably is the result of 17 years in the field of education. So perhaps today I can stimulate some to think about your importance as a leader in today's world and, at the same time, encourage you to reexamine your significance, perhaps stimulate some to acknowledge the greater challenge of today's environment and, since the precepts of "Leader of Leaders" are directed toward the young, to commit to being more positive influences upon our youth.

It is important in establishing that significance, acknowledging that challenge and committing that influence, that we first recognize that the world we inhabit today is a world distinctively different from the one once known—much different even from the world into which we were born. Just contemplate what you have observed in changes experienced in your lifetime.

Shakespeare wrote:

Tomorrow, and tomorrow, and tomorrow,
Creeps in this petty pace from day to day,
To the last syllable of recorded time....

My friends, tomorrows may have crept in Shakespeare's time, but they creep no longer. Instead, they rush past and carry us forward whether we want to or not, into a future radically different from the past we knew or the present we know. This future is going to be one filled with pitfalls, challenges and opportunities. It is our responsibility as leaders to prepare others to deal with them.

When I was teaching, I told my students, who probably thought I was a dinosaur, "Just wait, because if you think I am out of a distant past, wait until your children observe you."

Because of the geometric progression in the development of knowledge, we have run headlong into an environment with which we are unprepared to deal—to deal with ethically, morally, legally or any other way. We have already encountered legal and ethical challenges in many fields, such as medicine, biology, chemistry and law and we do not have the answers.

Modern technology may speed up the mechanical

application to problem-solving, but it also speeds up the development of issues and offers nothing in the way of ethical, moral or legal answers for coping with them. The future of this world, therefore, is totally in the hands of today's leaders—in our hands, my friends, and that places upon us an awesome responsibility.

I have, for a great portion of my life, watched the changes occurring in this world with a sense of detachment, almost as if they didn't affect me. I tended to think that what was happening was a temporary phenomenon, a reversible transition into a world which I had trouble accepting. Now I realize that I am traveling on a one-way track, as we all are, into a world in which we must live and lead whether we want to or not.

Looking back, there are still times when I feel that I was born too late in history, and yet there are so many great challenges to confront today. I don't know whether we are blessed with the challenges or condemned to live with them. Blessing or scourge, they are here and can be expected to increase as time goes on. But, then, it is the challenges in life that produce greatness in men. There are few great leaders who became great without great challenges to stimulate them.

I find myself still longing for the past where heroes set examples to be followed, where moral and ethical principles were inherent in the personae of most leaders, and where great men felt a commitment to be a positive influence upon the minds of the young.

It is tragic that the youth of the world are losing touch with the character of positive heroes in our leaders. There are today even attempts to destroy the image of those who were a positive influence on society when they lived and whose memory remained such. The tendency in today's world to fail in development of heroes must be indicative of leadership failure.

But, we cannot afford to dwell upon the past. As Long-fellow wrote, "Look not mournfully to the past - it comes not back again." We must not forget the past, but it cannot become a barrier that prevents us from knowing the present and leading into the future.

It is evident on a worldwide scale, however, that there is a need for the class of leader who is committed to restoring that positive feeling that he can be trusted by those he leads; a leader whose very persona creates a positive image, one who becomes a building block rather than a stumbling block in an operational society. For, if he has no positive influence, we are worse off than if he had no influence at all. History is rife with the tyrant leader, and God knows we need no more.

We cannot afford to allow the young to think that the leadership of the world lacks the moral ethics to be both a success and a role model. We cannot permit the acceptance of the attitude of "win at any cost" to be the motto by which they live. There is far too much of this attitude found in too many of today's leaders. If we allow it, the challenge to them to lead into the increasingly complex world of the future, dooms it to moral and ethical decay.

We all have the potential to improve upon what we are as leaders. Now we must acknowledge the need. We must assume a greater mantle of responsibility to lead into a world where right and good are not lost in the confusion of technology.

Now we, who think of ourselves as leaders, must be prepared to face continuing challenges to our way of life. We must have the vision to see well beyond the present. The demand for qualified leaders with the vision to see the needs of the future are more evident today than ever in history. But count on it, that demand will increase, and this is where it is important that we establish the niche into which we will fit. For the world's future, this niche must include a goal beyond the simple limits to influence others. It must include the establishment of the principles which lead to a sound ethical and moral world.

In this world of the present, and certainly the world of the future, there is no longer room for the leader who lacks the moral and ethical fiber to be concerned more with his purpose than with himself. As leaders, we must avoid the self-centeredness that has caused many of the problems faced each day.

Unquestionably, the greatest driving force in any leader is ego. As much as we may try to convince ourselves that our efforts are dictated by some noble motive to benefit others, it is the sense of satisfaction of accomplishment that remains the primary motivator for us to be leaders. And yet, our ability to keep a rein on our egos may be the greatest determining factor of the type of legacy we leave. All of us have seen valuable leaders who created an impact and yet are remembered with a negative image. After a number of years working with many leaders, I developed a little prayer with two points. "Dear God, let me never forget where I came from and let me know when to quit." Does this jog the memory of one you know or one once known? The legacy left behind by many was affected by one or either point. And it is sad to put that much effort into life and be remembered as a failure as a leader because too much ego consumed the good intentions or the good leader stayed on too long.

Perhaps we have had life too easy. Prosperity has a way of dulling appreciation for leaders who gave their best. This should, however, increase the need for us to strengthen our resolve to project a positive image of what is right and good in the world.

We must have the commitment to lead, enough ego to be driven but not enough to be overwhelmed. Enough vision to project the future but not so much that we see beyond our ability to succeed.

We must understand our place in history. We must appreciate the significance of the position we hold. Where the world goes now is in our hands. That future that will change the world so rapidly will be shaped by the standards we establish today. We cannot permit technology to override the moral and ethical guidelines of a civil society.

So as we sit here today and acknowledge that we have succeeded in becoming leaders, let us think a little more about our leadership role. Let us consider adopting a broadened objective of being even more committed to a type of leadership that retains or regains the ethics and morals of a civil society.

Those we lead deserve that. The world needs that.

FIVE

International
Masonic
Jurisdictions

[1]

VII Conferencia Mundial de Grandes Logeas Masoncias II Diego Portales Convention Center

*Given the day preceding the opening
of the World Conference*

Mr. Ricardo Lagos Escobar, President of the Republic of Chile, Jorge Carvajal Mutioz, Grand Master of the Grand Lodge of Chile, representatives of this great Republic, my Brother Freemasons from around the world, ladies and gentlemen.

It is a great privilege and personal pleasure for me, as Executive Secretary of the World Conference of Masonic Grand Lodges, to stand before you today and to address this public opening ceremony of the VIIth World Conference. It is also a pleasure to be back in your magnificent country where I have experienced nothing but the greatest of hospitality and friendliness of the Chilean people.

The World Conference is the first and only organization of its kind, designed to provide an environment where in the leadership of worldwide Freemasonry might meet together to sit and discuss our relationship with today's world. It first met in Mexico City in 1995, and has met subsequently in Lisbon, Portugal; New York City, United States; Sao Paulo, Brazil; Madrid, Spain and New Delhi, India. Now, the country of Chile honors us by giving us the privilege to meet here, and to give our delegates the opportunity to experience the diverse environment that constitutes this great land. Mr. President, we thank you and the peoples of Chile, for that privilege.

Regretfully, many areas of the world today are fraught with an instability that prevents its citizens from living together in peace. Liberty, freedom and equality are unknowns in many lands and acts of terrorism are increasingly becoming a tool used by those who would deny these God-given rights, which should be inherent to all men.

I realize that many of you here today are unfamiliar with the philosophy and precepts of the organization called Freemasonry, but these precepts of freedom, liberty and equality are structural cornerstones upon which the fraternity is founded, and toleration is a key byword upon which it operates.

Freemasonry became one of the first organizations to provide an environment wherein men from all stations in life, from all economic strata, from all monotheistic beliefs and from all racial and ethnic backgrounds could sit together as equals, without the burden of acknowledging the differences but with the freedom of accepting the qualities of all men.

We may not have always succeeded in achieving our philosophical goals, but few, if any organizations created by the mind of man can lay claim to having created a greater impact on the evolution of civil society than has Freemasonry. It became an attractive force to some of the greatest men who ever lived and by doing so, played a major role in stimulating the minds of men to work together for the benefit of all mankind. During the age of Enlightenment, these men, in turn, became the greatest contributors to the intellectual thinking that changed the course of civilization.

Many of the great names etched upon the headstones of freedom throughout the world, are the names of Masonic brothers whose thinking was influenced by the philosophical precepts of Freemasonry and although it emphasizes the need to support and conform to the laws of the land in which it exists, Freemasonry cannot, and should never, escape the need to support higher rights granted by a power much greater than ourselves.

Thus, we find etched upon these headstones names like Bernardo O'Higgins, national hero of this great country, José de San Martín and Simón Bolivar, names with which I am sure all of you are familiar. They were not isolated, however, as leaders in the struggle for rights of man. We also find the names of George Washington in the United States, Lajos Kossuth in Hungary, Benito Juarez in Mexico, Giuseppi Garibaldi in Italy, and Theodore Kolokotronis in Greece, along with a host of others whose contributions and commitments to the cause of liberty are never to be forgotten.

Freemasonry claims as its functional purpose, to take good men and make them better, and since there is no restriction on membership other than being a good man with a belief in a Supreme Being, it lacks many of the limiting restrictions inherent in other organizations. As a result, it has included in its ranks many of the great leaders in a diverse array of fields, including government leaders and statesmen, business leaders, theologians, entertainers, scientists, artisans, poets and writers, musicians, sports figures, and of course military leaders.

Freemasonry can be traced back hundreds of years, but interestingly, we ourselves do not know our own origin. The Regius Poem, the first written manuscript regarding the Craft dates back to 1390.

It is generally accepted by our members as well as historians outside of the Craft that we developed out of the original stonemason guilds that were responsible for building the great cathedrals of Europe. There is, however, a small cadre of writers who feel that we originated from the remnants of the Knights Templar who reached Scotland from mainland Europe, or were influenced by them.

We do know that the first speculative Grand Lodge was formed in London, England in 1717. (Speculative is a term used to differentiate from operative masons.) Since that year, Freemasonry has spread over much of the earth where freedom of man has permitted it to operate. Where tyranny rules, however, Freemasonry has been persecuted and Freemasons killed by the tens of thousands. Rulers such as Hitler, Mussolini, Franco, Stalin, Tito and Khomeini sought to destroy Freemasonry because the fundamental precepts of the Craft are an antithesis to their style of rule.

Freemasonry has re-emerged In Russia, where it has perhaps existed quietly underground since the reign of Catherine the Great, as it did in many of the other Eastern European countries, and it is once again attracting, with renewed vigor, many who were denied the right to freedom of thought and participation as free men.

Those fortunate enough to escape the regime of the Ayatollah Khomeini in Iran found the opportunity to re-create their Grand Lodge in exile in the United States and we are fortunate to have with us today, representatives of the Grand Lodge of Iran in Exile including the Grand Master. These men represent a present-day example of the tenacity for which Freemasonry has been historically known along with their commitment to the principles of the Craft.

Freemasonry has encouraged toleration, when toleration and was almost an unknown. It has encouraged freedom of thought; in environments where such freedom was anathema to those in power. It has promoted an equality of man, where such equality was not an accepted norm.

Freemasonry is non-dogmatic, requiring only a belief

in a Supreme Being. Discussion of religion and politics is strictly forbidden in the lodge. Thus the environment we create is one where good men can work together for the benefit of mankind without the dissension caused by these issues. This is the primary reason that Freemasonry has had within its ranks so many great personalities in so many fields.

We must acknowledge, that even as evil can create evil men to perpetuate that evil, good can create good men to perpetuate that good, and the philosophy of Freemasonry is geared to receive and to build good men.

Even as history can list the enemies of the world, it can also list the champions, many of whom were Freemasons. Men like Francisco Miranda, Benjamin Franklin, Voltaire, Mozart, Rudyard Kipling, Charles Dickens, Winston Churchill, John Wayne, Kit Carson, Nat King Cole, Harry Truman, José Miguel Carrera, and thousands more, found a comforting philosophical environment of like-minded men to whom to relate.

Freemasonry has functioned for centuries as a magnet drawing into the brotherhood good men who were attracted to a philosophy that inspires not only the belief in a power higher than ourselves, but also in diffusing the light of that power and knowledge throughout the world by our actions for the welfare of all mankind.

Our goal remains only to provide the opportunity where great men and great minds can join together in an environment unhindered by the dividing issues that tend to limit the stimulus to excel. Hopefully, by doing so, we may make some contribution to a greater understanding of one another, which in turn may help in some small way to lead to a lasting peace in the world.

Mr. President, speaking for this World Conference, I again express our appreciation to you and to the citizens of Chile for the privilege of meeting in your great country. We wish for all of you the greatest peace and prosperity. Thank you.

[2]

Freemasonry—What It Has Meant to the World and Its Potential for the Future

Presented at Baja California, Mexico

I t is a great privilege and a distinctive pleasure for me to be able to address you tonight on the subject of Freemasonry, what it has meant to the world and its potential for the future.

I trust that when we depart tonight I will in some way have caused you to think a little more about the significance of Freemasonry in the evolution of the world's societies and at the same time challenge you to accept a greater mantle of responsibility in leading the Society of Mexico in its ongoing evolution.

Speculative Freemasonry, as we all know, came into existence in London, England in the year 1717 and therefore has existed in this form for close to 300 years. However, we also know that the first man to be recorded as being made a Freemason was in Scotland in the year 1646. During that span of time Freemasonry has spread around the globe impacting the evolution of civil societies in almost every country where freedom exists.

Freemasonry played a major role during the age of En-lightenment in the quest for human freedom, liberty and equality, as one of the principal organizations that provided an environment where good thinking men from numerous

disciplines and with enlightened minds could meet together isolated from fear of governmental suppression or
religious restraint that would seek to take away man's right
of freedom of thought. In this environment they shared
their thoughts and ideas, fusing their thinking into new
ideals that would alter the course of history and provide
the basis for intellectual, physical and religious freedoms
for humankind. Indeed, it is Freemasonry more than any
other organization that provided the present day format
for the structure of democratic thought.

However, with all the contributions that our Craft has
made through its members to the world, it remains an almost
unknown entity to many outside of it and is distrusted and
feared by many others. Indeed, many of our own members
continue to find it difficult to explain to others what it
really is and what its purpose is.

It has been defined by some of our greatest adherents
as well as some of our greatest enemies. One of the reasons
why it is difficult to explain is that Freemasonry is what
each individual brother makes it to be in his own heart.
Because it is an ever evolving entity, any definition that we
might give today might not have fit as snugly yesterday or
may not tomorrow.

There have been many definitions of our Craft given
by Masonic scholars over the centuries, each of which has
a definitive meaning and application as to what we are.
They all define the Craft and yet none do so, not totally.
Freemasonry almost takes on an ethereal aura when one
tries to define it to others. This aura has caused it to be
misunderstood almost since its inception and has resulted
in major opposition to its existence again almost since its
inception. Man tends to fear what he does not understand
and what he fears, he wants to destroy.

Freemasonry has been intimately involved in the quest

for freedom and equality in much of the world for several centuries. When one examines the contributions that Freemasons have made to the development and evolution of civil society, we must ponder the question, why? Why should there be any objection to our contributions in any civil society?

Consider for example the influence of Benito Juarez on Mexican society. Think of how much different your lives might be were it not for his involvement in Mexico. To expand even farther consider the contributions made by great leaders of South America Simón Bolivar, San Martin, and O'Higgins or those throughout the world. George Washington in the United States, Ataturk in Turkey, Theodore Kolokotronis in Greece, Lajos Kossuth in Hungary and Giuseppe Garibaldi in Italy. When contemplating the contributions that these Masonic brothers made to the development of this world, ask again the question, why? Why this opposition? Just try to contemplate what this world might be today had these men not have lived or if they had not received some influence from the philosophy of Freemasonry.

It is almost inconceivable that in any civil society of free men that there would be those who would object to its existence, but they do. The answer must lie in the ambiguity of our definitions as to what we are, why we are and what are our motives. Couple this with the enmity of those who wish to control the right of man's freedom of thought and we might be able to comprehend why Freemasonry has had to struggle in its attempt to benefit mankind.

Its unabashed support for the freedom and liberty of man makes it an enemy to all those who would seek to take away that liberty and freedom. And yet, with all the ambiguity of what it is to the outside world, and with all the attacks from governmental and religious entities who have sought to destroy it, and with the dearth of understanding of its purpose even by our own leadership, it is an organization that has changed the course of history.

Regretfully, the philosophical precepts espoused by Freemasonry carries with them a price. We find in the ranks of our enemies the names of some of the greatest tyrants in history; names like Hitler, Stalin, Mussolini, Tito, Mao, Franco, and Khomeini. In spite of all oppression that has confronted the Craft, if the greatness of an organization might be measured in the greatness of its composition then Freemasonry would have to be judged an unqualified success.

During my travels over much of the world, I have learned that even though the philosophical precepts of the Craft do not permit deviation from its purpose, the sociological pressures of each environment causes it to adapt to the needs of the society in which it exists. As a result, it has been able to contribute immeasurably to the needs of every society in which it was found.

Because it accepts good men from all stations in life, from all economic strata, from all religious beliefs and from all racial and ethnic backgrounds and places them together as equals without the burden of acknowledging the differences but with the freedom of accepting the qualities of all men regardless of those dividing characteristics, it has attracted into its membership some of the greatest minds who have ever lived. So our brothers have played a major role not only in leading in the struggles for freedom, liberty and equality but contributing in many diverse fields that makes up any civil society.

These observations make up the glorious history of the Freemasonry of the past but my Brothers, what of the Freemasonry of the future? Voltaire wrote, "That which has been bequeathed to us must be earned anew if we would possess it." There can be no doubt that we no longer hold the image we once held in North American society

466

nor do we have the influence we once had in directing its ongoing evolution. Mexican Freemasonry today has a far greater potential to do so than do we in United States or in Canada. It is quite evident, however, that we must seek to earn anew that which has been bequeathed to us.

Every Freemason is a living definition of the Craft by which it will be judged. It is very simply what each individual brother determines it to be in his own mind and how he reveals it to the world. It will never be more or less to each brother beyond what he makes it to be. This is why it is so imperative that due consideration be given to each man who petitions the Lodge. His commitment to the Craft, its philosophical purpose and precepts must be unquestionable. Remember, my brothers, societies tend to judge organizations, not on its best members but on its worst. A noted Filipino Masonic writer once observed, "One bad man in your Lodge will do you more harm than any ten good men will do you good.

In spite of all of the obstacles that have confronted Freemasonry; it has exhibited a phenomenal capability of survival. Today the Craft is probably expanding and growing at a more rapid rate that it has perhaps for more than a century. Much of this expansion is a result of the creation or revival of Freemasonry in Eastern Europe and its development on the continent of Africa. Its potential influence in those two environments upon the evolution of their societies opens a new vista for Freemasonry. Freemasonry has always been at its best when the challenges to it have been the greatest. Today the challenges of the development of Eastern European countries and in the countries of Africa place the potential of Freemasonry in the forefront to influence the evolution of civil societies for the benefit of its citizens.

I have been greatly impressed with the quality of the

brothers that I have met in both these environments and their commitment to improve conditions in their respective countries. I look for our Craft to be an influential guiding light in their ongoing evolution.

I do not need to tell you that Freemasonry in Mexico has been extremely confusing to most of us trying to understand it. There can be no question, however, of the potential that exists within the Craft to influence an ongoing evolution here. It is time now to earn anew that which men like Benito Juarez bequeathed to you and to the world.

We live in an age of rapidly advancing technology that is creating a world that finds it increasingly difficult to keep up with the legal, ethical and moral requirements of a moral and ethical society. For this reason, if for no other, the influence of the philosophical precepts of Freemasonry must play a vital role in helping to stabilize this evolution in the society of Mexico.

We today, have an enormous challenge before us to develop a leadership with a vision to see beyond self-satisfaction and a character of life dedicated to rising above the mediocrity of today's social structure. We need an organization dedicated to taking good men and making them better; making them better by injecting ethical and moral principles into whatever their profession.

We have been part of an intellectual ideal that has provided a stimulus for men to think beyond the artificial limits that have been imposed upon him by those who would control his freedom of thought. My Brothers, there is a wide open door in front of you, a door of opportunity, a door of challenge.

All you need do is walk through it and practice those philosophical principles and precepts that you learned from our Craft. If you do, you can rest assured that your society and the world will be the better for it.

[3]

Is Charity a Real Core Value?

Given as my concluding paper
to the All-Canadian Conference

This could very well have been the shortest paper that I would ever give. The answer to the title *Is Charity a Real Core Value* is emphatically "Yes" and that could be the end of my paper. However, it is not the real core value and therein is a dilemma for Freemasonry and the reason that I speak a little longer.

I mentioned this afternoon that I encountered difficulty developing enough material to speak about my view on the subject of the Masonic Charity. In fact in preparation of these two papers, it became the greatest challenge that I have faced in writing.

From listening to me earlier, you probably understand that even though I am an ardent supporter of Freemasonry's involvement in charitable programs, I have a great concern as to the extent that North American Freemasonry has carried the concept. We have made it the core value of the Craft and we have done so, simply because we have forgotten or have never known the more significant purpose of Freemasonry.

To summarize what I said in my previous paper, Freemasonry in North America has become so deeply involved in charitable objectives that we have created a different and autonomous image of Freemasonry by which we are now known and which is distinctive to North America. Even though this image in itself is not a bad image, indeed, it is a good image, it fails to support the weight of the character by which the Craft has been known in the past and by which present-day historians are acknowledging us to be. As significant as this charitable image may be, it is not nearly as significant as the image for which we have been known on a worldwide level.

Freemasonry has had a magnificent past. The magnitude of its accomplishments for those who might not know them, and very few do, is almost beyond comprehension. Freemasonry's impact on the evolution of civil society cannot be overstated. It has been, and is, deeply concerned with the welfare of our fellow man but this concern in North America has carried it into an exaggerated commitment to the support of charity.

We must have a deep concern today as to whether this commitment is interfering with our basic purposes and whether it is worth it, if it results in our willingness to lower our standards to support this commitment. I asked our Grand Officers last year, if any of them could name one major project of North American grand lodges that was not directed either to increasing numbers of members or to raising money to give away to others. They could not name one.

I am talking about major projects of a magnitude that will serve to perpetuate an image that will be as long-lasting as that created by our brothers in the past. We are capable of developing long-range visionary programs that will not only benefit Freemasonry but will go a long way to ensuring our survival and what is even more important, will continue to develop leaders to guide the world. It will not happen, however, until we divest ourselves of our vision limiting hang-up on the need for high numbers or our ill-fated attempts to buy an image.

Charity is definitely a core value of Freemasonry, but we have other core values that have created an organization the likes of which have not been not seen before nor matched since. If there was any one criterion fundamental to the development of the Craft, it was the quality of its composition. The numbers of members was not an issue at any time, and a charitable image was not the intent at any time. Without the great men who have been part of us, it is inconceivable that we ever could have accomplished what we have. Now we seem not only willing but also eager to accept any level of quality simply to acquire numbers and to support our objectives whether they are an integral part of Freemasonry or not.

In another paper, I made the observation that I felt that Freemasonry gained its greatness for three primary reasons. First, it was probably the first organization to accept the men from all walks of life as equals. Second, it attracted some of the greatest men and greatest minds who ever lived. Third, it remained selective of the quality of the man whom it would accept.

These criteria as core values have more far-reaching ramifications than the core value of Masonic charity. It is therefore imperative that we place and keep in proper perspective, the relationship of charity to Freemasonry. If our charitable objectives in any way distract us from these three criteria, they interfere with our primary purpose as a Craft and cannot be ignored or tolerated.

Freemasonry in North America is at a critical crossroads in its life. Whether we realize it or not, we, its present leaders are being forced to determine what it is that we really want it to be and where we really want to go. For over thirty years we have been drastically declining in numbers but more importantly we have been reducing our image in society.

After my 40 years in Freemasonry as a profession-al Freemason, I am firmly convinced that we have been concentrating our efforts in the wrong direction. We have been experiencing a quarter-century panic attack because we are losing numbers that is caused by a sociological phenomenon over which we have no control. We have not reduced the loss by increasing the amount of money we contribute to charities, although Lord knows we tried. We have weakened the guard at the west gate as an act of desperation, and continue to weaken it and that has gained us nothing other than diluting our quality. Isn't it interesting my Brothers that our decreasing numbers have been followed by a decrease in quality and that in turn, by a reduced capability of raising money for charity? If charity therefore were the core value, we would still be reducing our capability of fulfilling that value.

This loss of quality is not only reflected in the decline in ability of our membership but in the decline in will-ingness. I must assume that every one of us here today has both the ability and the willingness or we would not be here. Therefore the mantle of responsibility is resting upon our shoulders. The decision of what we want to be as a Craft is in our hands. Do we want to remain a viable force for good in the world, as we have been for centuries? Do we want Freemasonry to continue to develop men who will lead in the world's struggles for freedom, liberty and equality? Do we want to remain the greatest organization ever developed by the mind of man, or are we willing to rest upon the laurels of our Brothers of the past as we've been prone to do for a long, long time? Do we have a vision to see the forest instead of the trees? If we do, we have some serious decisions ahead of us, for we must change the course of direction that we have been taking for at least the past quarter-century.

We must now examine all of our core values, see which ones have carried us for centuries and determine if this is a pathway we wish to take into the future.

Yes, charity is a core value of Freemasonry but we must place it in its proper perspective with the other core values of the Craft.

[4]

Banquet in Moscow

Again it becomes my pleasure to be in your company, and to speak to you regarding the future of Freemasonry in your countries. My Brothers, we represent the current leadership of an organization that changed the course of evolution of civil society.

We have been structured by some of the greatest minds that ever lived and walked this earth, and it was those men and those minds that carried us to greatness.

Freemasonry provided an environment wherein these men with enlightened minds might fuse their ideas into a form that could alter the course of history for the benefit of all mankind. Present-day civil society is the result, Masonic ideology was the course, the Masonic Lodge the catalyst.

But, we must never forget our purpose, to take good men and make them better. It is then, that these better men lead in the making of a better society and we make these men one at a time.

Does this philosophy make us elitist? Damn right it does. When we limited our organization by definition, to good men, we became elitist, and there is nothing wrong with that.

A minister challenged me one day, because we say we take good men and ignore the bad men. My response to him was that it is not our purpose. One cannot make fine porcelain out of bad clay. We do not reform, that is a function of the church.

We cannot be a totally introverted organization and succeed, but nor can we fail to develop our Brothers. To paraphrase our Brother, Rudyard Kipling, then you will be a better man, my Brother.

Russia is a society with a unique relationship of Freemasonry to society. With early Freemasonry, we find that society structured Freemasonry; but in Russia, early Freemasonry was used to structure the Russian society. What this shows to the world, is the flexibility and diversity of the influence of our Craft. In both cases, however, the end result was the benefit received by the society in which it existed, and even though it is our goal to make one man at a time a better man, we have, and can continue to alter the course of human society.

Each one of you sitting here today will create an impact upon the direction of Freemasonry in your countries. You can impact it much more because of the evolutionary change you are experiencing in your countries.

If I could offer you any advice above all else; it would be to seek out the good man and make him a better man. That is your goal and the world will remember you for it. The quantity of your membership is of little consequence if it carries with it no influence in society. Freemasonry did not impact the world by running over it; it impacted the world by the influence of one man at a time. Take the good man, cause him to learn, teach him the philosophy of the Craft, and stimulate him to think, make him a better man.

We have and we can, change the world. In your country, it is now in your hands. If we do not succeed in making better men, then we have lost our heritage and failed our past.

The world needs us. Let the world know.

[5]

Sibiu Conference:
Bridging the Orient and the Occident

*The Global Future of Freemasonry and Fraternalism
and Its Potential Contribution to Evolving Eastern
European Societies*

I regard it as a distinct honor to be asked to address this distinguished group of academic personalities on the subject of the global future of Freemasonry and Fraternalism and Its Potential Contribution to Evolving Eastern European Societies.

Only a decade or so ago, my presence here would have been a virtual impossibility. The ideological and sociological changes that have taken place in this part of the world in this short span of time have given rise to a hope for a far more stable future with a greater degree of freedom than has been known for generations. At the same time, we must recognize that it also brings greater challenges requiring greater commitments on the part of those who would lead their societies in this new-found freedom.

I was told one time when I was to be a keynote speaker that it was my responsibility to motivate, stimulate and inspire. Well, my friends, I'm not sure I have that capability to motivate or stimulate or inspire those of you sitting here. You represent some of the most significant personalities and great thinking minds in your society today and have already been motivated, stimulated and inspired or you would not be here but hopefully I will provide some points for you to think about.

With the exception of North America, I have spent more of my time in Eastern Europe over the past ten years than in any other area of the world. For me to say that I have been very much impressed with what I have found in Eastern Europe would be a gross understatement. I have not only learned to appreciate deeply the history of your countries, the beauty of your environment, and the cultures of your peoples, but I have also developed a deep admiration for their commitment to participate in the ongoing evolution of your societies. For me to take part even in this small way is an honor that I do not take lightly. I can only hope that my small contribution might provide some additional knowledge and encourage you to continue to lead the way in structuring an environment that is beneficial to all members of society.

An observation that I made in working with Eastern European leaders was that I was working with a different mindset from what I have been used to. This is not a criticism but rather an acknowledgment that one must comprehend when working with the leaders of Freemasonry or, for that matter, the leaders of any organization in Eastern Europe. This mindset is a totally understandable result of the societal systems that dominated the environment under which you lived for so many years. It will take years to totally reconstruct and develop the trust and faith in the brotherhood of man. Meanwhile, an organization like the Masonic fraternity offers a guideline based upon the very precept of trust and commitment to one's fellow man.

My subject today deals generally with the global future of Fraternalism and Freemasonry but more specifically with the philosophy and principles of Freemasonry and the potential contribution that its precepts can make to the ongoing evolution of societies in Eastern Europe. Freemasonry existed in most countries in Eastern Europe at some time in the past but was forced into extinction, or at the least into being a clandestine operation, as a result of oppressive Nazi and/or Communist regimes. It is a remarkable testimony to the tenacity of Freemasonry that it became constituted or reconstituted in most countries in Eastern Europe in such a short span of time following the collapse of these oppressive regimes. It is to the credit of the leadership that they had the vision to grasp the opportunity to use Freemasonry as a medium through which they could contribute to the rebuilding of society in their countries.

To understand this phenomenon and to understand the potential that Masonic philosophy has to become a major influence in the development of your societies, it is necessary to understand some of the history of this Craft, its philosophical purpose, its historic composition and its contribution in developing other societies.

As illogical as it may seem for an organization as old and as prominent as Freemasonry has been, no one knows for certain, its age or its origin. The first written manuscript regarding the Craft dates back to the year 1598, but we do not know how much farther back it may go. A principal cause of this lack of knowledge of our own heritage is that very little was ever recorded in written form and most of what was written has either been lost or destroyed.

What we do know is that the first speculative Grand Lodge of Freemasonry had its origins in London, England, in the year 1717. Since that year, Freemasonry has spread over much of the earth where freedom of man has permitted it to operate. Where tyranny ruled, however, Freemasonry has been persecuted and Freemasons killed by the tens of thousands. The countries in Eastern Europe have not been immune to this persecution. It is estimated that over

100,000 Freemasons died in the Nazi gas chambers along with the Jews during the Holocaust.

Even during the early days of Freemasonry, persecution in many countries became a way of life for the membership. Lodges and Grand Lodges were forced to close in some European countries as a result of both religious and civil persecution. When Catherine the Great came into power in Russia she shut down all Masonic lodges, even though it was through their efforts that Russia gained its greatest introduction to civility.

This persecution continues even to this day. The tragic bombing of the Masonic Temple in Istanbul several years ago killed two members of the fraternity, and the Grand Master of Venezuela was assassinated a little over a year ago. These actions must serve as a reminder that the philosophy of the Craft remains under attack by those whose own philosophy fails to provide for the inherent rights of men.

Perhaps just as illogical as the lack of knowledge of our origin is our failure to develop an all-inclusive definition of what we are and what is our purpose. Freemasonry has been defined by Masonic scholars in many ways throughout its existence. They all define the Craft—and yet none do so, at least not totally.

Unfortunately, most definitions are ambiguous enough that few understand them. It is extremely difficult even for most Freemasons to define Freemasonry in such a way as to make it understandable to those outside of the membership. In fact, emphasis placed upon its operation in various parts of the world renders definitions unreliable. Indeed, today only a relative small percentage of the members themselves truly understand the significance of the purpose of the Craft. Understanding must transcend words. This has historically been our greatest failure in attempting to create an atmosphere of acceptance in many world societies.

Our origin, however, is not relevant to our success as a fraternity, for regardless of how Freemasonry came into being, its significance lies in the impact that it has created on the evolution of civil society for several hundred years. It was one of the principal organizations that provided an environment during the Age of Enlightenment for great minds to come together and to share their thoughts and ideas with at least a limited fear of governmental suppression or religious restraint. (This limited fear, of course, was dependent upon the rule of the country and the dominance of the religion.) This environment has been greatly significant in many parts of the world. In my country, it contributed considerably to the development of a whole new concept of what a nation should be and what the freedom of man truly means.

Freemasonry claims as its functional purpose, to take good men and make them better, and since there is no restriction on membership other than being a good man with a belief in a Supreme Being, it lacks many of the limiting restrictions inherent in other organizations. It became one of the first organizations to provide an environment wherein men from all stations in life, from all economic strata, from all monotheistic beliefs and from all racial and ethnic backgrounds could sit together as equals without the burden of acknowledging the differences but with the freedom of accepting the qualities of all men.

Globally, Freemasonry is showing one of the greatest surges of interest by the public that has taken place since its very early existence. This interest is principally the result of a greater degree of freedom occurring in this part of the world, along with consecrations of new Grand Lodges in African countries. In addition, as a result of the writings of Dan Brown, author of *The da Vinci Code* and *The Lost Symbol*, there has been a proliferation of interest in many countries resulting in television programs and movies that in turn are creating an even greater interest. There has been a marked increase in petitions for membership being submitted in North America by young professional men.

Historically, Freemasonry's greatest impacts have taken place in environments where the need of its ethical principles and philosophical intent has been the greatest. It should, therefore, be of no surprise to observe this resurgence of the Craft in Eastern Europe. It also should be of no surprise that it is attracting some of the greater thinking minds from this part of the world. The same phenomenon is characterizing Freemasonry on the continent of Africa even as it has in every environment where it was permitted to develop. For this very reason, its potential contribution to the ongoing evolution of civil society in Eastern Europe will be limited only by any constraints imposed on it along with the commitment of the membership and the caliber and dedication of the leadership. The philosophy of Freemasonry could very well serve as a template for structuring a lasting civil society as well as for world peace. This philosophy, however, will only be as influential as those who lead the Craft.

If we choose to use as a barometer to measure its success as a fraternity the historical composition of its membership, it is probably the greatest human-created success story in the history of mankind. As a result of its willingness to accept good men from all walks of life, its composition reads like a Who's Who in more diverse fields than any organization that has ever existed, including government leaders and statesmen, business leaders, theologians, entertainers, scientists, artisans, poets and writers, musicians, sports figures, and military leaders. Fourteen of the Presidents of the United States have been Freemasons and I am certain that there are many great Freemasons from this part of the world who could be named. Many of the historically significant figures who led their countries in their struggles for freedom were undoubtedly influenced by their relationship with Masonic philosophy. They also read like a listing of the Who's Who of the liberators of the world. It is illogical to consider that so many of the great patriotic leaders of the world who led in struggles for freedom and the rights of man were Freemasons and would not have been influenced by its philosophy.

These men are universally revered in their countries for providing the leadership to rise above the tyrannical suppression that dominated the freedom of thought in the minds and bodies of their citizens. Even to this day where freedom does not exist, Freemasonry cannot exist, and where Freemasonry cannot exist, the environment is not conducive to world peace.

Even as this attractive force for great men created an environment that provided a template for forging societies that in turn provided for the rights and freedoms of man, it also, however, attracted its greatest enemies. These men who so adamantly opposed the rights and freedom of man certainly were committed to opposing the Masonic fraternity whose very philosophy supported those rights and freedoms. It is ironic that this genre of men who were such bitter enemies of the fraternity should give cause for decent freedom- loving men to appreciate its existence.

But also listed among the greatest opponents of Freemasonry have been some of the religious leaders of the world. They find great objection to the fact that Freemasonry promotes toleration and freedom of thought embracing all people and all religious dogmas testifying to a belief in a Supreme Power. It is a tragic commentary that the enemies of the Craft have been the world's greatest tyrants and some of the world's prominent religious leaders, major antagonists of each other.

Freemasonry's one requirement which causes it not only to be linked to religion, but to be opposed by some religious leaders, is the requirement of a belief in a Supreme Being that Freemasons refer to as the Supreme Architect of the Universe. There is no religious line drawn in the sand to prevent great thinking minds from working together toward a common goal. Therefore, Freemasonry serves not as a barrier to bringing men together but rather as an attractive force. It is non-dogmatic, requiring only a belief in a Supreme Being. Discussion of religion and politics is strictly forbidden in the Lodge. Thus the environment created is one where good men can work together for the benefit of mankind without the dissension of these issues.

Freemasons have been part of an intellectual ideal that has provided a stimulus for men to think beyond the artificial limits that have been imposed upon him by those who would control his freedom of thought. Our goal remains to provide the environment where great men and great minds can join together unhindered by the dividing issues that tend to limit the stimulus to excel. The world has always needed the guidance of great minds and many have been molded by the precepts characterized and tempered in the conclaves of Masonic ideology.

There has never been a time, when, if this philosophy and these precepts were applied, that peace could not have been an alternative to war and conflict. There can never be a time, no matter how long this world may exist, that Freemasonry's philosophy would not be applicable to the morals and ethics of any society. It has impacted the evolution of civil societies for several hundred years. It has changed significantly the course of civilization. It has influenced the development of some of the greatest men who have ever lived and it has been a bulwark in support for the rights and freedoms of all people.

The very nature of fraternalism requires a compatibility that may not exist outside of a fraternal structure. Fraternalism has played a vital role in helping to shape societies and has been especially significant in times of stress. Thus, one finds a marked increase in fraternal interest following times of war as well as during times of social struggle.

The fraternalism of Freemasonry offers the bonus of philosophical precepts specifically dedicated to improving the man and through the man the society. Fraternalism provides a binding force. The fraternalism of Freemasonry supplies a moral and ethical stimulus to that force.

The philosophical purpose of Freemasonry, however, is not to become directly involved in shaping society. The purpose of Freemasonry remains to shape the man. The man then shapes the society. By simply looking at the number of great personalities who have been responsible for shaping so many of the world's societies and who were Freemasons should provide evidence of the potential contribution that Freemasonry can make in shaping the societies in Eastern Europe.

But my friends, Eastern European society does not exist in a vacuum. Issues do not wait to be resolved and problems do not wait to be solved. So even as you struggle to resurrect your societies you will be challenged to keep up with an ongoing metamorphosis that the world is experiencing that is impacting the way we live along with the morality and ethics of civilization itself. The concept of political correctness that permeates much of the world today is influencing many societies and justifying a degradation of those morals and ethical values upon which most civil societies are founded. It is an issue that all societies are facing but it will offer an even greater challenge to those that are facing major adjustments to a way of life and that of course, include Eastern Europe.

Along with the need for leaders in societies experiencing a greater degree of freedom to provide guidance in adjusting to this newfound phenomenon, it will be extremely important to retain those principles upon which lasting successful civil societies must be grounded. Freemasonry has been not only a significant modifying influence during the metamorphosis of the past; it has been a driving force.

Freemasonry has been able to transcend the variances with which it has been confronted in the environments in which it existed. Because of the universality of its purpose coupled with the constancy of its zeal and the stability of its requirements, it has risen above those restrictive barriers that have hindered societal evolution for several hundred years and stimulated the leadership to rise with it. It has stood the test of time and has impacted the world in general, probably more than any other organization conceived by the mind of man and hopefully it will be able to play some role in the metamorphosis of your societies today.

Even though interest in Freemasonry is experiencing resurgence globally, it has been subject to a decline in interest and influence in some parts of the world partially due to sociological changes in society and a lesser need for its direction in more stable environments.

I have been emphasizing for more than a decade that the great future of Freemasonry will lie in Eastern Europe and Africa. I am convinced of this not only because these areas of the world are experiencing newly consecrated or re-consecrated Grand Lodges, but because Freemasonry has historically functioned best where its challenges have been the greatest. In areas of the world where Freemasonry has existed for hundreds of years, its influence on the evolution of the societies has lessened simply due to the sustained stability in those environments.

Freemasonry is a fraternity whose character is molded

by the demands of the environments in which it exists. Although it plays a major role in shaping the society, its character that I refer to as "style" of the Craft is to a great extent, shaped by that society. A great opportunity now exists for the societies of Eastern Europe to utilize the philosophy of an organization that has proven itself consistently for several hundred years, to lead the way in a quest for freedom and equality of all of its citizens.

It would be interesting if we could look back a hundred years from now and observe how much of an influence Freemasonry has had on the shaping of the societies in Eastern Europe and at the same time to observe the style of Freemasonry that was determined by those societies.

There is no doubt, my friends, that fraternalism can play a significant role in the ongoing evolution of Eastern European societies. This role will be dependent upon the vision, commitment and intellectualism of the leadership. Freemasonry certainly has established itself as a significant fraternal player in evolving societies in the past and hopefully may do the same in Eastern Europe while at the same time reestablishing its position as a vital cog in the wheel of evolving civilization.

[6]

Freemasonry, Fraternalism, and the Authoritarian and Dictatorial Regimes of the Twentieth Century

Bucharest, Romania—2011

Once again I am afforded the privilege of being able to participate in the projected annual conference that will deal with Freemasonry and fraternalism and its potential impact upon the ongoing evolution of civil societies. More explicitly, this conference will focus on specifics impacting Eastern Europe and the Mediterranean region but ranging further into the West, hence "Bridging the Orient and the Occident."

Let us establish before we proceed, that fraternalism does not necessarily guarantee assurance of a positive influence on any society. There have been many organizations that grouped men together into what may be regarded as a form of fraternalism for the significant purpose of creating what was to become a very negative influence on the society in which it existed. Indeed, that is what precipitates the structure of this conference today.

It was my pleasure and honor to be present last year in Sibiu/Hermannstadt to speak on the subject of The Global Future of Freemasonry and Fraternalism and Its Potential Contribution to Evolving Eastern European Societies. There, I was privileged to associate with many significant participants in what projects to be a scholarly program that should help guide the contributions of Freemasonry into the future of these evolving societies. We must comprehend that the direction of civil evolution in Eastern Europe will have a far-ranging impact on all world society so that any positive influence cannot be minimized, not only as a force for the benefit of mankind but also as a deterrent to future authoritarian/dictatorial powers.

Freemasonry is a global phenomenon that has been contributing a philosophical roadmap to the structuring of civil societies for several hundred years and is in a position, as in the past, to play a similar role in Eastern Europe. I must emphasize that this was not the intent when Freemasonry had its speculative beginnings in 1717, nor is it the specific intent today. The goal of Freemasonry is not to improve the society but rather to improve the man. It is then the man, influenced by Masonic precepts, who improves the society. Fortunately for humanity, the Masonic organization has probably had a greater positive impact on global societies than has any organization outside of some organized religions.

Regretfully, this roadmap and the philosophy of Freemasonry have not been universally accepted throughout its history and as a result the fraternity and its membership have paid a very dear price for its attitude of toleration and its promotion of the rights and equality of man. The theme for this, the second conference, *Freemasonry, Fraternalism, and the Authoritarian and Dictatorial Regimes of the Twentieth Century*, becomes a theme that reflects the persecution of the Craft and the price paid.

I am probably the least qualified of the participants in this conference to speak to the subject. I have never personally experienced any of the repression or suppression that has been placed upon you and your environments by authoritarian/dictatorial regimes, nor has my country been subject to that type of repression. Many of you have personally lived through the dogmatic dissection of fraternalism in general and Freemasonry in particular in your countries and if you have not personally experienced it, your nation certainly has. There are very few countries in the Occident or the Orient where Freemasonry has not been subject to authoritarian suppression and limitations during the several hundred years of its speculative existence.

For the European continent, the twentieth century probably ushered in a new low regarding the freedom and liberty of its citizens. The rise of dictatorial regimes has almost universally brought with them a confrontational attitude toward Freemasonry. I am not familiar with persecution of other fraternal organizations during this period in history, but I am aware of what happened to Freemasonry.

The attitude of dictatorial regimes should come as no surprise since the core philosophical structure of the Craft is one that would be an antithesis to any power dedicated to the suppression of freedom of expression of thought and to what should be the inherent rights of the liberty of man.

It is therefore not without a certain amount of pride that Freemasonry claims as its greatest enemies those who would deprive their citizens of those freedoms and rights. Hence, during the twentieth century, we find the greatest persecution of Freemasonry on the European continent during the Nazi regime as existed in Germany and its conquered lands, the National Fascist Regimes in Italy and Spain, the Communist regime in the Soviet Empire and lesser dictatorial powers as existed in the eastern European Communist bloc countries such as Ceausescu's here in Romania.

For that reason, on the historic roll of enemies of Freemasonry we not only find the names of Hitler, Stalin, Mussolini, Franco, Tito and Ceausescu among others on the European continent, but also the names of Hirohito, Mao and more recently Khomeini, Hussein and Qaddafi among others elsewhere in the world. It is significant that dictatorial powers outside of the European continent were just as oppressive to Freemasonry as those on the continent but the European continent seems to have fermented the greater diversity of dominating egos.

It is, however, with an even greater amount of pride that Freemasonry claims within its membership rolls, some of the greatest names that have been recorded in the annals of history of those who have opposed authoritarian/dictatorial powers and who lead their countries during their struggles for freedom, liberty and equality.

Dating back to its early history, philosophical values of the Craft have contributed to the development of such great patriots as Washington, Bolivar, O'Higgins, San Martin, Juarez, Garibaldi, Kolokotronis, Kossuth, and Ataturk along with a host of other lesser-known names who nonetheless played major roles in their countries' struggles for the rights of its citizens.

I pointed out last year that just two short decades ago, it would have been a virtual impossibility for me to be standing in the position that I stand today. It would also have been just as impossible for you to be sitting here either representing an organization dedicated to the principles exemplified by the Masonic fraternity or participating in a seminar involving it. Indeed as a result of authoritarian/ dictatorial rule, this organization and this conference simply could not even exist.

It is almost inconceivable that a transformation of this magnitude covering such a large geographical area and encompassing so many different countries could have taken place in this short period of time. The ideological and sociological changes that have taken place have now given rise to a hope that could not have even been conceivable in the not too distant past.

I also made the observation last year that I have found a different mindset in the citizens of Eastern Europe than what I have been accustomed to in most of the rest of the world. This mindset is structured as a result of the societal systems to which you have been subjected for many years and it will take time to redevelop trust and faith in the brotherhood of man. For Freemasonry to exert its most beneficial influence, however, it will require a dedication of the leadership to the future of the Craft as well as to the future of their societies.

Freemasonry and Masonic ideology are not new to much of Eastern Europe, however. In some Eastern European countries they have existed for more than a century. Nevertheless, their repression by authoritarian/dictatorial rule has resulted in their presence today to appear as new phenomenon rather than a reappearance of an old creation.

Freemasonry did not disappear from your landscape completely, however, during this period of oppression. Back in the early 1980s while I was serving as Grand Secretary of a Grand Lodge, a man from Russia came into my office and told me that he was a Freemason in that country. I asked him how that could be possible under the Communist regime existing there. Historically, the Masonic fraternity was banned in Russia during the reign of Catherine the Great and continued through Communist rule. It was not re-consecrated until 1995. His response was that Freemasonry continues to exist in Russia but that it was not practiced openly and there was no operating Grand Lodge.

This singular display of one man willing to risk his very survival to claim membership in an organization that in essence played a major role in converting Russia into a civil society reveals the tenacity and survivability of an organization through a membership that paid with their lives during the authoritarian regimes of the twentieth century.

It is not easily understood why historians have chosen to ignore Freemasons as a persecuted group who were sacrificed during the Holocaust along with the Jews and other groups. Perhaps it is a result of less dramatic numbers than those of the Jews. The Holocaust Museum in Washington, D.C., does include in some of its displays a record of Freemasons who were confined to and perished in concentration camps.

Robert L.D. Cooper's recently published book, *The Red Triangle: A History of Anti-Masonry*, which he refers to as "masonophobia," delves extensively into this subject to lay the foundation for the anti-Masonic activity in the British Isles. Cooper, a long-serving curator of the Grand Lodge of Scotland's Museum and Library, is an author of note and well-versed in Freemasonry. In this extensive study, he has extrapolated the information that he obtained to conclude that approximately 80,000 Freemasons were put to death on the European continent during this period in history simply because they were Freemasons and that is perhaps a very conservative conclusion.

Cooper's work may well be the most thorough analysis that has been made on this specific subject. He made the observation that the anti-Masonic feelings that developed early in its history were conceivably a result of the leadership's attempt to create a society without divisions, therefore eliminating any need of intervention by the dominating religious or political establishments whose livelihood depended upon that intervention. Controlling people's activities tends to become inherent in these professions. Freemasonry was not within the political or religious system and its philosophy was an unknown aberration in the eighteenth century. If that observation is accurate, it certainly gives cause for authoritarian powers to attempt to destroy or control it.

Following World War I, in an attempt to justify Germany's defeat, Ludwig M. von Hausen published the infamous and enduring *The Protocols of the Elders of Zion*, laying the blame for the defeat on a Jewish-Masonic conspiracy. This publication, although debunked in most of the civilized world, festered internally resulting in supposed justification of the mass extermination of the Jews during the regime of Hitler that carried along with it, the Masonic fraternity.

Cooper has been able to demonstrate that the Nazi regime under Adolph Eichmann's leadership, actually determined that Freemasonry was a primary target even before the "Jewish problem was considered." The Nazis made the distinction between Jews as a racial enemy of the German people and the Freemasons as an ideological enemy.

As the authoritarian/dictatorial powers expanded their control over the European continent, persecution of Freemasonry expanded along with it. Freemasonry in France was dissolved. The fascist regime of Benito Mussolini in Italy declared Freemasonry and fascism incompatible. The Grand Lodge in Czechoslovakia was dissolved and the property and assets seized; the Grand Lodge in Serbia was prohibited and all property and assets confiscated, members were removed from their jobs and some shot. In Spain, Franco established discrimination against Freemasonry as a state policy. In all countries where Nazism and Fascism gained control, Freemasonry was banned and when these dictatorial powers were defeated and Communism gained control, Freemasonry continued to be banned.

When dealing with the subject of authoritarian powers and their impact upon fraternalism and Freemasonry, it is significant that we establish the understanding and not lose sight of those who would be opponents of Freemasonry and who were not authoritarian/dictatorial powers of governments.

Regretfully, some who historically have been and remain opponents of Freemasonry have been some whose position benefited the most from its existence. Some prominent religious leaders have positioned themselves in direct opposition to Freemasonry and ironically they have opposed the Craft for the very same reason that the authoritarian powers did: their desire to control the thinking and actions of those under their power. They also find a great objection to the Masonic precept of toleration and freedom of thought embracing all people and all religious dogmas that testifies to the belief in a supreme power.

It is paradoxical that an organization that requires a belief in a Supreme Being and encourages its members to support the religion of their choice, should need to include upon its rolls of enemies some prominent religious leaders along with the most inhumane despots who ever soiled the Earth by their presence and who are major antagonists to each other. I emphasize, however, that no religion opposes Freemasonry. Only religious leaders oppose Freemasonry.

It has been well stated that those who do not recall history will be doomed to repeat it. It would be well for us not to lose sight of the fact that this pattern of anti-Masonry, although perhaps most pervasive during the twentieth century, began in the eighteenth and ninteenth centuries and has carried on into the twenty-first century. Recall the tragic bombing of the Masonic Temple in Istanbul a few short years ago and the assassination of the Grand Master of Venezuela just two years ago.

Historically, however, Freemasonry's greatest influence has taken place in environments where its ethical principles and philosophical precepts have been the most needed. Its attractive force to some of the best thinking minds in the world continues today, and therefore its potential contribution to evolving societies remains as a potential hope in much of the world. Freemasonry's intent remains to improve good men and to provide the opportunity where great men and great minds can join together in an environment unhindered by the dividing issues that tend to limit the stimulus to excel.

So long as human life exists in the world, there will be those ego- driven tyrants who will see themselves in their justifiable position to dominate the minds and actions of those over whom they have control. There never will be any guarantee that it will not continue into the future and that Freemasonry or some other fraternal organization will serve as the scapegoat either to justify their persecution or hopefully give cause for their defeat. We must always assume the potential and be prepared for it.

[7]

World Conference—Delhi, India

The country of India is a remarkable and fascinating location for us to meet, and I hope that you will take advantage of your time here to explore the unique and diversified cultures that is to be found

The complexity in preparing for this conference became compounded many times in consequence of the 9-11 terrorist attack in New York City. It became further compounded due to the tensions and conflict that took place in northern India along the border with Pakistan

When I spoke to you in Madrid, last year, I emphasized the need for us to recognize and realize that we were living in a rapidly changing environment that was going to force us to re-examine the way that we operate and the way we relate to one another in this environment. The time of isolationism of Freemasonry, within individual Grand Lodges is gone. The relative unknown quality of our Craft to those outside of it has been replaced by the public's demand for, and our willingness to give more extensive public knowledge. These characteristics of our past, although eroding for decades, have been rapidly swept aside by the technologies of the present, and there is nothing we can do to change this fact. Those Grand Lodges failing to acknowledge this evolution will in all probability become a footnote on some historian's writings in the future.

A great concern that we must face now, however, is the

impact that this change is creating on the fundamental purposes of Freemasonry. Decisions are being reached by Masonic leadership today that is restructuring and remolding our institution into something that we have never been, nor never meant to be. The results are evident by the dilution of our influence to use our philosophies and precepts in the development of what is good and right in the evolution of civil society. We as leaders of World Freemasonry have an obligation to do all within our power to curtail this dilution, to contribute to the perpetuation of our ideals and cause them to be diffused throughout the thoughts of future generations. If we fail in this purpose, we fail in our commitment to our Brothers of the past whose contributions are etched upon the headstones of freedom of which we all are a part. More importantly, however, we fail in our commitment to society in general and to world peace and understanding.

The World Conference has provided an opportunity for many of our leaders to meet together and to discuss not only mutual problems which confront us, but also to recognize unique problems confronting Freemasonry in different areas of the world. It has provided an environment wherein the bonds of brotherhood have been greatly expanded, and friendships created that will last the lifetime of those experiencing the feeling of this expanded brotherhood. Far more important, however, is the providing of opportunity for us to understand one another, to resolve issues before they become irresolvable, and to stimulate us to work more fully together to spread our philosophy for the good of mankind.

Many of us have become more cognizant of the operating variances that exist in the Masonic Fraternity in different parts of the world. These variances are the result of environmental differences in which our Craft operates.

It is therefore significant that we all understand that there may be differences in Freemasonry's operating philosophy but not in its structural philosophy, its precepts, or its fundamental purposes.

We must understand, recognize, and accept that each Grand Lodge is an independent sovereign unit unto itself and has the right to make decisions and take actions that it deems appropriate within its operation, so long as it does not violate this philosophy or these precepts. This is an undeniable and inalienable right of a "Grand Lodge."

With that in mind this Conference will operate within parameters where the rights of no Grand Lodge will be infringed upon. We must keep in mind that operating philosophies may vary resulting in emphasis being placed on different societal aspects in different parts of the world. We, therefore, must remember that when establishing goals we should aim to the universality of interest of the Craft everywhere.

I express again, that it is my sincere pleasure and privilege to be seated in a room with men such as you. You represent the epitome of the leadership that has assumed the mantle of responsibility to lead Freemasonry at the beginning of this century. One hundred years from now, historians will be writing about the impact of what you have crafted, even as they are today writing about our predecessors. What they write is now in your hands. I sincerely hope that this World Conference may serve as a contributory factor and positive influence upon what you Craft.

Let us now divest ourselves of any self-limiting egos that we may have acquired and work together upon that level that causes us all to be Brothers, and to circumscribe our desires to work toward a common goal of perpetuating the unifying philosophy of Freemasonry throughout a world that is in desperate need of it.

[8]

Freemasons' Obligation to Society

Given to the Grand Lodge of Romania

I recall an old Cherokee Indian proverb, "When you were born you cried and the world rejoiced. Live your life so that when you die the world cries and you rejoice."

If each of us as Freemasons lived our lives in such a way that when we died the world cried we could probably claim success of our life not only as citizens of the human society but as Freemasons in improving that society for all people. Is that not our purpose?

We have proclaimed to the world for many generations that the fundamental purpose of the Craft is to take good men and make them better. It is then our hope that these better men will become integral players in the ongoing evolution of civil society. There has been no organization created by man that has shown a greater success in achieving that goal than has Freemasonry.

Every man when he chooses to become a Freemason must assume the obligation that for him will become a life-changing experience that will cause him to devote more effort to the benefit of mankind in general and to the society in which he lives in particular.

I had the great privilege recently of speaking at the Sibiu Conference with the theme "Bridging the Orient and the Occident." In the paper I presented, I emphasized the diversity in the fields of endeavor of a number of the significant men who were Freemasons and who contributed greatly to creating the world societies that we now know. These Freemasons would claim a prominent position in a listing of a "Who's Who" of the greatest men who lived in the last 300 years.

Now, each of you stands on the threshold of opportunity to contribute to the continuing evolution of your society. The opportunities for you to participate are vaster due simply to the dramatic—and probably for many, traumatic—change that your society is experiencing. The obligation that you assumed on becoming a Freemason has a greater potential for you to impact society than of those of us who have not faced the suppression of freedom that you have. The eternal quest of man to seek to live outside the bonds of restraint to his freedom of "life, liberty and the pursuit of happiness" is far fresher in your memory.

It is imperative, however, not to assume that because the opportunities are so visible that the journey will be an easy one. I recall another saying that I will paraphrase, "It is difficult to free fools from the chains they revere." You will encounter those who find difficulty adjusting to a more free society. This will result in a greater challenge for understanding the brotherhood of man under the fatherhood of God but then the greater the challenge, the greater the potential reward.

This has been especially true for those who have participated and contributed to society's evolution in the past and who were influenced by the philosophic principles of Freemasonry. That is the reason you would find in that unwritten "Who's Who" of the greatest men who lived in the last 300 years the names of so many significant Freemasons. Their names are etched upon the headstones of eternity and as a result of the contributions of these Freemasons, the reputation of the Craft was born and has endured.

Each of us who takes that Masonic obligation assumes the responsibility of perpetuating the meaning of the Craft and ensuring its continuance as long as humanity survives. There can never be a time when the philosophy and precepts of Freemasonry would not be applicable as a guide to the evolution of civil society. The evolutionary direction that Romania now takes could very well be shaped by the contributions you now make.

Even as the age of Enlightenment opened a new vista of opportunity to Freemasons of the past to participate in an evolutionary change in society's conception of the meaning of freedom, this dramatic change in the concept of individual freedom in Eastern Europe offers a new opportunity for participation for Freemasons of the present to contribute to the evolution of their societies.

It is important, however, to not lose sight of the fact that our goal remains to improve the man. Freemasonry as an organization does not get involved in issues that tend to divide, but we trust that these resultant better men who were shaped or altered by Masonic philosophy will continue to be involved in shaping and altering Romanian society for the betterment of all citizens.

I have had the pleasure and privilege of meeting and associating with Romanian Freemasons and Masonic leadership for the past six years and have been very much impressed with the commitment and dedication of those I have met. There is reason for great confidence in the future of Romanian Freemasonry.

You have traveled far in your journey to reclaim your rightful heritage as Freemasons in your country after decades of repression, but your journey is far from complete. You will continue to be confronted with obstacles and you will experience disappointments. However, your future and the future of your children and your children's children could very well depend upon your ongoing commitment to the principles and precepts that you have obligated yourself to as members of the greatest fraternity ever conceived by the mind of man.

I offer my congratulations to Most Worshipful Brother Eugen Chirovici for his accomplishments in his service to Romanian Freemasonry. You have brought your Grand Lodge into visibility and acceptance on a world level. You have performed your task well and have proven my early evaluations of your commitment to Freemasonry. Now as you step down as Grand Master, you can rest comfortably in the knowledge that the Craft in Romania is better off for your having served.

I thank all of you for your kindness, hospitality and brotherly love that I have always experienced in my travels in Romania. The comfort that I find in Romanian Free-masonry and the intellectualism and commitment to its future is as good as I find anywhere else in the world. The Craft in Romania is indeed, in good hands.

[9]

Opening Address for
the Xth World Conference
Gabon, Africa

I t is a great privilege and a great pleasure for me to be able to welcome you to this the first World Conference to be held on the continent of Africa. It is of pronounced significance that we meet in Africa the birthplace of humanity and the continent where Freemasonry is perhaps growing the most rapidly.

Sadly, the conference is taking place with the absence of the Past Most Worshipful Grand Master, Omar Bongo Ondimba. It was his choice in setting the theme of the conference to be, "The Art of Building Our Environment Together." This theme was a reflection of his great interest as the President of Gabon to preserve not only the environment of his country but also of the world in general. There are few issues today that are of a more paramount importance for our future than is preservation of the environment. This visionary leadership style shown by our Past Grand Master is of extreme importance for human survival and although Freemasonry does not become involved in politics, we as Freemasons must be concerned with the contribution we can make to this preservation. It is, therefore, suitable that we dedicate the actions of this conference to his memory.

As we all now know Most Worshipful Brother Ondimba completed his journey here on earth and surrendered himself to the Supreme Architect of the Universe several months ago and his son Ali Bongo succeeded him as both President of Gabon and as Most Worshipful Grand Master of the Grand Lodge.

Unfortunately, distractions resulting from his death and the contribution of time put into the presidential elections along with the disturbances following the election had a negative impact upon those Grand Lodges in attending this conference. A number of cancellations and withdrawals of intended reservations has reduced the final count present here today. In addition, the difficulties encountered in creating an inclusive website have proved frustrating to some wishing to attend.

Nonetheless, the Brothers of the Grand Lodge of Gabon extend a warm and brotherly welcome to all of you sitting here today. It is their intent to see that your time spent at this X[th] World Conference will be enjoyable, educational and satisfying to you.

Fourteen years has elapsed since the first meeting of the World Conference was held in Mexico City. During that time the conference has provided the opportunity for the leaders of world Freemasonry to meet together and discuss mutual problems and issues that confront our fraternity. More importantly perhaps, has been the creation of an understanding within the leadership of Freemasonry of the nuances within the operational philosophies on a worldwide scale. This understanding is probably more important today than it ever has been in our past. We need to recognize that because operational styles vary it does not imply that they are irregular unless it violates the protocols or "landmarks" of regular Freemasonry. Regular Freemasonry must support regular Freemasonry or weaken our potential to fulfill our philosophical purpose. We must not permit our personal egos to dominate our thinking in making decisions within our own jurisdictions nor our relationships with other Grand Lodges.

We continue to have schisms within regular Freemasonry in a number of jurisdictions and in spite of all efforts, egos tend to interfere, limiting resolution. Appendant bodies persist in exerting or trying to exert a controlling influence over Craft Freemasonry. Irregular forms of Freemasonry continue to become more organized and expand into territories in which regular Freemasonry has existed for decades or even centuries. We cannot afford to ignore these issues hoping they will go away. It is of paramount importance that we unite our efforts in dealing with them. It is imperative that all Regular Grand Lodges work together in dealing with any issue which would tend to divide and destroy us.

We must work together in establishing a unified effort to regain our rightful image in society. There's probably been no organization ever created by the mind of man that has exerted a greater influence on the evolution of the civil society that has structured the modern-day world than has Freemasonry. And yet, in many parts of the world our attractiveness to quality men is declining, our image is diminishing and our impact on evolving society is lessening. While this is occurring we continue to find regular Freemasonry in conflict. The future the Craft lies in your hands, my brothers, and in the hands of other leaders like you who will determine the direction that we will go.

Much of our future lies in the success of the Grand Lodges being consecrated or re-consecrated in jurisdictions in which it has not existed or in jurisdictions where it has been suppressed for decades. This basically means that much of our future success will lie in Eastern European countries and on the continent of Africa. It is therefore more than symbolic that we are meeting here under the auspices of the Grand Lodge of Gabon. Freemasonry in these jurisdictions has a far greater potential to impact the development and evolution of their societies than does Freemasonry in the more settled environments and my brothers, it was the impact on society that has granted Freemasonry its greatest contribution to mankind. It will also be this present-day impact that will expose the Craft more significantly to present-day society. The fact that much of society has failed to recognize that contribution does not make it any less important to the world.

For this reason the need for a conference such as the World Conference becomes more significant. The responsibility of the older Grand Lodges to advise the new Grand Lodge leadership and to direct them away from the pitfalls we have known is of a vital importance. In this present age of advanced technology we no longer have the luxury of waiting that we once had. Decisions made today are around the world today. If we are to recapture the visual image of the Craft that once permeated world society regarding Freemasonry and if we are to assist new Grand Lodges to establish theirs, then we must work together and rationally examine our options.

I have recently written a review on Dan Brown's new novel, *The Lost Symbol.* This book is going to stimulate an increased interest in Freemasonry in the young men of our present day world, even more so than did *The da Vinci Code.* This increased interest will provide for us an opportunity to reestablish some of the quality for which Freemasonry has been historically known but it is going to take a commitment of the leadership to use this opportunity to reestablish those esoteric qualities. The onus of responsibility that is heaped upon our shoulders today is not only to provide leadership into the future but to reestablish the intellectualism and philosophical characteristics that has been bequeathed to us by our brothers of the past. Therefore, let us use these few days that we will be together to create bonds of understanding, to acknowledge the commitment we have made to future generations, and to recommit Freemasonry to the continuing evolution of civil society which must out of necessity involve an understanding of the preservation of our environment. The world needs Freemasonry, my brothers, perhaps more than ever in our past. We must make sure that the world knows.

As always, it is a great privilege for me to be here with each one of you. You represent the nucleus of the leadership that will assume the mantle of responsibility to lead Freemasonry into the future. It is you who must accept the dedication to preserving the heritage that our brothers in the past have provided for us. It is you who must comprehend and accept the need of divesting all personal egos in devoting yourselves to our common cause. It is you who have been given the opportunity to influence the evolution of our civil societies into a world more tranquil than the present. What the world is today is to a great extent a result of the influence of the Freemasonry of the past. What the world will be tomorrow may very well be determined by the contributions that you make in providing the leadership of the Craft today.

[10]

The Challenges of Masonry
in the Twenty-First Century

Izmir, Turkey—2013

Most Worshipful Grand Masters, distinguished colleagues and my brothers, it is a great honor and distinct privilege to be with you today and to address the subject that is the theme of this conference "The Challenges of Masonry in the Twenty-first Century." Indeed, since the beginning of this century the challenges of Masonry have been a major topic of discussion by Masonic leaders of the world as well as by the individual brothers who comprise our lodges. It is also a subject which I have placed a great deal of emphasis on in my position as Executive Secretary of the World Conference of Regular Masonic Grand Lodges.

Keep in mind that the observations that I present to you today will not be applicable to every jurisdiction or even to every part of the world. I write from the cumulative experiences which I have had and the knowledge that I have gained from the privilege of being able to travel over a great portion the world for the purpose of Freemasonry.

This is a remarkable age for Freemasonry. Our fraternity is expanding and establishing roots in relatively untouched environments. It is achieving success in its influence in parts of the world where it has not existed in the past or where it has been rejuvenated following the demise of repressive regimes. There have been 26 consecrations of new Grand Lodges since the beginning of this century. This represents perhaps the most rapid rate of expansion over that span of time that we have seen in our history. There has been a rebirth of interest in the potential of our Craft to contribute to a new societal evolution in much of the world. I have been greatly impressed and stimulated by the development of the interest seen in the leaders of countries striving to enhance the evolution of their societies and looking at the potential for Freemasonry to participate in that enhancement.

In many stable societies, however, the potential influence of Freemasonry has become less than what it was. This is simply a matter of fact due to those societies, having evolved to a level of stability where future evolutionary change will be limited or at least slowed in its development. This does not mean that the need for the philosophical purpose of Freemasonry has in any way become less but its ongoing influence will be more subtle than in the past. It means that the needs for dramatic societal changes are no longer paramount in these environments. But where Freemasonry is now rising there exists fertile fields to be cultivated by those dedicated to a society in need of the gentle guidance of our Craft.

And yet, along with this glowing future for our Craft in some parts of the world, we continue to acknowledge the ongoing challenges we are facing in other parts. The search for the ultimate solutions to the challenges of Free-masonry might almost be likened to the search for the elusive "Holy Grail." Facing challenges and searching for solutions is nothing new to Freemasonry. Challenges to our integrity have been part of Masonic history even before we were formerly structured in 1717. We have searched for solutions for centuries and yet challenges remain. However, our survival over those centuries is indicative of our success as an institution. Every challenge, large or small, became temporary because our philosophical purpose never wavered and the leadership of the Craft never lost vision of its purpose. The very fact that it continues to thrive throughout the free world is undeniable evidence that its purpose is universal and undying.

In the present age, however, there seems to be a prevailing attitude by many of our leaders that the Freemasonry of those past centuries is not a good fit for modern society and that we must change our operational precepts to adapt to this society. In spite of all of the changes that have been made in recent years, however, with our attempts to reshape Freemasonry to fit into this "modern" world there has been little success. Indeed, many of the attempts have resulted in an increase in failure.

One of the causes for our failure to find a universal answer is that the challenges are not universal and leaders of the Craft differ considerably in their thinking on the solutions to these challenges. In our attempt to regain our prominence and visibility, we have become far too willing to surrender the integrity and character that made us prominent and visible to begin with, simply to satisfy demands from the profane world.

Certainly the environment in which we must operate today is different from the environment of the past but environment has constantly changed. Is the societal change required to advance into today's age of technology any more dramatic than the societal change required to advance into the age of the industrial revolution? Is it necessary for us to become fundamentally different from what we have been for 300 years?

Are the environmental changes of the modern world so much different from those of the past that the philosophy of Freemasonry with its emphasis on morals and ethics is no longer applicable? Perhaps the changes are not so much needed in Freemasonry as they are in the society in which it exists. Because society lowers its values does not mean that we must lower ours to fit in. I would suggest that the problem is not with us and our philosophy but rather with society and its values. Our concern today must not so much be with the challenge of the changing environment in which we operate but rather our reaction to it.

Organized Freemasonry has survived and indeed has flourished in a constantly changing environment for close to three centuries and has been a dominant player in the evolution of civil society during that period of time. It has changed over these three centuries but never in the form or magnitude that we are seeing in the present age in some areas of the world.

Freemasonry has never been a stagnant institution but an issue that we should always be concerned with would be our refusal to consider change if it benefits our Craft. Any change we choose to make, however, must not be as a result of pressures from the outside world. The changes we made in the past in our operational procedures were changes that were made because we wanted them made for the benefit of the Craft resulting in a benefit to society not because those from the profane world wanted them made. Now, however, many changes we are making is our attempt to satisfy external demands which we are now willing to make to satisfy the "political correctness" attitude of present-day society and I find myself to be out of step with this attempt.

I have found myself to be in disagreement with many of today's leaders of Freemasonry, especially in my home country where our desperate attempt to secure numbers has resulted in a catastrophic loss of our image and influence in our society. Now we spend far too much time making excuses to justify our failings instead of working to maintain our successes.

I am not in accord with the rationalization that the protocols of regularity, recognition, right to visit, and territorial sovereignty are unable to shape today's world and I readily admit that I do not accept that these fundamental precepts that defined and served as a stabilizing factor for Freemasonry for centuries are outmoded vestiges of our past. For some reason or reasons we seem to have adopted the attitude that dramatic changes are not only desirable but necessary for our survival in a society that desperately needs an injection of the ethical and moral values of Freemasonry. These protocols under which we have operated for three centuries and that we are now implying do not fit into today's world have provided a protective umbrella, shielding the Craft from those who would attempt to dilute its values.

Why have we become so willing in recent years, to submit to the liberal thinking elements of society that the Freemasonry we have known for 300 years, the Freemasonry that has been a major contributor to the shaping world society as we know it today, the Freemasonry that has participated in so many struggles for liberty, freedom and equality for so many peoples, indeed, the Freemasonry whose philosophy could serve as a template for world peace is no longer applicable?

Freemasonry did not survive by bowing to the wishes or the demands of a society sadly lacking in many ethical and moral values that are foundation stones to our Craft. Freemasonry did not thrive by subjugating the Craft to dictatorial regimes or to oppressive religious powers. Freemasonry did not become the greatest organization conceived by the mind of man by lowering our standards and sacrificing our principles in order to receive greater numbers or acceptance from the profane world that makes no attempt to understand us. No, my brothers, Freemasonry became what it became due to of our commitment to retain those qualities which made it great and made it a benefit to civil societies.

A very good friend of mine, a Christian minister, once asked me why we defined ourselves as an organization with a goal to accept only good men and make them better, choosing to ignore those who need our help the most. My response to him was that fine porcelain cannot be made from bad clay. It was the responsibility of religious institutions to reform men, not ours. We are not a Reformation society; we seek to better men and it was that resulting better man who structured much of our civil society.

I fear that Freemasons today, in many areas of the world are forgetting that purpose and as a result the visible image that we are projecting to society is an image with much less prestige than we were able to exert in our past. As that prestige diminishes our influence to impact the ongoing evolution of civil society also diminishes and that is a tragic loss to the world. Freemasons exemplified those moral and ethical characteristics that tended to elevate societies, simply by emulating what was good and what was just and right in man. In so doing, Freemasonry served as a pattern that resulted in a new vision of the rights of humankind. In a broad sense it has served as a foundation for the concept of democracy.

As our overall influence may be decreasing, our potential to impact the world is increasing. But even as that potential is increasing, we are experiencing dissension within our ranks that also may be approaching a zenith. Internal issues within Grand Lodges resulting in Schisms and confrontations between Grand Lodges are increasing.

Too many of our members are developing the attitude that the Freemasonry that has existed for 300 years is not compatible with what they perceive as Masonic philosophy. Historically, the greatest challenges facing Freemasonry were external. Our greatest enemies have been oppressive leaders of governments and oppressive leaders of religions. You will note that I referred to leaders of governments and religions not governments and religions. Governments do not oppose us nor do religions oppose us. It is the leaders of these institutions who have been our opponents.

It is also worth noting that both these entities, even when in opposition to each other, opposed us for the very same reason, a desire to control the bodies and minds of those under their control and with intent to destroy any organization tending to interfere with that desire. They would take away from their adherents everything that Freemasonry stands for, the right of the liberty of man to think and to live, free from repressive political constraint and with the freedom to worship God as their consciences dictate.

Today, however, they are not the greatest threats that we are facing. The greatest threat to our future today is internal not external. There are far more divisive issues for Freemasonry today existing within inflated egos of the leadership and the liberal attitudes of the membership of the Craft than from challenges from forces outside of it. Neither repressive governmental systems nor any oppressive religious regime has been able to defeat the philosophy of Freemasonry. In spite of all of the attempts from these powers, none have destroyed us. Many have tried and many have failed. Now, however, in some areas of the world we are accomplishing what they could never do.

For years, I have been emphasizing several of the greatest threats to our integrity as an institution. They are the interference of appendant bodies with Grand Lodge operations, the spread of irregular forms of Freemasonry and our willingness to accept it and our enthusiasm to encourage exposure of Freemasonry to the public generally through the development of modern technology.

To this list should be added those leaders of the Craft whose abilities can never match the size of their egos and those members of the Craft whose ignorance of the true philosophical purpose of Freemasonry reduces the potential for us to continue to impact the evolution of world societies.

Any organization requiring Masonic membership as a prerequisite is subordinate to the Grand Lodge in that jurisdiction. The Grand Lodge is the supreme authority over Freemasonry in all jurisdictions and any interference by an appendant organization must be unacceptable. There have been far too many Grand Lodges in recent years struggling to compete with these organizations whose members feel that higher degree numbers means higher status. There is no Masonic degree higher than that of Master Mason. All other degrees are superfluous to the third.

Irregular Freemasonry is nothing new in the Masonic world. It has been in existence for almost as long as has regular Freemasonry but has never been a serious threat to our stability. Now, however, it is spreading into environments where regular Freemasonry has existed for centuries. It is now developing into a competitive threat to mainstream, regular Freemasonry. It has become a major obstacle in stabilizing Freemasonry in Eastern Europe and in some parts of Africa. We must be concerned today, with the willingness of some of our leadership to accept and grant recognition to those bodies that are not governed by the same protocols as are we. In lacking those protocols, they present to the world a different visual image from what we attempt to project and the world sees us all simply as

Freemasons.

Regularity of origin is a constitutional assurance that those who are seeking recognition are indeed, Masonic. Regularity in practice forms a basis for granting recognition and assures us that Grand Lodges remain in compliance with the principle landmarks of the Craft. Regularity is a right based upon origin and practice. Recognition is a privilege granted by each individual Grand Lodge and must be based on regularity.

Recently posted on the internet was this comment by a former and well-known member of the United Grand Lodge of England, "It is my belief that there is no such thing as clandestine or irregular Freemasonry. Such labels belittle the rich tapestry of our traditions both contemporary and historical. Further, such attitudes directly contradict the premise of brotherhood and fraternalism which is the foundation of Freemasonry."

I could not disagree more with that quotation. How could the writer possibly understand Freemasonry and write that such attitudes contradict the premise of brotherhood and fraternalism which is the foundation of Freemasonry? A founding principle of Freemasonry requires the belief in a Supreme Being. Many forms of irregular or clandestine Freemasonry do not. The required belief in a Supreme Being is one of the major factors that distinguish us from other fraternal, civic and social bodies. Were we to delete the requirement of the belief in a Supreme Being for one to become a Freemason, we would be deleting one the distinguishing characteristics of the Craft and perhaps the most revealing bond that unites us. Also, how could these labels belittle contemporary and historical traditions, when regularity has been consistently required and enforced for centuries?

In our present age, there has been a willingness of much

of our leadership to submit to the demands of society to lift the veil of mystique and secrecy that has made us such a unique organization. That uniqueness is what helped to differentiate us from others and made us the most outstanding and significant organization that the human mind has ever structured. Never has there been any organization that could approach the positive influence that Freemasonry has had on the evolution of civil societies. It laid the foundation for Democratic thought and provided an environment to stimulate it.

Now for some reason or reasons many of our present-day leaders feel the need to expose to the public that which we have concealed or attempted to conceal for several hundred years diluting our uniqueness and eliminating the aura that surrounded us and that tended to lift us to a higher plane than other fraternal organizations. This newfound motivation has had a major impact upon those who were attracted by the mystique and the unknown of the Craft. The result has been that many who might have petitioned for that reason have no longer the stimulus to affiliate.

Ignorance of the membership of the true significance and purpose of Freemasonry aided by their access to the Internet has facilitated the decline of the mystique. It is appalling to read some of the information that is put on the Internet by well-meaning brothers who have all the answers but have never heard the questions.

Inflated egos of far too many Masonic leaders today, along with their exposure to the public is negatively impacting the accepted image of Freemasonry by society of the true intent of Freemasonry. We have watched in recent years, a Grand Master almost totally destroy a highly respected and honored Grand Lodge. This became the most visible image of the damage that can be inflicted by one man but there are numerous less visible examples scattered throughout the Masonic world.

We also live in a world society today dominated by the concept of political correctness wherein everyone should have the right to have the same as everyone else regardless of their ability, initiative or work ethic. Masonic leadership in parts of the world has bought into that concept resulting in a devastating effect upon the quality of the Craft followed by a concomitant decline of our image in society.

The greatest challenges that Freemasonry faced in our historic past will be quite different from those we will face in the 21st century because most will be caused internally. We will probably continue to face challenges from leaders of governments and leaders of religions, but they will not be our greatest concern. We have faced these external challenges for centuries.

We have also faced internal challenges in the past. However, the internal dissensions that are tending to divide Grand Lodges, the increased egotism's that are tending to weaken Grand Lodges, the advancement of modern technologies that are providing for the diffusion of misinformation and our willingness to surrender our protocols should be our greatest concerns.

The 21st century could very well be the most critical period of time of our existence. We have in this century the potential to accomplish great successes but we also have the potential to accomplish what no other entity has been able to do, facilitate our own extinction. We have spent far too much time parasitizing the greatness of our past. We must appreciate and respect the past but we cannot continue to dwell upon its greatness while continuing to ignore the need to create our future. Our concern must now be our future and our greatest hurdle to get over, will be us.

The time has come for us to deposit our egos at the door and dedicate ourselves to the unity of regular Freemasonry. It is time for us to repay our brothers of the past who have given an unsurpassed legacy to each of us and to the world. We will not accomplish this by sacrificing the protocols that have created that legacy. We, the present-day leaders of this heritage must assume the responsibility of perpetuating it and carrying it into the future.

If Freemasonry is not succeeding anywhere in the world, it is not the failure of Freemasonry, it is the failure of Freemasons. Freemasonry does not fail. Freemasons fail.

[II]

Leadership in Freemasonry

Given to a Masonic Forum in Romania

Shortly after assuming the position as Grand Secretary, I wrote this little prayer: "Dear God, let me never forget where I came from and let me know when to quit." One of the greatest concerns that we should have today relative to Masonic leadership is with those leaders who forget their origins and with those who stay on too long.

In all probability, we all have met Masonic leaders who before acquiring the powers that we gave to them were decent and humble, gentle men. Upon assuming this power, however, they forgot "where they came from" and left behind a legacy of arrogance for which they will be forever known.

Other leaders who contributed so much to the fraternity of Freemasonry and paved the way for the rest of us to follow also left behind a legacy they structured for those who will remember them simply as old men and not as the great leaders they were. What a tragedy to be remembered for what they were at the end of their lives rather than for what they gave in the prime of their lives.

In preparing this paper on the subject of Leadership in Freemasonry, I found that it is not the easiest subject on which to write. There is not a great amount of written material available. Therefore, what I write is based on my observations and analysis over the 46 years I have spent in the Craft, all of those as a leader in some capacity.

The great Masonic leaders who preceded us must have been leaders of outstanding vision to have structured an organization the likes of which had never been seen before and has not been seen since. There are no organizations outside of organized religion that has ever impacted the evolution of civil society as has Freemasonry. In that statement I am eliminating those "organizations" that were structured by tyrannical and oppressive powers that limited the rights of man and contributed negatively to that evolution.

The Masonic leaders, however, did not receive their powers through political or religious domination. Masonic leaders could be removed from office by action of the majority of the membership. This in itself was a unique concept back in our earliest days. Indeed, this concept perhaps paved the way for democratic thought. Freemasonry was one of the enclaves during the Age of Enlightenment where men could gather and discuss progressive thinking with limited fear from the world outside of the lodge room. From these enclaves, leaders arose, not only leaders of Freemasonry but leaders of the world in multiple disciplines. Some of their names will forever resonate throughout the free world for their contributions to the rights and liberties of man.

Today, however, the Age of Enlightenment is over. The right to the freedom of thinking is no longer a new phenomenon. Although limitations continue to be imposed by some religious doctrines and some dictatorial powers, these restrictions no longer exists in the free world. Thus, my Brothers, leaders of Freemasonry today have a far greater opportunity to extend their visionary powers far into the future. For this reason, when any Masonic leader assumes office, he also assumes the overwhelming responsibility of directing this noble Craft along a pathway that will be to the uplifting of mankind and to influencing the ongoing evolution of civil society.

For this to happen, however, today's leaders need to develop a far greater vision than we are presently experiencing. They also need to have a far greater understanding of not only the significance of Freemasonry but also of the purpose of Freemasonry than they now have. They need to understand the ramifications of failure to promote the basic precepts of the Craft and the benefits of success. We have within our grasp the opportunity and the capability of creating an impact on the ongoing development of civilization simply because of the reputation of the great Masonic leaders of the past. But this heritage will only benefit us and the world if we have the Masonic leadership with the vision and understanding to see its potential.

Freemasonry in Eastern Europe today is afforded the opportunity as well as the responsibility to play a major role in this evolution. The strength of the philosophy of Freemasonry has always been greatest where the need of society was greatest. The influence of the leadership of Freemasonry in Eastern Europe should play a vital role in the direction the societies will take in the development of the rights and freedoms of all of its citizens. The philosophy of Freemasonry could very well serve as a template for world peace and for this reason, the leadership in Freemasonry will be extremely important in Eastern European society even as it has in so many societies of the world.

However, this will not be a simple task. As Nietzsche observed: "Life gets harder toward the summit; the cold increases, the responsibility increases and there is never any guarantee of success." The challenges facing Masonic leadership in Eastern Europe as well as in other areas of the world where freedom of thought and action is a relative new experience could be enormous.

It is imperative that when assuming office, the Masonic

leader must be fully committed to the principles of Freemasonry and not to the development of his own image.

Even as Freemasonry develops leadership to lead Freemasonry, it develops leadership to lead society. Freemasonry has been able to claim many great leaders of the free world among its members and there is nothing wrong with Masonic leaders becoming world leaders as long as Freemasonry is not used as a political tool for self-promotion. If it is our goal to take only good men and to make them better, is it not logical that these better men would make great leaders of the free world? In America, we take great pride in the fact that fourteen presidents of our country have been members of the Craft along with many other prominent leaders in various political positions.

Unquestionably, the greatest driving force in any leader is his ego. Every leader becomes a leader because he has an ego driving him to excel. And yet, one of the greatest issues facing Freemasonry today is the damaging effect that is caused to the Craft by excessive ego in Masonic leadership. Very few organizations confer the amount of power on their leadership as does Freemasonry. Unrestrained ego is very much an ongoing dilemma for Freemasonry. It is therefore extremely imperative that we seek a quality of beneficence in our potential Masonic leaders. The Masonic leader's commitment must remain a commitment to his Craft, to his brothers and to his society, and not to himself.

One of the primary reasons that I have been supportive of your present Grand Master is as a result of his coming to me shortly after being elected to the position, and telling me "that if I thought it would benefit Romanian Freemasonry, he would be willing to step down as Grand Master." My Brothers that is commitment to the Craft.

There is nothing wrong with having our egos drive us. We have all achieved what we have in life because we had driving egos. It made us what we are but the legacy we leave behind will depend far more upon our ability to rein in our egos than to use our egos. Masonic leaders must have the capability of avoiding that self-centeredness that has become almost a way of life in present-day world society.

It will always remain a challenge to search out those qualities in brothers that will make them Masonic leaders. They are intangibles, however, and difficult to find because there are no definitive qualities for which to look. There will be nothing specific to him as a potential Masonic leader. It is not a visible characteristic that he will possess but he will be a man capable of using his knowledge and imagination along with modern tools without losing sight of the ideals and principles upon which Freemasonry was founded.

This world is today to a large extent because Freemasonry lived and because it had great visionary leaders in the past. The world of the future may very well be in the hands of the Masonic leaders of the present. That means for each of us that it is in our hands whether we lead or whether we seek the leader, it places upon us an awesome responsibility. For society's sake, we cannot afford to fail.

[12]

European Masonic Forum

Given at a symposium in Prague, Czech Republic

I t is a great privilege for me to be with you in the city of Prague. Most of you know I am a firm believer in the need to sit together and to discuss mutual problems confronting Freemasonry at various levels. We cannot choose to ignore issues that impact Freemasonry elsewhere in the world. This is the major reason that I serve as the Executive Secretary of the World Conference.

I did not attend the first meeting of the World Conference when it met in Mexico City, and I found myself at odds with some of the decisions made at that conference. I also found it difficult to recognize the need of a conference composed of so many different operational philosophies that comprise World Freemasonry. My Brothers, I was wrong.

After declining to attend a second meeting to be held in Lisbon, Portugal, I was convinced to change my mind by the then Grand Master of that Grand Lodge, when he wrote to me and told me, that opinions like mine should be heard and discussed, not abstained. I realized then, that if I was not willing to participate, I had little credibility for my analyses of outcomes. I was very much impressed at that conference with the potential of what could be gained by a closer understanding of Freemasonry by our world leadership.

And yet, I can understand the concern that has been

so eloquently expressed regarding potential threats to the structural and functional integrity of individual Grand Lodges here in Europe. No conference that I am aware of, however, has ever impinged upon the authority or the inherent rights of any Grand Lodge. Indeed, it is my feeling that the World Conference has generated a respect by the participating Grand Lodge officers for the variations they have observed in global Freemasonry.

The Inter-American Confederation (CMI) is probably the oldest and perhaps the most viable conference in generating inter-Grand Lodge cooperation without in any way interfering with or causing animosity among the participants.

The North American conference of Grand Masters and the Conference of Grand Secretaries have been functioning for a considerable number of years without impacting the variances that occur in individual Grand Lodges. In a number of instances they have created a point of focus that has benefited Craft Masonry in North America.

I cite, for example, the creation of the Foundation for Children that has benefited both Freemasonry and the children of North America. This could never have been accomplished without the structure provided by the Conferences.

Several years ago when a North American Grand Lodge chose to grant recognition to an irregular Grand Lodge, it was the action of the conference that prevented this divisive action from becoming a reality. There are simply some issues that require a unity of purpose.

I understand fully that a comparison of the North American Conference and a European Conference is not necessarily comparing like entities. North American Freemasonry is more open than European Freemasonry, and we have never experienced the extent of the persecution of the Craft that you have.

We have also, however, never restricted and in fact, have welcomed attendance by other World Grand Lodge officers so that we might more fully understand world issues. Indeed, the Conference of Grand Secretaries of North America creates honorary membership for visiting Grand Secretaries. At the same time, I was never permitted even to sit and observe the Grand Secretaries' meetings in Europe, even after members tried to intercede on my behalf.

This is not meant to imply that our system is more correct than the system applied here. In fact, as many of you know, I am quite critical of the direction of North American Freemasonry. It is simply an observation of a difference in our ways of thinking.

I suspect that we should like nothing more than to be able to exist and operate in the glorious semi-isolationism that we have experienced through most of our existence, and be able to again contribute our influence to the evolution and development of civil society. This was our heyday. This was a time in our history when the great minds found in Freemasonry, were vital players in the age of Enlightenment. This was the period in which Freemasonry made its greatest contributions to that evolution of civil society. We have been fortunate to have carried our isolationist attitude into almost the present day. But, my brothers, like it or not, it is over. Modern technology along with present-day leadership attitudes, are removing that choice from us.

I have been expressing for several years, a great concern with major issues that have been impacting World Freemasonry. One of these is the spread of and inclination to; organize irregular forms of the Craft. This issue, along with the creation of new grand lodges, which, according to our protocols may be regarded as regular (created by three or more regular lodges) must be cause for concern. When a new grand lodge operates in a jurisdiction in which a regular grand lodge already exists, and it receives recognition from regular grand lodges, it dilutes any united effort of the Craft and weakens our potential to provide philosophical influence in the society.

A second concern is the impact upon the operation of Craft Freemasonry by appendant bodies, an untenable situation that all Regular Craft Freemasonry must oppose. The impact that has been created by this interference in Eastern Europe and in Africa has impeded the progress of the Grand Lodges in a number of jurisdictions. Perhaps, a conference of this type might have been able to play a role in preventing this from occurring.

The third concern may well be what should be our greatest, because it not only impacts the newly consecrated Grand Lodges but also many of our older Grand Lodges. We all recognize that our accomplishments in life are, in general, the result of our egos driving us. But, the legacy that we leave behind will far more depend upon our ability to limit our egos. The legacy that is meaningful to the world is the legacy of Freemasonry, not an ego-bloated legacy of ourselves. Much of our potential progress today is impeded by our concerns for our own images.

It is doubtful whether there is anyone sitting here today that can deny the reality of these issues. They must be acknowledged, discussed and plans of action developed to deal with them. This will never be accomplished by refusing to talk with one another or refusing to work together toward a common goal. By providing an environment wherein such discussion can occur, is perhaps the greatest benefit that can be provided by any conference.

Please understand that I'm not here to speak on behalf of the European Masonic Forum. I am here to encourage all regular Freemasonry to work together toward what we should be striving for and to assist one another to regain our rightful place in society.

Many Grand Lodges represented here today have been in existence for a very short period of time when compared to the age of our Craft, but they could very well represent the greatest exposure for our future in Society. They possess the potential, more so than do the older Grand Lodges, to impact the evolution of their civil societies and to create a more visible image to the world of the future. They do not, however, nor can they, have all the answers. This is where guidance through a conference by older and more established Grand Lodges can be invaluable to the future of the Craft.

I am in full accord that "Masonic awareness, cooperation, exchange of information and opinions in Masonry have always been one of the landmarks within (international) Masonry" but there seems to be more of an intent today to violate protocols that have sustained us, due to lack of commitment or lack of knowledge on the part of our leadership. A conference should never prevent nor interfere with any unique development within its structure. The diversity of Freemasonry, driven by the sociology of the environment in which it exists, is in itself one of the unique characteristics of the Craft

The greatest concern that I have heard expressed concerning the European Masonic Forum is a perceived appearance of individual grand lodges or of individuals within grand lodges attempting to control it. Any semblance of this occurring could spell disaster for any conference. My Brothers, you simply cannot permit this to happen. It would be totally counterproductive to what you hope to achieve, and I would oppose any conference or individual attempting to do so.

In addition, we must recognize and acknowledge that

recognition is part of the rights of a Grand Lodge and must be the result of a real relationship between grand lodges and not automatic because of regularity.

It is imperative therefore, that every grand lodge understands and respects the rights of every other grand lodge. A conference must be non-dogmatic. No decision can be made by the conference that infringes upon the integrity or rights of any grand lodge. Its purpose must simply be to provide an environment where in a mutual benefit exists for all, but more specifically for the Craft.

The influence of Freemasonry has altered the course of human progress. It does not matter whether your grand lodge has an ancient history or a more recent history; we all are the recipients of a heritage left by our past brothers. With that heritage, we assume the responsibility to carry the light of the philosophy of Freemasonry into the future. We cannot do otherwise.

[13]

The Grand Lodge of Chile

I t is a distinct honor for me to be with you today in Santiago. I wanted to be with you last year but an airline delay prevented me from making my connections. I especially wanted to be with you at the time when mutual recognition was to be established between the Grand Lodge of Chile and the Grand Orient of Brazil. More than fifteen years ago I made my first inquiries into the establishment of recognition with the Grand Orient, and the State Grand Lodges of Brazil. What took place last year was a continuation of a beginning which occurred in São Paulo during the fourth World Conference, when it was first announced that the Grand Orient and the state Grand Lodges of Brazil were establishing mutual recognition. It is the continuation of a dream which I hoped I would live long enough to see occur.

It was, however, just the beginning of my dream. My dream is to see the day when all regular Freemasonry in the world is in mutual recognition of one another and what we refer to as a brotherhood of men truly becomes, a brotherhood of men and when all regular Freemasonry can work together toward common goals. My dream is to see the day when a common bond that unites us becomes more significant than the individual egos that divide us. My dream is to see a day when what is good and right about Freemasonry can become the driving influence in the continued evolution of civil society, as it was in the past.

The success story of Brazilian Freemasonry must become a prologue to many success stories, a prologue to a long-range goal of achieving universality of regular Freemasonry. My Brothers, during my travels in recent years, I've been able to make observations concerning our Craft which are significant enough, that it behooves us to take the time, and to make the effort to understand Freemasonry. It is simply not enough in today's world to be able to say, "I am a Freemason." It is not enough to pay our dues, attend our meetings, keep our philosophy to ourselves, and ignore the world around us. The world has always needed the philosophy of Freemasonry. The world has always needed the guidance and leadership of great minds, which characterized Freemasonry from its inception. Make no doubt about it my brothers; this organization has played a major role in the evolution of civil society. The world is as it is today because of the influence of Masonic philosophy, and the leadership which guided that philosophy.

For Freemasonry to continue to play a major role in the ongoing evolution of civil society, it must continue to attract and develop the style of leadership that characterized it in the past. Our leadership must understand that even while the philosophy of Freemasonry is universal and remains the same throughout the world, the forces driving it varies its image depending upon those forces. Thus, the philosophical image of early Freemasonry still survives in Europe. In North America, however, its image is more of that of a charitable organization, while in South and Central America its image is molded more by the sociological demands of that environment. The basic purpose of Freemasonry, however, must remain; the taking of good men and making them better. These better men then will lead the world. These images, in no way, diminish the significance of the Craft in their regions, but it does require for all of us to understand the forces that are driving it. Only through understanding can we hope to unify our force for good. We may well find that the tragic events that occurred in my country on September 11, 2001, may serve as a unifying force for an ongoing development of our Craft.

Freemasonry has always functioned best during times of adversity. This is probably the primary reason why so many of the world's great leaders who led their countries in their struggles for freedom, and liberty were members of the Masonic fraternity. But, even as the world will require and demand more greatness from great men, Freemasonry will, and should, require more from its members. This is a different world today, made different in just a few short minutes, and created by just a few acts. Freemasonry now has a great opportunity to demonstrate to the world what it was that made it great in the past and why it is so significant in the present. We now have the opportunity to contribute to the creation of a brighter future. That opportunity is probably greater now than it has been perhaps for decades. How we respond will determine how we will be perceived by society in the future.

Historians will analyze us in the future, even as present-day historians are analyzing us now. The impact of our past brothers in the development of the present world has been magnificent and magnanimous. How we respond to the challenges of the present will determine how historians will write about us in the future. Present-day Freemasonry has the opportunity to leave a legacy that may also be judged as magnificent and magnanimous. Historians of the future may very well write about the significant contributions by Freemasonry of the present-day world, but that will be up to us. Our past Brothers left us with a great legacy. We have an obligation not only to support it, but also to make certain is one that continues for generations to come. We must now minimize our differences and maximize those characteristics which made us great. We must stop bickering amongst ourselves and work toward universality of all regular Freemasonry. We must understand one another, our unifying similarities, as well as our distinctive differences. We must work within the established protocols that have stabilized Freemasonry for over 300 years. Then, and only then, will we display our greatest assets, utilize our greatest strengths and make our greatest contributions to the world.

Very frankly, the future is in our hands. We must now assume that awesome mantel of responsibility to continue our heritage. We owe this much to our past Brothers. They deserve it, and the world needs it.

[14]

The Grand Lodge of Peru

Many times when I speak elsewhere in the world I point out the great feeling of brotherhood that characterizes the Freemasonry in both South and Central America. You have a potential for the Craft that probably exceeds that of anywhere else in the world. You have created a style of Freemasonry that is unique while retaining much of the philosophical qualities and intellectualism for which it is generally known.

When I inquired as to on what subject I should speak, I was asked to speak on the World Conference of Masonic Grand Lodges and its purpose. I have been serving as the Executive Secretary of this conference since the constitution was first structured in New York City. I am firmly convinced that this conference can play a vital role in creating a greater understanding of Freemasonry on a world level. There can be little doubt that if we could ever unify the influence of Masonic philosophy, we could be a major factor in working toward universal peace.

The contribution that Freemasonry has made in the evolution of civil society can never be overstated. I have been a student of our Craft for many years and I never cease to be impressed with its significance in the world.

Some of the greatest minds that ever lived, men who were giants in so many diverse fields, were members. The contributions they have made molded civilizations into what they are today. Many of the most notable leaders during the age of Enlightenment, who were responsible for stimulating cosmopolitan thinking and for impregnating society with the desires for what should be the inherent rights of all men, were inspired by the philosophical precepts of the Masonic fraternity.

The World Conference had its beginning in 1995 and my relationship with it is somewhat unique. The first meeting of what was then known as the World Conference of Grand Masters was held in Mexico City. I was not present at that meeting and I had some serious misgivings when I read the report that came out of it. A charter was developed there that was approaching far too closely to the realm of political and religious involvement.

The second conference was scheduled to be held in Lisbon, Portugal. I received a request from the Grand Master of Portugal asking me to attend and to address the conference. I responded to him, declining to be present. His observation was that opinions like mine should be heard and discussed, not abstained.

As a result of his observation, I attended the second World Conference, presented a paper and moderated two discussions. I left Lisbon with the feeling that there could be a great value in a conference such as this, so long as it served as a non-dogmatic forum to create a mutual understanding among World Grand Lodges.

At the third conference held in New York City, a constitution was crafted and I reluctantly agreed to accept the responsibility to serve as the first executive secretary, a position I continue to hold today. It was during this conference, that the change in title to the World Conference of Masonic Grand Lodges was agreed upon to provide for participation by Grand Secretaries for the continuity and stability they provided. The constitution defined the purpose of the conference as being to share information and to discuss issues, which promote the stability, progress, and universality of Craft Masonry.

In order to comprehend the significance and importance of a World Conference, it is important to understand the variations of style that are found in world Freemasonry; it is also of great importance to keep aware of changes and challenges facing Freemasonry today.

I have been afforded the great opportunity to be able to meet with most of the major leaders of the Craft over the past quarter-century. In my journeys, I have been continually impressed with the significance of our brothers and their dedication not only to Freemasonry but to the improvement of society in general. Freemasons remain the movers and shakers in much of world society. I have become more conscious of the constancy of the philosophical purpose of the Craft but I have also become more cognizant of the operational variances in different areas of the world.

I have placed the Freemasonry of South and Central America into a category I call a sociological style. I do so because your Freemasonry here seems to be more driven by the sociological demands of the societies in which you live. It is a form of Freemasonry that has retained much of the philosophical and intellectual qualities of the Western European style, while at the same time infusing an idealism that causes you to think and aim higher toward goals that are not sought elsewhere in the world.

I have great admiration and respect for what you have been able to achieve in providing a stabilizing influence in your societies in spite of the challenges and odds with which you are confronted. The only concern that I could express with this style, is that you might set unachievable goals. We must never forget, however, that our philosophy should ever stimulate us to pull society in general up to meet our standards, not climb down to meet its.

Initially I included the Freemasonry of Mexico in the sociological style. However I have reclassified Mexican Freemasonry as a political style because of the tendency for the Craft there to become more involved in the politics of the country.

This observation does not mean that I oppose Free-masons being involved in politics. Indeed, we should hope that if our goal is to take the best men we can find and improve those best men, that they would be involved with running our countries. This involvement, however, must be as the man not as the fraternity.

I have thus far been unable to place the Freemasonry of India, Africa or the Far East into any category that distinguishes them as being unique to that part of the world. This is probably as a result of my having spent less time there to observe. It is significant to note, however, that they do have a very vital and important position in society and have made considerable contributions in its evolution.

Freemasonry has existed in Africa for many years as provincial lodges or District Grand Lodges working under European Grand Lodge constitutions. Freemasonry is now, however, beginning to come into its own on the African continent. Grand lodges have been created in most of Northwestern Africa including Ivory Coast, Senegal, Benin, Burkina Faso, Mali, Morocco and others. In addition there are grand lodges in South Africa, Congo, Madagascar, Gabon, and Guinea. Other grand lodges are in the process of being consecrated.

I have been fortunate to experience the Freemasonry in some of these African countries and have again been greatly impressed with the caliber of the brothers with whom I have associated while there. There is no way, at present, to determine any specific style that they might adopt but certainly, along with Eastern Europe, they have a remarkable opportunity to impact the direction of the ongoing evolution of civil society in their respective countries. Indeed, I look at Freemasonry in these two environments as holding much of the potential of the future of Freemasonry.

Unfortunately, our Craft remains absent from most of the nations of the Middle East. One of its strongest positions probably existed in Iran prior to the return of Khomeini. The Grand Lodge of Iran now operates in exile and is headquartered in the United States with its members scattered throughout the world. Some of the most ardent Freemasons that I have had the privilege of knowing belong to this Grand Lodge. But then, I have learned in my travels that the greatest appreciation of the Craft lies in the members whose freedom to practice it was taken from them.

The World Conference has offered the first opportunity for the leadership of world Freemasonry to get together in one location and begin to understand that even though the philosophical purpose for Freemasonry is universal, the operational styles of the Craft vary within societies. This knowledge becomes vitally important in our ever-shrinking world. The isolationist attitude that has permeated our grand lodges for most of its existence is no longer applicable in the technologically-driven world of today.

The environment in which we live today has changed and it is going to change more rapidly in more ways than we have ever known. We are experiencing a metamorphosis that is impacting the way we live along with the morality and ethics of civilization itself. Freemasonry was not only a vital modifying influence during the metamorphosis of the past, it was a driving force and we could very well be a driving influence in the future, but it is going to require a united effort on behalf of our grand lodges.

Modern technology has swept aside in just a few short years, a system of operation that has characterized us for most of our existence. It is now far more important for us to understand each other and to work together for the perpetuation of a system that has made this world what it is. This rapidly changing environment is forcing us to realize and to recognize that we must re-examine the way we operate and the way we relate to one another. It is now more imperative than ever that we are aware and understand what is happening involving Freemasonry in all parts of the world. The relatively unknown quality of the Craft to those outside of it has been replaced by the demand for, and our willingness to give, more extensive public knowledge. This, out of necessity is going to force us to re-examine our position in modern-day society. The World Conference has given us the opportunity to become more acutely aware of the challenges confronting the Craft in today's world.

With the development of the World Wide Web we are being confronted not only with increasing attacks by our enemies, but we are being assaulted by the ignorance of our own members, who post inaccurate information concerning the Craft. Because they are members, however, the general public reads and accepts it as fact. Again, this is an issue that we cannot choose to ignore and it places a greater responsibility upon Masonic leadership, who must attempt to monitor and correct this misinformation.

Another problem that is becoming more pronounced to Regular Freemasonry today is the development and expansion of Irregular Freemasonry into many parts of the world where it did not exist in the past. The general public will have no conception of the difference between Regular Freemasonry and Irregular Freemasonry.

Finally, what is becoming a greater problem today than it has been in the past, is the issue of Regular Grand

Lodges being created in jurisdictions that already have a Regular Grand Lodge existing there. The issue becomes compounded when the new Grand Lodge is granted recognition by other Regular Grand Lodges. This situation can do nothing positive for the Craft and will tend to divide Regular Freemasonry into two separate camps.

Even though no binding decisions can be made on the floor of the World Conference that will impact grand lodges, the environment exists for discussions at least with individual leaders attending. These issues can be brought into focus on the floor the World Conference and provide a greater understanding of the impact that they may create if we choose to ignore them.

There is no question that via the World Conference there exists a greater understanding of World Grand Lodges by world leaders and appreciation of issues that are confronting us now and will continue to confront Freemasonry in the future.

It is my sincere hope that this short paper has served to provide a better understanding of the purpose and function of the World Conference of Masonic Grand Lodges.

[15]

The Grand Lodge of Romania

Romania has a heritage of Freemasonry tracing back to a lodge started by the Grand Orient of France in 1856. Since that time, you have experienced a sporadic and somewhat chaotic existence even though you could not practice Freemasonry. You have lived through the negative impact of the Nazi regime during the Second World War and the Communist regime following it. You have faced challenges most other Grand Lodges in the world have never faced, and you have faced them successfully. Your desire for the freedom and the rights that should be inherent to all men, along with the tenacity of Freemasonry, has resulted in the Craft once again being practiced in your country. I found it interesting, in reviewing your early Freemasonry from 1880 until 1905, that it probably damaged itself by a proliferation of "higher" degrees, resulting in degeneration, until it ceased to exist in 1913.

With your re-consecration in 1993, you now represent one of the earlier grand lodges constituted in Eastern Europe following the dissolution of the Soviet Union. Regretfully, your country has again experienced Masonic discontent, and again possibly as a result of the impact of "higher" degrees.

You sit today on the threshold of opportunity. Your Grand Lodge, along with many other newly constituted or reconstituted Grand Lodges in Eastern Europe, has the opportunity and the potential to play a major role in impacting the ongoing evolution of civil society in your country. Freemasonry in the past has probably had a greater impact in this evolution than any organization outside of organized religion. This is an opportunity that does not exist with the same magnitude in countries with a longer-lasting stable form of government.

You have, however, the additional opportunity to look back into the history of Freemasonry to see where we have succeeded and where we have failed. You have an unprecedented privilege to learn from our past. You can build upon our strengths and avoid the pitfalls of our weaknesses. My recommendation to you is to study the Craft and emulate only where the Craft has and is succeeding.

Do not become enamored with the Freemasonry of North America. We have permitted the philosophy of the Craft to become secondary to the charity of the Craft, and in doing so have lost much of our visibility and image in society. Wealth does not insure success. Build upon the character of the quality member. All of the wealth in the world cannot buy respect: it must be earned!

In order to take full advantage of this opportunity and to be recorded in the annals of history as a major player in your country's struggles for the rights and freedoms of man, however, will require the necessity of eliminating that which divides and preserving that which unites.

There can be no place in our great Fraternity for one who leads for the sake of himself. Great leaders, who will be remembered, will be those who lead for the sake of the Craft. The dissension that has occurred in some of the Eastern European Grand Lodges has served to discredit the commitment of some of the leadership to the principles of Freemasonry. It is imperative that if you are to participate as a Craft, you must assimilate and use the philosophy of

Freemasonry to remove the dissension that divides and adopt the brotherhood that unites. Then, and only then, will you realize the full potential that you have inherited from your Brothers of the past.

You have now taken on a mantle of responsibility to preserve not only a philosophy that has characterized some the greatest minds that ever lived but a philosophy that has changed the course of history by changing the men who created it.

Never forget that the basic purpose of our Craft is to take good men and make them better. These better men have led their respective countries for generations in an ongoing search for freedom, liberty and equality. With this mantle you have assumed, you have also assumed the awesome responsibility to represent the Craft of Freemasonry as an ongoing force for what is right and just in the world.

Do not concentrate your efforts on becoming a large grand lodge; concentrate your efforts on becoming a good grand lodge. Seek out the best men you can find, one at a time, and make him a better man. Thus you fulfill your responsibility to your Brothers of the past, to the philosophical intent of the Craft, to your country and to the world: for these better men will then lead.

[16]

The Grand Lodge of Greece

O ne of the inherent greatnesses of Freemasonry
is providing that opportunity to travel the globe
knowing that in all free countries, there will be
men with the same thoughts, the same principles, the
same brotherly love as we have. No organization outside
the Craft can provide the same.

I am saddened by some of the controversy existing in
Eastern Europe in Freemasonry today. Internal dissension can do nothing but hurt the Craft. We must look for
strength of unity to provide to the world the meaning of the
philosophy of this Brotherhood of Man. Today we watch
the emergence of Freemasonry in the former Soviet-bloc
countries. With it Freemasonry has a great opportunity to
grow and to provide incentive for moral insight and guidance in their development but we cannot hope to provide
to others what we cannot provide to ourselves.

I had the privilege to meet both your Grand Master
and Brother John in our Grand Lodge last December
and again in Washington, D.C., in February. While with
them, I learned of their concern for Freemasonry and their
Grand Lodge.

We Freemasons of the United States recognize the
tremendous contribution of Freemasonry in the making
of America. Many of our greatest patriots and heroes
were members of the Craft, men like George Washington,

Benjamin Franklin (who was two times Grand Master of the Grand Lodge of Pennsylvania), Paul Revere, and more recently President Harry Truman, Gen. Douglas MacArthur, and both presidents Theodore and Franklin Roosevelt.

For me to be in Greece is indeed a humbling experience. I knew that some of the earliest concepts of democracy originated here. Your country has a great heritage, one of the greatest.

One question I asked and received the answer I was looking for is, "What was the influence of Freemasonry on Greek freedom?" Your great General Brother Theodore Kolokotronis is not at all unlike our Brother George Washington. The culture you are heir to is one that you must be very proud of and one that Freemasonry has made a contribution to retain.

We recognize, my brothers, that just a little over 200 years ago when the early Freemasons in America were struggling for existence and freedom, Greece was already over 4000 years old. To see Greek history as revealed in its monuments and archaeological ruins is an awe-inspiring experience we will never see in America. But to feel the love of Brother for Brother as Freemasons, we can and do, just as in America

Freemasonry has been an attractive force for some of the greatest men this world has ever seen. It transcends even religions in its philosophy and practice of the Brotherhood of Man under the Fatherhood of God. It has carried man beyond the ravages of war, and even nationalistic enemies are still Brothers. It is a beacon of hope in an ever-increasing chaotic world. With its emphasis on toleration, it offers what may truly be the greatest solution for universal peace.

I attend meetings in a little Lodge in Chambersburg, Pennsylvania that was spared in the burning of the town during our Civil War. The commanding officer of the

Confederate forces, a Brother, stationed a cordon of soldiers around the Temple preventing it being burned. It stands today as the oldest building in the State built solely for Masonic purpose.

The Grand Lodge of Pennsylvania presented and dedicated a monument last year on the Gettysburg battlefield which exemplified the essence of the Brotherhood of Man. Prior to the war, Generals and Brothers Armistead and Hancock were classmates at the military Academy and fought together in battles prior to the Civil War. When the Civil War began, Armistead went to the south, Hancock to the North. They never met again and both were wounded yards apart at Gettysburg. Hancock survived; Armistead died.

The adjutant to Gen. Hancock, brother and Captain Bingham, observing a Mason in distress administered aid to Armistead and received his personal effects to convey to Hancock. These effects included his Masonic pocket watch and fob. Our monument depicts Bingham administering aid to Armistead and receiving his personal effects. The monument is called, "Friend to Friend a Brotherhood Undivided," both examples of the transcending power of the Brotherhood of Freemasonry.

This, if for no other reason, is why we must survive. If all mankind practiced the philosophy of Freemasonry, war would be known but in history. The world needs us, my Brothers. We must make sure the world knows.

But for now, we can bask in the knowledge that where freemen live, we will find our Brothers. There will always be a Christos Maneas, a John Souvaliotis, and you my brothers, my friends, because we are all Freemasons.

I thank you for being my brothers. I thank God for Freemasonry. While we live, freedom can never die. And while freedom lives, we cannot afford to die.

[17]

Grand Lodge of South Africa

Masonic Conference

W hat a great privilege and pleasure it is for me to be back in Africa. This is the first that I will have spent much time in South Africa, however. I look forward with great anticipation to the experience of this trip and the opportunity that I will have to meet with my Masonic brothers from this part of the world.

I have developed some great friendships with brothers whom I have met in Ivory Coast, Mali and Morocco as well as with brothers from other African Jurisdictions whom I learned to know while attending other Grand Lodges. One of the great honors that I have experienced was being made a chief of the village of Nigua-saff, the home village of the Grand Secretary of the Grand Lodge of Ivory Coast. My Brothers, I am honored to be with you and I express my most sincere appreciation to the Grand Lodge of South Africa for the invitation to address this conference. The continent of Africa holds such great potential for the future of Freemasonry. Here lies some of the most fertile ground for our future. I have been expressing the opinion for at least the last decade that the greatest potential for our Craft lies in the emerging Grand Lodges in Eastern Europe and in Africa.

Freemasonry is reemerging in Eastern Europe in countries that have either never had it or in countries in which it has been repressed for decades. In Africa, with the general exception of the existence of Provincial or district lodges or grand lodges, Freemasonry is just now establishing roots in relatively untouched environments. What this can mean to the world is immeasurable.

There can never be a time, no matter how long this world may exist, that Freemasonry's philosophy would not be applicable to any society. A change in leadership style has reduced our philosophical influence in some areas of the world and made us less visible in society. But here in Africa, there exists the fertile fields to be cultivated by those of you dedicated to a society in need of the gentle guidance of our Craft.

Freemasonry has impacted the evolution of civil society for several hundred years. It has changed significantly, the course of civilization. It has influenced the development of some of the greatest men who have ever lived, and therein lies our purpose beyond any other: to continue the development of great men. These great men will then influence the continuing evolution of civil society.

I firmly believe that Freemasonry on the continent of Africa has probably the greatest potential to impact its peoples, to contribute to the evolution of its societies and probably to alter the future of this world beyond any other. It, through you, has the opportunity to show to the world what a philosophy like ours can contribute to mankind.

It also, however, is perhaps going to meet some of the greatest challenges that it has ever experienced. For you, must deal with not only what might be one of the greatest diversities of societies, cultures and religious beliefs located on one continent, but you must also deal with the pressures which will be impressed upon you by outside influences.

But, the philosophy of Freemasonry has always, and must always; transcend the variances with which it will be confronted in the environment in which it exists. Because of the universality of its purpose coupled with the constancy of its zeal, it has risen above those restrictive barriers that have hindered societal evolution for several hundred years. The very fact that it continues to thrive throughout the free world is un-debatable evidence that its purpose is universal and undying.

I have been a member of the Masonic fraternity for forty-five years, twenty of those years as Grand Secretary of the largest Grand Lodge in North America, two additional years as Grand Secretary for foreign affairs, and am now serving my ninth year as Executive Secretary of the World Conference of Masonic Grand Lodges. There has been only a period of three months in my forty-five years that I did not sit in an office of at least one Masonic body. In addition, I have been writing the book reviews for the Scottish Rite for 18 years resulting in a continuing examination of our Craft. I tell you this not to inflate my significance. I tell you this to qualify why I was asked to speak to you today on the subject of World Freemasonry.

For most of our existence, even though there was that "Mystic Tie" binding us together in a universal brotherhood, there was a great tendency toward a provincial attitude in our Grand Lodges. We operated in a form of hierarchal isolationism. Today, however, modern technology has driven us to become a more visible organization, forcing us away from our isolationism and causing us to be more exposed and subject to more external examination.

This, however, in no way decreases our capacity of exerting our influence on society. What it does mean, however, is that we must face reality, confront the complexities it brings with it and adapt to using the technologies to further our goals which in turn must contribute to the betterment of mankind. We first, however, must understand ourselves and our goals. I have traveled extensively throughout the world for the past two decades for the purpose of Freemasonry and have been afforded the opportunity that few have, to study our present-day Craft and its methods of operation. I have been granted the privilege of meeting with some of the greatest men and in developing some of the greatest friendships that one could ever wish for. In doing so, I have observed the universality of the philosophical purpose of our Craft regardless of where it operates in the world. This I refer to as its structural philosophy.

I also, however, have become very cognizant of the differences that exist in the operational philosophies of Freemasonry. Where the structural philosophies are an integral, inherent and unchangeable character of the Craft, the operational philosophies seem to be more driven by the characteristic of the environment in which it exists. These operational variances are worthy of note, especially in areas where Freemasonry is in a developmental stage.

From my studies and observations, I have concluded that the personality of Freemasonry in different parts of the world is driven and shaped by the environment in which it exists. Based upon these operational variations, I have been attempting to categorize the Freemasonry in different parts of the world in what I refer to as styles of the Craft. Thus far, I have distinguished, at least for myself, four distinctive styles but I am sure that others, perhaps less distinctive, may exist or evolve into being. Please keep in mind that these styles are my creation and there could be those who disagree with me.

When looking at Western European Freemasonry we find that it retains more of the basic philosophical and intellectual qualities that characterized Freemasonry from its inception than may be found elsewhere in the world. This would be expected since its survival from the beginning has been dependent upon this style. External as well as internal pressures, although excessive at times and variable in their origins dictated an intellectual elitism dominated by secrecy for its very survival. Thus, I have classified Western European Freemasonry as a Philosophical Style.

When Freemasonry migrated into the South and Central American countries it retained much of the Philosophical Style that characterizes Western Europe. It did, however, change over the years by adopting a more idealistic attitude as to what it can accomplish than is to be found anywhere else in the world. The external pressures of society with which Freemasonry was confronted, although not totally unlike those of Western Europe, stimulated the creation of a uniqueness that I refer to as a Sociological Style. It is perhaps more driven by the society in which it exists than anywhere else in the world.

Mexican Freemasonry has more of a tendency toward a political activism and although I have many friends in Mexican Freemasonry, I frankly find it difficult to understand. For want of a more definitive term, I refer to Mexican Freemasonry as a Political Style of the Craft.

North American Freemasonry has diverged farther from its roots than any Freemasonry in the world. Much of the intellectual elitism that contributed heavily to the creation of what might arguably be referred to as the most influential organization ever conceived via human thought has been sacrificed in a support of charitable objectives. Therefore I categorize the Freemasonry in North America as a Charitable Style.

Before I go farther, let me clarify what I mean by elitism as it impacts Freemasonry and intellectual elitism as it has impacted Freemasonry. My Brothers, there is a tendency today for some to frown upon elitism. I have found myself at odds with some North American leadership by the use of this term. And yet, the day that we said that our goal was to take good men and make them better, we became elitist and there is nothing wrong with that form of elitism. In addition, one of the greatest reasons we became the major influential organization that we have, is that we attracted some of the greatest minds that ever lived and that, my brothers, is intellectual elitism. Subtract that factor from the equation and we are not what we are, nor could we have been what we were.

Present-day Eastern European Freemasonry has not been in existence long enough to show whether it will retain the philosophical style of its Western European creators. A different mindset seems to exist in these countries as a result of fascist and communist suppression that might stimulate it to evolve into something distinctive as a result of the different societal pressure where it exists.

Although I have spent some time in the Far East, India and the Philippines as well as in Africa, I have not discerned a specific style which differentiates and defines it. In these locations, as a result of operating under Provincial or District Grand Lodges for a prolonged period of time, there has been a tendency to take on the characteristic of the mother grand lodge, but we should expect a modification as a result of the independent operation that is now occurring. I have been watching Africa with great interest to see if there is any distinctive style of the Craft emerging. I feel certain that that will happen as a result of social needs in many African societies. I would expect in time, that there will be a more definitive character developed by the social requirements in these localities. Indeed, there might well be several different styles evolving into being as a result of the influence of different mother grand lodges as well as different social environments.

For you, Freemasonry, as it evolves on the continent of

Africa, has a distinct advantage that was necessarily lacking in the early life of our Craft: You have the opportunity of examining World Freemasonry and learning from its successes as well as its failures before reaching any decision on the direction you want to go. I would strongly encourage African Grand Lodges to examine very closely the different styles of the Craft operating in the world today and study their past histories before trying to shape your own.

If it is the intent of Freemasonry to remain a driving intellectual force in the evolution of civil society, if we wish for future historians to acknowledge our contributions in the developing world for the betterment of mankind, if we want to continue toward our goal of taking good men and making them better, then whatever style we choose must lead us on a pathway to that end.

Upon examining the different styles that I have presented to you, we can measure degrees of success in World Freemasonry.

The Philosophical Style has been in existence for the longest period of time and has paved the way in every other environment. Therefore, differences in style have all evolved from it. It has certainly stood the test of time and has impacted the world in general, probably more than any other. It was this style that became an integral part of the cornerstone of the Enlightenment and it was the Enlightenment that served as a pathway out of the ignorance of the Dark Ages.

The Sociological Style, found in Central and South America, has not deviated extensively from it. The infusion of the idealism has not in any way harmed the Craft's potential in the society in which it lives. I am not convinced, however, that it could thrive as well in other parts of the world. The strength of this Freemasonry is a result of the continuing struggle to operate within its environment.

I have great respect for both the Philosophical and the Sociological styles of the Craft.

As I have indicated earlier, I do not really understand Mexican Freemasonry, but I do have a fear that it places itself in jeopardy by coming close to violating a basic Masonic protocol. Keep this in mind my brothers. We do not fear Freemasons becoming involved in political activity, but we must never permit Freemasonry to become involved.

I am a North American Freemason and therefore belong to the Charitable Style of Freemasonry. I look at Canadian Freemasonry — although part of North America — as a modified version of both the Philosophical and Charitable styles. Canadians retain more of the Philosophical style from their origin but have been greatly influenced by the Charitable.

Freemasonry in the United States, however, is purely a Charitable Style today. Interestingly, the change into this style took place over the last 30 to 35 years. It began its life as a philosophical style as brought over by the early settlers from the British Isles and the European continent. There can be no doubt that its impact on the creation of the United States of America was extraordinary. The intellectual stimulus of the Enlightenment played a vital role in the idealistic structuring of this country and more than a few of the enlightened thinkers who played a role in this structuring were Freemasons.

But, North American Freemasonry has changed. As a result of never having to face the great challenges to its existence that most of the world has faced, it has not only failed to become stronger, but as a result of complacency, it has become weaker. And now, present-day leadership lacks the vision of our forefathers who structured our great society. Today our goal is not to change society but simply to become visible to society. We were an organization, respected beyond any other in America and one whose members were responsible for the structuring of a society that has been emulated by many others.

Freemasonry for the past thirty years in the United States has concentrated a vast amount of its energies on recruiting membership and raising money to give away to charities. We have become one of the greatest charitable organizations in the world at the sacrifice of our intellectual integrity and influence in society. We are trying to buy back, through charitable programs, that which we lost through ignorance. The result is that the membership has declined over 50% and we have lost most of our influence and prestige in society.

This does not mean that charity has no place in Freemasonry. Indeed, charity has been a core value of the Craft from its beginning, but this charity was in support of its brothers, wives, children and widows. Now, however, it has become the core value in North America with a face almost of a public charity.

What this all means, is that numbers of members and financial wealth is not a visible sign of long term success in Freemasonry. The United States had both and now is rapidly losing both. So, in studying the styles of Freemasonry do not become blinded by the numbers of its members or by the magnificence of its structures. Freemasonry changed this world not by large numbers or by buying its influence. Freemasonry changed the world by improving good men one at a time.

There is a movement now in the United States to change the style of Freemasonry and return to what we once were. Interestingly, the Freemasonry in Australia paralleled closely the Freemasonry of North America and the result has been the same. It is my understanding although I've never been there, that it is gradually improving in some areas by attempting a style change also.

In reviewing the history of World Freemasonry it doesn't take long to realize that it had its detractors and enemies almost from the beginning of its existence. Among those who became its greatest enemies were political leaders and leaders of religious institutions. Upon discovering the motivation for what caused this enmity in such different entities, you will find that they are the same. Both have a desire to control the bodies and minds of those under their dominion.

Almost universally, dictatorial and despotic government leaders have opposed the Craft but it is significant, that there is no religion that opposes Freemasonry: only religious leaders oppose it. The major objection that they have to us is that we accept membership from all monotheistic believers while requiring a belief in a Supreme Being.

Even though this opposition from both groups continues to exist today, Freemasonry has never been destroyed by the forces of either. It has been suppressed at times, driven underground and even forced to cease operation in some areas, but it has risen like a phoenix from the ashes when the tyranny was destroyed.

Looking at the condition of Freemasonry on a world level today in general, and disregarding the English-speaking jurisdictions, we continue to find a thriving organization continuing to exert influence in the evolving society. There does seem to be greater problems in some English-speaking Grand Lodges especially in number loss. Perhaps it has been willingness in these Grand Lodges to lower standards and to adopt a more charitable style of the Craft that has resulted in the decline and loss of influence in society. This is unquestionably true in North America.

I have been greatly impressed almost everywhere I travel, not only with the quality of the men I have found comprising the Craft, but also in the positions of influence that they hold in their societies.

Now, however, Freemasonry is being confronted with challenges unlike any that we have faced in the past and will require a continuing re-examination of our methods of operation. The greatest enemies threatening us today lie not in the leadership of governments or religious institutions, although some remain enemies of the Craft. Our greatest enemy today is ourselves.

The three greatest challenges that I see confronting Freemasonry today are expansion of Irregular Freemasonry, development of modern technology and ignorance of our membership.

Of course, Irregular Freemasonry is nothing new in the Masonic world. It has been around almost as long as has Regular Freemasonry and it has never been a major obstacle to us. The concern regarding it today is the rapidity of its growth and expansion and the tendency to become more organized than it has been in the past. What was once a quiescent separate style of Freemasonry is now develop-ing into a competitive threat to mainstream and Regular Freemasonry. It almost appears as a race to see which form of the Craft can occupy new territories first. This is an issue that we cannot choose to ignore, because it presents a different face of the Craft to society, one not bound by the protocols that define the Freemasonry we know.

What is of an even greater concern and is something totally new to our noble Craft, is the impact that is being felt via the use of the World Wide Web. The Internet has created a new atmosphere that is causing considerable problems for us and is one that is not going to go away or one that we can eliminate.

In 1998, I participated in an Oxford style debate in Washington, D.C., on the issue, Resolved: "The Internet

Will Make Grand Lodges Redundant." Each participant was a recognized scholar of Freemasonry. In the debate I was on the opposing side of the resolution.

From my position as a Grand Secretary I had made the observation a number of years earlier, that as a result of the Internet, Freemasonry would never be the same. I, therefore, had strong feelings on the resolution being presented.

I pointed out during the debate, that Grand Lodges today are being bypassed by ignorant Freemasons, and that ignorant Freemasons constitute the majority of our membership. Please note that I said ignorant, not stupid, although today from what I read on the net, I am not sure anymore.

I never cease to be amazed at how much misinformation is placed on the web by some of our members who become impressed with what they think they know. I now spend a considerable amount of my time responding to brothers who have become instant experts on the Craft.

The lack of Masonic knowledge by our own membership is one of the greatest threats to our survival. For an institution that impresses upon its membership the need for the acquisition of knowledge, the Internet reveals a considerable dearth of success on our part. It reminds me of a quotation I once read: "Let he who does not know, shut up and learn."

In addition to the damage that is being caused by our own members on the web, whose statements, because they are Freemasons, are accepted as fact by the non-Mason as well as our own members, more damage is caused by those who would destroy us. Our enemies have found fertile ground on the web to dissipate their vitriolic hate of our fraternity. This we cannot contain any more than we could contain it in the past, but we must understand that it is there, and educate our membership concerning it.

The Internet will demand even more the organization of the Grand Lodges to maintain the stability necessary for Freemasonry to function as a unified whole. The web will not make Grand Lodges redundant; it will make them more necessary.

We have been fortunate to have carried our isolationist attitude into almost the present day. But, like it or not it is over. This modern technology along with present-day leadership attitude, is removing that choice from us.

One of our glaring weaknesses as leaders today has been our inability to see the big picture of the Craft. We have a tendency to lose sight of the great accomplishments for which Freemasonry has been known, and concentrate our efforts on issues not paramount to our existence and of little consequence to society. This is not a viable option. We simply cannot afford to fail to understand the diverse impacts that we have created and continue to create on human society.

For 300 years our past brothers worked to develop an unparalleled organization whose philosophical purpose could easily be used to structure world peace. There has probably been no time in our existence that the influence of that philosophy was any more needed in the world that it is today.

I am tremendously pleased to see the creation of this conference here in Africa. There is a commanding need for Freemasons to sit together to discuss our Craft and the problems confronting it today. I made the observation many years ago, that anything that affects Freemasonry in the world today affects Freemasonry everywhere. The web has assured us of that. By talking together we may be able to resolve issues. By not talking together we can resolve no issues.

As Freemasonry continues to develop on this continent,

the Grand Lodge of South Africa, as a result of its longevity and knowledgeable leadership, may possibly shoulder a greater responsibility to provide guidance in this development. You may be asked to accept a disproportionate share of responsibility in continuing to perpetuate an organization that contributed greatly to making this world what it is.

It has been a great honor for me to be here with you today. As we acknowledge and recognize our place in the world as Freemasons we must also acknowledge and recognize our responsibility to the world as Freemasons. Our brothers of the past have done their job exceedingly well. They have placed it in the forefront as an elite organization, one respected highly for its contribution in developing world society. It is now up to us to continue to build upon what they established. The very least we must do as Freemasons to contribute to a better world is to live as Freemasons. My brothers, so mote it ever be.

[18]

SPI Conference—Serbia

As I have intimated to you in the past, it is my belief that many of you sitting here today represent Grand Lodges with a potential for Freemasonry to participate in the reshaping of societies that it has not participated in for many decades, or if so, only marginally.

You should also be sitting here with a far greater appreciation of the privilege of being a member of this Craft than those of us who have not experienced the oppression and limitations of a dictatorial form of rule. With that appreciation and the newfound freedom to practice Freemasonry again, there must also, however, be a dedication and commitment to the principles and precepts for which it is known.

This dedication and commitment necessitates the divestiture of any ego that might serve as a barrier to releasing the full potential of the Masonic philosophy. I have been very impressed with the quality that I have observed in much of the leadership, but am concerned, as I have indicated in the past, with the instability that affects some Grand Lodges. Most of the instability is the result of uncontrolled egos of those challenging legitimate Grand Lodge leadership. This is an intolerable situation because it weakens Freemasonry's potential, not only in the jurisdiction in which it exists, but also in the Craft in general. Modern technologies preclude the isolationism that characterized Freemasonry for much of its history, so that what impacts Freemasonry anywhere in the world today, impacts Freemasonry everywhere in the world.

This conference is at least as important as any Masonic conference functioning today, because the Grand Lodges represented here must have the opportunity to sit and discuss mutual problems characterizing your early struggles. It is imperative that you understand, generate and support a cohesive force for regularity in Freemasonry! This conference could play a vital role in developing that force. It is important that a united front be generated in this section of the world not only to support regular Freemasonry, but also to combat irregular Freemasonry.

The expansion of irregular forms of the Craft is one of the greatest threats to our integrity as a viable institution today, not only in areas of the world were Freemasonry is reemerging or just starting, but in all areas of the world. With the use of modern technologies such as the World Wide Web, forms of the Craft lacking some or all of the basic Landmarks that constitute regularity, such as the belief in a Supreme Being, or the Volume of the Sacred Law being upon the altar, or the admission of female members are making inroads into jurisdictions where it has not been seen before.

We, as leaders, cannot afford to ignore these activities. It is more important today than perhaps at any time in our past that we work together in supporting those characteristics that made us the greatest organization ever conceived.

Far too much negative impact has been created by some appendant bodies in your jurisdictions. Every organization that requires Masonic membership as a prerequisite to its membership must remain under the control of the Grand Lodge. Interference in Craft Masonry by any other Masonic body is intolerable. Freemasonry has been seriously damaged in some jurisdictions by an ego-bloated leadership who feel that because they have a degree number higher than the third, that they outrank the grand lodges. We cannot permit this interference to weaken the integral structure of Craft Masonry. Concentration of effort must focus on strengthening grand lodges and their image in society, and if there is any force impeding this process, it cannot be ignored.

If Freemasonry is to be a major player in the structuring of society, it must be through the structuring of the man. This is, and has been, the philosophical intent of Freemasonry for several hundred years. Through this intent, it has changed the course of civilization in many areas of the world by the development of its members to a commitment to the basic principle of the inherent rights of man. Its identity as a Brotherhood of Man under the Fatherhood of God with the right of all men to worship a Supreme Being in accordance to the dictates of their own conscience could well be used as a template for world peace.

Now, once again, we are being afforded the opportunity to spread that cement of brotherly love in a region that has historically lacked it. Our success is going to be measured in the future by the standards and commitment you place into it. You have become its variable. Its future in your country is in your hands. It behooves all of us to reexamine our commitment to the principles of the Craft and to reinforce that commitment, or step aside so that others may lead. Freemasonry is just too important to this world to do otherwise.

I caution you once again not to use North American style of Freemasonry to emulate as yours. I am one of a nine member steering committee for a new foundation in North America called The Foundation for Masonic Reconstruction. Our purpose is to develop a different style of Freemasonry in North America. Quantity and wealth are not an assurance of success. Through our style, we have surrendered much of our image and influence in society. I also caution you to avoid being enamored of organizations appendant to Craft Masonry that will serve to dilute your leadership pool, something that is needed to strengthen Craft Freemasonry.

My congratulations on what you have accomplished in a short time span, but avoid complacency: you have a long way to go.

[19]

SPI Conference — Russia

It is indeed a sincere privilege and pleasure to be here in Moscow. You may recall that I was scheduled to be with you for the SPI conference in Sophia, Bulgaria in September 2001. Unfortunately, I was unable to travel at that time due to the terrorist attack on September 11 of that year.

The Grand Lodge in Russia is in a unique position when compared with most other Grand Lodges in the world, having been re-consecrated in recent years. You have the opportunity of retrospectively examining Freemasonry as it functioned in its speculative form for almost 300 years. You have the opportunity to see it for its greatness, for the contributions it has made to the development of civil society, and to observe the characteristics of the Brothers who made it into the highly respected institution it became. The influence of Freemasonry has altered the course of human progress.

You also have the great opportunity of seeing where we might have been better, where we have made mistakes and where our leadership has failed. Having seen, you need not repeat failures. You have the opportunity to learn from our past mistakes so that your progress will be less hindered.

Many of the world's greatest heroes who led their countries in the struggles for freedom were men whose images were crafted within the confines of a Masonic Lodge. They were men whose ideologies were tempered within those same hallowed walls. They were men of courage, with a will to promote the basic philosophies of Freemasonry, and these men were our Brothers.

It matters not if your grand lodge has an ancient history, interrupted by interference from outside forces, or whether you are a newly-created grand lodge, with a limited history. We are all recipients of a heritage left to us by our past brethren. Each of us has inherited an awesome responsibility, for we are now the caretakers of perhaps the greatest organization ever conceived by the mind of man, a force for good that changed the direction of the evolution of civil society. Where this Craft goes from here is now in our hands. Where it goes in your country is now in your hands. You have the potential to contribute to the formation of its greatness in your country as it has in other countries of the past.

In the message that I sent to you for the Sophia conference, I made the observation that the greatest potential for the growth and advancement of Freemasonry in the world today, exists in the countries of Eastern Europe and Africa.

I also expressed, however, that I had a great concern with the dissension that existed within some Grand Lodges, either as a result of uncontrolled ambition within the leadership, or the interference of appendant bodies. These dissensions continue to exist in some Grand Lodges, and must be unacceptable to regular Freemasonry everywhere.

In addition, the expansion of irregular Freemasonry with its aggressiveness on the Internet is creating a threat to the integrity of regular Freemasonry on a worldwide level. Even as regular Freemasonry is regaining a position in your countries, irregular Freemasonry is doing the same. We cannot afford disunity within our ranks, or we shall become a factor in its spread.

Unity of purpose which has been a fundamental cornerstone of our Craft for hundreds of years cannot be permitted to deteriorate as a result of unabated ego within a few of our leadership, nor can we permit the creation of Masonically affiliated organizations to interfere with, or weaken the power of the Grand Lodge. Let no one fail to recognize that the Grand Lodge is the supreme authority in any jurisdiction, and all appendant bodies are subject to its control.

To the world, you represent Freemasonry as it is in your country. You are its visible image. You have within your hands the potential to make this Craft a contributing force to the advancement of civil society in your country. As I said in my message in 2001, "you can make Freemasonry great, or you can contribute to its failure." Today, this world needs Freemasonry, perhaps more than ever in the past. Its principles, its philosophies and its precepts have never been outdated, nor can they ever be. Good in mankind is eternal. Now, it is in your hands. Our one hope my bothers, for immortality, beyond spiritual immortality, lies within the influence we create in the minds of others. May yours be a positive one, and may the Great Architect of the Universe always be your guide.

[20]

SPI Conference—Italy

*Message sent to Rome due to my being
unable to be present*

It is with sincere regret that I am not present with you today for your conference. I made a commitment over a year ago to be at another function, and I must honor that commitment. Please realize, however, that I am with you in spirit.

I am sure that you are aware of my great interest in Freemasonry in Eastern Europe. This is evident in my having have spent more time there in recent years than any other part of the world.

I am convinced that much of the future of our Craft will lie in the direction that Freemasonry takes in this part of the world. You hold within your hands the potential to not only impact Freemasonry's future but also the future of your country with the influence of the philosophy of the Craft, as it has done in so many other parts of the world.

The rebirth of Freemasonry in Eastern Europe is providing you with a potential to utilize this philosophy to a far greater degree than perhaps anywhere else on the globe. This potential carries with it a responsibility to utilize Freemasonry's philosophy for the benefit of the Craft as well as for the society.

It is also, however, placing upon your shoulders a commitment to leadership that requires you to shed personal ambition and to direct your efforts to the greater good of our Craft and our fellowman.

As many of you are discovering, this is not an easy task but it is imperative that you remain committed to the principles that has made Freemasonry the magnanimous structure of the ages. Each of us has assumed a mantel of responsibility that requires us to be better than the average man. It requires us to shed, the vices and superfluities of life, as our ritual states, and to serve as an example to society of what Freemasonry makes of good men. You are the visible image of the Craft in your countries. Our intent of taking good men and making them better means that the leadership should be the best of the good.

It is doubtful that any organization in the history of mankind has ever impacted the evolution of civil society, as has speculative Freemasonry with the exception of organized religion. Freemasonry has, however, the great advantage of working without the built-in bigotry that out of necessity exists in organized religions. We hold within our hands, therefore, the potential to use our influence for the promotion of human understanding and far more than any organization in existence today. Every Masonic leader in Eastern Europe has the great opportunity to contribute to the building or rebuilding of their society with that template.

One of the saddest commentaries of human experience is that the greatest manifestation of man's inhumanity to man has been carried out in the name of God. It has been a characteristic of the past is certainly evident in our present and will in all probability carry well into our future. If for no other reason, this abomination to the Supreme Being provides to us, the opportunity to present to the world an alternative to this way of life that can benefit no man and could well lead to the destruction of human existence.

But, we must not forget that there is an inherent hazard

for the misuse of influence in all organizations but even more so in an organization that grants so much power to its leadership as do we. If the leadership fails to use its capacity to do good it can do much harm. The future of Freemasonry in your countries and also in the society itself, quite possibility lies in the decisions you make today. Do not ever underestimate your potential to do neither good nor the harm you may cause if you fail.

I expressed early on when Eastern Europe was first regaining its freedom to practice Freemasonry, my greatest concerns with what could negatively impact the success of your Grand Lodge operations. Regretfully, those concerns have become realities in some of your Grand Lodges.

I was concerned with the development and interference by appendant Masonic bodies in Grand Lodge operations. This is happening. My brothers, Craft Masonry has been the bulwark in the development of civil society for several hundred years. Historians are now writing about the contribution of Freemasonry to the evolution of civil society but they write about Craft Freemasonry. We must not permit Masonic bodies' appendant to Craft Masonry to interfere with Grand Lodge operation and keep in mind that when I speak, I speak as a member of over 40 appendant bodies so I am not in opposition of them.

No Masonic body is superior to the Grand Lodge. It must be your goal to strengthen your Grand Lodge and the Craft Lodges in your jurisdictions. Then and only then should you be concerned with other Masonic bodies.

Secondly, I was concerned with a willingness to accept those who should never have been Freemasons in order to grow larger. My brothers, the quality of the member not the quantity of members is what changed the world.

No organization has attracted the number of great men, as has Freemasonry. These men then contributed to making the Craft great. Great men can make an organization great and great organizations can contribute to making men great. Only by accepting good men can you hope to make them the better men to fulfill our purpose.

Finally, I was concerned with the potential of the leadership of the newly established Grand Lodges becoming more dedicated to their own image than to the future of the Craft and my brothers that has been a problem in some of your Grand Lodges. Ego can be a great asset, but the control of ego can be an even greater asset. All of us are driven by the sense of accomplishment. That is our ego driving us, but the legacy we leave behind will depend much more upon our ability to control our ego.

I wish you the very best for the success of this conference. I extend my greatest hopes for the future of Freemasonry in your respective countries, and I pledge to you my assistance and support to achieve the purpose of the Craft, that of making good men better men and contributing to the welfare of mankind in your countries and the evolution of civil society.

[21]

Inter-American Masonic Confederation

Given in San Diego, Chile

I speak to you today as significant leaders of the Masonic world. I speak with the hope that what I say will cause you to think a little more about your importance to the ongoing evolution of a civil society that desperately needs that leadership.

It is a privilege of great importance for me to be here with you, to greet you, as prominent leaders of Freemasonry in your respective countries. I have never failed to notice during my twenty years as Grand Secretary, and have always been impressed with, the display of brotherhood that came out of the Freemasonry of Central and South America. I thank you for having me with you.

Our Craft has been faced with many challenges over the years of our existence, but perhaps no more so than today. We are being challenged by our enemies in many areas of the world, not only in areas where we have become accustomed to the challenges, but in areas where Freemasonry has operated in relative peace in the past. We are being challenged by irregular Freemasonry at a pace probably never seen in our past and is offering a threat to our stability as a regular institution. Of an even greater concern, however, is the challenge we are facing by the ignorance of our own membership.

Your Grand Lodges have lived as ongoing institutions

with greater challenges to your integrity than have many Grand Lodges in the world, and have succeeded in doing so very well. Your form of Freemasonry is more idealistic than that found in most areas of the world, and is something to be admired and probably emulated.

We all must realize, however, that we do not live in a vacuum. The isolationism of the past that tended to protect us is no longer a viable alternative in the present-day world. We can no longer ignore the threats in the rest of the world, thinking that it is their problem. The World Wide Web has created a new challenge, a new environment, which we must face, for it is here that gives the greatest exposure to our ignorance. We should be appalled at the information that is being placed on the web by our own members.

We have known our great Masonic heroes of the past; men like San Martin, Bolivar, Washington, Juarez, Garibaldi, and so many others whose names are emblazoned forever in the history of mankind. We can also readily recognize the names of many of our greatest enemies. We also know those enemies who have probably benefited the most by our existence. These are some of the leaders of the free world and some of the religious leaders of the world who have chosen to oppose us rather than appreciate us.

All of our heroes and all of our enemies have embraced or opposed us for the very same reason, the Masonic premise that every man should be free, with the right to worship his God as his conscience dictates and our teaching of toleration of these rights. It is significant that none of our enemies have had any great and long lasting impact on our integrity as an institution or upon our ability to impact the ongoing evolution of civil society. The ignorance and lack of quality of our own membership, however, may accomplish what our enemies have been unable to do. It is imperative for our future that we become more cognizant of what is happening with respect to membership and become involved in the education of those who belong.

Each of us as leaders of the Craft has assumed the awesome responsibility of preserving the qualities of Freemasonry that have been handed down to us by our brothers of the past. Now, with the expansion of irregular Freemasonry compounded by the ignorance of our membership, our task has become more complex. It is now more imperative that we are aware and understand what is happening involving Freemasonry in all parts of the world.

The environment in which we live today has changed, and it is changing more rapidly than ever in our history. We are experiencing a metamorphosis that is impacting the way we live along with the morality and the ethics of civilization itself. Freemasonry has been not only a modifying influence during the metamorphosis of the past several hundred years, but has been a driving influence. We could and may be a stabilizing influence in the future, but we certainly will not be if we cannot stabilize ourselves.

The unity of regular Freemasonry is a must if we are to accomplish our goals and continue to be an influence in society. We cannot tolerate or ignore deviation from our accepted protocols that have sustained us for hundreds of years. We must stand firm against the expansion of irregular Masonry. Ignoring it will not make it go away. We must also continue to work to eliminate Masonic ignorance of our own membership. If we do not understand ourselves, how can we expect the outside world to understand us?

If we are to continue to play a viable role in the world of the future, then we must expand our vision. We must remove the self-imposed constraints through ignorance of what we were, what we are, and what we can be. We must acknowledge that the organization is much greater than the sum of all its components parts. Self-limiting egos must become a characteristic of the past, and dedication to the Craft the cornerstone of the future. We must communicate with one another, so that we understand one another. We must work together for the benefit of Freemasonry, for that is also for the benefit of the world.

We are also being challenged by the needs of the world even more today. There has never been a time when the world has not needed the philosophy of Freemasonry. There has never been a time when the precepts of the Craft have not been applicable to the morals and ethics of society. There has never been a time, when, if this philosophy and these precepts were applied, that peace could not have been an alternative to war and conflict. The world has always needed the guidance of the great minds that have been molded by the professions forged by Freemasonry and tempered in the conclaves of Masonic ideology. Do not ever doubt my brothers, that this world needs us, needs our philosophy, and needs our precepts.

Our present was left to us by the brothers of the past. What we do today will determine the value of what is left to the brothers of the future, and that value will impact the value of society. My brothers, we as leaders cannot fail, for if we do, the world is the loser.

[22]

The Association of Masonic Arts

Given at First Conference in Brasilia, Brazil

I t is a great privilege to be here representing the Association of Masonic Arts. When I was asked to assume the position as honorary chairman, I expressed hesitancy because I feel very inadequate to be a representative of the arts in any form. I indicated at that time that there were probably many other brothers far more qualified than I, but that if I could benefit the organization, I would be willing to do so.

When I received an email from Brother Dimitar asking me to address you today, I was in Romania and did not return home until last Thursday. I then had a brother from Belgium who is traveling around the world for the next six months producing a film for the 300th anniversary of organized Freemasonry, stay with me at my home for three days. As a result, I only had a day and a half to write this paper, so I apologize for any deficiency in the quantity and quality of what I say.

My background and training is in the fields of science but I have always had great appreciation of the arts in its multiple forms as well as for those who have the talents and abilities to express themselves through those forms.

At the same time I recognize that most of the original prominent personalities who structured the first Freemasonry were found in the fields of the sciences. Many of them were members of The Royal Society of England and were the leaders in the advancement of scientific thinking and discoveries, when the world was emerging from a period of darkness where learning was repressed into a bright new vista and was encouraged and promoted. These were the great thinking minds that created the concept of our Masonic fraternity. They were the men with the vision to see into the future of what could be. They were the men laying the foundation of our speculative fraternity and they were the men responsible for the development of phenomena that changed the world.

However, much of the luster, much of the attention, much of the attractive force to our Craft came not only from the scientific mind but from the minds and the skills of the artisan. These were the brothers in that age who had the greatest exposure to and appreciation of society. After all, we acknowledge and rightly so, that we evolved from the stonemason who was an artisan in his own right.

So, even as we acknowledge our origins from the thinking of the scientific communities, we must acknowledge that we had our early origins from the artisans who built the great cathedrals and structures of Europe. Following that origin much of the luster that we have gained has been the result of the artisans of that day whose presence in our Craft served as an attractive force for others to want to become part of us and indeed, that force continues to this day.

Our Craft has taken great pride in being able to proclaim that upon our membership rolls have been those brothers whose names are some of the greatest artists who have ever lived in a diversity of fields. Brothers like Amadeus Mozart, Marc Chagall, Alphonse Mucha, Franz von Liszt, Franz Joseph Haydn, John Philip Sousa, William Hogarth, Rudyard Kipling, Robert Burns, and Alexander Nasmyth. These names have reverberated and will continue to reverberate so long as human appreciation of the arts survives. We have a grand officer of the Grand Orient here in Brasília, a noted conductor and friend, Tullio Colacioppo, whose life has been expressed in the Masonic arts.

Do we not admonish our brothers today, to be a lover of the arts and sciences and take it all opportunity to improve themselves therein? If that, indeed, is our intent, then we have the responsibility of infusing into the minds of our adherents an increasing appreciation of the position of the arts in Freemasonry.

This is a reason that we are sitting here today in Brasília as an acknowledgment of the need of the arts not only within the parameters of Freemasonry but within our lives. Indeed, this is the very reason why we have The Association of Masonic Arts. It is the culmination of the thinking of a few dedicated Freemasons who saw the need to promote a greater understanding of the significance of the arts in our lives. I deem it a great privilege to be associated with these brothers who had not only the vision to see the need but the artistic talent to contribute to that need.

I spent my youth in a relatively uneducated and poor environment and thus never had great exposure to the arts until I began my academic studies at the University level where the study the arts was required to obtain my degree. I now, highly value that requirement and my membership in Freemasonry has greatly enhanced that value.

I recall several years ago an experience in Warsaw, Poland when I was standing outside of the hotel where I was staying. A symphony and ballet performance was being given to the general public. In the listening and watching of that performance I stood with tears in my eyes, experiencing an appreciation I had never had before. Freemasonry gave to me that experience and that appreciation.

I have been very fortunate in my life to have been able

to travel over much of the world for Freemasonry and have been very much impressed with many of the brothers I have met, who have the innate ability to express themselves throughout the spectrum of disciplines that we refer to as the arts. I have found this to be especially true in some of the Eastern European countries where Freemasonry has once again become able to exert influence in societal evolution. I regard it as a unique privilege to meet with these young brothers who express themselves through their music, their painting and their writings. They, in their societies present a visual image of the Masonic fraternity, displaying the character and the quality of the Craft.

A discovery I have made in my years of travel and through those brothers who I meet, is that there is no sharp line of demarcation distinguishing the individual as a scientist or an artist. Indeed, some of the great scientific thinking minds were also some of the great artistic producers. Take for example Leonardo da Vinci.

What this means is that Freemasonry has the opportunity and the potential to impact the thinking and the development of the minds of its members through our precepts and disciplines, a greater appreciation of the Masonic arts. This was the vision of those few brethren who entered into the creation of The Association of Masonic Arts. I take no credit for this creation but I do give considerable credit to them for what they have accomplished.

This Association, as you know, is a new (founded in 2013) and unique corridor offered to the members of the Craft, that will provide for many, a greater comprehension of the uniqueness of our fraternity as a pathway to understanding the fuller meaning of the Brotherhood of man under the Fatherhood of God.

We have been extremely fortunate in being able to gain the support of our ambassadors in numerous countries throughout the world. It will be through these brothers that the Association will become known and through the Association the artistic character of Freemasonry will be preserved as an integral part of our Craft.

There can be little doubt that over the 300 years of our existence as a symbolic fraternity that the appreciation of its artistic qualities has waned as our societies have become more embedded in the technology of the modern world. It is the purpose of The Association of Masonic Arts to reignite the flame where-in the acquisition of knowledge and the appreciation of the arts with it symbolic meanings, may once again become a significant element in the structure of the Craft.

My travels have taught me that even in the poorest of nations, even in the most primitive of societies existing in today's world, admiration of the arts has constituted a part of the basic fabric of those nations and societies. It should therefore be an inherent responsibility of all Freemasons to cultivate and encourage a greater appreciation of the arts in the society in which they live. Freemasonry has since its inception, exemplified an appreciation of the fine arts that is reflected in the architecture of their edifices and the artistic decorations both within and without these edifices. Perhaps time has dulled some of our commitment to maintain this vision in some areas of the world, but my brothers, I have found it to continue to exist, especially in societies where Freemasonry is a new phenomenon.

The Association of Masonic Arts is dedicated to the retention of the appreciation where it does exist and hopefully restore it to those environments wherein time has dulled the appreciation.

I want to personally express my very sincere appreciation to the Grand Orient of Brazil and to Grand Master Marcos José da Silva for serving as the host jurisdiction for this, the first conference meeting of the Association. I have had a great appreciation for the Grand Orient and for the brothers and friends that I have met over the years.

I wish for you all, the blessings of the Grand Architect of the Universe and solicit his blessing for the success of The Association of Masonic Arts.

[23]

History: Myth and Reality

Given at the University of Bucharest

My Masonic brothers, ladies and gentlemen, it is a distinct honor and personal privilege for me to be able to stand before you today in your country and to speak to you regarding the subject of Freemasonry. It has not been many years ago that this would not have been possible.

This privilege to be here is indicative of many ideological changes that have rapidly taken place in many parts of the world in recent years and certainly in Eastern Europe. It is indicative of an ongoing desire for man in his quest for intellectual freedom as well as for an equality of humankind on all levels of life.

Hopefully, I will convey to you today a greater understanding of what Freemasonry is: its origins, its philosophy, its purpose, its successes, and even its failings.

Freemasonry has been intimately involved in this quest for freedom and equality in much of the world for several centuries. It was perhaps the first organization ever developed by human thinking to impart equality without regard to social status, occupation or religious persuasion. Its philosophical intent is to accept good men and then contribute to making them better by infusing into them the ethical and moral principles that we profess and to prove to them that they were much more capable than they thought themselves to be.

It played a major role during the age of Enlightenment in this quest as one of the principal organizations that provided an environment in which great minds from numerous disciplines could gather together share their thoughts and ideas and fuse their thinking into ideals that provided the basis for intellectual, physical and religious freedoms for humankind. Indeed, it is Freemasonry more than any other organization that provided the format for the structure of democratic thought.

Illogically perhaps, even the greatest of Masonic scholars do not know for certain, our origins. The most widely accepted theory is that Freemasonry is an evolutionary product growing out of the early building guilds responsible for constructing the great cathedrals of Europe during the age of the Renaissance. However, there are also those theorists who feel that Freemasonry had its origin with the remnants of the Knights Templar or is a resultant merger of these remnants and the early Freemasons. Recently there has been a proposed theory that Freemasonry is a result of Isaac Newton's quest for knowledge that led to its foundation and is the result of the development of intellectualism and freedom from the religious constraints placed upon freedom of thought.

However, this lack of knowledge of our origins has not interfered with the capability of the Craft to create perhaps the greatest impact upon the evolution of civil society of any organization ever conceived.

We do know that the first man recorded as having been made a Freemason was in England in the year of 1646 but some of the early manuscripts trace it to a much earlier date in Scotland. The first organized form of speculative Freemasonry originated in the year 1717 when four lodges in London met together to create a Grand Lodge to oversee the increasing number of lodges that were developing.

From that date Freemasonry spread rapidly throughout Europe and much of the rest of the known world. It continues to expand today into areas where it has had limited existence for a many years such as on the continent of Africa. It also continues to appear or reappear in most of the Eastern European countries where it was repressed for decades.

Not only do we have no definitive knowledge of our origins but we find it difficult to define what it is and its purpose in such a way that is easily understood by those outside of it. Its most descriptive definition is that it is a "beautiful system of morality, veiled and allegory and illustrated by symbols." Its most simple and definitive expression, however, is that we are an organization designed to take good men and make them better.

These are the realities as we know them but Freemasonry has been veiled in myths regarding its origins as well as its motives and purposes almost since the beginning of its existence. There are those within the Craft who have created some of these myths tracing its origins back to the Egyptian dynasties and beyond. The fact remains, however, that there is no supportive evidence to trace it back any farther than the dates that I have just given to you.

Almost from its inception it has had its supporters and it has had those who have sought to destroy it, those who loved it and those who hated it. Its tenacity for survival is almost legendary when one considers who its enemies have been.

Freemasonry's greatest enemies have been those who oppose its philosophical precepts of the freedom of man to think and to be free as well as to worship their God as their consciences dictate. Its unabashed support for the freedom and liberty of man makes it an enemy to all those who would seek to take away that liberty and freedom. As one might expect, therefore, dictatorial and oppressive regimes have opposed the existence of Freemasonry for centuries. Freemasonry has been outlawed in almost all countries where under repressive regimes thousands have been imprisoned or executed for simply being Freemasons.

Regretfully, some religious leaders of the world have also opposed Freemasonry. It is a tragic commentary that the enemies of the Craft have been the world's greatest tyrants and some of the world's prominent spiritual leaders, both antagonists to each other. It is even more tragic that they oppose us for the very same reason, our support for the freedom of thought and our philosophical principle that man should not only have the right to worship God but the right to worship God as he sees fit.

Freemasonry's only religious requirement for membership is the belief in a Supreme Being. I have been in grand lodges that had five Volumes of the Sacred Law lying upon the altar, one for each major religion in the country. Therefore religious belief serves not as a barrier to bringing men together but rather as an attractive force.

In spite of all the repression that has confronted the Craft, it has not only survived, it has thrived and continues today to promote its philosophy throughout the free world.

But even as there have been those in leadership positions that have opposed Freemasonry there have been many of the greatest leaders of the world who led in their country struggles for freedom who were members of the Masonic fraternity. It would not be logical to think that the philosophy of the Craft did not have some influence on their way of thinking, all of them Freemasons and all of them revered in their respective countries for providing the leadership to rise above the tyrannical suppression that dominated the freedom of thought in the minds of its citizens.

If the greatness of an organization might be measured in the greatness of its composition then Freemasonry would have to be judged as an unqualified success. There have been more great men in more diverse fields that have been dedicated to the principles of Freemasonry than any organization that has ever existed. Masonic philosophy has served as an attractive force to bring together some of the greatest personages that have lived over the past 300 years. Fourteen presidents of the United States have been Freemasons and Winston Churchill in England was also a Freemason. In Africa today the presidents of at least seven countries are members of the Craft and two are serving as Grand Masters. Historically many members of royal families have been and remain members. But perhaps even more significant are the prominent men in so many diverse fields that found an attractive force in Freemasonry.

Freemasonry has had its successes as well as its failures for at least three centuries. Its greatest accomplishments can be measured in the millions of men and women who live today in an environment of freedom and they can worship God as they choose. It of course has experienced its failures revealed in the deaths of thousands of its members who died in promoting these freedoms.

My friends, Freemasonry's philosophy has had a fundamental impact over evolving civil societies for several hundred years influencing some of the greatest men that this world has ever known to lead their countries in this ongoing quest for the rights of man. There can be no doubt that had Freemasonry never existed, this world would be a markedly different place today and by the grace of Almighty God it will continue to do so.

[24]

Freemasonry's Values:
An Impact on the Past and Potential
for the Future

Given in Budapest, Hungary

I regard it a great privilege to be asked to address this 1st European Conference on Masonic values. I congratulate the Symbolic Grand Lodge of Hungary along with the support of the United Grand Lodges of Germany for taking the initiative to develop a program that will continue to expose to the European world, not only the great societal contributions of our past, but the potential for contributions to European society in the future.

Please keep in mind, as I speak that I have a tendency to look at Freemasonry on a different level than do most leaders of the Craft. Because of my lengthy exposure to international issues confronting Freemasonry, I consider Freemasonry, not only on a grand lodge, country or continental level but on a world level with the understanding that in today's world, an impact on Freemasonry anywhere is an impact on Freemasonry everywhere. I also speak as one from outside your societies and therefore unaffected by any personal bias generated within the environment.

Freemasonry on the European continent is in a unique position today, as a result of the historic division between the East and the West for over fifty years. Most of Western Europe has been able to practice Freemasonry with limited interruption for approaching three centuries while the countries that comprise Eastern Europe, even though they may have had the Freemasonry of the past, have lacked that freedom for those fifty-plus years.

Freemasonry is truly experiencing a remarkable resurgence of significance in today's world, and European Freemasonry is the major participant in that resurgence. Twenty six new grand lodges have been created since the beginning of this century, with the majority of them as a result of consecrations or re-consecrations of grand lodges in Europe; others had been consecrated in the last decade of the twentieth century. It is an interesting phenomenon that although most of these new grand lodges are in Eastern Europe, there have been new consecrations in Western Europe also, even though the Freemasonry there is some of the oldest in the world.

Only on the continent of Africa does Freemasonry have the potential to create a comparable impact on evolving society. Indeed, it is in these two locations that Freemasonry is expanding most rapidly into new environments. Just last month, we received a request to support a new grand lodge re-consecrated in Egypt.

Although our Craft has faced multiple challenges on numerous fronts since its inception, The Freemasonry in Europe has faced what perhaps might have been the greatest challenges anywhere in the world. Latin American Freemasonry has faced ongoing challenges but with the exception of Brazil, Latin American countries all speak a common language, not the multiple languages as found in Europe, nor have they experienced as great a diversity of cultures as exists in Europe.

This unique position in which European Freemasonry finds itself offers an opportunity for its members to create a far greater impact upon society than exists in most of the world. However, this greater opportunity carries with it greater challenges. It places upon the leadership a burden of responsibility to present a positive image of our Craft to their countries and a commitment to improve the moral and ethical values of the society in which they lead.

For many years, I wondered why historians did not write about Freemasonry until I began to comprehend that historians wrote about the lives of national leaders and their influence on society, not the organizations to which they belonged. More than a few of those leaders were Freemasons!

In the last two decades, however, historians have been writing about the impact of Freemasonry upon the lives of those great leaders and heroes who led in their countries struggles for freedom and liberty. I have not seen an account written by these historians concerning the influence of Freemasonry that has not been positive. That places an additional onus of responsibility upon those who are leaders today, for what the historians write in the future may well depend upon the image that you present to your society today.

Many of those national heroes were European Freemasons and they created an image that will benefit today's leadership in assuming responsibility in your society. However, you cannot live by parasitizing the past. You must be an active participant in the present and not base your success upon reputations created by the brothers who preceded you. There tends to be an adopted tendency for Freemasons today to lean upon the persona created by the brothers of the past, but a future cannot be built by a dependency upon our past.

Historically, there were of course, those who were enemies of Freemasonry, almost from its inception. But that was part of the challenge that contributed to making

Freemasonry into perhaps the greatest organization ever conceived by human thought. The image of Freemasonry was forged and tempered in conflict and adversity, and the Craft has always been at its best when its challenges were the greatest. The lack of challenge tends to produce a complacency that can readily evolve into apathy.

Freemasonry did not survive by bowing to the wishes and demands of a society sadly lacking in the ethical and moral values upon which this Craft was structured. Freemasonry did not thrive by subjugating the Craft to dictatorial regimes or to oppressive religious powers. Freemasonry did not become this eminent organization by lowering its standards and sacrificing its principles in order to receive acceptance from a profane world that makes no attempt to understand us. No, my Brothers, Freemasonry became what it became due to our commitment to retain those qualities that made it great and made it beneficial to civil society.

In our global society which is rapidly losing those moral and ethical values that sustained it in the past, are those who feel that Freemasonry's values are out of touch with today's reality and that its philosophical purpose of promoting those values are antiquated standards of ages past. There can never be an age in which the values of Freemasonry would not be applicable to any civilized society, but society has to know that. It is the responsibility of every Freemason to set the visible image that society will see as Freemasonry.

When we examine the declining values of the present age, I would suggest that it would be more prudent for society to adopt the standards of Freemasonry rather than for Freemasonry to adopt the values of present-day society. We cannot afford to surrender to the demands of the profane world. Were the world to live by the philosophy promoted by Freemasonry, it could very well indeed, serve as a pathway for world peace.

But now, when we look at the failure of Freemasons and its leadership to practice our own values, how can we expect the profane world to adopt them and to grant us the respect that we carried in the past? Never forget, that each Freemason is the visible image of Freemasonry to the public. So the commitment accepted by the leadership of Freemasonry places them on a higher level of responsibility than the average citizen.

I have been a student of Freemasonry for many years and the more I study the Craft the more impressed I become with how much its presence meant to the development of civilization. Now, however, I am increasingly alarmed by the willingness of today's Masonic leaders to violate the protocols that have sustained us for three centuries. This organization was created by some of the greatest minds who inhabited the world of our past. The success of what they created generated the visible image that the world accepted as Freemasonry. Today, there are leaders who feel that that their thinking is superior to that of these great men and that they can mold us into something superior to what we are.

It is a tragic commentary when we recognize that the greatest challenges to our success in the past have been external challenges chiefly presented by religious leaders and government leaders, none of whom were able to destroy the Craft or restrain its continued success in society, while the greatest challenges confronting us in the 21st century are internal challenges. There are far more divisive issues existing within the inflated egos of Masonic leadership and the liberal attitudes of the membership than those from challenges outside of it. Dissension between grand lodge leaders and dissension within grand lodges has become an increasing issue confronting Freemasonry's success in the present age. The Freemasonry developing in Eastern

Europe has not been immune to these challenges and it should be incumbent upon Freemasonry everywhere to aid in the confrontation to solve these issues.

The challenges, of course, exist beyond the borders of Eastern Europe. We have recently watched the ego and action of one man come close to destroying a highly respected grand lodge that has existed for many years. That also, must be unacceptable to world Freemasonry. The unparalleled egos of too many Masonic leaders today are providing the potential for us to accomplish what our enemies could never accomplish; extinction.

Masonic leaders buying into the political correctness concept has impacted many grand lodges and lowered the quality of the organization.

Well, not every man deserves the same as everyone else unless he earns it and not every man deserves to be a Freemason. One of the reasons that Freemasonry became the great institution that it became was its philosophical intent to accept good men from all social strata and seat them in the lodge room as equals. However, a second reason for its success was its commitment to accept only good men. This attractive force to great thinking men was primary in causing our Craft to become a force unlike any other seen in the world; one that has served as a beacon to the developing world societies.

Freemasonry was one of the primary enclaves that provided the environment during the age of Enlightenment that attracted great minds and laid the framework for a Democratic society. Consider men like Benjamin Franklin, Wolfgang Amadeus Mozart, Giuseppe Garibaldi, George Washington, Sir Christopher Wren, Simón Bolívar, Alexander Fleming, Lajos Kossuth and so many other great men and what their membership meant to our Craft. Without them, it is highly doubtful that we would have become the world's most renowned fraternity nor even survived to the present age.

The leaders of Freemasonry evolving in Eastern Europe have the distinct advantage of being able to study and to learn from the history of Western European Freemasonry, but it is of significant importance to recognize the challenges of the present era, which, while similar in many ways, are distinctively different in others. Freemasonry in Eastern Europe is operating in a different environment as a result of surviving oppressive forms of government, and with a different mindset of its citizens than existed in Western Europe. One must face the challenges of leading an organization that promotes the freedom and equality of man in environments where freedom and equality were unknown for decades and where individual struggle to achieve success was at best, a muted phenomenon.

Nonetheless, the philosophical intent of Freemasonry remains the same as it is in Western Europe, and as it was in our past, to take good men and make them better men. These better men must then assume the responsibility of leading their societies. You, as leaders cannot ignore the needs of the society in which you live. Ultimately, you have a responsibility to improve that society through the good men that the Craft has improved and although charity has been a core value of Freemasonry since its inception and an inherited quality that has distinguished us, it is not the core value of Freemasonry. The core value is the improved man. Freemasons improved societies by becoming part of them and leading them into a better future than their past had been.

Dr. and Brother E. Scott Ryan in his book, *The Theology of Crime and the Paradox of Freedom* observed, "The wonderful work of Masonic charity is by no means synonymous with the wonderment of Masonic spirituality—and that is a shame, when one considers how many fine charities there are and how few fine spiritualties there are." The respect that Freemasonry has received in other environments was earned, not bought, and if that mantle of respect is to be placed upon you, it must be earned.

Although I have developed a great respect for much of what I have observed in the development of Freemasonry in Eastern Europe, I have also developed a great concern with the inflated egos that are interfering with the potential to meet the challenges that are required to sustain its greatness. My Brothers, there is no room in the brotherhood of Freemasonry for egos so large that they interfere with the philosophical intent of our Craft. It is incumbent upon every one of us as leaders in Freemasonry, to divest ourselves of any limiting ego that may interfere with our commitment to the goals of Freemasonry and frankly, I see that as perhaps your greatest challenge.

Regular Freemasonry must be united in its common goal to improve good men, and consequently society. Divisiveness can only weaken that potential. Concentration must be made to continually improve the quality of the organization through accepting only good men. The quantity of the membership is not nearly as important as the quality of the member, and membership numbers will increase in direct proportion to the quality of the organization you present to society.

There has been possibly no time in history that the philosophy of Freemasonry is more needed than it is today. Freemasonry in Eastern Europe now stands on the threshold of opportunity for the membership to contribute to the ongoing evolution of your societies and the Freemasonry of Western Europe must provide a gentle guidance in that contribution.

This conference could very well contribute to the understanding of the challenges and problems of our era, but only if you participate with a willingness to learn. It is incumbent upon each of you as leaders to stimulate your members to seek the knowledge to promote a respect for human dignity and peace as stated in the purpose for the conference.

This world is as it is today because Freemasonry lived and Freemasonry lived because it undertook the responsibility of taking the good man and making him a better man, by teaching him the philosophy and precepts of the Craft. These better men then became the leaders that created modern-day civil society. That must be your goal. Freemasonry's future in Europe is in your hands. What will the historians write about you?

[25]

Masonic Academy of Serbia

It is a great pleasure for me to be able to address this opening of your Masonic Academy. Fifteen years ago with the support of the Grand Master, we created the Academy of Masonic Knowledge in my home grand lodge. The mission statement for that Academy is, "It will strive to create an environment that will encourage Masons to seek a greater understanding of the nature and purposes of Freemasonry in all its many aspects-past, present, and future-and to share that understanding with others. This Academy is designed to offer learning opportunities in which Masons may participate in dialogues with similarly inclined brothers and, witness prominent Masonic scholars discussing various aspects of Freemasonry, and pursue home study at their own pace."

Our Academy has been extremely successful in creating an environment for learning. In the fifteen years of our existence, four of our members have published books on Freemasonry and we find an increased interest of our members who have been stimulated to understand the significant contribution that Freemasonry has made to the evolution of civil societies for three centuries. In addition, it has been the function of the Academy to infuse in the minds of our members their responsibility as Freemasons, their responsibility to their God to their society and to their fellow man.

I have not seen a mission statement or stated purpose of the Academy now being created in Serbia but in communication with Most Worshipful Brother Ranko, I would have to assume that the end result that you seek would be the same, through the intellectual improvement of the Serbian Freemason. Thus your Academy would contribute in fulfilling the primary purpose of the Craft, to make good men better. We would then hope that those better men would assume the responsibility of contributing to the ongoing evolution of your society, your country and to the world.

There are many pathways that can be followed in your Academy toward the same end, just as there are numerous pathways that may be followed through the rituals to become a Master Mason. You must determine the pathway that you will follow. I have brought with me a copy of the system that we are using to give to your leaders that hopefully may provide suggestions that may be of some help to you.

It is almost unfathomable the number of books that have been written on the subject of Freemasonry during our three centuries of existence. It is doubtful that any other private organization has ever generated that degree of interest. Some of the books have been written by those who oppose the existence of the Craft but the vast majority has been written by those acknowledging and supporting our contribution to the improvement of man and thus the improvement of society. For many years, I pondered and puzzled over the lack of acknowledgment by historians of our contribution to that improvement. In fact, I wrote a paper around thirty years ago that I titled, "How Can They Ignore Us?" It seemed totally illogical to me, with my studies of Freemasonry, why we were not credited as an organization for what we had accomplished. And then, after reading the report following the first World Conference of Masonic Grand Masters (the title of the World Conference for the first three meetings), I finally began to comprehend. A Mexican Grand Master at that conference referring to a great Mexican leader proclaimed, "Benito Juarez, the great figure of a Mason who led our countries struggles for freedom and liberty." I suddenly realized, why historians did not write about Freemasonry. They wrote about men. It was not Benito Juarez, the great figure of a Mason who led in his Country's struggles but Benito Juarez the great figure of a man who happened to be a Freemason.

However, I have been extremely pleased to realize that in the last two decades, historians are now writing about Freemasonry. They are acknowledging that the man could not be separated from the organizations that inspired him. They are writing about the influence that Freemasonry had upon society through the men who were Freemasons. They are crediting the impact of Freemasonry upon the men, who then became involved with the ongoing evolution of civil societies in many diverse fields.

I have been emphasizing for many years that Freemasonry as an organization, does not become involved in political affairs or religious affairs. Freemasons may get involved but not acting for Freemasonry. Freemasons should become involved. If it is our goal to take the best man we can find and improve that man, we should sincerely hope that these better men would be leading our countries in their development of a civil society. Indeed, in spite of the great beneficial impact that we have had upon society, that is not our purpose. It may be our intent, but not our purpose. Our purpose remains to improve the good man.

This is why the Freemasons of Serbia and the Freemasons of all of Eastern Europe have such a great opportunity to make a major contribution to this part of the world.

With the consecration and re-consecration of Freemasonry in Eastern European countries, you and your grand lodges have a far greater potential to accept that mantle of responsibility, than have the grand lodges that have been in existence for long periods of time and in more stable environments. There are times that I look upon you with envy, recognizing your potentials to contribute to the evolution of change in your countries. Within these environments are fertile fields open to cultivation and be sown with the seeds of Masonic philosophy. You also have the privilege of studying the successes of Freemasonry and also its failures in other parts of the world. This should help you avoid the pitfalls that the Craft has encountered over the last 300 years.

It is important to realize, however, that growth and advancement does not take place overnight nor will it come easily. There is much to learn and the learning takes time. Mistakes will be made and have been made. There are hurdles to get over and there will be barriers placed in your way, but Freemasonry has always been confronted with hurdles and barriers and as the challenges arose, Freemasonry rose with those challenges.

It is not going to be an easy journey. As a result of your recent past, there is an inherent distrust of organizational powers by much of the populace and indeed even with Masons of one another. There is a different mindset in Eastern Europe that may result in a different style of Freemasonry being developed than exists elsewhere in the world. Styles of Freemasonry result from the environment in which it exists and I would expect a variation in style from that of Western European Grand Lodges.

I have received communications from brothers in Eastern Europe accusing Masonic leaders of using their position to further them in the political arena. I am not doubting that this may happen but I found the information I received in the past to be false.

A newly elected Grand Master of an Eastern European country, in response to a letter I received accusing him of that offense, volunteered to resign the office if I felt that it would be to the benefit to his Grand Lodge and his country. I knew at that time, that he was the brother who should be in that office and I advised him not to resign. He served two very effective terms as Grand Master and made major contributions to the visibility and viability of his grand lodge.

There is nothing wrong with Masons being involved in the politics of their countries, so long as the Craft is not being actively used to gain political position. We Masons in the United States, recognize the vital contribution that Freemasonry made to the development of our democratic society. Moreover, we take great pride in being able to claim that fourteen of our presidents have been Freemasons and lest you think that Freemasons contributed only to the struggle for liberty and the development of civil society in North America consider the contributions made by Giuseppe Garibaldi in Italy, Kemal Ataturk in Turkey, Theodore Kolokotronis in Greece, Simon Bolivar in South America, Benito Juarez in Mexico, O'Higgins in Chile, San Martin in Argentina, to name but a few.

In addition to those brothers who excelled in fields of the military and politics we may add the names of Robert Burns, Charles Dickens, Rudyard Kipling, Alexander Pushkin, Johan von Goethe, Luther Burbank, Sir Alexander Fleming, Amadeus Mozart, Franz Liszt, John Wayne, and we could go on and on. We have barely scratched the surface of listing those names whose lives made major contributions to the world as we know it, names etched upon the headstones of eternity.

Permit me to quote the first president of the Philippines,

Emilio Aguinaldo, to show how much this Craft meant to the Filipino independence: "The successful revolution of 1886, was Masonically inspired, Masonically led, and Masonically executed. And I venture to say, that the first Philippine Republic of which I was the humble president, was an achievement we owe largely to Masonry and the Masons." Speaking of the revolutionist, he added, "With God to illumine them, and Masonry to inspire them, they fought the battles of emancipation and won." Please note, Masonry inspired them, an act of making good men better.

In considering the contributions that Freemasons made to the development of world civilization, consider now your assumed responsibility to follow in their footsteps. You have within your grasp in Serbia today, as well as in all countries where Freemasonry is becoming a visible and viable institution, the opportunity to join the ranks of so many great men in so many diverse fields who paved the way for you by creating and nurturing the greatest organization ever conceived by the mind of man.

I have watched the development of Freemasonry in Eastern Europe almost from its beginnings following the collapse of dictatorial powers that prohibited its existence. I've been greatly impressed with the achievements that you have made in a relatively short period of time. I have appreciated the intellectualism that I find within the leadership and the dedication within the membership.

I have observed the great interest that is being shown by some of the political leaders in Eastern Europe of the potential for Freemasonry to become a player in the struggles to recover from the impact of these dictatorial powers and in the development of a new horizon of the rights and liberties of the citizens.

Many of you sitting here today, indeed probably most of you sitting here today have experienced the futility in a life lacking the freedom of thought as well as the freedom of expression. This should have stimulated a greater appreciation of the privilege of being able to say, "I am a Freemason." Freemasonry cannot exist where freedom does not exist.

However, I have also observed with great concern the internal struggles within the Craft itself. I have watched in far too many countries the schisms that have occurred as a result of inflated egos of individual brothers who find the transition from the realism of the past into the idealism of the present, overpowering. When this dissension occurs, the result is a weakening of the potential of Freemasonry to perform to its full intent and to the benefit of society. In far too many jurisdictions, lack of knowledge and bloated egos, have resulted in the failure of the Craft to achieve its possibilities. Masonic protocols have sustained Freemasonry for three centuries and we must not let the actions of a few alter those standards that have made us great.

To fully appreciate our responsibilities as members of this Craft, we must understand the significance of its contributions in the development of civilized society, and to fully understand this significance requires an educated brotherhood. The formation of this Academy should be major step in this understanding.

Those of you who have become affiliated with this Masonic Academy have now placed yourselves in a position of greater responsibility of studying the past, of observing the present and of comprehending the future for Freemasonry in Serbia. The magnitude of the resources available to you is far beyond anything available in the past and is expanding every day but you must make the effort to receive it. There is no osmotic process by which it can be achieved.

Freemasonry has been intimately involved in the development of intellectualism even before its formal structure began in 1717. It played a major role during the age of Enlightenment in the quest for knowledge as one of the principal organizations that provided an environment in which great minds in numerous disciplines could gather together and share their thoughts and ideas and infuse their thinking into ideals that provided the basis for intellectual, physical and religious freedoms for humankind. Our ritual requires for us to be a lover of the arts and sciences and take every opportunity to improve ourselves therein. Therein, lays the primary function of your Academy.

Freemasonry is the most successful fraternal organization that has ever existed and if there was a way of determining it, it could very well be the most successful organization of any kind that is ever existed. It has impacted the world well beyond any other institution created by the mind of man. It has existed longer and has grown larger. It has caused change in the direction of the development of civilization. It has promoted civility, in civil society. And now, it has given you the opportunity to make your mark in this world.

Many men, indeed probably most men will finish their tour of life in this world leaving very little evidence that there were even here. Freemasonry will give you a greater opportunity to leave your Mark. This Academy will give you an even a greater opportunity to make your presence known. Now, it is in your hands. The future of the Craft in Serbia is up to you. I wish you great success. I wish for this Academy the greatest success in stimulating you to be a better man.

[26]

The Growing Threat

Romanian Institute Lecture

Freemasonry as a regular institution has been operating under a set of protocols that has sustained it as a speculative Craft for almost 300 years. By accepting and maintaining those protocols, our institution has become, perhaps, the most significant factor in the evolution of civil society outside of organized religion. Today historians are acknowledging the impact of Freemasonry's philosophy has had on individuals, and in turn, those individuals have had on the development of the standards by which society is judged. Our Craft has been a major player for several hundred years in creating the stimulus for men to learn and to develop and has served as a catalyst to bring together great men and to contribute to making men great. We have taken good men and have made them better men while instilling in them a dedication to rights and freedom of all men.

World Freemasonry today, however, is in a greater state of instability than it has been for probably the greater part of its existence, and for a number of reasons.

First, Freemasonry is expanding more rapidly than it has probably for well over 100 years, and maybe 200 years. With the emergence of Freemasonry in Eastern Europe and the development of new grand lodges on the continent of Africa, Freemasonry is experiencing a surge of growth

605

unseen for many decades. It is significant that irregular forms of Freemasonry are also expanding probably more rapidly than they have in their entire history. This is a major concern for the stability of regular Freemasonry. It has become almost competitive to see which style of the Craft can be established first.

Second, ignorance of the Craft and its purpose has become a way of life for many Freemasons.

Third, the Internet has become a valuable tool to spread misinformation and the ignorance of others to our brothers and to anyone else who reads it and who lack the knowledge to reject it. The subject of regularity in Freemasonry is not a recent phenomenon, although there are some of our members today who think they have discovered something new in the Masonic world. It was probably one of the first major considerations to confront early speculative Freemasonry. As a result, specific criteria have been established to which any Masonic Grand Lodge must conform and adhere to, to be regarded as regular.

Today, we acknowledge that a grand lodge's regularity is contingent upon it having been created by another regular grand Lodge, or by the action of three or more regular subordinate lodges. Regularity is also dependent upon adherence by a grand lodge to established practice and compliance to specific requirements.

The Craft established the system of granting warrants to grand lodges and lodges around 1731 and thus created a method early in speculative Freemasonry that was adhered to as a worldwide standard. Regularity of Freemasonry is the structural base upon which we have erected our edifice to protect the constancy of purpose to the world outside of our Craft. Those grand lodges not operating within these standards, have not adopted or have eliminated some of the basic landmarks upon which we exist, i.e. the required belief in a Supreme Being, the Volume of the Sacred Law upon the altar, the avoidance of involvement in politics and religion as an organization, and the restriction of male-only membership.

Regularity in Freemasonry has been accompanied by irregularities since close to its inception. There have been and are regular grand lodges in origin that became irregular in practice. There have been, and are grand lodges that comply with some of the requirements for regularity, but not all, and there exists grand lodges that have never been regular in either origin or in practice. Masonic leaders have dealt with these issues effectively for almost 300 years. Now, there are some of our members who have developed an attitude that regularity is not significant to the Craft.

Now, there is a pervasive attitude beginning to permeate our Craft regarding regularity and fraternalism that none of us can choose to ignore. There are those within the fraternity today who have developed the attitude that anyone calling themselves Freemasons should be regarded as Freemasons. There are those, even including a small segment of our leadership who feel that almost 300 years of history, practice and tradition is no longer applicable in today's world. These brothers probably have no idea how many grand lodges exist in the world.

Unquestionably, this results from the ignorance of the vast majority of Freemasons concerning Masonic history, its contributions to the world and even its purpose for existence. Couple this ignorance with ego and we have a blueprint for disaster. Our leaders should be informed enough to know better, and it is difficult to comprehend the motives that inspire these men.

Lack of knowledge is certainly a major factor, but ego and arrogance is another, and present-day liberalism is probably a third. Whatever the motives, we cannot afford to ignore their actions. If permitted to continue, it will destroy Freemasonry as it has been known for almost three centuries. We simply cannot permit these attitudes against our protocols to exist in our membership. Our members, who choose to violate their obligation as a Freemason, should be removed before their destructive thinking is spread farther.

Present day leadership is being confronted with the need to make decisions that will impact our fraternity far into the future and many are ill-equipped to deal with them due to a lack of knowledge, not only in procedures required for recognition, but also concerning the grand lodges in question.

Freemasonry is the most successful fraternal organization that has ever existed. It has existed longer and has grown larger. It has caused change in the direction of the development of civilization. It has promoted civility, in civil society. And now, there are those in our fraternity today with the impression that they have a wisdom superior in our past brothers who have created and sustained it for 300 years.

The Internet is being used today by those within the Craft who feel they have a vision for the future of Freemasonry that lies beyond the parameters of what made and sustained our greatness. It is within this small cadré of our own membership that lies perhaps the greatest threat to our survival as a viable institution, and again we cannot choose to ignore it.

Personally, I would like nothing more than to see all Freemasonry in the world united is a like-minded brotherhood of men dedicated to a common goal. Such an entity could only contribute to the strengthening of our noble institution. It would increase our potential to be an influence for the ongoing evolution of civil society. This cannot happen, however as long as we remain ignorant of, or ignore the protocols of fraternal relations. Nor can it, nor will it happen so long as conformity to the protocols which has sustained us for almost 300 years are not complied with by those seeking recognition. We cannot be seduced into accepting anything less.

For the sake of Freemasonry it is therefore imperative that we become capable of divesting ourselves of our limiting egos and goals of creating self-aggrandizing images and become more aware of the foundations upon which we have thrived for hundreds of years. We must become more concerned about the future of Freemasonry and less concerned about our own images.

The subject upon which I speak is now one of the greatest threats to our survival, and our capability of impacting society in this millennium. Yet the problem confronting us is one that we ourselves are causing by creating or permitting disunity within the Craft, supporting irregular instead of regular Freemasonry, by reacting instead of acting, and by failing to recognize our own ignorance on specific issues.

If our Craft is to have a stable and contributory future we must support our requirements for regularity and for fraternal recognition. We must also be unwilling to accept deviations from these requirements we must be prepared to remove from our brotherhood those who choose not to conform to these protocols. Fraternal relations must be limited to Regular Freemasonry. Those grand lodges seeking recognition know what is required. If they cannot or will not accept these parameters then they fail to gain recognition and if regular grand lodges choose a divergent pathway then they must risk losing recognition.

We must remember that fraternal relations between grand lodges is not a right, it is a privilege. Every member has a right to accept what he chooses but he must also accept that his choice will determine his right to membership.

Each grand lodge is also free to choose but if that choice contributes to disunity then Regular Freemasonry has the responsibility to attempt reunification.

Freemasonry has been facing a loss of image in present-day society for decades and my Brothers, we are the cause. The philosophy has not changed. We are the variable. We have not only permitted but also stimulated the decline in the quality of the membership. We have required too little to be a member and far too little to remain a member. We have caused ignorance to become the norm in an organization that has always encouraged the acquisition of knowledge. We have cheapened our organization by being cheaper ourselves and now we are permitting egos rather than brains to lead us.

We must decide whether we wish to survive as an institution that will impact future society or choose to continue to slide into history as a once great society of men who changed this world but which no longer exists.

What do you want my Brothers? It will be you who will decide.

[27]

Opening Address

VIIth World Conference of Masonic
Grand Lodges—Santiago, Chile

I
t is again my extreme pleasure and great privilege to
be able to welcome each of you as significant Masonic
leaders in your respective Grand Lodges, and as leaders
in a world crying out in desperation for the practice of the
philosophy which characterizes our Craft.

This, the seventh meeting of the World Conference,
is pleased and honored to be hosted by one of the great
grand lodges in South America. The leadership of the
Grand Lodge of Chile has been working diligently since
the completion of the sixth World Conference held in
New Delhi, India, to assure each of you, not only a valuable
Masonic experience, but an enjoyable one as well. It is been
my good fortune to be in Chile on two other occasions, and
I have been greatly impressed with the dedication of those
who have been developing the program for these activities.

The country of Chile is an intriguing and diverse one
with intriguing and diverse people. The countryside offers a unique beauty stretching for many miles north and
south, and I would encourage you to take the opportunity
to experience the different cultures of this land. I would
also encourage you to take advantage of the side excursions
available, and to explore the uniqueness to be found in this
area of the world. One of the additional values that this

World Conference has provided to the participants has been to give them the opportunity to discover along with variations of Freemasonry, the variations in cultures and values of the peoples of the world.

Many of our leaders have expanded their horizons and established lifelong friendships from attending our conferences in the past. They have begun to understand and to extend more fully the bonds of brotherhood that distinguishes our Craft.

More importantly, however, is that the Conference has made us more aware of the challenging issues facing Freemasonry in today's world. We are observing expansion of Freemasonry into new areas, along with the problems carried with the expansion. We are more cognizant of the interference of appendant bodies with some grand lodge operations. We are being exposed more rapidly to the threat of irregular Freemasonry in our jurisdictions, and we are becoming more aware of the need to solve our problems before they become unsolvable.

The World Conference of Masonic Grand Lodges held its first meeting in Mexico City in 1995 and has progressed considerably since that time. Many Masonic leaders are for the first time, beginning to discover the nuances and subtleties that characterizes Freemasonry in different parts of the world.

Modern technologies offer expanding amounts of information to our membership, but even as these technologies serve as a valuable educational tool in the dispensing of information, they also have become a definitive threat to the structural integrity of regular Freemasonry. As the world continues to shrink and our Craft becomes more exposed, it becomes even more important that we recognize and understand not only the similarities but also the differences that characterize Freemasonry. The World Conference of

Masonic Grand Lodges has been at the forefront in promoting this understanding.

We are now opening our second meeting to be held in South America, the fourth Conference being held in Sao Paulo, Brazil in 1999. With all that we may have accomplished, however, my Brothers, ongoing issues confronting our Craft continues to arise and must be effectively dealt with if we are to preserve our heritage and pass our philosophy on to future generations.

The purpose of our Conference as defined in the Constitution is to discuss issues, which promote the stability progress and universality of the Craft. It is the intent of this Conference to provide the opportunity to learn from one another and to become more attuned to the needs the world. We cannot choose to ignore the issues impacting Grand Lodges outside of our own because that impact today reverberates throughout world Freemasonry.

The days of isolationism within individual Grand Lodges is part of our past. What impacts Freemasonry anywhere on the globe today, impacts Freemasonry everywhere on the globe. Within a day of the tragic shooting that occurred in a New York City lodge, I was receiving telephone calls and e-mails from many parts of the world expressing a concern and seeking answers to explain the cause.

The relatively unknown quality of Freemasonry that characterized it for over 250 years has been replaced in recent years by our willingness to give more extensive public information to justify our existence. Modern technologies have swept aside, with a heretofore unseen rapidity, any intent to preserve our isolationist attitude, and there is nothing we can do to change that fact. Those Grand Lodges that fail to comprehend and acknowledge this technological evolution may well become a footnote in some future historian's writings.

And yet, at the same time, it is our responsibility as leaders of this Craft to preserve its fundamental precepts and its philosophical purpose if it is to have any value as a major influence in the ongoing evolution of civil society in the future. No organization outside of organized religion has had a greater impact on the progression of civil society than has Freemasonry. Our Craft has altered the course of civilization. We are the recipients of a heritage that has given us a prestige never seen by any other organization, but along with it, the obligation to maintain it.

Recent decades, however, have shown a dilution of our influence to use these precepts and philosophy in some areas of the world and it is our responsibility as present-day leaders not only to curtail the dilution, but also to work to reposition the Craft to where it might again be a major player in service to mankind. It is our responsibility to contribute to the perpetuation of our ideals and to cause them to be diffused throughout the thoughts of future generations.

The philosophy of Freemasonry has never been insignificant to any civil society, but it is, perhaps, more important to the world today than at any time in our past. If we are to have any hope of providing guidance through our philosophy to the world outside of it, we must develop a greater understanding of one another along with our goals. We must work more closely together to preserve intact those characteristics that identified it as an organization of importance in the societal developments of past years. We must strive to restore the image as well as the influence we once had. This Conference has every opportunity to serve as a vital tool in our quest to regain our rightful place in society. Working together we can accomplish much. Failing to do so, in today's world, might well spell disaster.

The tragic bombing of the Masonic Temple in Istanbul

several months ago that killed two of our brothers must serve as a reminder that the philosophy of our Craft remains under attack by those whose own philosophy fails to provide for the inherent rights of men. It should, however, serve not as factor to instill fear in us, but as a stimulus to unite us in a resistance against any form of terrorism that would remove these God-given rights from man, even as did our brothers of the past.

There continues to exist within our Craft, however, a degree of instability that foments disharmony and prevents Regular Freemasonry from working as a unified force toward any common goal. Schisms continue to occur, leadership continues to fail, competing grand lodges continue to arise, standards for recognition continue to be ignored, and bodies subordinate to grand lodges continue to create internal dissention. Although these may be issues confronting individual grand lodges, they are issues that affect operating procedures in other grand lodges as well, and they are giving credence and strength to irregular forms of Freemasonry.

It is absolutely imperative that grand lodges establish or re-establish their position as the supreme authority in the jurisdiction over which they rule. We cannot permit any organization whose membership is predicated upon Masonic membership to interfere with the authority of the grand lodge.

Although irregular Freemasonry has existed for hundreds of years, it has become more aggressive in recent years in establishing themselves in jurisdictions where Regular Freemasonry already exists. This aggressiveness has been encouraged and even assisted by individual Masons whose egos are stimulated by exposure to misinformation and irregularity on the World Wide Web and utilized by those whose motives are to convert Freemasonry into an unacceptable form.

Failure to recognize or choosing to ignore this threat may prove devastating to our future. Likewise, failure to work together as grand lodges structured upon the protocols of regularity may be just as disastrous. As grand lodge leaders, it is our responsibility to provide the direction of whatever action is required to prevent this from occurring.

We are living in a different environment today than we have in the past, but the principles and precepts of Freemasonry are no less applicable today than they were 300 years ago, and will be no less applicable 300 years from now. What was important to society then is important now. There will never be a time that a demand for a quality organization will not exist. We must be committed to preserving it so that our children, their children and their children may experience the influence of an organization unique in the history of mankind.

We must expand our horizons and extend our vision beyond what we are, to see what we can be. Freemasonry has been a magnet to some of the greatest men this world has ever seen. It has influenced those minds that changed the world in an ongoing quest for civility. It has stimulated the greatest leaders in the world's struggles for freedom.

If its influence is not as great as it once was, then we have inherited the responsibility to restore that influence. The world needs our philosophy and us. We must make sure the world knows.

With this in mind, please recognize and understand that within this Conference, it is acknowledged that every Grand Lodge is an independent sovereign unit unto itself. It is an undeniable and inalienable right. The Conference will operate within parameters where the rights of no Grand Lodge will be infringed upon. Remember that operating philosophies in some areas of the world may vary, resulting in an emphasis being placed upon different societal aspects. We, therefore, must remember that when establishing goals, we should aim to the universality of interest to the Craft everywhere.

My Brothers, you represent to the present-day world the epitome of the leadership of the greatest organization ever conceived by the mind of man. You have taken upon yourself a mantle of responsibility under which your actions may very well impact the future of the world. The leadership of the past did so, and we may very well do so.

Historians of the present day are finally acknowledging the influence that Freemasonry has had in the development of civil society. There have possibly been more significant writings concerning Freemasonry in the last twenty years than are to be found in the prior 250 years. One hundred years from now, historians may be writing about the impact that our leadership created on the evolution of civil society. What they write about is now in our hands. We sincerely hope that this World Conference may serve as a contributory factor and positive influence upon what you Craft.

Let us now set our goals to work together upon that level that defines us as brothers, and circumscribe our desires so that we may work together toward the common purpose of perpetuating that unifying philosophy of Freemasonry and to diffuse it to a world desperately seeking a form of peace.

[28]

Opening Address

VIII th World Conference—Paris, France

I
t is a great privilege for me, as Executive Secretary of the World Conference to welcome you to Paris, the City of Light. We trust that your experience here will be not only beneficial to you and your Grand Lodge, but also will be one of great enjoyment. As many of our leaders have discovered in the past, lifelong friendships have been generated and their horizons have been expanded from attending this conference and enabled us to work together for a common goal.

As leaders on the highest levels of Freemasonry, you represent our greatest hope for achieving our goals as the Masonic Fraternity. It is our fervent wish that the environment of the World Conference will serve to stimulate you to a greater understanding of the purpose of Freemasonry and to the issues confronting the world of our Craft today and perhaps also to assist you in confronting them. We cannot choose to ignore issues impacting Grand Lodges outside of our own jurisdictions because the impact today will reverberate throughout the world of tomorrow.

It is never the intent of this conference or of its participants, to offend any regular grand lodge in the world or anyone attending the conference. We must, however, be free to speak openly concerning broad-spectrum issues that may be detrimental to Regular Freemasonry.

It is also not the responsibility of the Conference, in session, to deal with specific issues or disagreements between grand lodges. Any such problems must be resolved between the grand lodges involved but hopefully this environment might provide the stimulus and location to resolve such issues.

For a number of years now, I have been expressing a great concern with the spread of irregular Freemasonry and of our seeming lack of ability or at least interest in working together to solve mutual problems including this expansion. Frankly, my brothers, from my observations in recent years, I feel that our Craft is approaching a crisis standpoint in its existence and unless regular Freemasonry begins to work together to preserve what we are, our future may be very bleak indeed. My remarks are not meant as any specific criticism but rather as the stimulus to cause you to think about where we are and where we are going.

There has now arisen what could become an even greater threat to our integrity than irregular Freemasonry, as we have known it. This year a new "Masonic Grand Lodge" came into existence known as the "Regular Grand Lodge of England" and even though at the present time it offers little threat, it must be of a concern to us. They are claiming regularity of descent, which the other irregular grand lodges of the world, as far as I know, do not. According to their web site, they claim to be the "only grand lodge in England practicing and promoting English Craft Masonry" and they are establishing a new confederation of "regular" grand lodges throughout the world. They claim world distribution into twenty-five jurisdictions with a combined membership of over 500,000 members.

I find these claims impossible to accept but I find their philosophy as expressed on their web site impossible to ignore. I find it impossible to ignore, simply because I find it impossible to disagree with it. It is the same philosophy of the Craft Masonry, as I have known it.

They contend that the purpose for its creation is a result of deviation from the ancient usages of the Craft. This was the same reason given that resulted in the separation of the Grand Lodge of England into the Moderns and the Ancients in 1751. In addition, I have received several requests this year for advice from British Freemasons on how to constitute a new grand lodge. I received similar requests from North American Freemasons during my tenure as Grand Secretary. My advice to them constantly, is to work for change from within if there is dissatisfaction and that any separation is divisive to Freemasonry and to its goals.

This Irregular Grand Lodge expresses that "At the core of these concerns is the heartfelt lament that Masonry… has effectively degenerated into a social and dining, club, meeting upon the excuse of initiating yet another candidate into a society whose only apparent purpose is to carry out initiations, whilst seeking to justify its existence through the business of institutional charity." And "where the hierarchy classically maintains discipline through the assiduous manufacture of 'honours' whilst ignorantly sacrificing ancient form and spiritual value in obeisance to transient political correctness."

Although this dissatisfaction was aimed at the United Grand Lodge of England, it could just as easily have been directed to the Grand Lodges of North America and probably to other Grand Lodges in other parts the world as well. We in North America, in recent years, have certainly placed our greatest emphasis on carrying out initiations and raising money for charities and have dramatically increased the ease with which members may obtain honors. Political correctness also tends to dominate our actions. My brothers, we will never achieve our goal of making good men better with this approach to the Craft.

Regular Freemasonry is today experiencing what may be the greatest short term expansion that we have ever seen. The consecration or reconsecration of grand lodges in Eastern Europe and of new grand lodges being consecrated in Africa is providing us with an opportunity not only to display to the world the significance of the need for an organization with the philosophical purpose of Freemasonry, but also to use that influence in the development and evolution of civil society in their respective countries.

Even as our numbers are increasing throughout much of the world, our influence upon the world continues to decrease. Perhaps the major causes for this phenomenon are the distractions which, although not trivial, are not of the magnitude of others facing our Craft that we are ignoring because of those distractions, and which are affecting all of us. It will take unity and understanding of all regular grand lodges to deal with them effectively. When we fail to work together, we strengthen not only our enemies but also irregular Freemasonry.

North American Freemasonry is observing a phenomenon of public exposure that perhaps is greater than we have ever seen via books, movies and television programs. Historians the world over are finally acknowledging the significance of Freemasonry in the evolution of civil society. The need for our philosophy to influence world leaders is at least as great as it ever was. And yet, my Brothers, we are continuing to fail to work together in unity to take advantage of what may never again be presented to us.

The isolationism and provincialism that has characterized our past is no longer applicable in today's world. Modern technologies, with unseen rapidity, have swept aside any intent we may have had to preserve our isolationist attitude. Those Grand Lodges that fail to comprehend and acknowledge this technological evolution may well become footnotes in some future historian's writings.

In addition, our present-day willingness to provide extensive public information to justify our existence has probably provided little value to us and has quite possibly been counterproductive by reducing our attractive mystique.

It is imperative that we as leaders understand fully the ultimate purpose of Freemasonry as well as our responsibility in leading it to accomplish that purpose. There are far too many Masonic leaders today who are failing to comprehend the magnitude of the responsibility that lies within their hands nor do they understand the significance of our Craft with its potential influence on society. Egos too frequently become the driving force rather than the intellectual prowess of the leader.

Irregular Freemasonry is also expanding more rapidly than ever in its past and it is becoming more organized in its efforts. Not only is this creating a major problem with our new Grand Lodges, but it is also impacting jurisdictions that did not have to deal with it in the past. It is a monumental mistake if we choose to ignore them. Failure to recognize or choosing to ignore this threat to our veracity may prove disastrous to our future.

A major problem confronting many of the new grand lodges is the interference in Craft Masonry by appendant organizations whose leadership feels that they are superior to the grand lodge. Regretfully, the interference has led to competing grand lodges being created. This should be intolerable to Regular Freemasonry and yet we remain divided on the issues of recognition, giving hope and strength to the appendant leadership as well as weakening the influence of Craft Freemasonry.

It is also vitally important for new grand lodge leadership to understand that rapid growth is not a criterion for success nor is the development of appendant bodies. Both approaches have caused serious damage to some grand lodges.

As I stated in Santiago, at the VIIth World Conference, "There continues to exist within our Craft a degree of instability that foments disharmony and prevents Regular Freemasonry from working as a unified force toward any common goal."

Even though the environment today is different than it was 300 years ago, the precepts of Freemasonry are no less applicable today than they were back then. It is absolutely imperative that we as leaders be committed to preserving it so that our children, their children and their children may experience the influence of the most extraordinary organization ever conceived by the mind of man.

Historians are finally acknowledging us, my brothers, and our influence in the development of civil society. Let us, therefore, set our goals to work together in a manner that defines us as Brothers. Let us circumscribe our desires so that we move forward to the common goal of perpetuating that unifying philosophy of Freemasonry and to defuse it to a world desperately in need of it.

[29]

Opening Address

XIIIth World Conference—Bucharest, Romania

My brothers, it is my great pleasure to preside over this thirteenth World Conference of Regular Masonic Grand Lodges and to welcome each of you to the first to be held in Eastern Europe. The first World Conference was held in Mexico City in 1995 and was known then as the World Conference of Grand Masters. The conference held in Bucharest, Romania is the 13th and is now known as the World Conference of Regular Masonic Grand Lodges.

I hope you will take advantage of the opportunity to explore this beautiful country and discover what should make it one of the great tourist attractions in Europe. I have spent much time here over the past dozen years, and have come to appreciate the uniqueness and beauty in its mountains, its coast on the Black Sea, its ancient ruins, its old cities and of course, the legend of Dracula.

I have had the privilege of attending twelve of the thirteen World Conferences, and at the third one held in New York City in 1998, I was elected as Executive Secretary. Little did I know what that vote would mean to my life for the next 16 years. Much water has flowed over the dam in those ensuing years and the demands incumbent on the office has increased considerably.

Whereas, the function of the Executive Secretary was

to be simply, the coordination and assistance with the conferences every 18 months, it has taken on a much more significant role in world Freemasonry. A considerable amount of time that I now commit to the conference is in visiting and speaking at symposiums and conferences, negotiating and mediating and trying to assist in resolving divisive issues, interviews by the media and simply responding to the hundreds of emails that I receive in a number of different languages, each month.

We have seen many changes in Grand Lodge operations during these years, along with the consecration or re-consecration of new Grand Lodges. Indeed, the rate of expansion of Freemasonry in this new millennium may be the most rapid at any period in our history. This truly is a remarkable age for Freemasonry.

The very fact that we are being hosted by a grand lodge in Eastern Europe would have been an unheard-of phenomenon just a couple of decades ago. We have experienced within these decades, the extraordinary character of Freemasonry, to rise from the ashes of our past in this part of the world.

We have been able to experience the tenacity of an organization unparalleled in its survivability and influence. This is why we are the largest and the oldest fraternal organization in existence. This is why we have carried the respect of multiple societies for centuries. This is why we were able to impact the evolution of civil societies, indeed of civilization itself.

The establishment or reestablishment of Freemasonry in this part of the world, however, has not been without its challenges. There has been more dissension and more challenges to regular Freemasonry, resulting in schisms than anywhere else in the world, perhaps in our history. Although some of the dissension has been resolved, we still have a long way to go, and it will be the responsibility of the leadership to divest themselves of any limiting egos that interferes with these resolutions. It must also be the responsibility of the leaders of older established regular Freemasonry, to advise and assist with limited interference, these newly established grand lodges.

This Craft has attracted some of the greatest thinking men that have ever lived and it was these brothers who contributed greatly to the image of Freemasonry that became known to the world. Realistically, without this attractive force we could never have achieved the status that we have.

I look at three major reasons why Freemasonry was able to grow to its greatness. First of all, we did attract this caliber of man. Secondly, we provided an environment in which men of all class distinctions could sit in a room as equals. Finally, we remained constant on the quality of the man that we would accept. Without anyone of these three factors we could not have become what we became and if we fail to retain them, we will not remain as we are, in fact, we may not even remain.

This fast-paced world in which we find ourselves living today and the pressures of political correctness has had a tendency to cause us to warp our values, those same values that contributed to forming the image for which we were known. Well, Freemasonry is not, nor was it ever meant to be for every man. It was structured on the quality of the member that caused the profane world to respect it and for others to want to become part of it.

Modern technology out of necessity is causing us to change our operational procedures, but we cannot permit it to change our philosophical values. We must continue to provide an environment where men of all social classes can sit together as equals, but it is just as important for us to be able to attract the great men of today's world. We must remain selective on the quality of the man we will accept. By lowering our standards, we diminish our image and contribute to our own extinction.

The isolationist attitude that characterized Freemasonry for over two and a half centuries has now been overridden by modern technology and information on the World Wide Web. As we all are aware, much of this information is incorrect and has been placed there by those who have chosen to be our enemies, as well as by many of our own well-meaning members whose ignorance of the true significance of Freemasonry is exceeded only by their egos.

I made this observation at the VIIth World Conference: "There continues to exist within our Craft a degree of instability that ferments disharmony and prevents regular Freemasonry from working as a unified force toward any common goal. Schisms continue to occur, leadership continues to fail, competing grand lodges continue to arise, standards for recognition continue to be ignored and bodies subordinate to grand lodges continue to create internal dissension."

Ten years have passed and I make the same observation at this conference. Not only do the divisive issues continue to exist, but they have increased. My brothers, the responsibility must rest upon the shoulders of the leadership who have been either unable or unwilling to acknowledge and deal with them.

The World Conference has for nineteen years provided an environment where world leaders of Freemasonry can meet and establish an understanding of the issues that impact our Craft and yet instability within grand lodges continues to exist. Perhaps the phenomenon of rapid expansion of the Craft has destabilized the relative tranquility that we experienced in the not-too-distant past.

It is incumbent on each one of us to shoulder the mantle

of responsibility that we assumed when the Craft elected us to lead and if we will not or cannot, then we should walk away. I sincerely trust that this conference will serve as a positive influence, and as a stimulus to re-dedicate ourselves to the philosophical precepts of our Craft. We owe it to those brothers who have preceded us, and left us with this unsurpassed legacy. We also owe to the world.

We not only sit here as equals in accordance with Masonic precept, but we sit here as leaders of Masonic equals. We have each taken on a mantle of responsibility to perpetuate the precepts and goals of Freemasonry and to set the image of what we expect from those whom we lead. Egos that may interfere with our ability to set that image must be divested. So let us circumscribe our desires and dedicate ourselves to the work of showing to the world the true meaning of the Brotherhood of man under the Fatherhood of God.

[30]

Closing Address

XIIth World Conference—Chennai, India

O nce again, we come to the close of a World Conference. I trust that it has been a benefit to you
and certainly a contribution to the benefit of Freemasonry. As in past World Conferences, it is my fervent
hope that there have been friendships forged with brothers
whom, were it not for freemasonry, you would have never
known, and that will last conceivably for a lifetime.

It has been seventeen years since the first World Conference met and the world has experienced changes of a
magnitude perhaps never seen before in that short a span of
time. These changes have produced a world with a clouded
and very uncertain future and it is a world sadly lacking in
much of the moral and ethical values that characterized it
in the not too distant past.

What will these changes mean for or Craft? This is an
environment in which this Craft should thrive. Freemasonry has always been at its best when its challenges were
the greatest. Its potential contribution to the world has
increased considerably over these seventeen years. Perhaps,
the environments in which we live today may cause us to
shake off the apathy that has dominated much of Freemasonry over the past several decades.

Freemasonry was one of the primary enclaves that
provided an environment for men of thinking minds met

together during the age of Enlightenment and craft the concepts of human rights. Today, it might well provide the enclaves for men of thinking minds to gather together to reinsert those moral and ethical values back into a society that have been lost in this technological age. It will be a challenge, but also an opportunity to regain what we have given up. I remind you as I did in Cartagena at the last World Conference, "we cannot afford to let the young people of today think that the leadership of the world lacks those moral and ethical values to be both a success and a role model for them." Freemasons have been in the fore-front for several centuries in providing guidelines toward these values that are necessary for a stable environment. We cannot fail in providing them again.

However, we need to acknowledge that our leadership must use that mantle of responsibility placed upon them to guide Freemasonry in the direction that will be a credit to both Freemasonry and to civil society. Out of necessity, this concept will require that every one of us and every other Masonic leader divest himself of any ego that might cause him to forget that this mantle gives him the right of leadership to benefit mankind, not to benefit himself.

The theme of this conference, "The Role of Freema-sonry in Universal Peacekeeping" should be pertinent to every Freemason. However, lest we fail to comprehend the philosophical purpose of Freemasonry, I emphasize that it is never Freemasonry's role, as a fraternity, to be involved with universal peacekeeping. It remains Freemasonry's purpose to take the "good man" and make him a better man. It is then the responsibility of that better man to exemplify the philosophy of the Craft in his commitment for which Freemasonry is known.

You will make the difference. It is in your hands that the fate of Freemasonry lies today. Your decisions, big or small, are not insignificant. My dream remains to see regular Freemasons united and working together toward a universal purpose, and contributing to a universal world peace. As frustrating as I have found much of my effort to have been, I retain that dream.

As we leave here today, let us reanalyze the decisions we are making so that we may assure that our beloved brotherhood of men never need venture into that clouded Masonic future. The legacy of the Craft and our dedication to support it should wipe away any potential mists that might cloud our future and rededicate ourselves to the philosophy of Freemasonry and to a contribution of a peaceful future. May the Great Architect of the Universe watch over us and guide our actions until we meet again.

[31]

Closing Address

IXth World Conference—Washington, D.C.

We have come to the closing of the IXth World Conference and I trust that you have established a better understanding of world Freemasonry, its variations contained within its uniformity and the need for an ongoing commitment to the philosophical principles of our Craft. One of the greatest values of the World Conference is that it provides the only opportunity for the major leaders of all of world Freemasonry to assemble and to unite our thoughts and minds for a common purpose.

Just as important, however, is that it provides the environment for us to be exposed to issues that although confronting other Grand Lodges, will affect Freemasonry on a world level. There is no way in today's world that we can afford to fail to work together to resolve issues facing any regular grand lodge. The challenges confronting our Craft and its commitment to social stability are no less important today than it was at any time in our past. Freedom from all forms of oppression over both the bodies and the minds of man is not any less significant today than it ever was. The rise of terrorism in any form requires our commitment to support the liberty, freedom and equality that today writers acknowledge us as supporting in the past.

Last week I received a communication from the Grand Master of the Grand Lodge of Bolivia informing me that both he and the Grand Treasurer would have to cancel their plans to attend this conference due to the "unexpected social turmoil affecting his country." His final sentence was: "We all hope in Bolivia that this state of affairs will be just a 'shooting Star,' and I think that I must stay as the head of the Grand Lodge of Bolivia in the event of any troubles we could face."

The issue in Bolivia is not an isolated incident in the world and Bolivian Freemasons are not isolated brothers in this fraternal network of ours. Freemasons must be dedicated to a united effort to support, if not in a material sense at least in a spiritual sense, every brother who needs our assistance.

So long as any Grand Lodge fails to operate under the landmarks and parameters that establish regularity, there can be no unity. Nor can there be unity so long as there is more than one regular Grand Lodge operating in the same geographical location without mutual recognition. It should be our goal to resolve issues that separates regular Freemasonry into opposing camps. It should also be our goal to work to bring regularity to irregular grand lodges and stimulate it to become part of the Freemasonry that we know.

I have expressed in my opening address a concern with inflated egos of some of our leadership that contributes negatively, not only to any possible hope of a resolution to restore regularity but also to even cement commitment of the members of their own grand lodges. I acknowledge that it is difficult for any one of us to recognize within ourselves the existence of this as a problem. We always seek to leave a lasting legacy but that legacy will depend much upon our ability to control and direct our egos.

We also cannot fail to be aware of the changing environment in which we live as a result of advancement in technology which resulted in the World Wide Web. We can no longer avoid the impact that it is creating upon the operation of our grand lodges. We must learn to live with it. It is not going to go away and we must be concerned with our future for we have the rest of her lives to live there.

I leave you with the admonition that even as Freemasonry is designed to take good men and make them better, we, as leaders have inherited the responsibility to then improve upon the better man and my brothers that includes each one of us. It has been my great privilege to have spent a few days with you and I hope that your Masonic experience has been enriched.

May you have a safe journey to your homelands and may the Great Architect of the Universe travel with you always.

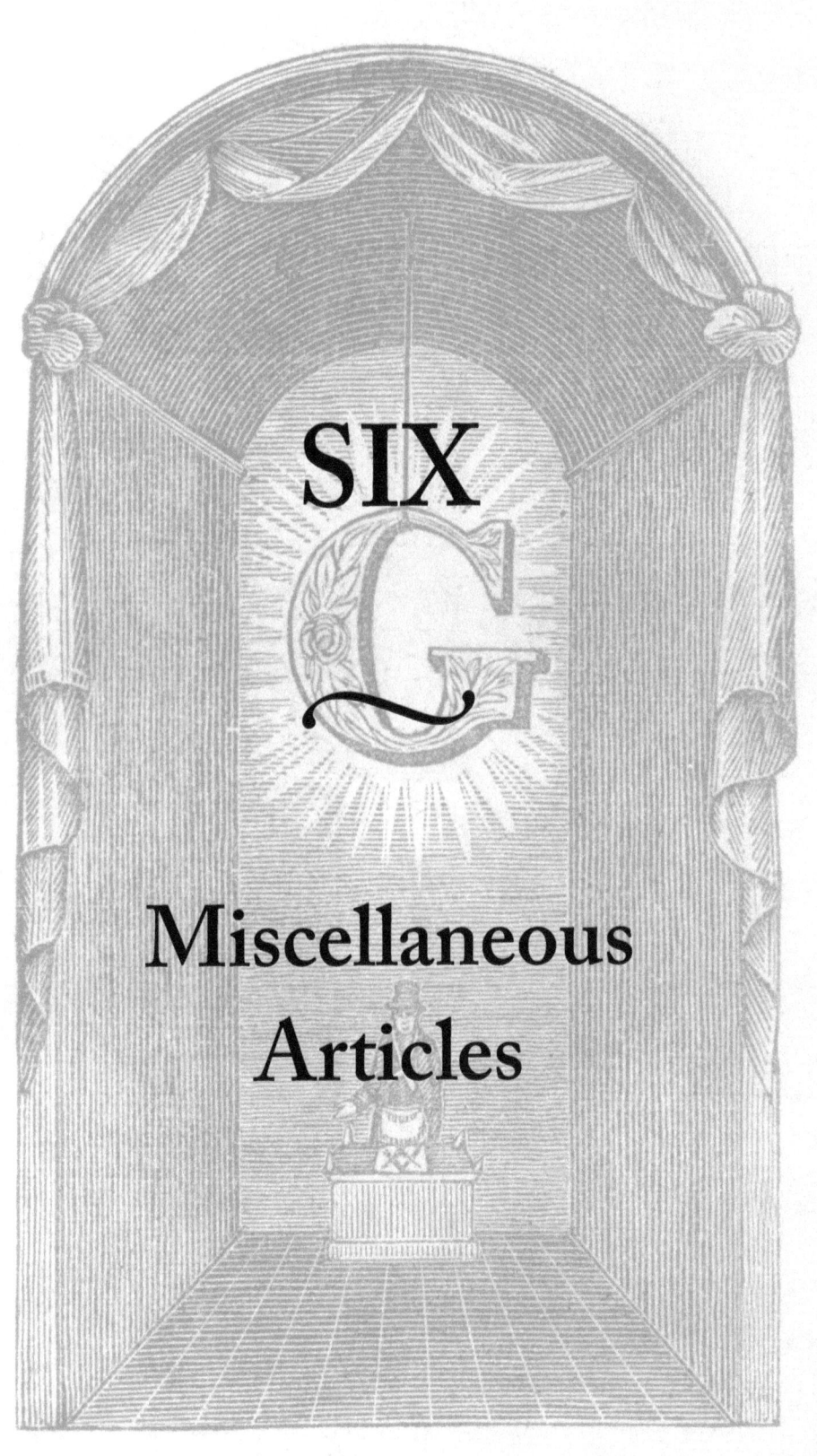

SIX

Miscellaneous Articles

[1]

On the Writings of
Christopher Knight and Robert Lomas

There have been very few authors and perhaps none other in the literature of Freemasonry who have managed to create more controversy than have Christopher Knight and Robert Lomas, notwithstanding the attempt by William Morgan to publish his exposé. They have co-authored three books and a fourth book was authored by Lomas alone.

When I was first contacted to present this lecture I readily committed to it. For some reason I misunderstood the subject topic request and I thought I was speaking on *The da Vinci Code*. So, when I started to prepare this paper, I was preparing it on *The Da Vinci Code*. Fortunately, I went back and read the e-mails I received in time to start over, so I will address you tonight on the writings of Knight and Lomas.

Nonetheless, when I started to think about delivering a lecture on either one of these subjects, I began to realize that I was venturing outside of my realm of expertise.

Several years ago I was asked to present a paper at a symposium at UCLA on the subject of the American Enlightenment. Again, I readily agreed.

Upon thinking about it, however, I realized that I knew next to nothing about the American Enlightenment. I called the individual who had requested it and told him that perhaps he asked the wrong man, and that I didn't even know that there had been an American Enlightenment. He convinced me, however, to proceed with it and I found it to be a stimulating experience, mainly because it forced me to do research again, which I hate to do, and also to learn, which I love to do.

So, here I am this evening speaking to you about the works of two authors who have far more knowledge and capability than have I. If these authors have accomplished nothing else, they have generated controversy and therefore stimulated their readers to think, and there is nothing wrong with thinking.

In order to evaluate the books and the authors it is necessary to read and review what they have written. I will therefore draw extensively upon my evaluations of the books and the authors that I found in preparation of my book reviews for *The Northern Light*.

When I wrote a review of Knight and Lomas' first book, *The Hiram Key*, I made this observation. "If I were attempting to write a book to aggravate the greatest number of people, I would consider using this book as a template. The authors will probably manage to stir up enmity in the vast majority of Christians, Jews and Freemasons who read it." Indeed, that proved to be true. Their second book, *The Second Messiah*, continued to fuel the flames of controversy.

I expressed a concern at that time, that there would be those who would accept their words as dogma on Freemasonry since the authors were Freemasons. That also proved to be true. A conference minister of the Conservative Congregational Christian Conference wrote in a newspaper that, "It confirmed everything I have read by Freemasonry's critics" and referred to the authors as "two obviously prominent Freemasons." It is a sad commentary, that in supposedly intellectual circles, we must be concerned by what we write or what we say because of close-minded bigots. Nonetheless, it is a true commentary. I can only wish that Freemasonry could be as significant as many authors imply we are, or have as much power as our enemies say we do.

I also emphasized, however, that it is every author's right, to publish what he pleases so long as it is not an inflammatory pack of lies. What Knight and Lomas have written is unquestionably a result of extensive research and considerable thought. Much of it is also, in my opinion, the result of much fanciful conjecture. Regardless, it is their right to develop that conjecture.

It is the responsibility of the reader to accept or to reject what he finds in the written word. Many times I have expressed that the only thing that I know for sure is what I have seen within my lifetime. Everything else that I know, I have had to accept from what I have read or from what someone told me and that is true of every person.

My educational training is in the field of the sciences where theories are an operating norm. I suspect that this is the reason that I am more prone to accept the privilege of authors to propose fanciful speculation than are most reviewers. When John Robinson published his first book, *Born in Blood*, Masonic book reviewers almost universally condemned it. Even though I did not accept all of his conclusions, I gave the book a decent review. Robinson, as you know, went on to become one of the most influential North American Freemasons in the past century. We became close friends, and I was privileged to sign his petition to join the Craft and also to give a eulogy at his memorial service.

To this day, I value the relationship we developed, because I was able to accept venturing outside the norm of traditional thought.

So too, do authors Knight and Lomas deserve the right

to be read and their theories considered. As Brother Voltaire once wrote, "I detest what you write, but I would give my life to make it possible for you to continue to write." Knight and Lomas in turn, along with many other authors, owe a debt of gratitude to their predecessors like Robinson and Baigent, Leigh, and Lincoln, the authors of *Holy Blood, Holy Grail.* These authors blazed the trail that stimulated an interest in the subject and resulted in numerous books being written. Indeed, perhaps Dan Brown's books *The Da Vinci Code,* and *Angels and Demons* along with the movie *National Treasure* might be an indirect result of their earlier works.

I readily acknowledge that I'm not qualified to sit in judgment as to the accuracy of the conclusions reached by Knight and Lomas nor any of the other authors. However, I suspect many of the current authors see a dollar sign in this subject. Certainly the quality of some of the books being written reflects a lack of academic capability of the author.

Now, with that qualification stated, I will attempt to give you my evaluation of Knight and Lomas and the books that they have written. Please keep in mind, that what I say is nothing more than that, my evaluation. John Robinson once said that "he was only an expert on his own personal opinion." That is also true of me.

The first book, *The Hiram Key,* was published in 1996 and I met with Christopher Knight at a reading in one of the major bookstores in Philadelphia several months before I wrote my review. I told him at that time that I would not guarantee him a good review but that I would guarantee a fair review. Following publication of the review, I received a letter from Knight informing me that I had misquoted a part of the text. I replied to him, stating page number and paragraph from where I had taken my information. I have not been in communication with either author since that time.

My basic evaluation of this text was that, if the writings were true, they would have had to represent the culmination of possibly the greatest piece of detective work in the history of mankind. If they were not true, they would have had to represent the greatest use of the imagination for the creation of fiction as to equal the greatest novelists of the past. Today, I probably regard their first two books as a combination of both. I also stated, however, that I found the book to be fascinating reading — but then I probably found Mother Goose fascinating reading when I read it.

Let's take a look at some of the conclusions at which Knight and Lomas arrive in *The Hiram Key*. First, they trace the origin of Freemasonry back to the ancient Egyptians. They not only determine that Hiram Abif was a historical living human being, but they determined that he was an Egyptian King, by the name of Seqenenre Tao. In addition, verification was made of the cause of his death. A photograph in the book of his purported mummy displayed injury signs, interpreted by the authors as relating to Masonic legend. In addition, another photograph was purported to be that of the mummy of Jubelo, his assassin. This proposition alone is so farfetched as to damage their credibility.

It is, however, not the most extreme of the conclusions they had reached. They also proposed that Jesus Christ was a Freemason and that America, created by Freemasons was named not for Amerigo Vespucci but for an evening Star called "Merica." Also concluded was that the face on the Shroud of Turin is that of Jacques DeMolay. These conclusions do nothing to improve their credibility.

Some other suppositions and conclusions they reached are not nearly as implausible nor are they necessarily new proposals to the world. They have, for example, stated that the early Knights Templar had uncovered tablets (Nasorean

Scrolls) from beneath Herod's Temple, and that they are currently deposited beneath the floor of Rosslyn Chapel in Scotland. In addition, they also conclude that Templars visited America long before Columbus. Neither of these proposals is new, and present-day writers are reaping a harvest using the subjects as a basis for their writing. Even Dan Brown incorporates Rosslyn Chapel into his novels.

In addition to the astounding conclusions reached by the authors, they also made some observations regarding Freemasonry that were not only inappropriate but disconcerting when coming from Brothers. For example, they referred to the Craft as "sheer pointlessness." Granted, its image and influence does not carry the impact now that it did at one time, especially in North America, but it certainly retains great potential to impact continuing evolution of civil society and even lacking that potential, does indeed influence the membership to become better men and leaders in society. Even though I have been an outspoken critic of our failure to educate our membership in the significance of our ritual, and have classed North American membership as the most ignorant Freemasons in the world, their observation that "our members do not understand a word of the ceremonies they participate in," implies that our membership must be composed of total imbeciles, and provides a great disservice to our Brothers.

A statement made by the authors referencing the writers of the early books of the Old Testament reads, "Different authors filled the gaps in different ways depending on their political view of the world and their opinion as to how it should have been." That statement could be applied quite literally to *The Hiram Key*.

The Second Messiah, published in 1997, is a sequel to *The Hiram Key*, and shows the same intent and style. The research and thought that went into both books, however, would be admirable in any field of endeavor; but the conclusions remain debatable and highly questionable.

Even though Knight and Lomas imply in the introduction that their findings revealed in *The Hiram Key* were warmly received by many biblical, Templar and Masonic scholars, as well as several Catholic priests, I must seriously question the accuracy of the statement. Certainly, the reactions that I heard were not supportive. Their second book was even more inflammatory to theologians and Freemasons in general and the hierarchy of the Roman Catholic Church in particular.

In essence, both of these books are committed to tracking the continuing evolution of the beliefs and teachings of the original Jerusalem Church, as the authors perceive them. As disconcerting as the conclusions were in The Hiram Key, they tend to be even more so in *The Second Messiah*. Knight and Lomas have managed to tie in the Arthurian legend and the search for the Holy Grail. They also offer the concept that Tarot cards were the creation of the Templars — used to convey messages while reducing risk to them. The book also further discusses the origin of the shroud of Turin and they conclude that Jacques de Molay was not only the face on the shroud, but in reality is the second Messiah. It also expands upon their conclusion that the purpose of the original Knights Templar was to excavate beneath Herod's Temple in Jerusalem where they discovered scrolls that, "with certainty," are contained in vaults beneath Rosslyn Chapel. They then develop a fascinating tale to support this conclusion. It is with the presenting of their findings as dogmatic conclusions instead of theories that I have the greatest difficulty. It's fascinating fiction, but there are too many people who don't know the difference—and maybe they don't either.

According to Knight and Lomas, the scrolls removed

from the vault were recordings of the genealogies of the children of the priests tracing lineage back to David and Aaron. The survivors, following the destruction of the Temple, assumed the designation of, "Rex Deus" (Kings of God) and passed this information through succeeding generations. It is the author's contention that the Rex Deus family was then the driving force behind the Crusades for the purpose of reclaiming their inheritance.

The book is highly critical of the United Grand Lodge of England. It states that "The Grand Lodge of London" was nothing more than a gentleman's dining club with credibility built on the reputation of their predecessors, and that the Duke of Sussex undertook a project of erasing all original meaning of the degrees throwing away the whole purpose of the organization.

Frankly, there may be some element of truth in this accusation. They are not the only authors who question the motives and purpose of early English Grand Lodge leadership. They also brand Albert Pike as being "unashamed of his appalling ignorance and arrogance," and again there may be a fragment of truth in this evaluation.

Knight and Lomas' analysis becomes more questionable, however, when they make the observation that there were no journalists in the crowd the day that DeMolay was burned at the stake, and go on to state that the words he spoke were not of a Christian order because "nowhere in his 103 word parting speech did he mentioned Jesus Christ." Who recorded what DeMolay said that day and who counted the words?

Both books contained enough readily avoidable errors as to justify questioning the credibility of the authors' conclusions. Among others, for example, Knight and Lomas refer to the author of *The Sirius Mystery* as "a direct descendant of George Washington." Most schoolchildren know George

Washington had no children, making a living descendant highly unlikely. He also places George Washington as a Master of Alexandria Lodge Nº 22 on the rolls of the Grand Lodge of New York. Alexandria Lodge, since 1788, was under the Grand Lodge of Virginia.

Although I continue to support the prerogative of an author to present his conclusions, as a reader, I retain the right to evaluate these conclusions. It is my evaluation that many conclusions were reached then theories developed to support the conclusions, instead of developing theories and then seeking support for them.

If we regard the first two books as pushing credibility, Knight and Lomas' third book, *Uriel's Machine*, with its questionable propositions, will not improve their creditability, although it is probably the best publication of the three due to the extent of scientific research involved. This book offers the reader more of a challenge to understand what the authors are saying, and requires a greater concentration to follow their intent in drawing conclusions.

The title of the book is a reference to a device; knowledge of which is given to Enoch by the "angel" Uriel: the "machine" was a "simple but highly accurate means of measuring the declination of any heavenly object, in essence, a celestial computer." With it, Uriel was supposedly able to plot celestial orbits including the orbits of comets and to predict eclipses. This information is taken from the Book of Enoch that was discovered in the mid-1700s and supported by the Dead Sea scrolls.

According to Knight and Lomas, Enoch was taken to Europe by Uriel to be taught lessons in astronomy that would give him the opportunity to observe and predict a striking of the earth by a comet. They then imply that many of the megalithic sites, including Stonehenge, were constructed for that purpose of observation. They discuss the significance of the earth being struck by two comets, the first being the one that caused the flood in 7640 BC. as recorded in the Bible, the second the one concerning Enoch's involvement in 3150 BC.

It is their contention that the Book of Enoch is an actual historical record of his experiences with Uriel's guidance to produce a machine—to rebuild civilization following a global catastrophe. This global catastrophe was a flood resulting from the earth being hit by a comet. It was Uriel's intent to give to Enoch the opportunity to assist survivors to re-establish an agricultural civilization in the shortest possible time.

The seemingly scientific application applied to their suppositions was impressive to me, even though their conclusions sound outlandishly farfetched. Frankly, I found the book to be fascinating reading.

All three books credit Freemasonry with far more responsibility than lies within the minds of present-day Freemasons, and probably more than ever lay within the minds of any Freemasons. They contend that the Craft is "the unwittingly repository of much of the knowledge of the past." According to the authors, this same information was carried by the oral traditions of Freemasonry for centuries and was part of Masonic tradition even before the Book of Enoch was discovered. In fact, according to Knight and Lomas, the knowledge of Uriel's people survived in Freemasonry and was even embodied into the capital city of Washington, D.C. They state that Freemasons are "the only major living oral tradition in the Western world" having been "based on once secret information - that had been taken directly from Jewish traditions that predated the fall of Jerusalem in A.D. 70."

They also conclude that, entire Masonic degrees of the Ancient Accepted Scottish Rite that are no longer used, are devoted to Enoch and reveal his story of being told by Uriel that he must save the secrets of civilization from global disaster.

The authors again use their writing to criticize leadership within the Masonic Fraternity. They unhesitatingly accuse Masonic leadership of either deliberately or ignorantly destroying the knowledge they inherited, or diluting it to a state of uselessness. They may not be totally incorrect in their analysis of our present-day Masonic structure. I have felt for a number of years that there has to be much more to Freemasonry than we credit it with today. This does not mean that I support their suppositions or conclusions but I do believe that in reconstructing and redeveloping degree ritual, we are destroying much of the intent of the purpose of the Craft. Unfortunately again, enough errors appear in *Uriel's Machine* as to cause question of the extent of research of some of the subjects. Certainly Knight and Lomas must have been able to determine with little effort that former President George Bush was not a "senior Freemason." Nevertheless, I found *Uriel's Machine* to be compelling reading and worthy of our effort. It does offer a greater opportunity to challenge scientifically many of the author's suppositions and conclusions than did their previous two books.

All three of the books written by Knight and Lomas became international bestsellers and created a considerable stir in the Masonic world. Robert Lomas alone wrote the fourth book relative to the Craft, *Freemasonry and the Birth of Modern Science*. In addition, he authored the book, *The Man Who Invented the Twentieth Century: A Biography of Nikola Tesla*. Both of these books are more closely related to his academic background. He holds first class honors in electrical engineering and a Ph.D. in solid-state physics.

Freemasonry and the Birth of Modern Science is a combination of historical text coupled with well researched speculation that Freemasonry played a major role in the creation of the Royal Society (the oldest and most respected scientific society in the world), and the Royal Society in turn helped give birth to modern science. This theory is not a new one, but more acceptances probably lie in the reverse of the supposition. As may be assumed by the title, this book deals more specifically with the subject of Freemasonry than did the prior three books. Lomas delves deeply into the origin of the Masonic fraternity, its evolution into a speculative form, and its major impact upon what the world of science has become today.

Lomas reveals personalities who were known Freemasons and who were, according to Lomas, directly involved in the creation of the Royal Society. He also reveals the operational requirements incorporated by the Royal Society as well as the terminology that was directly indicative of a knowledge and relationship with Freemasonry.

Perhaps one of the greatest achievements of the Royal Society and also the Masonic fraternity was to provide an environment wherein great minds of that age from various disciplines were able to gather together and to develop creatively those theories that lead to the betterment of mankind and to the development of modern science. In essence the theories were involved in the creation and nurturing of the Age of Enlightenment.

This may seem to us today, a relatively uncomplicated task, but we must comprehend not only the need to bring together into a working relationship the great minds in varying fields of science but those who were also on opposing sides of the political conflicts of the day. Discussion of political subjects would not have been conducive to peace and harmony and should alert us to the similarities in the operating procedures of Freemasonry even to this day. Not only would the philosophy of Freemasonry be an asset but also it was, according to Lomas, utilized in creation of the society.

We must also understand that the conditions existing at that time were not conducive to this type of organization. Repressive rulers and Christian dogma were still stifling the freedom of open thought and reason. Science as we know it today did not and could not exist. According to Lomas, and he may be correct, credits Freemasonry with bridging the chasms that separated those with the potential to create, construct, and operate the Royal Society, thus leading to the birth of modern science. It is Lomas' contention that the Royal Society "borrowed a philosophy from early Freemasonry and turned it into a force which changed the very nature of the world."

It is also significant that he observes the while the Royal Society is still a major force for science, modern Freemasonry cannot create the climate necessary to promote such scientific creativity today, due to our loss of professional classes of young scientists. This issue is one of the most recognizable threats to the survival of Freemasonry in North America.

I respect Lomas for his willingness to take on the "Giants." These include the hierarchies of Freemasonry and the Christian church. Although none can deny the negative influence that the early Christian church had on the advancement of civilization by stifling the freedom of man to think, there are few with a willingness to express it is boldly as Lomas. In addition, even though being a member of the Lodge operating under the United Grand Lodge of England, he expresses freely his disagreement with some of the teachings, including the place and time of origin of Freemasonry.

I found this book to be extremely interesting, filled

with intrigue, reading more like a historical novel than a book on Freemasonry.

Freemasonry and the Birth of Modern Science, unlike the previous three books, carries more credibility, offers less speculation and less questionable conclusions than did they. According to Lomas, "The Masonic philosophy inherited by the new society led to the nurturing of the most important scientific developments of all time." Also, "What they (Freemasons) did was much greater and created a system that developed the possibilities of a vast increase in human well-being more than any other in recorded history." Lomas could be incorrect in his analysis, but it is my opinion that he could also be correct. I give much more credence to the conclusions reached in this book than in the prior three.

One cannot analyze or write regarding Knight and Lomas and their works without invoking criticism by those who oppose any new theoretical propositions that impacts what to them is an accepted norm. In addition, there are those waiting in the wings to condemn anyone they feel is supporting in any way what Knight and Lomas propose.

At the beginning of this paper I indicated, that if I wished to aggravate the greatest number of people I might consider using the works of Knight and Lomas as a template for my approach. I in no way endorse their theories and conclusions; and perhaps the greatest objection that I find in the writing is that they offer few theories and many conclusions. At the same time, I do not write them off as totally unworthy of any consideration.

I hasten to reiterate that I am not qualified to sit in judgment of the accuracy of their work. I also do not, in any way, purport to be an authority on Freemasonry, its origins or most of its history. I was not there to observe and therefore am subject to accepting or rejecting what others have written. My greatest concern about the works of these authors is that it provides fodder to our detractors and enemies, but in no way, do I feel the books should not have been written. They have stimulated thought both within and outside the Fraternity. They may be the greatest fairy tales of all time, but they also might just contain some element of truth. *Uriel's Machine* deserves credence for some possible accuracy and should stimulate unbiased research. *Freemasonry and the Birth of Modern Science* could well be a historical analysis of the creation of an organization that led to some of the greatest discoveries of all time.

In short term, these books probably cause Freemasonry some harm. In the long run, however, they quite possibly could be a benefit. They certainly caused more people to become aware of our existence and I'm not sure that being ignored is any less harmful than being condemned. These writings might also serve to stimulate us to move off our complacent backsides and to rethink our significance in the evolution of civil society. With that being said, bring on the critics.

[2]

The Second Amendment

*Given at a dinner following a lodge meeting
at the request of the Master of the Lodge
who also served on the Board of Directors
of the National Rifle Association*

B efore I begin, permit me tell you a little bit about myself so as to qualify who I am before I speak. I grew up in the small town of Shippensburg where I earned the second Eagle Scout rank in that district and the first God and Country Award. I was on the high school football and wrestling teams. I carried the flag for many years to lead in the Memorial Day parade into the cemetery to honor the veterans and chaired the program to decorate their graves. I was in essence, the All-American boy in this little town.

I went on to college earning a bachelor's degree in chemistry and biology and a Masters degree in zoology. I was Amateur Athletic Union and All-American weightlifting champion. I served on numerous civic boards and committees in the community. I have been Grand Secretary of the Grand Lodge now for 17 years and I am also, a gun owner.

When I was asked to speak on the subject of the Second Amendment, I agreed to do so as long as it was not speaking in the Lodge room and I was giving my own opinion and not speaking as a Grand Lodge officer.

"A well regulated militia being necessary to the security

of a Free State, the right of the people to keep and bear arms shall not be infringed."

The Worshipful Master of this Lodge is a board member of the National Rifle Association. He asked me to speak on the subject of the Second Amendment. This will be the first time that I have ever spoken on this topic. I am also a life member of the National Rifle Association and the 2nd Amendment Taskforce although I may not always agree with some of their positions; I am an ardent supporter of this organization.

I have been a hunter for over fifty years. I do not enjoy killing but I dearly love hunting, and this probably applies to all true sportsman, and by the way, I favor gun control. This comment probably shocks the "hell" out of most gun owners but let me proceed.

Let us go back to the reference of a "well-regulated militia." To most anti-gun activists the word "militia" means military. Section 311, title 10 of the U.S. Code reads:

> (a) The militia of the United States consists of all able-bodied males at least 17 years of age and under 45 who are citizens of the United States. (b) The classes of militia are: (1) The Organized Militia (2) the unorganized militia which consists of the members of the militia who are not members of the National Guard or the naval militia.

Take a look at China's attempt to enforce "freedom" in their country as well as in Russia when the government required the surrender of all arms, or when Hitler required gun confiscation. How do you appreciate the freedom found there? Is this the freedom that we want here?

John Adams in his expression of the right to bear arms wrote, "Arms in the hands of citizens to be used at individual discretion, in private self-defense." Thomas Jefferson said, "No free man shall be debarred the use of arms in his own lands or tenements" and Patrick Henry put it this way, "Guard with a jealous attention the public liberty." Suspect everyone who approaches that jewel. Unfortunately nothing will preserve it but downright force. Whenever you give up that force, you are ruined. The great object is that every man be armed."

I do not own an AK assault rifle, and I probably never will. I do not own a "Saturday Night Special," and I probably never will. I do not own an Uzi, and probably never will. That does not mean others should not.

I was in California recently and read in the newspaper that red colored cars were involved in more violations than any other color of automobile. The result, of course, means that all insurance premiums are higher as a result of the violations of red colored cars.

Should that be a justifiable reason to ban red automobiles? Surely many innocent people were killed because of them. The question becomes not whether the red automobile should be banned but whether the government has the right to tell the general public they cannot have one? The same issue applies to the gun.

I have many concerns about those using guns. I was a deputy sheriff in one county and a special deputy sheriff in another. I have had my life threatened and the window was shot into in my Philadelphia office. But these are guns in the wrong hands. It is not the fault of the gun. I have in my home close to fifty guns. Does that predispose me to become a criminal in the future? Does that make me a threat to humanity?

I said I believe in gun control and I have not supported that claim. Now I will. 1. I believe in controlling gun sales to minors. 2. I believe in prohibiting gun sales to convicted felons. 3. I believe no drug addicts or mental incompetents should possess guns. 4. I believe gun owners should be required to use firearms with discrimination. But, my friends, these laws already exist.

I also support any laws that will more stringently prevent criminals from obtaining guns, so long as they are not infringing upon the rights of all free honest people from obtaining guns. I support mandatory prison sentences for those committing crimes using a gun and, I mean enforce those laws. Punish the criminal, not the honest person who owns guns. Criminals will always get guns. Computerized record checks are expensive and since criminals get guns from criminals, they do not work.

If I can buy anti-ballistic missiles, or bazookas on the open market today; what is a gun? As for the required waiting period; Patrick Purdy, in California who killed those children was up on felony charges seven times before he went to Stockton schoolyard. Five times he bought guns under California's waiting period law, and it is one of the toughest in the nation.

Is there any significance to note that those states with the toughest gun laws tend to have the highest crime rate? These include California, New York, Washington, D.C., and New Jersey. It is long past due for our government to attack the criminal not the gun.

I have absolutely no reservation in telling you now that if the government were to tell me that I had to surrender my guns, I would become a criminal. I stand with Charlton Heston when he says, "I will give up my gun when they pry it from my cold dead fingers."

[3]

Club des Cinquantes

Given to a luncheon club in New York City

Good afternoon. I regard it as a distinct pleasure to be with you and to be asked to speak to your group today. Brother Ted Harrison has made me aware that this club is made up of what is regarded as regular as well as irregular Freemasons. I have no great concern whether those attending agree or disagree with me. I only wish to stimulate thinking.

I have been a member of what is regarded as regular Freemasonry for over fifty-two years. However, I have no problem in relating to what is looked upon as irregular forms of the Craft so long as it does not require me to sit in a tiled Lodge. Indeed, I have been on speaking engagements in the past with leaders of female Masonic bodies as well as co-Masonic bodies.

Ted has informed me that many of you here today are members of the Grand Orient of France and I have had great respect for this Grand Lodge for many decades. I have been with your Grand Masters on a number of occasions and respect their commitment and accomplishments. It is the oldest and largest Grand Lodge operating in France and perhaps the most prestigious. It began its life as a regular and recognized Grand Lodge. However, the decision was made a couple centuries ago to operate in a style that was not compatible with the requirements of regular

Freemasonry and thus it is regarded today as an irregular form of the Craft.

I respect the position they take. They know they are regarded as being an irregular form but have no problem existing as such, and seek no recognition from regular Freemasonry. There are other irregular grand lodges that consistently seek recognition from regular Freemasonry while retaining their irregular practice. One cannot be both.

So that all here might fully understand the difference between being regarded as regular or irregular, one must recognize that regularity is based upon two criteria, origin and practice.

To be regarded as a regular Grand Lodge by origin, it must have been created by one or more regular grand lodges or by a minimum of three regular subordinate lodges within a jurisdiction that has no regular Freemasonry or the grand lodge in that jurisdiction grants them recognition and authorizes them to share territory.

In North America, most "mainstream" grand lodges, after many years, have agreed to share territory with, and recognize the Prince Hall Grand lodges, regarded in much of the past as being irregular. They are now regarded as regular. However, they were consecrated as a regular lodge in the 1700s by the Grand Lodge of England and have now healed the schism that caused them to be removed from the rolls. (Prince Hall Freemasonry is composed of principally black members.)

For your information, there is only one jurisdiction in the world in which three regular grand lodges share the same territory. That is in the state of California where the mainstream Grand Lodge, (I refer to the regular grand lodge recognized in any jurisdiction, as mainstream) the Prince Hall Grand Lodge and the Grand Lodge of Iran in Exile, all share the same jurisdictional territory.

Now, lest you challenge me, there are jurisdictions in the world in which more than one Grand Lodge has lodges operating in the same geographical jurisdiction. A classic example would be South Africa, where there is a Grand Lodge of South Africa and also provincial lodges of England, Scotland, Ireland and the Netherlands. However these are provincial grand lodges, not grand lodges.

In order to be regarded as regular by practice there is a required compliance to principal landmarks. Landmarks are adopted fundamental characteristics by regular Masonic grand lodges that require all seeking recognition to comply with. However, grand lodges have varied in what constitutes and are adopted as landmarks. There are those acknowledging less than a dozen and those who have accepted over fifty. Albert Mackey, the great Masonic scholar listed twenty-five areas that he considered landmarks. Many jurisdictions have these landmarks written, while others may never have a written list of landmarks.

There are, however, regardless of the jurisdiction's accepted numbers of landmarks, specific landmarks that every grand lodge seeking recognition must comply with. For example, the belief in a Supreme Being, the Volume of the Sacred Law placed upon the altar in all open lodges, the prohibition of women admitted to membership, along with others. Failure to comply with any of these landmarks would rule the grand lodge as being irregular in practice and denied recognition by all regular Freemasonry. Any recognized grand lodge eliminating the requirement for the practice of any one of these landmarks, subject themselves to having recognition withdrawn. The reason the Grand Orient of France lost recognition by regular Freemasonry is the removal of the requirements for the belief in a Supreme Being and the Volume of the Sacred Law.

I emphasize, however, that Regularity is a right by

consecration, Recognition is a privilege granted by grand lodges. You may therefore, have grand lodges that have been regularly consecrated but not necessarily recognized by all other regular grand lodges. There are also, grand lodges that are irregular in consecration and/or in practice that have received recognition by some regular grand lodges. This constitutes a serious breach of protocol, however, and can subject the grand lodge granting recognition to suspension of recognition by other grand lodges.

There are probably very few members in either form of Freemasonry today who recognize that the growth of the Craft in recent years has probably been greater than any time since shortly following its inception and structuring, as a speculative form of Freemasonry. There have been twenty-seven new regular grand lodges consecrated since the turn-of-the-century and although I have no way of knowing the number of irregular grand bodies that have been created in that same period of time they are, likewise growing. While I was Grand Secretary of the Grand Lodge of Pennsylvania I became aware that there were at least eighteen grand lodges operating in New York City and six headquartered on Broad Street in Philadelphia.

Consequently sixteen in New York City were irregular as well as four on Broad Street in Philadelphia. I do not know how many Grand Lodges operate in Italy today but I was informed that at one time there were 91. Any organization or group of men can claim to be a Masonic organization, and many have. For a couple of centuries there have been those organizations or men who have conferred degrees using the name Freemasonry, to profit themselves. They have been referred to as degree mills. This type of fraudulent selling of degrees is indicative of the prestige of Freemasonry, resulting in men willing to pay a fee, simply to say that I am a Freemason.

Ted suggested when he asked me to speak to you today, that you might be interested in my feelings both pro and con of any possibility of coming together of the various obediences for inter-visitation or to establish a world conference including all major obediences and I will respond to that.

As I have mentioned, I have participated in discussions and symposiums with representatives of what was regarded as irregular Freemasonry. Approximately twenty years ago, I took part in a symposium held at UCLA that was composed of the Grand Masters of the female Masonic grand lodges of Belgium and France and the Grand Master of the co-Masonic grand lodge of France.

It has always been my conviction that to resolve issues, discussion must be encouraged. However, for the ongoing success of the influence of Freemasonry certain criteria for regularity must be nonnegotiable. Approximately five years ago Lord Northampton, then, Pro Grand Master of the United Grand Lodge of England, instituted a conference of European Grand Masters that included all Grand Masters of regular Freemasonry in Europe, whether recognized or unrecognized. This conference has proven valuable and continues to meet in different European countries. It, however, did not involve irregular grand lodges.

It has been my dream for many years to see all regular Freemasonry united in a common effort. I have been involved, as Executive Secretary of the World Conference of Regular Masonic Grand Lodges for sixteen years in attempts to see that achieved. During that period of time I have mediated and assisted in negotiations to effect mergers, validate elections and simply to establish compatibility within world leadership. What a challenge this has been. If we cannot unite regular Freemasonry, how much more difficult it would be to unite regular and irregular Freemasonry.

Historically, the greatest challenges to Freemasonry have been oppressive leaders of governments and repressive religious leaders. Today and into our future, the greatest challenges to our integrity are and will be internal. These challenges lie within the uncontrolled egos of our leaderships. Those of you who are here today from France, should know well, how the unbridled ego of one man came close to destroying the only Grand Lodge in France presently recognized as being regular in both practice and origin.

It is my conviction that the great future for Freemasonry lies in environments where Freemasonry is being newly established or re-established. Following oppressive dominations in Eastern Europe and the rise of Freemasonry in the indigenous populations of Africa there exists fertile fields for the Craft. It is in these locations that are evolving into more civil societies that the philosophical precepts of the Craft with its moral and ethical emphasis can play a major role in the direction of this evolution. Freemasonry has always been at its best and has been most successful when it was needed the most and its challenges were the greatest. I have found in these environments, a great interest in the leaderships of the countries, in the potential of Freemasonry to contribute to this ongoing evolution. Regretfully, in many of these environments and especially in Eastern Europe there have been major schisms resulting in a splitting of grand lodges, which out of necessity results in one of them being regarded as regular and entitled to recognition, the other although perhaps regular in consecration, not entitled to recognition. The major cause of the schisms in most of the cases has been the result of the leadership of organizations appendant to Freemasonry assuming that their higher degree numbers make them superior to the grand lodges. Both in regular and irregular Freemasonry the highest degree one can receive is the 3rd, that of Master

Mason. There may be higher degree numbers but there is no higher degree. There can be no higher authority in any jurisdiction than that of the Grand Lodge.

There is great respect shown to Freemasonry in many African countries. Indeed, when the World Conference was held in Gabon, there were presidents of four countries in attendance and two of the presidents were Grand Masters of their respective grand lodges. When we consecrated the Grand Lodge of Mozambique, the installed Grand Master was the Prime Minister of the country. However, on the continent of Africa, Freemasonry will face challenges unprecedented, as a result of the great diversity of cultures, languages, religions and distrust of much of the population.

It should be of interest to us, that many of these African countries are predominantly composed of those practicing the Muslim religion. I sat in a lodge in Bamako, Mali where I and a friend of mine were the only two non-Muslims sitting in that Lodge that evening. It is worth noting however, a significant and very active grand lodge in a principally Muslim country, not in Africa, is the Grand Lodge of Turkey that is over 100 years old.

While attending the 275th anniversary of the United Grand Lodge of England, I was talking with a young brother from Malaysia who told me that the only location that all members of his country could sit together without animosity was in a Masonic Lodge.

Whether those of you sitting here today belong to what is regarded as regular Freemasonry or irregular Freemasonry, it is important that you appreciate the privilege that you have, to belong to an organization that has been responsible for the structuring of world societies for several hundred years. Some of the greatest men and greatest minds the world has ever seen have been Freemasons. A list of these men could be regarded as a Who's Who of world history.

I said that it is been my dream that all regular Freemasonry could unite for a common purpose. It is also my fervent wish that all irregular forms of Freemasonry could someday unite in regularity.

In response to Brother Ted's thoughts, it is my opinion on the potential of regular and irregular Freemasonry coming together, is that it will not happen. We may associate with one another. We may relate to one another but we cannot merge with one another nor do I believe that we can visit with one another. Indeed, even if I wanted to visit an irregular or an unrecognized grand lodge, I am prohibited by my obligation from doing so. I have had to turn down on a number of occasions, invitations to attend and to speak at unrecognized grand lodges in Latin America. I have many friends who belong to these lodges, but I cannot attend their tiled meetings.

Many irregular grand lodges do not require the belief in a Supreme Being, which is one of the strongest binding requirements of regular Freemasonry. It is probably one of the greatest forces that separate us from other social or civic organizations. Because we are not dogmatic nor do we support any specific religion it gives us the opportunity beyond all religions, to unite people all over the world and to exemplify the meaning of a brotherhood of man under the fatherhood of God. Although irregular Freemasonry that does not require the belief in a Supreme Being does not have to deal with the issue of religious divisions, it lacks that bond that unites regular Freemasonry.

I realize that I will never live long enough to see my dream nor my fervent wish come true—but it remains mine.

[About the Author]

Right Worshipful Brother Thomas W. Jackson is an eminent Freemason, recognized around the world for his work encouraging and supporting the Masonic fraternity. Bro. Jackson was made a Mason in Cumberland Valley Lodge № 315 of Shippensburg, Pennsylvania, and served as its Worshipful Master in 1969. He went on to serve a twenty-year tenure as the Grand Secretary of the Right Worshipful Grand Lodge of Free and Accepted Masons of Pennsylvania, retiring in 1999.

He was also the first Executive Secretary of the World Conference of Regular Masonic Grand Lodges from 1998 to 2014, and is now Honorary President ad Vitam of that organization.

R.W. Bro. Jackson is a strong supporter of Masonic education and research, serving as the Warrant Master of the Pennsylvania Lodge of Research, a Fellow of the Philalethes Society, a Founding Fellow of the Masonic Society, a member of the Board of Directors of the Scottish Rite Research Society, and a member of the exclusive Society of Blue Friars.

He has also held leadership positions in many other organizations concerned with the culture of the Craft, including president of the Conference of Grand Secretaries of North America, board member of the Masonic Information Center of North America, the Masonic Restoration Foundation, the Masonic Relief Association of North America and chairman of the board of directors of the Association of Masonic Arts.

He holds honorary membership in 111 grand lodges in the world, is the only American Freemason holding Grand Rank in the United Grand Lodge of England, and holds Honorary Grand Rank in 42 grand lodges including Honorary Grand Master in 16 jurisdictions.

He has presided over 18 local, state, national and world Masonic bodies. He has spoken in over 40 countries and had articles published in educational, scientific, and Masonic journals, newspapers, and publications in more than thirty countries, and has had his papers translated into more than a dozen languages.

www.ingramcontent.com/pod-product-compliance
Lightning Source LLC
Chambersburg PA
CBHW031123180526
45160CB00005B/66/J